SILVER BURDETT
English

Marian Davies Toth
Nancy N. Ragno
Betty G. Gray

SILVER BURDETT COMPANY   MORRISTOWN, NJ

Atlanta, GA · Cincinnati, OH · Dallas, TX · Northfield, IL · San Carlos, CA · Agincourt, Ontario

Centennial Edition

Acknowledgments

Cover: Tom Stack/Tom Stack & Associates.

Contributing Artists: Karen Ackoff, Michael Adams, Robert Blake, Harry Borgman, Marie De John, Bert Dodson, Nancy Hannons, Chris Holzer, Robert Jackson, John Jones, Jane Kendall, Francis Livingston, Michelle Noiset, Taylor Oughten, Beverly Pardee, Norma Rahn, Sally Schaedler, Nancy Schill, Steven Schindler, Den Schofield, Samantha Smith, Susan Sturgill, George Ulrich, Gary Undercuffler, Herman Vestal, James Watling, George Wenzel

Unit 1 3: © Bill Wison/Photo Researchers, Inc. 30: Silver Burdett. 32: © P.B. Kaplan/Photo Reseachers, Inc. 33: Edith Haun/Stock, Boston. 36–39: Silver Burdett. 41: E.R. Degginger. 43: Silver Burdett. **Unit 2** 49: © Earl Dibble/Photo Researchers, Inc. 77–80: Silver Burdett. **Unit 3** 87: Dan De Wilde for Silver Burdett. 114–115: Silver Burdett. 117: Dan De Wilde for Silver Burdett. 122–125: Silver Burdett. 127: Photo Courtesy Bausch & Lomb. **Unit 4** 141: Mosallem/Atoz Images. 166: Walter Chandoha. **Unit 5** 177: Walter Chandoha. 197: *t.* Peter Guntner/Shostal Associates; *m.* Thomas R. Taylor/Shostal Associates; *b.* John Bacchus for Silver Burdett. 207: Silver Burdett. 209: Jonathan Wright/Bruce Coleman. **Unit 6** 213: Craighead/Atoz Images. 230: NASA. 236: Silver Burdett. 240: Wendell Metzer/Bruce Coleman. 241: Jeff Simon/Bruce Coleman. 243: Eric Carle/Shostal Associates. 248: Silver Burdett. **Unit 7** 257: Tom Stack/Tom Stack & Associates. 287: Dan De Wilde for Silver Burdett. **Unit 8** 293: Edward Lettau/Peter Arnold. 312: © Junebug Clark/Photo Researchers, Inc. 313: Willinger/Shostal Associates. 314: Jorgenson Photography/Shostal Associates. 315: Winston Pote/Shostal Associates. 317: *t.* Robert Pelham/Bruce Coleman; *t.m.* Harald Sund; *m.m.* W. Hodge/Peter Arnold, Inc.; *b.m.* Clyde Smith/Peter Arnold Inc.; *b.* Rod Planck/Tom Stack & Associates; *m.* Peter Menzel/Stock, Boston. 318–321: Silver Burdett.

PERMISSIONS: We wish to thank the following authors, publishers, agents, corporations, and individuals for their permission to reprint copyrighted materials. Page 2: Poem "Advice to a Bird, Species Unknown" from *Have One on Me* by Georgie Starbuck Galbraith. Page 28: This Key to Pronunciation is adapted from *Scott, Foresman Intermediate Dictionary*, by E.L. Thorndike and Clarence L. Barnhart. Copyright © 1983 by Scott, Foresman and Company. Reprinted by permission. Page 86: Poem "The Wind" from *The Wandering Moon* by James Reeves. Published 1960 by E.P. Dutton & Co. Reprinted by permission of William Heinemann Limited. Page 130: Poem "The Pasture" from *The Poetry of Robert Frost* edited by Edward Connery Lathem. Copyright 1939, © 1967, 1969 by Holt, Rinehart and Winston. Reprinted by permission of Holt, Rinehart and Winston, Publishers. Page 138: Poem "Cat" from *Menagerie* by Mary Britton Miller. Reprinted by permission of the Estate of Mary Britton Miller. Page 152: Excerpt from *Island of the Blue Dolphins* by Scott O'Dell. Copyright © 1960 by Scott O'Dell. Reprinted by permission of Houghton Mifflin Company. Pages 156–161: Excerpt from the book *The Key Word and Other Mysteries* by Isaac Asimov. Copyright © 1977. Used with permission of Walker & Company. Page 176: Poem "I Wouldn't (text only) from *You Read to Me, I'll Read to You* by John Ciardi (J.B. Lippincott). Copyright © 1962 by John Ciardi. Reprinted by permission of Harper &

Contributing Writers: Duncan Searl ; Michael Quinn

Acknowledgments continued on page 330

C O N T E N T S

UNIT ONE

GRAMMAR *Sentences*   2

  1 What Is a Sentence?   4
  2 Four Kinds of Sentences   6
  3 Capitals and End Punctuation   8
  4 Complete Subjects and Complete Predicates   10
  5 Simple Subjects   12
  6 Simple Predicates   14
  7 Locating Subjects in Sentences   16
  8 Commas in Sentences   18
  9 Synonyms and Antonyms   20
    Grammar Review   22

  Grammar and Writing Workshop:
    Sentence Combining   24

COMPOSITION *Classifying*

  10 Finding Words in a Dictionary   26
  11 Using a Dictionary   28
  12 Using a Thesaurus   30
  13 What Is a Paragraph?   32
  14 Topic Sentences and Supporting Sentences   34
  15 The Writing Process: A Photo Essay   36
  16 Writing Project:
    Writing a Paragraph of Contrast   40

Worktable: A Dictionary Calendar   44
Building Bridges to Social Studies   45

Checkpoint: Unit 1   46

UNIT TWO

GRAMMAR *Nouns*   48

    1 Nouns   50
    2 Common and Proper Nouns   52
    3 Capitalizing Proper Nouns   54
    4 Abbreviations   56
    5 Singular and Plural Nouns   58
    6 Possessive Nouns   60
    7 Compounds   62
    Grammar Review   64

    Grammar and Writing Workshop:
    Writing with Nouns   66

COMPOSITION *Persuading*

    8 Listening for Facts and Opinions   68
    9 Having a Discussion   70
    10 Writing a Persuasive Paragraph   72
    11 The Parts of a Newspaper   74
    12 Writing Project:
    Writing a Newspaper Editorial   76

Worktable: Persuasive Advertisements   80
Building Bridges to Health   81

Checkpoint: Unit 2   82

CUMULATIVE REVIEW: Units 1—2   84

UNIT THREE

GRAMMAR *Verbs*   86

1 Verbs   88
2 Linking Verbs   90
3 Helping Verbs and Main Verbs   92
4 Verbs with Direct Objects   94
5 Tenses of Verbs   96
6 Principal Parts of Verbs   98
7 Using Irregular Verbs   100
8 Using Irregular Verbs   102
9 Troublesome Verb Pairs   104
10 Troublesome Verb Pairs   106
11 Prefixes   108
Grammar Review   110

Grammar and Writing Workshop:
Writing with Verbs   112

COMPOSITION *Informing*

12 Writing an Explanatory Paragraph   114
13 Using the Telephone   116
14 Friendly Letters   118
15 Business Letters   120
16 Writing Project:
Writing a Letter of Information   122

Worktable: A Commemorative Stamp   126
Building Bridges to Science   127

Checkpoint: Unit 3   128

UNIT FOUR

GRAMMAR *Pronouns*   130

   1 Pronouns   132
   2 Subject Pronouns   134
   3 Object Pronouns   136
   4 Possessive Pronouns   138
   5 Predicate Nominatives   140
   6 Using Pronouns Correctly   142
   7 Contractions   144
   8 Homophones and Homographs   146
   Grammar Review   148

   Grammar and Writing Workshop:
   Writing with Pronouns   150

COMPOSITION *Narrating*

   9 Writing a Narrative Paragraph   152
   10 Writing Quotations   154
   11 Reading a Story   156
   12 Writing a Book Report   162
   13 Writing Project:
   Writing a Personal Narrative   164

   Worktable: A Class Story Chart   168
   Building Bridges to Mathematics   169

   Checkpoint: Unit 4   170

   CUMULATIVE REVIEW: Units 1—4   172

UNIT FIVE

GRAMMAR *Adjectives*   176

   1 Adjectives   178
   2 Proper Adjectives   180
   3 Predicate Adjectives   182
   4 Demonstrative Adjectives   184
   5 Comparison of Adjectives   186
   6 Comparison of Adjectives   188
   7 Adjective Suffixes   190
     Grammar Review   192

   Grammar and Writing Workshop:
   Writing with Adjectives   194

COMPOSITION *Describing*

   8 Writing a Descriptive Paragraph   196
   9 Listening for the Main Idea and
     Descriptive Details   198
  10 Using Space Order in Paragraphs   200
  11 Interviewing   202
  12 Writing Project:
     Writing a Character Sketch   204

Worktable: A Coat of Arms   208
Building Bridges to Social Studies   209

Checkpoint: Unit 5   210

UNIT SIX

GRAMMAR *Adverbs*   212

    1 Adverbs   214
    2 Adverb Location in Sentences   216
    3 Comparison of Adverbs   218
    4 Avoiding Double Negatives   220
    5 Using Adjectives and Adverbs   222
    6 Context Clues   224
    Grammar Review   226

    Grammar and Writing Workshop:
    Writing with Adverbs   228

COMPOSITION *Researching*

    7 Choosing a Topic   230
    8 Using the Library   232
    9 Using an Encyclopedia   234
    10 Using Other Reference Materials   236
    11 Using the Parts of a Book   238
    12 Taking Notes and Paraphrasing   240
    13 Outlining   242
    14 Giving Oral Reports   244
    15 Writing Project:
    Writing a Three-Paragraph Report   246

Worktable: A Call Number Guide   250
Building Bridges to Science   251

Checkpoint: Unit 6   252

CUMULATIVE REVIEW: Units 1—6   254

UNIT SEVEN

GRAMMAR *Conjunctions and Prepositions* 256

1 Conjunctions 258
2 Prepositions 260
3 Prepositional Phrases as Adjectives 262
4 Prepositional Phrases as Adverbs 264
5 Using Prepositional Phrases 266
6 Parts of Speech Summary 268
7 Idioms 270
Grammar Review 272

Grammar and Writing Workshop:
Sentence Combining 274

COMPOSITION *Reasoning*

8 Writing Directions 276
9 Recognizing Propaganda Techniques 278
10 Making Analogies 280
11 Making Common-Sense Decisions 282
12 Writing Project:
Writing a Cause-and-Effect Paragraph 284

Worktable: A Puzzle Potpourri 288
Building Bridges to Computers 289

Checkpoint: Unit 7 290

UNIT EIGHT

GRAMMAR *Sentences*   292

    1 Compound Subjects and Compound
       Predicates   294
    2 Compound Sentences   296
    3 Subject-Verb Agreement   298
    4 Subject-Verb Agreement   300
    5 Sentence Errors   302
    6 Using Commas   304
    7 Word Connotations   306
    Grammar Review   308

    Grammar and Writing Workshop:
    Sentence Combining   310

COMPOSITION *Creating*

    8 Reading Imaginative Poetry   312
    9 Listening for Sounds in Poetry   314
    10 Using Figures of Speech   316
    11 Writing Project:
       Writing a Poem   318

Worktable: A Greeting Card   322
Building Bridges to Music   323

Checkpoint: Unit 8   324

CUMULATIVE REVIEW: Units 1—8   326

REVIEW AND PRACTICE HANDBOOKS   331
   Grammar Handbook   332
   Young Writer's Handbook   390
THESAURUS   414
PLANNING AHEAD
  1 Diagraming Subjects and Verbs   434
  2 Diagraming Sentence Parts   436
  3 Diagraming Other Sentence Parts   438
  4 Indirect Objects   440
  5 Perfect Tenses of Verbs   442
  6 Clauses   444
INDEX   446

Grammar
Sentences

Composition
Classifying

Advice to a Bird, Species Unknown

Listen to me, you silly bird,
Has no one told you? Haven't you heard
That the winters here are long and cold?
Then harken, bird. You are being told.
Be on your way! Go south! Get going!
Any time now it may be snowing,
Sleet and hail and a mean wind blowing.

Winter is here. Didn't you know that?
And winter's a crusty old gray cat,
Ice on his whiskers, frost on his paws.
He'll gobble you up in his freezing jaws!
He'll snap you up in his arctic mouth!
I'm telling you, bird, be bright. Go south!

—*Georgie Starbuck Galbraith*

1 — **What Is a Sentence?**

> ● A **sentence** is a group of words that expresses a complete thought.

Read the groups of words below.

Not Sentences	**Sentences**
1. Begins at home.	1. Charity begins at home.
2. Still waters.	2. Still waters run deep.

The word groups on the left do not express complete thoughts. The first group of words does not name who or what *Begins at home*. The second group of words does not tell what *Still waters* do. The word groups on the right answer these questions. The first group of words names what *begins at home*. It is *Charity*. The second group tells what *Still waters* do. They *run deep*.

Groups of words that are not sentences do not make sense by themselves. The word group below does not make sense.

In small packages.

Adding more words gives it meaning and makes it a sentence. Always begin each sentence you write with a capital letter.

Good things come in small packages.

Skills Tryout

Tell which of the following groups of words is a sentence, and which is not a sentence.

1. Too many cooks spoil the broth.
2. A stitch in time.
3. The squeaky wheel gets the grease.
4. Is worth a thousand words.
5. A barking dog seldom bites.

Practice

A. Write *sentence* or *not a sentence* for each group of words.

1. Many hands make light work.
2. Lost time is never found again.
3. All work and no play.
4. Haste makes waste.
5. A bad worker.
6. Will be a new day.
7. In the bush.
8. Love will find a way.
9. Fortune helps the brave.
10. In glass houses.

B. Add words to make each group of words a sentence. Try to make a proverb, or wise saying. Then write the sentence.

EXAMPLE: _____ grow from tiny acorns.
ANSWER: Tall oaks grow from tiny acorns.

11. _____ flies.
12. April showers _____.
13. _____ is the best policy.
14. Birds of a feather _____.
15. A new broom _____.
16. _____ has a silver lining.
17. An apple a day _____.
18. _____ catches the worm.
19. _____ are better than one.
20. One good turn _____.

Application WRITING SENTENCES

Choose three proverbs from this lesson. Then write two sentences for each telling what it means. To check a proverb, use *Bartlett's Familiar Quotations* in the library reference room.

2 — Four Kinds of Sentences

- A **declarative sentence** makes a statement.
- An **interrogative sentence** asks a question.
- An **imperative sentence** gives a command or makes a request.
- An **exclamatory sentence** expresses strong feeling.

Does it really weigh 100 tons?

Look at the whale's tail.

Please let me see.

The blue whale is the largest animal.

Blue whales are so gigantic!

The children in the picture used the four kinds of sentences. Paco used a declarative sentence to make a statement, or tell something. Bea used an interrogative sentence to ask a question. Cal used an imperative sentence. He commanded the others to look at the whale's tail. Pat's sentence is also imperative, but it makes a request. A request usually has the word *please* in it. Ann used an exclamatory sentence to show her strong feeling about the whale's size.

Skills Tryout

Tell which kind of sentence each of the following is.

1. Listen to this, everybody.
2. The blue whale is bigger than thirty elephants.
3. How much does it eat every day?
4. It eats from four to eight tons of food a day.
5. What a huge appetite it has!

Practice

A. Write each sentence. After each sentence write *declarative, interrogative, imperative,* or *exclamatory.*

1. A blue whale is about twenty-five feet long at birth.
2. What a big baby that is!
3. How much does a baby blue whale weigh?
4. Please read the sign to find out.
5. It weighs about two tons at birth.
6. Can a blue whale stay underwater for a long time?
7. Some have stayed underwater for almost an hour.
8. What huge breaths they must take!
9. Tell me more about these amazing animals.
10. Blue whales often dive to depths of several hundred feet.

B. Write which kind of sentence each of the following is. Then tell the purpose of each sentence.

EXAMPLE: Whales breathe air through their blowholes.
ANSWER:　declarative (makes a statement)

11. A spout of water vapor shoots into the air.
12. Look at the blue whale's spout.
13. How high it is!
14. Do you know the length of this blue whale?
15. Please ask Mr. Carlotti.
16. This whale is almost 100 feet long.
17. Can you see the two flat flukes on the whale's tail?
18. These strong tail fins push the whale forward.
19. Its streamlined body glides smoothly through the water.
20. What an extraordinary animal the blue whale is!

Application　WRITING SENTENCES

Pretend that you are a giant blue whale. Write four sentences that tell about your watery world. Write one declarative, one interrogative, one imperative, and one exclamatory sentence.

3 — Capitals and End Punctuation

- Begin every sentence with a **capital letter**.
- Use a **period** (.) at the end of a declarative sentence or an imperative sentence.
- Use a **question mark** (?) at the end of an interrogative sentence.
- Use an **exclamation mark** (!) at the end of an exclamatory sentence.

Anita and Julia are members of an astronomy club. Anita just received this note from Julia.

My new telescope arrived yesterday.
Do you want to watch the comet with me?
Come to my house at 8:00 P.M. on Friday.
What an extraordinary sight it will be!

Capital letters help readers understand written language. Julia has begun each sentence with a capital letter. The capitals show Anita when a new sentence is beginning.

End punctuation also helps readers. A period indicates the stop people make naturally after a statement or command. A question mark indicates that a question is being asked. An exclamation mark shows the writer has a strong feeling or is excited about something.

Skills Tryout

Tell how each sentence should begin and end.

1. a comet is a giant ball of frozen gas and dust
2. have you ever seen one
3. look through this telescope
4. how bright it is
5. the comet's center is called the nucleus

Practice

A. Write the sentences using capital letters and end punctuation correctly.

1. tell us more about comets
2. the fuzzy area around the center is the coma
3. what do you call the long trailing part
4. it is called the tail
5. one famous comet has a tail 200 million miles long
6. that's unbelievable
7. did you know the word *comet* originally meant "long-haired one"
8. explain how comets are like planets
9. most comets revolve around the sun
10. however, some travel far beyond the solar system

B. Write the sentences using capital letters and correct end punctuation. After each sentence write *declarative, interrogative, imperative,* or *exclamatory.*

11. do you have any other questions about comets
12. how often does a comet orbit the sun
13. some comets orbit the sun every few years
14. others take thousands of years to make one orbit
15. what a long time that is
16. let me look through the telescope now
17. show me how to focus it
18. are new comets still being discovered
19. astronomers find new comets every year
20. how beautiful this comet is

Application WRITING SENTENCES

Imagine that a spectacular comet is passing through the sky over your neighborhood. Write four sentences that tell what you think and feel about it. Use the four kinds of sentences.

4 Complete Subjects and Complete Predicates

> - The **complete subject** is all the words in the subject part of a sentence. The subject part names someone or something.
> - The **complete predicate** is all the words in the predicate part of a sentence. The predicate part tells what the subject is or does.

Every sentence has two main parts—the complete subject and the complete predicate. Both parts are necessary to make a complete sentence. In each of the following sentences, the complete subject is shown in blue. The complete predicate is shown in green.

> Columbus Day is a popular October holiday.
> The people of America celebrate.
> Christopher Columbus was born in Genoa, Italy.
> The great explorer landed in the New World.
> He arrived on October 12, 1492.

The complete subject can be one word or many words. However, it always names someone or something. The complete predicate can also be one word or many words. It always tells what the subject is or does.

Skills Tryout

Name the complete subject in each sentence.

1. The sun set at 5:30 P.M. on October 11, 1492.
2. Three small ships sailed west into the sunset.
3. They had been at sea since August 3.
4. Anxious sailors searched the red horizon.
5. No land was in sight.

A. Read each sentence. Then write the complete subject of each sentence.

1. The evening of October 11 passed.
2. Columbus stood alone on the deck of the *Santa Maria*.
3. The time was 2:00 A.M.
4. The small ship *Pinta* sailed ahead of Columbus's ship.
5. The lookout on the *Pinta* was Rodrigo de Triana.
6. He rubbed his eyes suddenly.
7. A white sand cliff was gleaming in the distance.
8. The young man yelled the Spanish word for land.
9. Captain Pinzón of the *Pinta* fired a signal cannon.
10. The powerful explosion echoed over the moonlit ocean.

B. Write each sentence. Underline the complete subject once. Underline the complete predicate twice.

11. The sound thrilled Columbus.
12. His long journey into the unknown was a success.
13. Columbus shouted to Captain Pinzón.
14. A night landing would be too dangerous.
15. The hours until dawn crept by.
16. The three ships found a suitable harbor at daybreak.
17. Small boats carried the sailors ashore.
18. Tears of joy filled Columbus's eyes.
19. The thankful sailors fell on the beach.
20. Columbus named the island San Salvador.

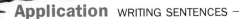

Application WRITING SENTENCES

Pretend you were on the *Santa Maria* with Columbus. Write six sentences that tell your hopes and fears. Be sure each sentence includes a complete subject and a complete predicate.

5 — Simple Subjects

- The **simple subject** is the main word in the complete subject.

You have already learned that the complete subject of a sentence is all the words in the subject part. One word in the complete subject, however, is more important than the rest. This main word is called the simple subject. Like the complete subject, the simple subject names someone or something.

Read the sentences below. The simple subject of each sentence is in a blue box.

Complete Subject	Complete Predicate
1. The game of table tennis	was first played in 1889.
2. James Gibb	invented the game.
3. He	made paddles from cigar boxes.
4. Old bottle corks	served as the first balls.
5. Gibb's dinner table	was the playing surface.

Notice in sentence 3 that the complete subject is just one word. In such cases, the simple subject is the same as the complete subject. In sentence 2, the complete subject is a name. This name is also the simple subject, although it is made up of two words.

Skills Tryout

Name the simple subject in each sentence.

1. Gibb called his game Gossima.
2. The English inventor developed better balls and paddles.
3. The new game was not popular at first.
4. Gibb's lawyer renamed the game Ping-Pong a few years later.
5. People in Europe played the game enthusiastically.

Practice

A. Write the simple subject of each sentence.

1. Joseph Merlin was the world's first roller skater.
2. This Belgian musician skated into an English ballroom in 1760.
3. The young skater was also playing a violin.
4. The guests stared at the strange sight.
5. Tragedy struck almost immediately.
6. The musical athlete smashed into a giant mirror.
7. Bits of glass littered the ballroom floor.
8. A valuable violin was broken.
9. Poor Joseph was badly injured.
10. The new sport was not tried again for fifty years.

B. Write each sentence. Underline the complete subject once and the simple subject twice.

11. One popular American sport is almost 100 years old.
12. A Massachusetts college teacher invented basketball in 1891.
13. His name was James Naismith.
14. The young coach needed an indoor sport for his athletes.
15. The new sport had only thirteen rules at first.
16. The first basketball was a soccer ball.
17. Two old baskets were nailed to the wall as goals.
18. A janitor with a ladder got the ball after each goal.
19. The players loved the game from the beginning.
20. Only one goal was scored in the first game.

Application WRITING SENTENCES

Invent a game, and then write five sentences about it. Use each of the words below as the simple subject of a sentence.

game   ball   rules   equipment   players

6 Simple Predicates

> ● The **simple predicate,** or verb, is the main word or words in the complete predicate.

You have already learned that the complete predicate of a sentence is all the words in the predicate part. One or more words in the complete predicate, however, are more important than the others. This main word or words is called the simple predicate. The simple predicate is always a verb. A verb expresses action or being.

Read the sentences below. The simple predicate of each sentence is in a green box.

Complete Subject	Complete Predicate
1. A coyote	**is** a sly animal.
2. It	**runs** faster than rabbits.
3. The doglike mammals	**can catch** snakes with no trouble.
4. A crafty coyote	**has crept** into our yard.

Sometimes the simple predicate, or verb, is made up of more than one word. In sentence 3, the main verb *catch* is helped by another verb, *can.* In sentence 4, the main verb *crept* is helped by the verb *has.*

Skills Tryout

Name the simple predicate, or verb, in each sentence.

1. The coyote carries its bushy tail quite low.
2. The ears of a coyote are short.
3. It has slender legs.
4. The coyote inhabited the plains originally.
5. It is found in mountain areas, in valleys, and in other places now.

Practice

A. Write the simple predicate, or verb, of each sentence.

1. A coyote likes fresh game of any kind.
2. It can survive on a diet of insects.
3. Many farmers complain about coyotes.
4. The sly beasts steal poultry and baby lambs.
5. Some coyotes have raided vegetable gardens.
6. Few people mistake the howl of a coyote.
7. A coyote's wail cuts the night like a knife.
8. The howl has a lonesome sound.
9. Coyotes are not lonely animals.
10. They live in family units most of the time.

B. Write each sentence. Underline the complete predicate once and the simple predicate twice.

11. Coyotes make their homes in underground dens.
12. Some have chosen natural caves in rocky areas.
13. The female coyote guards her pups with care.
14. The babies stay near the den.
15. A mother coyote will fight all intruders savagely.
16. Coyotes hunt at night in populated areas.
17. They search for food at all hours in the wild.
18. Desert coyotes may rest during the hot midday.
19. Prairie coyotes are a brownish color.
20. The fur of some other coyotes is gray.

Application WRITING SENTENCES

Write six sentences about your favorite animal. It can be a wild animal or a pet. When you have finished writing, underline the simple predicates in your sentences.

7 Locating Subjects in Sentences

- Change an interrogative sentence into a declarative sentence to find the subject.
- *You* (understood) is the subject of an imperative sentence.

You know that the subject part of a sentence names someone or something. In declarative sentences the subject part usually comes first.

Subject Part	Predicate Part
The leaves	are turning red and gold.

In interrogative sentences, however, the subject part often comes after the first word of the sentence. To find the subject of an interrogative sentence, change it into a declarative sentence.

Are the days getting shorter?   The days are getting shorter.

The subject of both sentences above is *days*. When the word *subject* is used by itself, it means simple subject.

In imperative sentences the subject is always *you*. However, the word *you* is not usually stated. It is understood. In the sentences below, the subject is understood to be *you*.

(You) Put on a sweater.   (You) Help pick the apples.

Skills Tryout

Tell the subject of each sentence.

1. Is autumn beginning already?
2. Turn on the furnace tonight.
3. Will we harvest the corn on Saturday?
4. Do you want to help?
5. Buy a big pumpkin for Halloween.

Practice

A. Write the subject of each sentence.

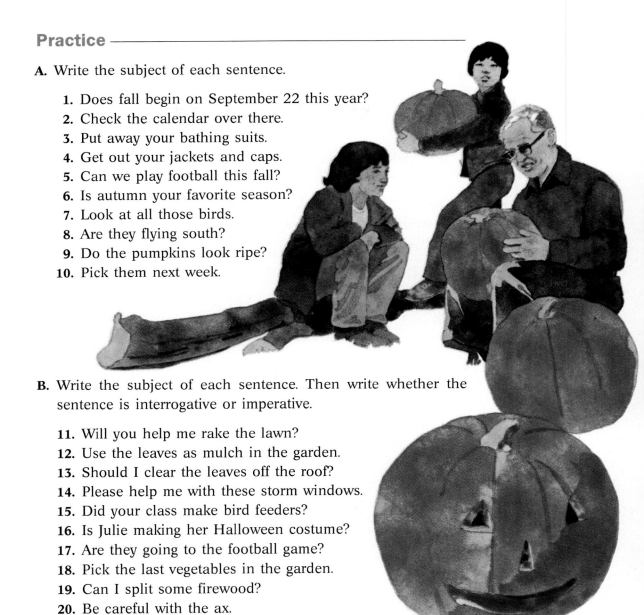

1. Does fall begin on September 22 this year?
2. Check the calendar over there.
3. Put away your bathing suits.
4. Get out your jackets and caps.
5. Can we play football this fall?
6. Is autumn your favorite season?
7. Look at all those birds.
8. Are they flying south?
9. Do the pumpkins look ripe?
10. Pick them next week.

B. Write the subject of each sentence. Then write whether the sentence is interrogative or imperative.

11. Will you help me rake the lawn?
12. Use the leaves as mulch in the garden.
13. Should I clear the leaves off the roof?
14. Please help me with these storm windows.
15. Did your class make bird feeders?
16. Is Julie making her Halloween costume?
17. Are they going to the football game?
18. Pick the last vegetables in the garden.
19. Can I split some firewood?
20. Be careful with the ax.

Application LISTENING

Write four interrogative sentences and four imperative sentences that you might hear in autumn. Underline the subject of each interrogative sentence.

Commas in Sentences

> ● Use a comma to separate words in a series.
> ● Use a comma to separate the date and year.
> ● Use a comma to separate the name of a city from a state or country.

Commas (,) make written language clearer. They separate certain words within a sentence and show a reader when to pause. The chart below explains rules for using commas.

Explanation	Examples
1. A comma separates words or groups of words in a series. A series is made up of three or more items. No comma is placed after the last item.	People set records in baseball, football, and swimming. Records for eating spaghetti, toppling dominoes, and balancing coins also exist.
2. A comma separates the date and the year. If the year is not at the end of a sentence, use a comma after it also.	Errol Bird yodeled for over ten hours on October 6, 1979. On October 13, 1979, Tom Kuhn tested a 256-pound yo-yo!
3. A comma separates the name of a city from the name of a state or country. If the state or country is not at the end of the sentence, use a comma after it also.	Mollie Jackson swung on a swing for 185 hours in Tarrytown, New York! Newell Banks of Chicago, Illinois, played 140 games of checkers at the same time!

Skills Tryout

Tell where commas belong in these sentences.

1. Records are set for walking running and crawling.
2. Lang Martin of Charlotte North Carolina set a record.
3. On February 9 1980 he balanced seven golf balls.
4. He used no glue tape or other adhesives.
5. Will he ever balance eight nine or ten of them?

Practice

Write the following sentences. Add commas where needed.

1. Jane Dorst of Atherton California released a balloon on May 21 1972.
2. On June 10 1972 it was found in Pietermaritzburg South Africa.
3. It had gone over mountains past cities and across the sea.
4. John Marino bicycled from Santa Monica California to New York City New York in thirteen days.
5. He completed the trip on August 26 1978.
6. His legs knees and back all must have hurt by then.
7. The largest dance ever held was in Houston Texas.
8. The date of the big event was February 8 1969.
9. Thousands of people danced the waltz the polka and the jitterbug at the Astro Hall that night.
10. Peter Dowdeswell has set records for eating sandwiches drinking milk and consuming other foods.
11. On February 9 1977 he ate sixty-two pancakes in just under seven minutes.
12. People set records for fun money and attention.

Application FILLING OUT FORMS

Pretend you are applying for a job as a newspaper carrier. Copy the form below. Then fill in the information that is required. Application forms should always be filled in neatly and accurately.

```
                     APPLICATION FOR PAPER ROUTE

    Name_____

    Address_____

    City & State _____ ZIP_____

    Phone_____ Age_____

    School_____

    Days and hours available_____

                 Signature_____

                      Date_____
```

9 — Synonyms and Antonyms

- **Synonyms** are words that have similar meanings.
- **Antonyms** are words that have opposite meanings.

Imagine how dull your world would be if the weather were always cloudy. Even the weather report would sound dull:

Expect another <u>cloudy</u> day today. The sky will be <u>cloudy</u> all day. Tomorrow and the weekend will be <u>cloudy</u>, too.

The weather report would sound more interesting if the person who wrote it used synonyms for *cloudy*. Synonyms are words with similar meanings. Learning to use synonyms can help make your writing more interesting. The synonyms for *cloudy* are underlined in the weather report below.

Expect another <u>gray</u> day today. The sky will be <u>sunless</u> all day. Tomorrow and the weekend will be <u>hazy</u>, too.

If the weather were to change suddenly, the weather reporter could use antonyms for *cloudy*. Antonyms are words with opposite meanings. The antonyms for *cloudy* are underlined below.

Expect another <u>clear</u> day today. The sky will be <u>sunny</u> all day. Tomorrow and the weekend will be <u>bright</u>, too.

Skills Tryout

Tell whether the underlined word in each sentence is a synonym or antonym for *rainy*.

1. Bring an umbrella, since it's going to be <u>damp</u> today.
2. Another <u>drizzly</u> day is forecast for Thursday.
3. By Sunday we should see <u>fair</u> weather return.
4. Look for mostly <u>dry</u> days next week.
5. Then <u>wet</u> winds from the south will return.

Practice

A. Write whether the words in each pair are synonyms or antonyms.

1. hot/cold
2. story/tale
3. love/hate
4. smart/intelligent
5. unusual/common

6. give/take
7. rug/carpet
8. help/aid
9. odd/even
10. talk/speak

B. Write the word in parentheses ( ) that is the synonym for the underlined word.

11. Chilly winds blew during March. (cold, hot)
12. The rain stopped at lunch time. (started, ended)
13. I quickly got a tan in the bright sunlight. (slowly, rapidly)
14. The heavy snow made driving difficult. (easy, hard)
15. The fog lifted at 10:00 A.M. (mist, sunlight)

C. Rewrite each sentence using an antonym in place of the underlined word. The antonym will make the sentence a true statement.

16. Winter days are longer than summer days.
17. The warm sunlight will freeze the ice.
18. The wetness of very cold air makes snow unlikely.
19. Winter days are long and dark.
20. A bright red sunset means bad weather is coming.

Application USING LANGUAGE

Write a synonym and an antonym for each word. Then use both words in one sentence. In all, you will write six sentences.

    big   old   happy   remember   near   friend

Four Kinds of Sentences   *pages 4–7*

A. Write *declarative, interrogative, imperative,* or *exclamatory* to show which kind of sentence each is.

1. Have you ever heard of Mount St. Helens?
2. This peak is in the Cascade Mountains in Washington.
3. Don't climb Mount St. Helens now.
4. What a powerful and dangerous volcano erupted there!
5. The volcano first erupted in May 1980.

Complete Subjects and Complete Predicates   *pages 10–11*

B. Write each sentence. Underline the complete subject once and the complete predicate twice.

6. Several scientists watched the peak before the blast.
7. A huge bulge was growing on the mountainside.
8. Tremendous pressure was building up inside.
9. The north side of Mount St. Helens exploded on May 18.
10. The powerful explosion shot out tons of ash and stone.

Simple Subjects and Simple Predicates   *pages 12–15*

C. Write each sentence. Underline the simple subject once and the simple predicate twice.

11. The force of the blast was very great indeed.
12. People heard its sound 200 miles away!
13. A giant plume of ash billowed into the air.
14. It darkened the sky far to the east.
15. Inches of ash fell on cities and countryside.
16. The volcano's heat melted snow on the mountain.
17. A muddy flood rushed down the mountainside.
18. The powerful flow destroyed whole forests.
19. The barren landscape looked like the moon.
20. The terrible volcano lowered the mountain's peak.

Grammar Review

Locating Subjects in Sentences   *pages 16–17*

D. Write the subject of each sentence.

    21. Are you leaving for camp tomorrow?
    22. Tell me all about camp in a letter.
    23. Can we visit you there soon?
    24. Is your suitcase in the car?
    25. Don't forget your toothbrush.

Commas in Sentences   *pages 18–19*

E. Write the following sentences. Add commas where needed.

    26. Sue's parents brother and sister drove her to camp.
    27. They left Albany New York at 8:20 A.M. on July 1.
    28. Near Bennington Vermont the car had a flat tire.
    29. Sue's father lost the map made a wrong turn and followed the wrong road for miles.
    30. Everyone was surprised to be in Adams Massachusetts.
    31. They bought some fruit cheese and bread for lunch.
    32. Then thunder lightning and heavy rain made driving slow.
    33. "It will be August 1 1999 when I get to camp!" said Sue.
    34. At midnight they reached the camp near Burlington Vermont.
    35. By that time everyone was tired hungry and uncomfortable.

Synonyms and Antonyms   *pages 20–21*

F. Decide whether the word in parentheses ( ) is a synonym or an antonym for the underlined word. Write *S* or *A*.

    36. The days at camp were <u>bright</u> and happy. (dull)
    37. Sue swam in the <u>deep</u> cold lake. (shallow)
    38. She took hikes in a <u>huge</u> forest. (large)
    39. The campers put on <u>funny</u> skits and plays. (humorous)
    40. Sue will never <u>forget</u> her wonderful summer. (remember)

See also Handbook pages 332–339, 403, 405–406.

Grammar Review

Sentence Combining

Grammar and Writing Workshop

> ● Sentences with repeated ideas can be combined.

Read the sentences below.

> A. Richard saw the space shuttle.
> B. Nancy saw the space shuttle. (and)
> A + B. Richard and Nancy saw the space shuttle.

Sentence **A** tells that Richard saw the space shuttle. Sentence **B** tells that Nancy also saw the space shuttle. The word *and* was used to combine, or join together, these two short sentences into one longer sentence in **A + B**. Sentence **A + B** was made by combining the subject of sentence **A**, *Richard*, and the subject of sentence **B**, *Nancy*. The repeated idea in sentence **B** was removed.

Now look at the following sentences.

> C. Richard toured the museum.
> D. Richard met the scientist. (and)
> C + D. Richard toured the museum and met the scientist.

Sentence **C** and sentence **D** tell what Richard did. Sentence **C + D** tells the same thing in one sentence. The word *and* was used to combine the predicates of the two sentences in sentence **C + D**.

Three or more sentences that express similar thoughts can also be combined.

> E. Nancy bought photographs of Venus.
> F. Nancy bought photographs of Mars. (,)
> G. Nancy bought photographs of Jupiter. (, and)
> E + F + G. Nancy bought photographs of Venus, Mars, and Jupiter.

Commas and the word *and* were used to combine three sentences into one sentence. Recall from Lesson 8 how commas are used to separate words in a series.

Using Clues Combine the following sentences. Use the clues in parentheses ( ) the way they were used on page 24. Write each new sentence.

1. Roger Crippen traveled on the first space shuttle.
   John Young traveled on the first space shuttle. (**and**)
2. The space shuttle flies like a rocket.
   The space shuttle lands like an airplane. (**and**)
3. Modern satellites are carried aboard the shuttle.
   Important experiments are carried aboard the shuttle. (,)
   Special instruments are carried aboard the shuttle. (, **and**)
4. Newspapers interviewed Sally Ride.
   Magazines interviewed Sally Ride. (,)
   Television networks interviewed Sally Ride. (, **and**)
5. She is an experienced scientist.
   She is a trained astronaut. (,)
   She is the first American woman in outer space. (, **and**)

Using No Clues Combine each pair of sentences without clues. Write each new sentence.

6. Weather satellites observe hurricanes.
   Weather satellites photograph thunderstorms.
7. Satellites send telephone messages.
   Satellites study the stars and planets.
8. Weather satellites orbit the earth.
   Television satellites orbit the earth.
   Other special satellites orbit the earth.
9. Schools may one day get information directly from satellites.
   Homes may one day get information directly from satellites.
   Businesses may one day get information directly from satellites.
10. Satellites have been launched by the United States.
    Satellites have been launched by the Soviet Union.
    Satellites have been launched by France.

10 — Finding Words in a Dictionary

> • The words in a dictionary are arranged alphabetically. Each word that is defined is called an **entry word.**

Of all reference books the dictionary is probably the one people use most often. If you know the shortcuts to finding words in a dictionary, you can quickly locate the words you want.

The first shortcut is to think of the dictionary as divided into three parts: the front, *a–g*; the middle, *h–p*; and the back, *q–z*. Decide in which part your word is listed. Then open to that part. See how close you can come to opening to the first letter of the word you want. In which part of the dictionary would you look to find each of these words?

install   geyser   Norse   dory   renew   uneasy

Another shortcut is to use the guide words at the top of a dictionary page. They show the first and the last entry word on the page. If your word falls between the guide words alphabetically, or if it is a guide word, it should appear on that page. If the word does not fall between the guide words, decide if it comes before or after that page.

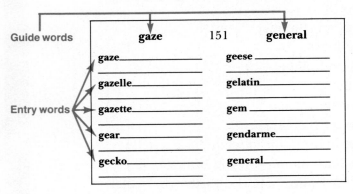

Guide words: **gaze**   151   **general**

Entry words:
gaze
gazelle
gazette
gear
gecko

geese
gelatin
gem
gendarme
general

Skills Tryout

Tell whether each word comes *on*, *before*, or *after* the page with the guide words **equip** and **error.**

1. equator   **2.** err   **3.** erupt   **4.** eraser   **5.** equine

Practice

A. Write the following words in alphabetical order. Then write *front, middle,* or *back* to show in which part of the dictionary each word would be found.

1. cutter   **4.** shadow   **7.** cutlet
2. usher   **5.** medical   **8.** eagle
3. predict   **6.** predicate   **9.** shade

B. Guide words for dictionary pages 436–439 are shown at the right. Write words 10–25. Then write the page number for each entry word.

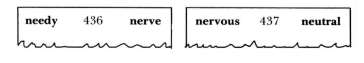

| needy | 436 | nerve | | nervous | 437 | neutral |

| neutron | 438 | newt | | next | 439 | nimble |

10. nickel   **14.** newcomer   **18.** next   **22.** nest
11. neighbor   **15.** nerve   **19.** neuter   **23.** neigh
12. nettle   **16.** neglect   **20.** nephew   **24.** nibble
13. newsreel   **17.** neurotic   **21.** niece   **25.** never

C. Look up these words in a dictionary. For each word write the guide words from the page on which the word appears.

26. practical   **31.** notch   **36.** sparrow   **41.** xylem
27. saunter   **32.** remedy   **37.** bolt   **42.** yen
28. fiendish   **33.** sponsor   **38.** ail   **43.** zebu
29. sergeant   **34.** exploit   **39.** hyena   **44.** quaff
30. gopher   **35.** mirage   **40.** walrus   **45.** jetty

Application   USING STUDY SKILLS

Write ten words from the glossary of a social studies or science book. Scramble the alphabetical order. Then exchange papers with a classmate. See who can most quickly alphabetize the words and write the dictionary page number where each one appears.

11 — **Using a Dictionary**

> ● A dictionary gives spellings, pronunciations, meanings, and parts of speech of words.

Does *recommend* have two *m*'s or two *c*'s? What does *migrate* mean? What is the correct pronunciation of *amphibian*? As you read, write, and speak, many questions about words arise.

Fortunately there is one book that can help you answer these questions—the dictionary. Study the entries below. Notice the kinds of information that dictionary entries contain.

Pronunciation   Part of speech

Accent marks

Entry word—**ir ri gate** (ir′ə gāt), *v.* To bring water to crops, usually through canals or pipes.

i so therm (ī′sə thèrm), *n.* A line on a weather map connecting areas that have the same temperature.

Definition

isth mus (is′məs), *n.* A narrow strip of land between two larger bodies of land.

i tin er ar y (ī tin′ə rer′ē), *n.* The route of a journey or a proposed outline of one. *Our itinerary lists the hotels we will stay at during our vacation.*

i vo ry (ī′vər ē), *n.* 1. The hard white material that composes elephant tusks. 2. A creamy white color.

Example sentence

Pronunciation key   hat, āge, cāre, fär; let, ēqual, tèrm; it, īce; hot, ōpen, ôrder; oil, out; cup, pùt, rüle; **ch**, child; **ng**, long; **sh**, she; **th**, thin; **ŦH**, then; **zh**, measure; ə represents *a* in about, *e* in taken, *i* in pencil, *o* in lemon, *u* in circus.

Skills Tryout

Use the dictionary entries above to answer these questions.

1. Which entry word is not a noun?
2. Which syllable is accented in the word *isthmus*?
3. Which word in the pronunciation key shows how to pronounce the *i* in *ivory*?
4. Which entry includes an example sentence?
5. What is the number of the meaning that *ivory* has in this sentence? *She ordered the sweater in blue and in ivory.*

Practice

A. Use these dictionary entries for questions **1–5.**

> **glad i a tor** (glad′ē ā′tər), *n.* 1. A person who fought another person or animal for the entertainment of an audience in ancient Rome. 2. A person who takes part in any kind of struggle.
>
> **glance** (glans), *v.* 1. To take a quick look. 2. To strike slantwise and go off at an angle. 3. To flash; glint. *The water glanced in the sunlight.*
>
> **gland** (gland), *n.* Any special organ or tissue in the body that makes chemical substances.

1. What part of speech is *gland*?
2. What is the number of the meaning that *glance* has in this sentence? *Hail began to glance off the window as the storm worsened.*
3. Which entry contains an example sentence?
4. Which entry word names a part of the body?
5. Which meaning of *gladiator* describes a football player?

B. Use a dictionary to answer these questions.

6. Which word is spelled incorrectly and how should it be spelled: *embarrass, license, occurrence, seige*?
7. Which word names a color: *flitch, dun, fain, coif*?
8. Does *feign* rhyme with *lean, pain,* or *sign*?
9. What part of speech is the word *plover*?
10. Which word has an accent on its first syllable: *oblivious, obscurity, obelisk, outlandish*?

Application USING STUDY SKILLS

Look up the words below in a dictionary. For each word write the part of speech, the pronunciation, and the definition. Then use each word in a sentence that shows you understand the meaning of the word.

dialogue	tyranny	scornful
buoyancy	flinch	migrate

12 — Using a Thesaurus

> ● A **thesaurus** contains lists of synonyms and antonyms.

The English language has the largest vocabulary and the most synonyms of any language in the world. One way to take advantage of the richness of the English language is to use a thesaurus. A thesaurus lists entry words in alphabetical order and gives synonyms and antonyms for each one. Use a thesaurus to find the exact word you want when you write.

Turn to pages 414–433 of this book and skim through the Thesaurus that appears there. After you have seen how the Thesaurus is organized, study this entry for *noise*.

Part of speech   **Definition**

Entry word — **noise** (n)—loud, confused, or irritating sounds.

Example sentence — The <u>noise</u> of traffic in the street made sleep impossible.

Synonyms —
clamor—a loud noise, especially shouting, that goes on continuously. the <u>clamor</u> of the crowd filled the air.
clatter—a rapid succession of sharp, rattling sounds. An awful <u>clatter</u> was coming from the kitchen.
din—loud noise that goes on without letup. The <u>din</u> from the stadium could be heard blocks away.
hubbub—a general, confused noise, as of many voices. The speaker waited for the <u>hubbub</u> to die down.

Informal — *ruckus* [informal]—a noisy uproar. After the game, the winning team raised a <u>ruckus</u> in the locker room.

Cross-reference — See also *sound* (n).

Antonyms — ANTONYMS: calm (n), quiet (n), silence (n), tranquility.

Skills Tryout

Use the thesaurus entry above to answer these questions.

1. What part of speech are *noise* and its synonyms?
2. Which words are antonyms of *noise*?
3. Which synonym for *noise* best describes the sound of banging pots and pans?

Practice

A. Write each sentence. Complete it with a synonym for *noise*. Use a different synonym in each sentence.

    1. The _____ of angry voices was heard outside the palace.

    2. The arrival of the king caused a _____ of excitement.

    3. The _____ from a nearby construction site interferes with my work.

    4. Did you hear the _____ of breaking dishes?

    5. The announcement that the concert had been canceled created an incredible _____ among the fans.

B. In each sentence below, replace the word *hot* with a synonym that makes sense. (Turn to *hot* in the Thesaurus for a list of synonyms.) Write the new sentences.

    6. Kim wasn't used to the hot jungle climate.

    7. Alan served us bowls of hot soup.

    8. Under the hot sun our lawn turned brown.

    9. The hot bedroom in the attic had only one small window.

    10. Now place the vegetables in the hot oil.

C. Find the five antonyms for *hot* listed in the Thesaurus. Write a sentence for each word. If you wish, you can write the sentences about a winter sport or activity.

D. Find the six synonyms for *grow* listed in the Thesaurus. Write a sentence for each word.

Application USING STUDY SKILLS

Choose a commonly used word and write a thesaurus entry for it. Set up your entry like the one on the opposite page. Write the word's part of speech, a short definition, and an example sentence for it. Then list as many synonyms for the word as you can think of. Be sure to include definitions for the synonyms, too. Finish the entry by listing antonyms for the word.

13 — What Is a Paragraph?

> ● A **paragraph** is a group of related sentences about one main idea.

When you write, you need to organize your thoughts in a meaningful way. You also need to write about one idea at a time. You do this by writing in paragraphs.

A paragraph is a group of related sentences about one main idea. Often a paragraph has one sentence that states the main idea. The other sentences give more information about the main idea. The first sentence of a paragraph is indented.

Read the paragraph below. The first sentence states the main idea. Notice that one sentence is crossed out because it does not relate to the main idea.

> The Smithsonian Institution in Washington, D.C., began as a gift from James Smithson. Smithson was an English scientist who never saw America. Yet when he died in 1829, he willed a huge fortune to the United States to start the Smithsonian. One popular exhibit there is the Wright Brothers' plane. Smithson did not say why he left his money to Americans. Perhaps he wanted to honor the new nation and its people.

Skills Tryout

Tell which sentences below belong in a paragraph about the National Zoo in Washington, D.C.

1. The National Zoo is part of the Smithsonian Institution.
2. The zoo is the home of more than 2,500 animals.
3. Its most famous residents are two giant pandas.
4. Pandas love to eat bamboo.
5. There are also elephants, giraffes, and monkeys in the zoo.

Practice

A. Write *yes* if a sentence tells about this main idea and *no* if it does not: *The White House grounds have been used by Presidents in different ways.*

1. Dwight D. Eisenhower played golf on the lawn.
2. John Adams planted peas and cabbages on the grounds.
3. The grounds are carefully guarded.
4. Thomas Jefferson kept grizzly bears on the grounds.
5. It takes many people to care for the White House grounds.

B. Write the following paragraph. Underline the sentence that states the main idea. Cross out the sentence that does not belong.

    The Smithsonian Institution is more than one museum. Altogether it has thirteen museums. Twelve of these are in Washington, D.C., and one is in New York City. New York City, like Washington, D.C., has many fine museums.

C. Write the following sentences as a paragraph. Write the main idea first. Then write the other sentences in an order that makes sense. Remember to indent the first sentence.

6. The collection grows by about a million objects a year.
7. Therefore, the Smithsonian's staff changes exhibits often.
8. The Smithsonian Institution has a vast number of objects in its collection.
9. Only a small part of the collection can be shown at one time.
10. It now has about 75 million items.

Application WRITING A PARAGRAPH

    Write a paragraph about an interesting place you have visited or would like to visit. Begin with a sentence that states the main idea. Add other sentences that tell more about the main idea.

14 Topic Sentences and Supporting Sentences

- The **topic sentence** states the main idea of a paragraph.
- **Supporting sentences** give details about the main idea.

You know that many paragraphs have a sentence that states the main idea. This sentence is called the topic sentence. A paragraph does not have to have a topic sentence, but a topic sentence helps to make the main idea of the paragraph especially clear. Although the topic sentence often comes first, it may come anywhere in a paragraph. The other sentences give details about the main idea. They are supporting sentences.

In the paragraph below, the first sentence is the topic sentence. The other sentences give details to support it.

Topic Sentence →

Supporting Sentences →

Many desert animals dig burrows to escape the scorching desert sun. In a burrow only four inches below the desert surface, the temperature is thirty-one degrees cooler than on the surface. In a burrow eighteen inches beneath the desert floor, the temperature can be over eighty degrees cooler than the burning desert sand.

Skills Tryout

The following sentences could form a paragraph. Tell which is the topic sentence and which are supporting sentences.

1. The Sahara is almost as large as the entire United States.
2. Africa's immense Sahara is the largest desert in the world.
3. It has a lake the size of New Jersey.

A. Use sentences **1–5** to write a paragraph. Begin with the topic sentence. Then complete the paragraph by writing the supporting sentences.

> 1. They are deserts because they get less than ten inches of rain a year.
> 2. Parts of the Arctic and Antarctic, for example, are considered to be deserts.
> 3. Deserts are always dry, but they are not always hot.
> 4. That is how scientists define a desert.
> 5. In fact, some deserts get bitterly cold.

B. Choose one of the following topic sentences. Write the sentence. Then develop it into a paragraph by adding at least two supporting sentences.

> 6. I would (would not) like to visit the Sahara.
> 7. Night is the best time to visit a desert.
> 8. A camel would probably (probably not) make a good pet.
> 9. Traveling on a flying carpet would have many advantages.
> 10. Water is one of our most precious natural resources.

C. Write a topic sentence for each of these topics.

> 11. A pet you would (would not) like to have
> 12. Things people collect
> 13. A character from a book you have read
> 14. Your favorite sport
> 15. An interesting (strange) hobby

Application WRITING A PARAGRAPH ───────────────────────

Imagine that you have visited a strange, exotic land. (You may choose a real or an imaginary place.) Write a paragraph describing it. Try to include at least four fascinating details in your paragraph. Underline the topic sentence.

15 — The Writing Process

What happens when you write? What really goes on when you write a story or a report? Have you ever thought about it? Take some time now to think about it and to discuss it with your classmates. Try to describe what happens when you write.

Everyone writes differently. In general, however, all writers follow four steps:

1. **prewriting** 3. **revising**
2. **writing**   4. **publishing**

This is "the writing process."

A description of the writing process begins on the next page. As you read, think about it. Does it describe what happens when *you* write?

1. Prewriting

Prewriting is getting and exploring ideas. This can be difficult, of course. Have you ever wanted to say, "I don't know what to write about"? If so, don't worry. All writers sometimes feel that way.

Here are just a few techniques for getting ideas:

- Notice the look, smell, sound, taste, or feel of something.
- Read a book and jot down your reactions to it.
- Interview someone about a subject they know well.

Almost any activity can provide an idea. Here is the surprise: One idea is all you need to start writing.

2. Writing

Is it true that you must know everything you will write before you start writing? No, you can start writing with just one small idea. You will get more ideas as soon as you start to write. Remember: Thinking helps you write, but also writing helps you think!

WRITER'S HINT: As you write, it helps to know two things:

1. **Purpose** Why are you writing? To tell a story? To persuade someone about an opinion you have?

2. **Audience** Who will read what you write? Will your reader be someone your own age? Someone younger? An adult?

Knowing your purpose and your audience helps you write more effectively.

This is the time to get all your ideas on paper. Don't worry about neatness or spelling. Don't worry about putting your ideas in the best order. Just keep on writing as long as ideas are coming. When you have written everything you want to say, stop. You have written your first draft.

3. Revising

Vision means "seeing." *Revision* means "seeing again." Revising is taking another look at what you have written, trying to see it through your reader's eyes. It is adding, subtracting, or changing to make clearer. It is rewriting to improve.

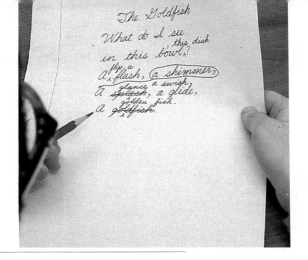

4. Publishing

Publishing is sharing what you have written. You can mail a letter to the editor of a newspaper or read a story to the class. You can place a collection of poems in the school library or post a report on the bulletin board.

Be courteous to your reader. Before you publish, proofread what you have written. Fix any errors, and make a neat and correct copy.

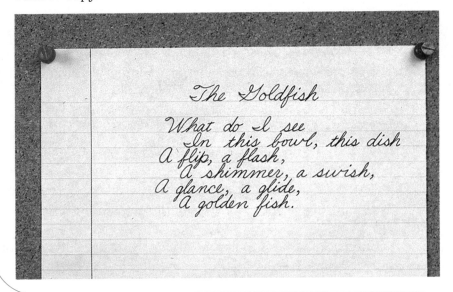

16 — Writing a Paragraph of Contrast

> ● A **paragraph of contrast** tells about differences between two objects, persons, places, animals, or ideas.

Differences are important. You think about differences, or make contrasts, whenever you must choose between two similar things. For example, you make contrasts to help you decide whether to buy sneakers or running shoes … whether to join the soccer team or the basketball team … whether to get a hamster or a gerbil for a pet.

Finding differences is important in school subjects, too. For example, in science you might be asked to tell how reptiles and amphibians are different. In social studies you might be asked to contrast forest regions with plains regions.

Making contrasts can sharpen your thinking skills and your powers of observation. In this lesson you will have an opportunity to sharpen both as you write a paragraph of contrast to share with your classmates.

1. Prewriting

Your paragraph will tell how two similar things are different. What two things could you write about? Brainstorming with your classmates is a good way to think of possible topics. The purpose of brainstorming is to get a lot of thoughts flowing. Everyone in the group tries to give many ideas quickly, without stopping to think about whether the ideas are good or not. When a suggestion is given, it is not discussed or judged. That would stop the flow of ideas.

▶ Brainstorm about pairs of things to write about. Both things should belong to the same category. Look at the examples on the next page.

- hamsters and gerbils (pets)
- science-fiction movies and comedy movies (movies)
- hang gliding and skydiving (air sports)
- wild animals and tame animals (animals)
- rock music and classical music (music)
- tornadoes and hurricanes (storms)

When you have finished brainstorming, think of the pairs that were suggested. Choose one of these or a pair of your own for your topic.

▶ Do your own brainstorming to think of the differences between the two things you have chosen. Think of as many differences as you can. Write the differences in a chart, as in the example below, or make notes about your topic.

gerbil

	Hamsters	Gerbils
Differences in appearance:	many colors and markings fluffy coats short, stubby tails	few colors and markings smooth coats long, hairy tails
Differences in movement:	creeps, crawls, and climbs on four legs	leaps, jumps on strong hind legs

hamster

2. Writing

What have you chosen to contrast? Let your readers know in your first sentence. You could begin with a question: "Do you know the differences between hamsters and gerbils?" Also consider beginning with a statement: "If you observe hamsters and gerbils carefully, you will notice differences in their appearance and movement."

Connecting words and phrases

although
however
besides
on the
other hand
even though
in contrast

▶ Begin your paragraph by stating the main idea. Then use the chart or the notes you made when you brainstormed. Write supporting sentences to illustrate the differences.

Read the connecting words and phrases in the box. These words and phrases will help you introduce supporting sentences that explain differences.

3. Revising

▶ Read your first draft to yourself. Think about changes you could make to improve your writing. Use this checklist as you revise your paragraph.

Revision Checklist

- Does my paragraph begin with a topic sentence that states the main idea?
- Did I write supporting sentences that tell more about the topic sentence?
- Did I contrast two things by telling about their differences?
- Did I use connecting words to introduce supporting sentences?
- Did I combine short sentences that repeat similar ideas?

Writers use editing marks when they revise their work. These symbols show what changes a writer wants to make. Read the sample paragraph and notice how editing marks were used to make changes. Also notice how the sample was improved by combining sentences.

If you observe
Look at hamsters and gerbils carefully. You will
differences
notice diffrences in their appearance. You will see
and   *fluffy*
that their movements are different. The coats of

If you observe hamsters and gerbils carefully, you will notice differences in their appearance and movements. The fluffy coats of hamsters vary more in color and markings than the smooth coats of gerbils. Hamsters have short, stubby tails that are barely visible. On the other hand, gerbils' tails are quite long and hairy. Using their two oversized back legs, gerbils leap and jump. In contrast, hamsters climb, creep, and crawl on four legs.

▶ Now make your changes, using the editing marks.

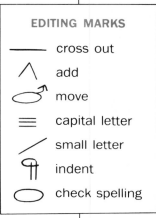

EDITING MARKS

——	cross out
∧	add
↻	move
≡	capital letter
/	small letter
¶	indent
◯	check spelling

4. Publishing

▶ Use the checklist below to proofread your writing, and use the editing marks to make corrections.

Proofreading Checklist

- Is the first word of the paragraph indented?
- Does each sentence begin with a capital letter and end with the correct punctuation?
- Is each word spelled correctly?
- Have I used my best handwriting?

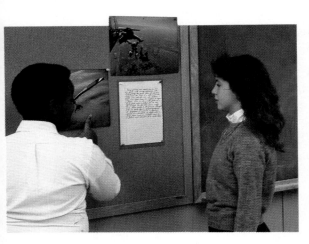

▶ Find pictures that illustrate the two things you wrote about in your contrast paragraph. Display your pictures and paragraph on a class bulletin board for others to enjoy. Take time to read your classmates' paragraphs and to tell the writers what you liked most about their work.

Writing Project

A Dictionary Calendar

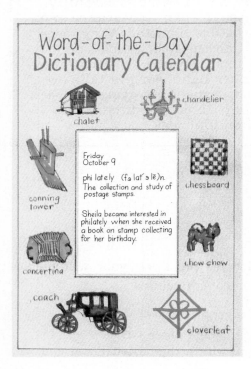

Make a word-of-the-day dictionary calendar to build your class's word power. Choose one school day in the month. Pick a day that no one else has chosen. Then make a calendar dictionary page to display on that day. The page should show the date, a dictionary entry, and an original sentence for the dictionary word. Try to choose a word that you think your classmates do not know but will be able to use. Check the word with your teacher first.

Each day read the word that is posted. Throughout the day try to use the word as often as you can in your speaking and in your writing.

Social Studies

Classifying is part of thinking. When you classify, you organize. You put things together that belong together. For example, you classify when you put words in alphabetical order. You classify when you group details that belong together in a paragraph.

Classifying is important in social studies. When you study the nations of the world, you will find they are classified into groups. One way of classifying some nations is shown below. This way of classifying groups the nations according to where they are located.

1. Western Europe
2. The Soviet Union and Eastern Europe
3. The Middle East and North Africa
4. Africa south of the Sahara
5. South Asia, East Asia, and Australia

▶ Try it. Use the five groups above to classify the nations listed on the right. Write the groups on a sheet of paper. After each one, list the nations that belong in that group. You may use an atlas or an encyclopedia if you need help.

Speakers at Work Teachers are concerned with helping students to think. They spend much time explaining classifications to their students.

▶ Pretend you are a first-grade teacher. You want to explain the classifications *city*, *state*, and *country* to your class. Prepare an oral explanation that will help the class understand these classifications. You might point out that a city is within a state and a state within a country.

United Kingdom
Turkey
Sudan
Hungary
Italy
Japan
Zaire
Egypt
Norway
Ghana
Australia
Senegal
France
Poland
Nigeria
Israel
Yugoslavia
India
China
Algeria
Austria
Tunisia
Romania
Thailand

Sentences *pages 4–17*

A. Write the sentences using capital letters and correct end punctuation. After each sentence write *declarative, interrogative, imperative,* or *exclamatory*.

1. get into the raft now
2. can you paddle faster
3. how cold the water is
4. rafting trips are exciting

B. Write each complete subject. Underline each simple subject.

5. Baron von Drais of Germany built the first bicycle.
6. This awkward machine was made of wood.
7. A handle on the front wheel turned the bicycle.
8. The baron's bicycle became popular for a brief time.

C. Write each complete predicate. Then underline each simple predicate.

9. Theresa is beginning a seashell collection.
10. She keeps her shells in a large box.
11. The collection includes starfish and sand dollars.
12. A friend has given Theresa some oyster shells.

D. Write the subject of each sentence.

13. Are the actors ready?
14. Open the curtains.
15. Change the scenery quickly.
16. Did Jamie forget his lines?

Commas *pages 18–19*

E. Write each sentence. Add commas where needed.

17. Paul Revere was born on January 1 1735 in Boston.
18. He became a skilled silversmith engraver and printer.
19. On April 18 1775 he made his famous ride.
20. The town of Revere Massachusetts was named for him.

Checkpoint: Unit 1

Synonyms and Antonyms *pages 26–29*

F. Write whether the word pairs are *synonyms* or *antonyms*.

21. tame/wild **22.** gaze/stare **23.** lid/cover **24.** halt/start

Dictionary *pages 26–29*

G. Use these dictionary entries for questions **25–28**.

pe cul iar (pi kyül′yər), *adj.* 1. Odd or strange.
2. Belonging to one group, person, place, or thing.
Feathers are peculiar to birds.
pen nant (pen′ənt), *n.* A long, narrow flag, usually
triangular in shape.
per suade (pər swād′), *v.* To convince by urging.

25. What part of speech is *persuade*?
26. Which syllable is accented in the word *peculiar*?
27. Which entry word names a type of flag?
28. Which entry contains an example sentence?

Thesaurus *pages 30–31*

H. Use the thesaurus entry for questions **29–31**.

sleek (adj)—smooth and shiny.
My cat's fur is <u>sleek</u>.
glossy—having a shiny surface
silky—soft and smooth
**ANTONYMS: coarse (adj), dull
(adj), rough (adj)**

29. What part of speech
is *sleek*?
30. Which words are
synonyms of *sleek*?
31. Which words are
antonyms of *sleek*?

Paragraphs *pages 32–35*

I. Write a topic sentence and two supporting sentences about
Why people enjoy vacations.

See also Handbook pages 332–339, 390, 402, 405–406.

Grammar
Nouns

Composition
Persuading

The Kayak

Over the briny wave I go,
In spite of the weather, in spite of the snow:
What cares the hardy Eskimo?
In my little skiff, with paddle and lance,
I glide where the foaming billows dance.

Round me the sea-birds slip and soar;
Like me, they love the ocean's roar.
Sometimes a floating iceberg gleams
Above me with its melting streams;
Sometimes a rushing wave will fall
Down on my skiff and cover it all.

But what care I for a wave's attack?
With my paddle I right my little kayak,
And then its weight I speedily trim,
And over the water away I skim.

—*Anonymous*

1 Nouns

> ● A **noun** names a person, place, thing, or idea.

Nouns are naming words. A noun may name a person, place, thing, or idea. The chart below shows examples of nouns.

Nouns	
Names of Persons	girl, boy, worker, Paul Bunyan
Names of Places	park, city, Minnesota
Names of Things	house, log, pen, Ohio River
Names of Ideas	honesty, kindness, love

Most nouns name things that can be seen or touched. For example, you can see a town or a lake. You can touch a child or a house. Some nouns, however, name things that cannot be seen or touched. These nouns name ideas, such as happiness, anger, and success.

Nouns can be made up of one word or more than one word. Look back at the chart. Which nouns are more than one word?

Skills Tryout

Name the nouns in each sentence.

1. Paul Bunyan is the hero of many tales.
2. Lumberjacks made up stories about his strength.
3. This powerful man could easily cut down a whole forest.
4. Paul was a fast runner, too.
5. The friendly giant could beat his own shadow!

Practice

A. Write the nouns in these sentences.

1. A great blue ox named Babe lived with Paul.
2. The very heavy pet left his footprints in solid rock!
3. The ox could haul a forest of logs.
4. The logger and his crew lived in a huge bunkhouse.
5. The chimney almost touched the sun.
6. Paul Bunyan cut down trees in Minnesota.
7. His sawmill was in Louisiana.
8. The giant needed logs for his mill.
9. No rivers or roads had been built.
10. So Paul and Babe dug the Mississippi River!

B. Write the nouns in these sentences. Then write whether each noun names a person, place, thing, or idea.

EXAMPLE: Paul made his own ax.
ANSWER: Paul (person), ax (thing)

11. Paul Bunyan had tremendous power.
12. His voice shook every tree in the forest.
13. Paul dug Lake Michigan for a bathtub.
14. His handkerchief was a sheet.
15. His bed covered a large field.
16. The giant used a tree as a comb.
17. For breakfast the great lumberjack ate 140 eggs.
18. Paul drank thirty buckets of milk.
19. The logger met Pecos Bill in Arizona.
20. The two men became friends.

Application WRITING SENTENCES

Paul Bunyan was many times bigger than an average man. Think about what it would be like to be the size of this imaginary giant. Write five sentences telling what problems you might have. Underline each noun in your sentences.

2 Common and Proper Nouns

- A **common noun** is the general name of a person, place, or thing.
- A **proper noun** names a particular person, place, or thing.

You know that a noun names a person, place, or thing. Notice the underlined nouns in the following sentences.

1. The <u>woman</u> loved her <u>state</u>.
2. <u>Martha Washington</u> loved <u>Virginia</u>.

The nouns in sentence 1 do not name any particular woman or state. *Woman* is a general name for every woman. *State* is the name for any state. These nouns are called common nouns. A common noun is the general name of a person, place, or thing.

The nouns in sentence 2 name a particular woman, Martha Washington, and a particular state, Virginia. A noun that names a particular person, place, or thing is a proper noun.

A proper noun always begins with a capital letter. Some proper nouns are made up of more than one word, but only the important words begin with a capital letter.

George Washington   **Washington and Lee University**

Skills Tryout

The nouns in the sentences below are underlined. Tell whether each noun is common or proper.

1. A <u>class</u> from <u>Ridgevale School</u> went to <u>Virginia</u>.
2. <u>Pupils</u> saw <u>Mount Vernon</u>, the <u>home</u> of <u>George Washington</u>.
3. The beautiful <u>Potomac River</u> flows near the <u>house</u>.
4. The <u>students</u> also visited the <u>Tomb of the Unknown Soldier</u>.
5. This <u>monument</u> is located in <u>Arlington</u>.

Practice

A. Write each underlined word. Then write whether it is a common noun or a proper noun.

1. <u>Virginia</u> has a rich <u>past</u>.
2. <u>Thomas Jefferson</u> was a famous <u>president</u> from that <u>state</u>.
3. He was the <u>author</u> of the <u>Declaration of Independence</u>.
4. The <u>class</u> saw <u>Monticello</u>, his <u>home</u> near <u>Charlottesville</u>.
5. They visited <u>Jamestown</u>, too.
6. <u>Settlers</u> from <u>England</u> arrived there in 1607.
7. Nearby <u>Williamsburg</u> is a historic <u>city</u>.
8. <u>Craft House</u> and other <u>buildings</u> have interesting <u>exhibits</u>.
9. The <u>battlefield</u> at <u>Yorktown</u> was the <u>scene</u> of a big <u>event</u>.
10. The last major <u>battle</u> of the <u>American Revolution</u> took place there.

B. Write each sentence. Draw one line under each common noun and two lines under each proper noun.

11. Norfolk is the largest city.
12. Ships from Norfolk sail across Chesapeake Bay to the Atlantic Ocean.
13. Nearby Virginia Beach is a great place for a vacation.
14. Ships are built in Newport News.
15. The Pentagon is in Arlington.
16. The students also visited the capitol at Richmond.
17. On Monument Avenue are statues of great heroes.
18. The trip ended on Skyline Drive.
19. The Blue Ridge Mountains can be seen from this road.
20. These mountains extend into North Carolina.

Application WRITING SENTENCES

Write six sentences about a place you have visited in your state. Use at least three common nouns and three proper nouns in your sentences. Underline the common nouns once and the proper nouns twice.

3 — Capitalizing Proper Nouns

> ● A proper noun always begins with a capital letter.

You have learned that a proper noun names a particular person, place, or thing. You also know that the important words in a proper noun begin with a capital letter. The chart below shows when to use capital letters in proper nouns.

When to Use Capital Letters	
1. Capitalize the names of persons and pets.	Anthony, Susan Ramos, John Paul Jones, Rover
2. Capitalize important words in the names of particular places and things.	Salt Lake City, Utah, Canada, Lake of the Woods, Maple Avenue, Golden Gate Bridge, World Trade Center
3. Capitalize months, days, and holidays.	November, Thursday, Fourth of July, Thanksgiving
4. Capitalize important words in the names of clubs, organizations, and businesses.	Maplewood Garden Club, Jackson Fire Department, Park Paint and Paper Company

Which words are not capitalized in the proper nouns above?

Skills Tryout

Name the proper nouns in these sentences and tell which letters should be capitalized.

1. Sixth graders at lamonte school studied careers last may.
2. One friday an officer from the ridgefield police department spoke to the class.
3. Students also visited ridge hospital on valley road.
4. linda harris, a doctor, described many health careers.
5. She studied medicine at the university of chicago.

Practice

A. Write the sentences. Capitalize the proper nouns.

1. A reporter from a newspaper spoke to the class may 15.
2. Students visited the newspaper's office on main street.
3. On thursday alan wess of micrex company told the class about careers in computers.
4. His company has offices in mexico, israel, and france.
5. Members of the lamonte computer club enjoyed the talk.
6. beth lang of the professional engineering society also spoke.
7. She showed her plans for the honey river bridge.
8. Finally, cara gray and her owl, charlie, visited the class.
9. She told about working at yellowstone national park.
10. After memorial day, students reported on other careers.

B. Write a proper noun for each common noun below.

EXAMPLE: state
ANSWER: Oklahoma

11. river
12. building
13. country
14. bridge
15. street
16. school
17. store
18. company
19. holiday
20. club

Application FILLING OUT FORMS

Copy this form and fill it out. Make up any information you do not know. Circle each proper noun.

```
                  DOG LICENSE APPLICATION
OWNER'S NAME_____
              First           Middle           Last
ADDRESS    _____
           Number   Street

           _____
           City                          State
DOG'S NAME_____AGE _____
MALE ☐    FEMALE ☐    COLOR _____
```

4 — Abbreviations

- An **abbreviation** is a shortened form of a word. Many abbreviations begin with a capital letter and end with a period.
- An **initial** is the first letter of a name. It is written with a capital letter and followed by a period.

Sometimes you do not have to write out a word completely. Instead, you can use an abbreviation. An abbreviation is a shortened form of a word. For example, *Sen.* is an abbreviation for *Senator.* Many abbreviations begin with a capital letter and end with a period. Here are some common abbreviations.

Titles of Persons	Dr.—Doctor Rev.—Reverend Gov.—Governor Mr.—Mister Mrs.—Mistress (a married woman) Ms.—for Miss (an unmarried woman) or Mrs.
Words That Mean *Street*	St.—Street Rd.—Road Ave.—Avenue La.—Lane Dr.—Drive Blvd.—Boulevard Pl.—Place
Days	Sun. Mon. Tues. Wed. Thurs. Fri. Sat.
Months	Jan. Feb. Mar. Apr. Aug. (Other months are Sept. Oct. Nov. Dec. not abbreviated.)
Times	A.M.—*ante meridiem* (Latin for *before noon*) P.M.—*post meridiem* (Latin for *after noon*)

Initials are sometimes used in place of complete names. The name *Sarah Brown Johnson* could be written *S.B. Johnson.* Initials are capitalized and followed by a period.

Skills Tryout

Tell what each abbreviation stands for.

1. Mr.   **2.** Ave.   **3.** Mon.   **4.** Apr.   **5.** P.M.

Practice

A. Rewrite the proper nouns below using complete words in place of the abbreviations.

1. Gov. Drew
2. Aug. 16
3. Thurs.
4. Dr. Bergstrom
5. Clay St.

6. Rev. John Diaz
7. Ark Ave.
8. Dec. 20
9. Mr. Breen
10. Sun., July 2

B. Write the abbreviation or initial for each underlined word.

11. Our dog Sparky got loose on <u>Tuesday</u>, <u>September</u> 28.
12. He ran down Park <u>Drive</u> toward Lincoln <u>Place</u>.
13. <u>Reverend</u> <u>Edward</u> Daly saw the dog go by.
14. Sparky chased <u>Mister</u> Newman's cat up a tree.
15. Then he ran to <u>Doctor</u> <u>Laura</u> <u>Ann</u> Polk's office.
16. <u>Doctor</u> Polk is a veterinarian on Myrtle <u>Road</u>.
17. She said, "Sparky's appointment isn't until <u>Wednesday</u>."
18. The doctor drove Sparky to our house on Elm <u>Street</u>.
19. "Bring Sparky to the office on <u>October</u> 6," she said.
20. After his adventure Sparky slept all day <u>Friday</u>.

Application FILLING OUT FORMS

Copy this application for a part-time job with Dr. Polk. Then fill it out. Use abbreviations for your street address and for months, days, and times.

```
                     JOB APPLICATION

Name_____
        Last                    First          Middle Initial
Address_____
         Number and Street
        _____
          City                        State        ZIP
Today's Date _____ Date of Birth _____
Days of the week you can work  _____
Hours you can work _____
```

5 — **Singular and Plural Nouns**

- A **singular noun** names one person, place, thing, or idea.

- A **plural noun** names more than one person, place, thing, or idea.

Rob knew that a singular noun names one thing and a plural noun names more than one. While using the dictionary one day, he learned that different nouns form their plurals in different ways. Most nouns add -s in the plural. Some change their spelling in the plural. A few have the same singular and plural.

Singular	Plural
boy girl dog	boys girls dogs
patch dish glass box	patches dishes glasses boxes
party lady hobby	parties ladies hobbies
toy tray monkey	toys trays monkeys
calf wife shelf	calves wives shelves
rodeo potato hero	rodeos potatoes heroes
tooth woman child	teeth women children
moose deer sheep	moose deer sheep

The rules for spelling plural nouns are on page 344 of your Grammar Handbook. Refer to the rules as you complete the practice exercises in this lesson.

Skills Tryout

Tell how you would form the plurals of these nouns.

1. tax
2. birch
3. cherry
4. cabin
5. potato
6. elf
7. moose
8. bee
9. man
10. guess

Practice

A. Write the plural form of each noun.

1. fox	**6.** cry	**11.** self	**16.** deer
2. body	**7.** lunch	**12.** radio	**17.** sky
3. stone	**8.** rodeo	**13.** hero	**18.** church
4. valley	**9.** eyelash	**14.** day	**19.** lock
5. thief	**10.** loss	**15.** tooth	**20.** play

B. Write each sentence using the plural forms of the nouns in parentheses ( ).

21. The (child) saw many (exhibit) at the county fair.

22. (Business) and farm (society) sponsored the event.

23. The (pen) of (calf) and (sheep) interested Elsa.

24. Kurt liked the (pony), (donkey), and (lamb).

25. One girl was brushing the (mane) of her (horse).

26. (Man) and (woman) were showing (duck) and (turkey).

27. The biggest and best (tomato), (cabbage), and (beet) were also on view.

28. These (vegetable) were stored in (box) on (shelf).

29. Kurt sampled some excellent (jam) and (jelly) made from (blackberry) and (peach).

30. Then Elsa and Kurt each drank two (glass) of milk and ate two (sandwich).

Application WRITING SENTENCES

Write six sentences about a fair or carnival you have attended. Tell what you saw and what you did. Use at least two plural nouns in each sentence.

6 Possessive Nouns

> ● A **possessive noun** shows ownership.

You know that a noun names a person, place, thing, or idea. A noun can also show ownership, or possession. The underlined nouns below are possessive nouns.

The colony had a harvest. It was the <u>colony's</u> harvest.
The Pilgrims had a feast. It was the <u>Pilgrims'</u> feast.
The children had a turkey. It was the <u>children's</u> turkey.

The chart below lists rules for forming possessive nouns.

Forming Possessive Nouns	
To form the possessive of a singular noun, add an apostrophe and *s* ('s).	a <u>child's</u> job Sue <u>Ashton's</u> house <u>James's</u> good luck
To form the possessive of a plural noun that ends in *s*, add only an apostrophe (').	three <u>farmers'</u> fields many <u>students'</u> books the <u>girls'</u> coats
To form the possessive of a plural noun that does not end in *s*, add an apostrophe and *s* ('s).	the <u>geese's</u> feathers the <u>women's</u> tools many <u>people's</u> efforts the <u>oxen's</u> tails

Skills Tryout

Name the possessive noun in each sentence. Then tell whether it is singular or plural.

1. Thanksgiving began with the Pilgrims' feast in 1621.
2. The settlers' harvest was poor the next year.
3. The celebration's date changed from year to year.
4. A few colonies' leaders decided against the holiday.
5. More than one Thanksgiving a year was common in some of New England's towns.

Practice

A. Write the possessive noun in each sentence. Then write whether it is singular or plural.

1. Our country's first nationwide day of thanksgiving was celebrated in 1789.
2. Each state's date for Thanksgiving was soon different.
3. It was Sarah Hale's idea to make Thanksgiving a national holiday like the Fourth of July.
4. Mrs. Hale was editor of a popular women's magazine.
5. Many of her magazine's articles were about Thanksgiving.
6. Sarah Hale sought important people's help.
7. Her plan for a national holiday had many governors' support.
8. Finally it attracted President Lincoln's attention.
9. He met Mrs. Hale and discussed the woman's plan.
10. In 1863 the President's proclamation made the last Thursday of November our national Thanksgiving Day.

B. Write the possessive form of each noun. Then write whether the noun is singular or plural.

11. house
12. mice
13. glass
14. men
15. plates
16. turkey
17. dish
18. cranberries
19. Mr. Jones
20. guests

Application WRITING SENTENCES

Choose six of the possessive nouns you wrote for **Practice B.** Use each in a sentence. You may want to write your sentences about a Thanksgiving dinner you remember.

7 — Compounds

- A **compound** is a word formed from two or more words.

This sign was posted at the Elmwood Swimming Pool. Can you find three nouns on the sign?

The three nouns are *show-off, horseplay,* and *swimming pool.* They are compounds. Many compounds are nouns. A compound is a word formed from two or more words. Notice that the compounds are written in three ways.

Some compounds, such as *horseplay, rainbow,* and *fireplace,* are written as one word. Other compounds are written as separate words. Examples are *swimming pool, post office,* and *junior high school.* Still other compounds are written with a hyphen or hyphens, as in *show-off, twenty-one,* and *sister-in-law.* A hyphen (-) is a punctuation mark used to connect words or word parts.

Skills Tryout

Name the compound in each sentence.

1. Swimmers should always obey the lifeguard.
2. Don't run around a pool or on a diving board.
3. Do you have a life jacket?
4. This one is a hand-me-down.
5. The buddy system can prevent many accidents.

Practice

A. Write each sentence. Underline the compounds.

1. Can you do a back dive?
2. We usually swim in the afternoon.
3. Don't swim during a thunderstorm.
4. Be careful with floats and inner tubes.
5. A current could carry you far from the beach or riverbank.
6. The ocean's undertow can also be dangerous.
7. Baby-sitters should always watch children carefully near a pool.
8. For safety, floodlights should light all parts of a pool at night.
9. Learn about lifesaving from a skilled teacher.
10. Artificial respiration can save a person's life.

B. Match the words in column **A** with the words in column **B** to form compounds. Write each compound as one word.

	A	B		A	B
11.	house	way	16.	rain	people
12.	saw	water	17.	tooth	father
13.	hall	craft	18.	grand	ache
14.	salt	mill	19.	pocket	book
15.	air	keeper	20.	towns	drop

C. Use these ten words to write five compounds. The compounds will be written as separate words.

school	gloves	tape	fiction	high
recorder	cash	science	boxing	register

Application USING LANGUAGE

Write three compounds that begin with the word *sun*. Write three compounds that end with the word *way*. Use each compound you wrote in a sentence.

Common and Proper Nouns   *pages 50–53*

A. Write each sentence. Draw one line under each common noun and two lines under each proper noun.

1. Bryan Allen made an unusual trip during one summer.
2. Bryan pedaled his bicycle from England to France.
3. The deep English Channel separates the two countries.
4. Bryan had a bicycle with wings like a glider.
5. The "flycycle" was called the Gossamer Albatross.
6. The frame was made from lightweight plastic.
7. The pedals of the cycle turned a propeller.
8. Paul MacCready built the machine with the help of a company in the United States.
9. The successful flight covered thirty miles.
10. Allen and MacCready won a prize for the feat.

Capitalizing Proper Nouns   *pages 54–55*

B. Write each sentence. Capitalize each proper noun.

11. Last summer jack and his family visited niagara falls.
12. These waterfalls are on the niagara river between lake erie and lake ontario.
13. The family was gone from august 15 until labor day.
14. On the first tuesday they asked directions at the lakewood fire department.
15. On the way home they stopped in several towns in new york and new hampshire.

Abbreviations   *pages 56–57*

C. Write the word that each abbreviation stands for.

16. Mr.   18. Oct.   20. Rd.   22. Sen.   24. Wed.
17. Dr.   19. Mon.   21. Ave.   23. Rev.   25. Feb.

Singular and Plural Nouns   *pages 58–59*

D. Write each sentence using the plural forms of the underlined nouns.

26. The puppy chased the pony into the alley.
27. The monkey hid the key in the trunk.
28. The snowman built by the child had no ear.
29. The moose saw the fox on the log.
30. The dish and the glass were left on the table.
31. The potato and the berry are on the shelf near the radio.
32. The duck won't sit on the bench with the sheep.
33. The family took their pet to the party.
34. The man put the watch in the box.
35. The deer jumped over the canary in the bush.

Possessive Nouns   *pages 60–61*

E. Write each sentence. Use the possessive form of the noun in parentheses ( ).

36. The (clown) dog stands on its head.
37. The (children) laughter rings out.
38. The (ponies) plumes bob up and down.
39. (Mr. Mills) brother is the ringmaster.
40. Everyone loves the (circus) color and excitement.

Compounds   *pages 62–63*

F. Write the compound in each sentence.

41. A hummingbird is the bird that flies backward.
42. These plants thrive in the humidity of the greenhouse.
43. My sister-in-law has written a book on exercise.
44. At any one time 1,800 thunderstorms rain down on earth.
45. Ted's jump shot landed just as the final bell sounded.

See also Handbook pages 340–347, 400–402, 404–408.

Writing with Nouns

● Use exact nouns to give details in your writing.

Read the sentences below.

1. **The room was filled with decorations.**
2. **The room was filled with streamers, balloons, and tinsel.**

There is nothing wrong with sentence 1. However, *decorations* is a vague noun. It does not really give a clear picture of what is filling the room. Sentence 2 is quite different. The vague noun *decorations* has been replaced by the exact nouns *streamers, balloons*, and *tinsel*. These nouns provide details that give a much better picture of how the room looks.

Different exact nouns would change how the room looks. Read the sentence below.

The room was filled with candles, paintings, and confetti.

Using exact nouns really makes a difference in your writing. They create details and make you a more interesting writer.

Using Nouns Below is a list of vague nouns. What exact nouns could replace each one?

Select a noun from the list and write it on a piece of paper. See how many exact nouns you can write in two minutes. Then try to use three of them in a sentence to provide more details about the vague noun.

location	book	entertainment
dance	flower	sound

How many exact nouns did you write? Find a classmate who chose the same vague noun. Did he or she think of any exact nouns that you didn't? Now select another vague noun from the list and begin again.

Replacing Nouns   Below are pairs of sentences. The first sentence contains an underlined vague noun. The second sentence contains a blank or blanks for exact nouns that can replace the vague noun. Write each sentence. Replace the underlined vague noun with an exact noun or nouns.

EXAMPLE: We found a <u>person</u> who fixed our lamp.
          We found a ⎯⎯ who fixed our lamp.
ANSWER: We found a technician who fixed our lamp.

1. Iris will have to stay in bed for a <u>while</u>.
   Iris will have to stay in bed for a ⎯⎯.
2. Paul bought the <u>ingredients</u> for a hot bowl of soup.
   Paul bought ⎯⎯ and ⎯⎯ for a hot bowl of soup.
3. It takes many <u>qualities</u> to be a mountain climber.
   It takes ⎯⎯, ⎯⎯, and ⎯⎯ to be a mountain climber.
4. We sat on the bench and played musical <u>instruments</u>.
   We sat on the bench and played ⎯⎯ and ⎯⎯.
5. I studied many <u>things</u> during the school year.
   I studied ⎯⎯, ⎯⎯, and ⎯⎯ during the school year.

Using No Clues   Find the vague word in each sentence. Think of a more exact noun that could replace it. Write the sentence.

6. Rosanna admired the beautiful scenery.
7. Bruce took his parents to the event.
8. I read about the election in the paper.
9. Do not leave your belongings lying about the house.
10. I look just like my relative.

Using the Thesaurus

Find the entry for the noun *help* in the Thesaurus that begins on page 414. Then write five different sentences, using a different synonym for *help* in each one. You may want to write your sentences about someone who is lost in your neighborhood.

- A **fact** is true information about something.
- An **opinion** is what a person *thinks* about something.

A VOTE FOR BROWN IS A
VOTE FOR A
BRIGHTER TOMORROW!

How can you judge the truth of the persuasive messages you hear every day? One way is to distinguish between opinions and facts.

Opinions often contain words such as *best, worst, like, should, probably, think*, and *deserves*. Words like these express feelings and judgments.

> Mayor Brown has done a <u>first-rate</u> job.
> She <u>deserves</u> another term as Roseland's mayor!

Facts contain information that can be proved. You can check facts in reference books or in other records.

> Mayor Brown has brought ten new industries to Roseland.
> Crime has decreased during her term of office.

Before you accept an opinion, listen for facts that support it. A valid opinion is usually backed by facts.

Opinion ——— ⎡ Mayor Brown has made Roseland a better place. She has
Facts ——— ⎢ raised money for our youth center, and she has had 70
        ⎢ percent of the roads in town repaved. She has reorganized
        ⎣ the police and fire departments, too.

If you are not sure whether a statement is a fact or an opinion, ask the speaker to clarify it. You can also ask for the sources of a speaker's facts.

Tell whether each statement is a fact or an opinion.

1. Roseland's merchants are outstanding citizens.
2. The new parking lot downtown cost $80,000.
3. The parking lot makes downtown shopping so convenient!
4. Merchants reported a 25 percent increase in sales.
5. These empty storefronts should be torn down.

Practice

A. Write *fact* or *opinion* for each statement.

1. Mayor Brown is a skillful, intelligent leader.
2. She has degrees in law and public administration.
3. Bryan Park is her most important achievement.
4. The park is located in northeast Roseland.
5. In one of her early campaign speeches, Ms. Brown had promised to build it.
6. Bryan Park provides first-rate recreation for all.
7. The mayor has greatly improved Roseland's schools.
8. The average class size is the smallest ever.
9. The new library opened in April.
10. The school should buy more computers.

B. Write an opinion based on each fact.

11. The mayor works from 7:00 A.M. to 9:00 P.M. every day.
12. Roseland's nearest hospital is thirty miles away.
13. Every morning the mayor jogs three miles.
14. Roseland's population has doubled in four years.
15. Anyone with a problem can telephone the mayor.

Application LISTENING

Discuss an issue that is important to your school or community. Listen to the opinions that different class members have on the issue. Then list facts that support each opinion.

9 ───── Having a Discussion ─────

> ● A **group discussion** is an opportunity to exchange
> opinions and information.

A class at Lawrence School is holding group discussions
about television. In a group discussion, people talk about a specific topic.

Before beginning, the class drew up these rules.

- Check your information before the discussion.
- Begin the discussion with a question.
- Back up your opinions with facts.
- Stick to the topic when speaking.
- Listen carefully to the comments of others.
- Do not interrupt a speaker.
- If you disagree with someone, politely explain why.

Here is a portion of the discussion at Lawrence School.

Joe: Should there be commercials on TV?
Brad: No. TV commercials are annoying. They interrupt programs
every ten or fifteen minutes.
Rita: But commercials pay for the TV shows you watch, Brad.
Gina: So many people buy things they don't need because of com-
mercials, though.
Rita: Actually, commercials are a good source of information
about products, and . . .
Ray: Sure, but the claims they make are impossible to check.

Skills Tryout ─────────────────────

Answer the following questions about the discussion above.

1. What is the topic of the discussion?
2. What is Brad's opinion?
3. What fact does he use to back up his opinion?
4. Does Rita share Brad's opinion?
5. What rule has Ray broken?

Practice

A. Read this discussion. Then answer the questions that follow.

Tad: Which reports the news better—TV or newspapers?
May: TV news is better because it is up to the minute.
Dan: Yes, but newspapers go into more depth and ...
Jan: Who cares about all the little details anyway?
Bob: Did you see Mayor Brown on the news last night?

1. What is the discussion group comparing?
2. What is May's opinion?
3. What fact does she use to back up her opinion?
4. Which discussion rule does Jan break?
5. What rule does Bob break?

B. Read more of the discussion. Then answer the questions.

Tad: Videotapes make TV news more exciting.
Guy: My uncle just bought one of those video cameras.
Dan: With newspapers, though, you can choose which stories
    you want to read about. I think newspapers are better.
Kim: Newspapers also give us a printed record of ...
May: Most of us don't have time to read the news.

6. Who does not keep to the subject?
7. Who interrupts a speaker?
8. Does Dan support his opinion with fact?
9. What opinion would you hold if you were in the group?
10. What fact would you offer to support your opinion?

C. Write a discussion question on some aspect of television.

Application SPEAKING and LISTENING

Working in groups, discuss television programs. First use a TV schedule to decide what show each group will watch. Take notes as you watch the show. Then discuss whether or not the show was worth watching.

10 — Writing a Persuasive Paragraph

> ● A **persuasive paragraph** tries to convince the reader to agree with the writer's opinion.

When you write, you write for a reason. Sometimes that reason is to persuade others. You want to share your opinion about something and convince the reader to agree with you. That is the purpose of a persuasive paragraph.

As with any other kind of writing, you should take time to think before you write a persuasive paragraph. Here are some suggestions to help you direct your thoughts.

How to Plan a Persuasive Paragraph

1. Jot down the different opinions people hold about your topic. Decide exactly what your opinion on it is.
2. Think about your audience. Whom are you trying to convince? A parent? A friend? Your classmates? Then think about how your topic affects them. Why would it be to their advantage to agree with you? (People are more likely to agree with an opinion if they see some benefit to them.)
3. Think of facts that support your opinion. (You may have to do some research.) Also, think of examples from your own experience that support your opinion.

When you are clear about what you want to say, you are ready to write your paragraph. Begin with a topic sentence that states your opinion. Then give reasons, facts, or examples to support your opinion. Consider ending your paragraph with a sentence that sums up your main points or that repeats the idea given in your topic sentence. Use the paragraph below as a guide.

To keep healthy you should eat a balanced diet. Fresh fruits and vegetables supply needed vitamins. Protein foods such as meat repair body tissues. Bread and pasta provide energy. Eating a balanced diet is the only way to be sure you are getting the nutrients you need.

Skills Tryout

Read this paragraph. Then answer the questions that follow.

Everyone should try to save and recycle wastepaper. Wastepaper can be used instead of trees to make new paper. Making paper from wastepaper uses less energy and causes less pollution. Recycling also saves land that would have been used for waste disposal. Therefore, it makes sense to recycle.

1. Which sentence is the topic sentence?
2. Which sentences give facts that support the topic sentence?
3. What purpose does the last sentence serve?

Practice

A. Write the following sentences as a persuasive paragraph. Write the topic sentence first. Then write the sentences that support the opinion in an order that makes sense. End the paragraph with the summary sentence.

1. Then we will take a boat tour in the Okefenokee Swamp.
2. First we will go flounder fishing off Georgia's coast.
3. You should spend your vacation down here in Georgia.
4. Those are just a few things you will enjoy in Georgia.
5. You will see unusual animals at the Okefenokee Swamp.

B. For each topic, write a topic sentence that states an opinion.

6. The length of the school year
7. Whether or not TV mysteries are too violent
8. The best time to exercise
9. Dress codes in schools
10. Whether or not people need eight hours of sleep

Application WRITING A PARAGRAPH

Develop one of the topic sentences you wrote for **Practice B** into a persuasive paragraph. Use the suggestions on page 72.

11 — The Parts of a Newspaper

> ● A newspaper contains information in different forms, including news stories, feature articles, and editorials.

Newspapers are designed to satisfy your natural curiosity about what is going on in the world today. You may want some facts about events in your town, your state, your country, or the world. You may also want to know what other people think about what is happening. You may want to read their opinions. To satisfy these needs, newspapers provide different kinds of information.

News stories present facts about important world, national, and local news. **Feature articles** give background information and lively, detailed accounts of the news. **Editorials** give opinions about the news.

The newspaper has other parts as well. Items such as letters to the editor and movie reviews offer opinions. Classified ads and TV schedules present facts.

Larger newspapers are divided into major sections. Each section is assigned a letter. Here is how one newspaper is divided.

A: **News Around the World** C: **Home and Entertainment**
B: **Local and National News** D: **Business and Classifieds**

Most newspapers have an index on one of the front pages to help the reader locate various items. The index usually shows the section letter and the page number of each item.

INDEX

Business	D1–2	Movies	C5–6
Classified Ads	D4–10	Music	C7
Crossword	C10	Restaurant Guide	C9
Editorials	A12	Sports	B8–12
Employment Outlook	D3	TV/Radio	C3–4
Home and Garden	C1–2	Weather	B13
Local/National News	B1–7	Your Health	C8

Skills Tryout

Tell whether each of these newspaper items is concerned with giving facts or with giving an opinion.

1. an editorial in favor of lowering the sales tax
2. a news story about a flood
3. a feature article about controlling mosquitoes
4. a favorable review of a new movie
5. a list of today's TV programs

Practice

Use the index on page 74 to answer these questions.

1. On which pages would you look for a sports article about last night's baseball game?
2. Which page might give information about exercise and physical fitness?
3. Which pages might have a feature article on growing corn?
4. Which page might contain a review of a new rock album?
5. Which pages would tell about a nationwide strike?
6. Which pages might tell in what new movie the actor Robert Redford is starring?
7. On which pages would you look to see if anyone is selling a used ten-speed bike?
8. How many pages are devoted to editorials?
9. On which page would you find a weather map?
10. What is the last page that might have a feature story about a basketball star?

Application FINDING FACTS AND OPINIONS

Cut out three articles from a newspaper: a news story, a feature article, and an editorial. Underline in blue sentences that give facts. Underline in red sentences that give opinions. Do news stories ever contain opinions? Do editorials contain facts?

12 — Writing a Newspaper Editorial

> ● A **newspaper editorial** gives an opinion and is often about a news event.

Writing Project

What opinions do you have about the news happening around you? Maybe you think the city should not raise the admission price to the public pool. Perhaps you agree with the new rule that requires a bicycle inspection every year. Maybe you disagree with the law that requires you to register pets.

In this lesson you will have an opportunity to express your opinion about a news event. You will try to persuade your classmates to agree with you by using reasons to support your opinion. When you express an opinion and support it with reasons, you are writing persuasively.

1. Prewriting

Newspaper editors and concerned citizens express their opinions about the news in a special section of the newspaper called the *editorial page*. The written opinions are called *editorials*. Since you are going to write an editorial about a news event, you need to know what is happening in the news.

▶ Check your local newspaper. Look for news stories on which you have strong opinions. Cut them out. Then reread the articles. Choose one for the topic of your editorial.

Now that you have a topic, you need to develop it. Making a cluster is a good way to help you find and organize ideas. Imagine, for example, that you are going to write an editorial about computers. You think computers can help students. To develop your opinion, you could make a cluster like the one shown below.

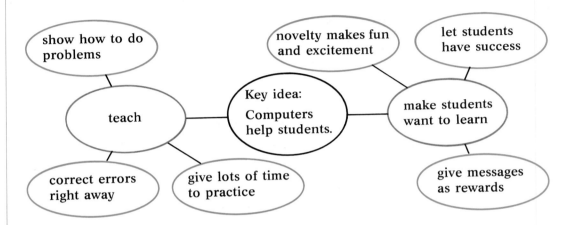

- Write your key idea in a large circle in the center: <u>Computers help students</u>.
- Think of reasons that support your key idea. How do computers help students? Computers can <u>teach</u>, and they can <u>make students want to learn</u>. As you think of each supporting idea, write it in its own circle.
- Write details that tell more about your supporting ideas. For example, look at the cluster of words around the supporting idea <u>teach</u>. How do computers teach? They <u>show how to do problems</u>. They <u>give lots of time to practice</u>. They <u>correct errors right away</u>.

▶ Make a cluster. Start with your key idea in the center circle. Add reasons, or supporting ideas, in their own circles. Surround each supporting idea with details. When your cluster is finished, show it to a classmate. Discuss your opinion.

2. Writing

Your opinion is valuable. It is worth expressing in writing. Use the cluster you have made to help you focus on your key idea, supporting ideas, and details as you write.

▶ Tell your readers your key idea in the first sentence, and then support your thinking with reasons. Give your strongest reason last. That way the last idea, your strongest idea, will stay with the reader. You could conclude with a question that restates your key idea. Here is an example: "Don't you agree that computers can be of great help to students?"

3. Revising

▶ Ask another person to read your editorial. Ask, "Do you agree with my opinion?" Discuss what you have written and what you intended to say. Listen to your reader's suggestions for changes. Use this Revision Checklist, too.

Revision Checklist
- Does my first sentence state my opinion?
- Did I give reasons to support my opinion?
- Did I place my strongest reason last?
- Did I use specific words?

Read the example on the next page. Notice how choosing specific words improved the editorial.

I believe computers can help ~~children~~ _students_ because they can teach and ~~make students want to learn.~~ _motivate_ By ~~showing~~ _demonstrating_ how to _solve_ ~~do~~ problems, ⟨they teach⟩ and

---

I believe computers can help students because they can teach and motivate. They teach by demonstrating how to solve problems, and students can go back and study the demonstrations as often as they want to. With a computer, students can practice as much as they need to, and the computer will correct errors right away.

Computers also motivate. Some programs give personal messages as rewards for right answers. That makes students want to try, and it makes them feel successful. Also, the novelty of computers adds fun and excitement to learning. Don't you agree that computers can be of great help to students?

EDITING MARKS

—— cross out

∧ add

↻ move

≡ capital letter

/ small letter

¶ indent

◯ check spelling

▶ Use the editing marks to make changes in your first draft.

4. Publishing

▶ Proofread your editorial before publishing it. Use the Proofreading Checklist in the Young Writer's Handbook on page 399. Make corrections with the editing marks.

▶ If you wish, send your editorial to your local newspaper. You can also publish your editorial in your classroom. Display your editorial with the newspaper story it was based on. Hang a blank piece of paper by your work and write _Comments_ on the top. Invite classmates to read your editorial and to respond to your opinion.

Writing Project

Persuasive Advertisements

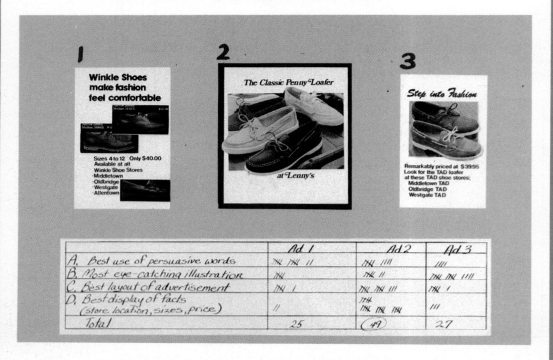

	Ad 1	Ad 2	Ad 3
A. Best use of persuasive words	𝇍𝇍 II	𝇍 IIII	IIII
B. Most eye-catching illustration	𝇍	𝇍 II	𝇍 𝇍 IIII
C. Best layout of advertisement	𝇍 I	𝇍 𝇍 III	𝇍 I
D. Best display of facts (store location, sizes, price)	II	𝇍 𝇍 𝇍 𝇍	III
Total	25	(49)	27

Look at advertisements in a newspaper. Cut out three different advertisements for similar products. Glue all three to one poster board. Then write 1, 2, or 3 next to each advertisement.

Make a score sheet similar to the one above. Glue the score sheet under the advertisements on the poster board.

Display your poster and those of your classmates around the classroom. Take turns voting for the most persuasive advertisement on each poster. Vote for one advertisement in each category: **a.** persuasive words, **b.** illustration, **c.** overall look, **d.** facts. Mark your votes on the score sheet.

When everyone has finished voting, add up the votes on your poster. Circle the winning total.

Health

Throughout the ages, people have held opinions about the benefits of certain foods. Today scientists test foods to find out their true nutritional values. Studies have shown that there is some truth behind many of the old beliefs about foods.

▶ Try it. Here are some sayings that have been used to persuade people to eat certain foods. Choose one of the sayings, or use another one you have heard. Then study the food chart below. In a paragraph, tell whether the saying is based on fact.

- Spinach makes you strong.
- Carrots improve your eyesight.
- Milk helps you grow.
- Eggs are good for hair.

Vitamin	Foods	Needed for
A	Green leafy vegetables, carrots, fruits, butter	Good vision; growth of bones and teeth
B_1	Green vegetables, pork, soybeans, liver, lamb, peas, whole grains	Healthy muscles; growth; release of energy; good digestion
B_2	Milk, eggs, green leafy vegetables, cheese	Healthy skin and hair; growth

© King Features Syndicate, Inc.

Writers at Work Doctors, dentists, and other health specialists often make up catchy sayings to persuade their patients to take good care of themselves. One dentist has the following saying hanging in his office.

You don't have to brush all your teeth-only the ones you want to keep!

▶ Try it. Pretend you are a doctor, dentist, nutritionist, or other health specialist. Write a saying that would encourage people to take care of their health.

Nouns   *pages 50–53, 58–59*

A. Write the nouns in each sentence. Then write whether each noun names a *person, place, thing,* or *idea*.

1. The heavy snowstorm caused problems in Windsor.
2. Workers driving plows had trouble clearing the streets.
3. The mayor advised citizens to stay in their homes.
4. Most of the windows and roofs were capped with snow.
5. Happy children brought sleds and skis to Holland Hill.

B. Write the plural form of each noun.

6. potato
7. ditch
8. tooth
9. mystery
10. pillow
11. chimney
12. knife
13. deer

C. Write each underlined word. Then write whether it is a *common noun* or a *proper noun*.

14. Meriwether Lewis and William Clark were famous explorers.
15. In 1804 they set out on an expedition from St. Louis.
16. This long journey took the men over the Rocky Mountains.
17. Their westward path led to the Pacific Ocean.

Capital Letters and Periods   *pages 54–57*

D. Write each sentence. Capitalize the proper nouns.

18. The brighton school of medicine is on elm street.
19. My sister myra takes a medical care course in lakeville.
20. Our class visited riga hospital on monday.
21. We talked to mr. chiu of the star ambulance company.

E. Write the word each abbreviation stands for.

22. Gov.
23. Pl.
24. Wed.
25. Feb.
26. Blvd.
27. Rev.
28. Aug.
29. Sun.

Apostrophes   *pages 60–61*

F. Write the possessive form of each noun. Then write whether the noun is *singular* or *plural*.

30. mule   **31.** feet   **32.** Thomas   **33.** nations   **34.** women

Compounds   *pages 62–63*

G. Write each sentence. Underline the compounds.

35. Where is the watering can?   **37.** Did you eat the leftovers?
36. My pen pal lives in China.   **38.** Our team needs a time-out.

Fact and Opinion   *pages 68–69*

H. Write *fact* or *opinion* for each statement.

39. The temperature today is 82°F.
40. It's too hot to go jogging.
41. It will be cooler tomorrow.

Persuasive Paragraph   *pages 72–73*

I. **42.** Write the sentences below as a persuasive paragraph. Write the topic sentence first.

Gym classes have limited space for sports.
Therefore, we need a larger gym for two important reasons.
We also have no area big enough for all-school meetings.
The Frances Perkins School needs a larger gym.

The Parts of a Newspaper   *pages 74–75*

J. Write the letter that matches each newspaper part.

43. index   **a.** presents facts about important news
44. editorial   **b.** helps readers find items in the newspaper
45. news story   **c.** gives an opinion about a news event

See also Handbook pages 340–347, 400–402, 404–406.

Sentences *pages 4–17*

A. Write the sentences using capital letters and correct end punctuation. After each sentence write *declarative, interrogative, imperative,* or *exclamatory.*

1. we enjoy violin music
2. play your violin for us
3. how well you play
4. do you practice every day

B. Write each complete subject. Underline each simple subject.

5. The idea of flying has excited people since ancient times.
6. Huge kites were the earliest flying machines.
7. An American inventor made a powered aircraft in 1896.
8. The first pilots were Wilbur and Orville Wright.

C. Write each complete predicate. Underline each simple predicate.

9. Elephants are the largest land animals in the world.
10. They live in many parts of Asia and Africa.
11. Wild elephants travel together in herds.
12. An adult elephant can eat up to 750 pounds of food a day.

D. Write the subject of each sentence.

13. Did Bob drop that bag?
14. Pick up the oranges.
15. Don't step on the grapes.
16. Are the bottles broken?

Commas *pages 18–19*

E. Write each sentence. Add commas where they are needed.

17. On November 29 1832 Louisa May Alcott was born.
18. She lived in Concord Massachusetts for many years.
19. Louisa wrote fairy tales magazine articles and books.
20. Her characters resemble her parents sisters and friends.

Cumulative Review

Nouns   *pages 50–53, 58–59*

F. Write the nouns in each sentence. Then write whether each noun names a *person, place, thing,* or *idea.*

   21. The wild beauty of Alaska attracts many travelers.
   22. Tourists sail along its coastline in large ships.
   23. Trains carry passengers to the major cities in the state.
   24. Mount McKinley tests the ability of brave climbers.

G. Write the plural form of each noun.

   25. leash   **26.** shelf   **27.** tomato   **28.** century

H. Write each noun. Then write whether it is a *common noun* or a *proper noun.*

   29. Hudson River   **30.** leopard   **31.** grocery store   **32.** Frisky

Capital Letters and Periods   *pages 54–57*

I. Write each sentence. Capitalize the proper nouns.

   33. Last may I visited my relatives in scotland.
   34. I walked along the coast of the north sea with aunt molly.
   35. We saw edinburgh castle and the port of glasgow.
   36. On memorial day I flew home to west virginia.

J. Write the word that each abbreviation stands for.

   37. Ave.   **38.** Sept.   **39.** Mr.   **40.** Thurs.

Apostrophes   *pages 60–61*

K. Write the possessive form of each noun. Then write whether the noun is *singular* or *plural.*

   41. people   **42.** Mr. Adams   **43.** ducks   **44.** coyote

Grammar
Verbs

Composition
Informing

The Wind

I can get through a doorway without any key,
And strip the leaves from the great oak tree.

I can drive storm-clouds and shake tall towers,
Or steal through a garden and not wake the flowers.

Seas I can move and ships I can sink;
I can carry a house-top or the scent of a pink.

When I am angry I can rave and riot;
And when I am spent, I lie quiet as quiet.

—*James Reeves*

1 — Verbs

> ● A **verb** expresses action or being.

You know that the simple predicate, or verb, is the main word in the complete predicate. In the following sentences the verbs are underlined.

> **An architect <u>draws</u> the plans for a house.**
> **Workers <u>pour</u> a concrete foundation.**

The verbs *draws* and *pour* are action verbs. The verbs express, or tell about, action that can be seen.

Some action verbs express action that cannot be seen.

> **The architect <u>thinks</u> about her plans.**
> **She <u>wants</u> a beautiful house.**

Other verbs do not express action at all. Instead, they state what is. These verbs are called state-of-being verbs.

> **The architect <u>is</u> famous.**
> **Those workers <u>are</u> plumbers.**

The following forms of the verb *be* are the most common state-of-being verbs.

be	is	was	being
am	are	were	been

Skills Tryout

Name the verb in each sentence.

1. Trucks bring lumber to the house site.
2. Carpenters lay long, thick beams across the foundation.
3. A power saw is a useful tool at this time.
4. The builders follow the architect's plans.
5. They enjoy their work very much.

Practice

A. Write the sentences. Underline each verb.

1. Carpenters build the frame of a house.
2. They construct each wall separately.
3. Then the workers raise the walls into place.
4. A steel beam supports the second floor of the house.
5. This beam is very strong.
6. Next the carpenters install windows and doors.
7. They also cover the inside walls with plasterboard.
8. Roofers nail shingles on the roof.
9. The shingles protect the wooden part of the roof.
10. The outer walls of this house are brick.

B. Write the verb in each sentence. Then write *action verb* or *state-of-being verb* after the verb.

11. That worker was a bricklayer.
12. She built the fireplace, chimney, and front steps.
13. The plumbers were here last week.
14. They connected the pipes for the kitchen and bathrooms.
15. The plumbers are also responsible for the heating system.
16. An electrician is in the house now.
17. He brought a truckload of electrical cable and light fixtures with him.
18. The painters, paperhangers, and carpet installers arrive next week.
19. Then the lucky owners move into the house.
20. They love their new home already!

Application WRITING SENTENCES

Write six sentences about something you have made or built. Tell the steps you followed to make it. Then underline the verb in each sentence.

2 Linking Verbs

> ● A **linking verb** connects the subject with a word or words in the predicate.

State-of-being verbs are also linking verbs. Linking verbs connect, or link, the subject of a sentence with a word or words in the predicate. In the following sentences the underlined words are linking verbs.

1. Jody <u>is</u> a gardener.   2. Her plants <u>look</u> healthy.

In sentence 1, the linking verb *is* connects the subject *Jody* with the word *gardener* in the predicate. In sentence 2, the linking verb *look* connects the subject *plants* with the word *healthy*. Below are some common linking verbs.

Forms of Be	Other Linking Verbs
be, am, is, are, was, were	appear, become, feel, look, seem, smell, taste

Read the sentences below. Notice that a singular noun is used as subject with *is* and *was*. A plural noun is used as subject with *are* and *were*.

That flower <u>is</u> a rose.   The garden <u>was</u> large.
Beans <u>are</u> vegetables.   The eggplants <u>were</u> purple.

Skills Tryout

Name the linking verb in each sentence.

1. Jody's garden is a sunny spot.
2. The land seems quite flat.
3. The soil appears rich and dark.
4. Those tomatoes are so red!
5. The tomato plants smell strong.

Practice

A. Write the sentences. Underline each linking verb.

1. That tool is a hoe.
2. It was very useful.
3. Those vegetables are squash.
4. They taste delicious with onions.
5. The pumpkins finally appear ripe.
6. The watering cans look heavy.
7. They were very full.
8. These peppers become red in October.
9. The herbs smell pleasant.
10. The garden feels especially peaceful in the evening.

B. Write each sentence. Draw one line under the linking verb. Draw two lines under the words that the verb connects.

EXAMPLE: The large orange flower is a zinnia.

ANSWER: The large orange <u>flower</u> <u>is</u> a <u>zinnia</u>.

11. These yellow roses smell so sweet.
12. Their petals feel very soft.
13. The marigolds appear dry now.
14. Yellow and white daisies are my favorite flowers.
15. That bench in the garden looks comfortable.
16. This garden becomes more beautiful every year.
17. Those white insects are mealybugs.
18. Flowers taste great to them.
19. The bees were busy earlier.
20. I am always happy in the garden.

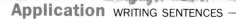

Application WRITING SENTENCES

Write five sentences about a flower, a vegetable, or your favorite food. Use a linking verb in each sentence. Tell how the item you choose appeals to the senses. You might tell how it tastes, feels, looks, or smells.

3 — Helping Verbs and Main Verbs

> ● A **helping verb** works with the main verb to express action or being.

A verb can consist of more than one word.

The batter is not hitting the ball.
The batter should have hit the ball.

When a verb is more than one word, the most important verb is called the **main verb.** The other words are called helping verbs. *Hitting* and *hit* are the main verbs in the sentences above. Notice that the word *not* can separate the helping verb and the main verb. It is not part of the verb. Below is a list of common helping verbs.

am	be	had	did	may
is	being	can	shall	might
are	been	could	should	must
was	has	do	will	
were	have	does	would	

Some verbs in the list, such as *is* and *has*, can stand alone. When they stand alone, they are the main verbs.

She is here.   He has the proof.

Skills Tryout

Name the helping verbs and main verbs in the sentences.

1. The crowd has left the stadium.
2. I must have lost my ticket.
3. Reggie did play yesterday.
4. The runner will steal second base.
5. The pitcher is being replaced.

Practice

A. Write the sentences below. Underline the helping verbs once and the main verbs twice.

  1. Our team did not score in the first inning.
  2. The ball was hit over the fence.
  3. Dominic had walked the first batter.
  4. The fans are walking on the field.
  5. The ball has bounced into the stands.
  6. The batter should have swung.
  7. A pinch hitter may bat for the catcher.
  8. The game was not shown on television.
  9. The Little League game is being postponed.
  10. The rain had started in the second inning.

B. Write the verbs in the sentences. Then write *MV* if the sentence has a main verb but no helping verb. Write *HV + MV* if the sentence has both a helping verb and a main verb.

EXAMPLE: The umpire has the ball.
ANSWER: has (MV)

  11. The umpire has called the pitch a strike.
  12. I am playing third base.
  13. The game is in extra innings.
  14. The manager would not agree with the umpire.
  15. The scoring cards are in the stands.
  16. The umpire always has the final word.
  17. Our local newspaper does not cover sports.
  18. Our team could play in a championship game.
  19. Jo Ann has the new uniforms.
  20. You must watch the World Series.

Application WRITING SENTENCES

Write six sentences about baseball or another sport. Use a helping verb and a main verb in at least four of them.

4 — Verbs with Direct Objects

> ● The **direct object** receives the action of the verb.

A bad winter storm caused a power blackout in Center City. Susan was watching a TV news program. Because of the blackout she didn't hear the end of this sentence:

Much of Center City has lost its _____.

The part of the sentence that Susan didn't hear was the direct object. Without the direct object the meaning of the sentence is not complete. A direct object receives the action of the verb. It is often a noun. In the sentence below, the noun *electricity* is the direct object. It answers the question *what* after the verb.

Much of Center City has lost its electricity. (has lost what?)

A direct object can also answer the question *whom* after the verb. In the following sentence *brother* is the direct object.

Susan called her older brother into the room. (called whom?)

You can find the direct object in a sentence by asking who or what receives the action of the verb.

Skills Tryout

Name the direct object in each sentence. Tell whether it answers the question *whom* or *what.*

1. Thick ice covered the trees.
2. A strong wind broke a large branch.
3. The falling branch tore an electrical wire.
4. The house suddenly lost its power.
5. The blackout worried Mother.

Practice

A. Write the direct object in each sentence. Tell whether it answers the question *whom* or *what*.

1. The power company received many calls.
2. The company sent out workers.
3. The workers repaired many wires.
4. By now the house had lost its heat.
5. Susan built a big fire.
6. She lit candles, too.
7. Mother telephoned the neighbors.
8. They had also lost their electricity.
9. The family cooked dinner over the fire.
10. Father watched the street from time to time.

B. Write the sentences. Underline each action verb once and each direct object twice.

11. He did not see any lights yet.
12. Mother piled more wood on the fire.
13. Susan found a radio with batteries.
14. She heard her favorite program.
15. The family invited some friends to the house.
16. Everyone sang songs by the firelight.
17. Mother and Father told long funny stories.
18. Susan suddenly noticed the television.
19. She saw a reporter on the screen.
20. The reporter at the TV station announced the end of the blackout.

Application WRITING SENTENCES

Imagine that there is a power blackout in your neighborhood. Write six sentences that tell what you and your family might do. Use an action verb and a direct object in each sentence. Underline each action verb once and each direct object twice.

5 — Tenses of Verbs

> • The **tense** of a verb shows time.

You probably use a clock, a calendar, and a watch to tell time. Did you know that verbs also tell time? You use verbs when you speak or write sentences. The tenses of the verbs you use show time.

A verb in the present tense shows action that happens now.

> **A huge sheet of ice <u>covers</u> the Antarctic continent.**
> **The scientists <u>arrive</u> at this icy glacier.**

A verb in the past tense shows action that already happened. The past tense of a verb is usually formed by adding *-ed.* If a verb ends in *e*, drop the *e* and add *-ed.*

> **During the Ice Age a glacier <u>moved</u> over North America.**
> **This glacier <u>melted</u> long ago.**

A verb in the future tense shows action that will happen. The future tense is usually formed with the helping verb *will* or *shall.*

> **The scientists <u>will measure</u> the glacier.**
> **I <u>shall join</u> the scientists next week.**

Skills Tryout

The verbs are underlined in the sentences below. Tell whether each verb is in the present tense, the past tense, or the future tense.

1. The scientists <u>drilled</u> a deep hole in the glacier.
2. They <u>measured</u> the ice.
3. The edges of the glacier <u>touch</u> the ocean.
4. Giant chunks of ice <u>form</u> icebergs.
5. These icebergs <u>will float</u> in the ocean.

Practice

A. Write the verb in each sentence. Then write *present tense*, *past tense*, or *future tense* after the verb.

1. Winds and ocean currents move the mountains of ice away from Antarctica.
2. In time the icebergs will reach warmer waters.
3. Then they will melt.
4. In northern waters, icebergs cause problems for sailors.
5. The famous ship *Titanic* rammed an iceberg in 1912.
6. Water poured into the ship.
7. Many people died in the tragedy.
8. Later the United States and England formed the International Ice Patrol.
9. Today the Coast Guard watches large icebergs.
10. Their work will prevent many tragedies in the future.

B. Write the past tense and future tense of each verb below. Use *will* with the future tense.

11. laugh
12. believe
13. show
14. invite
15. push
16. pour
17. count
18. watch
19. smile
20. crash

Application WRITING SENTENCES

Choose three verbs from **Practice B**. Write three sentences for each verb. The first sentence should be in the present tense, the second sentence should be in the past tense, and the third sentence should be in the future tense. You will write nine sentences in all.

6 Principal Parts of Verbs

- The **principal parts** are the basic forms of a verb. They include the present, the past, and the past participle.

All verbs have basic forms called principal parts. The first principal part is the present. The second principal part is the past. It is usually formed by adding -ed. The third principal part is called the past participle. The past participle is also usually formed by adding -ed. It is used with the helping verb *has, have,* or *had.*

Present: My brothers and I <u>raise</u> pigeons.
Past: People originally <u>raised</u> pigeons for food.
Past Participle: We <u>have</u> <u>raised</u> pigeons for three years.

When the past and the past participle of a verb are formed by adding -ed, the verb is called a **regular verb.**

Read the principle parts of these verbs.

Present	Past	Past Participle
ask	asked	(has, have, had) asked
laugh	laughed	(has, have, had) laughed
hurry	hurried	(has, have, had) hurried
stop	stopped	(has, have, had) stopped

Notice that verbs that end in a consonant and *y,* such as *hurry,* change the *y* to *i* and add -ed to make the past. One-syllable verbs that end in a vowel and a consonant, such as *stop,* double the final consonant and add -ed to make the past.

Skills Tryout

Tell the present, past, and past participle of each verb. Use the helping verb *has* with each past participle.

1. help   **2.** use   **3.** carry   **4.** trap   **5.** add

Practice

A. Write the three principal parts of each verb. Use the helping verb *has* with each past participle.

1. smile
2. drag
3. try
4. serve
5. walk
6. pass
7. snap
8. plant
9. supply
10. subtract

B. Write the verb in each sentence. Then write *present, past,* or *past participle* to show which principal part of the verb was used.

11. Pigeons race great distances.
12. The swift birds cover about 500 miles a day.
13. Owners have timed pigeons at speeds of eighty miles per hour.
14. The racers travel around storms and bad weather.
15. Homing pigeons always hurry back to their homes.
16. Many amazing stories have resulted.
17. One homing pigeon returned to China from France!
18. Pigeons have served as messengers throughout history.
19. In Greek mythology a pigeon acted as a guide for Jason and the Argonauts.
20. Ancient Egyptians carried the birds aboard their ships.
21. They communicated with their homeland by pigeon.
22. Soldiers have used pigeons during times of war.
23. Some Army pigeons have received medals for bravery!
24. Pigeon owners describe their pets as loyal.
25. Pigeons provide much pleasure for their owners.

Application WRITING SENTENCES

Write six sentences that tell how birds or other animals can help people. Use at least one verb in the present, one in the past, and one past participle in your sentences.

7 — Using Irregular Verbs

> ● **Irregular verbs** do not form the past and past participle by adding *-ed*.

You have learned how to form the past and past participle of verbs by adding *-ed*. Some verbs, however, do not follow this rule. These verbs are called irregular verbs. The chart below shows the principal parts of some common irregular verbs.

Present	Past	Past Participle
begin	began	(has, have, had) begun
blow	blew	(has, have, had) blown
do	did	(has, have, had) done
drink	drank	(has, have, had) drunk
eat	ate	(has, have, had) eaten
fly	flew	(has, have, had) flown
give	gave	(has, have, had) given
go	went	(has, have, had) gone
grow	grew	(has, have, had) grown
know	knew	(has, have, had) known
ring	rang	(has, have, had) rung
sing	sang	(has, have, had) sung
swim	swam	(has, have, had) swum
take	took	(has, have, had) taken
throw	threw	(has, have, had) thrown
write	wrote	(has, have, had) written

The irregular verbs *be* and *have* are especially important and deserve extra study. See page 356 of your Grammar Handbook for the special forms of these verbs.

Skills Tryout

Name the three principal parts of these verbs.

1. grow **2.** give **3.** take **4.** swim **5.** begin

Practice

A. Write the three principal parts of the verbs below.

    1. do   **3.** fly   **5.** throw   **7.** blow   **9.** go

    2. eat   **4.** ring   **6.** drink   **8.** know   **10.** write

B. Write each sentence using the past or the past participle of the verb in parentheses ( ).

    11. At last our vacation had (begin).

    12. The ride to our campsite (take) a long time.

    13. It (grow) darker and darker.

    14. We finally (begin) to unpack.

    15. Mother had (give) everyone a job to do.

    16. Father and I (take) the tent to the campsite.

    17. We (sing) our favorite songs.

    18. No one (know) the tent poles were still at home.

    19. By now it had (grow) even darker.

    20. Finally we (throw) the tent over a rope between two trees.

    21. A big bat (fly) overhead.

    22. Had it (fly) into our tent?

    23. We all (go) into the tent.

    24. Meanwhile our dog had (eat) all our sandwiches!

    25. I (drink) some water.

    26. Then the rain (begin).

    27. The wind (blow) harder and harder.

    28. Soon rainwater had (begin) to leak in.

    29. We (do) the only possible thing.

    30. We (go) to a motel for the night!

Application SPEAKING AND LISTENING

Tell a short story about something you did last summer. Use six irregular verbs from this lesson. Ask your listeners to raise their hand whenever they hear one of the irregular verbs.

8 Using Irregular Verbs

- Some irregular verbs follow a pattern in the way they are formed.

You know that irregular verbs do not form their past or past participle by adding -ed. Many irregular verbs, however, do follow other patterns when forming their principal parts. The irregular verbs below are grouped by patterns.

Some form the past participle by adding -n to the past.

Present	Past	Past Participle
break	broke	(has, have, had) broken
choose	chose	(has, have, had) chosen
freeze	froze	(has, have, had) frozen
speak	spoke	(has, have, had) spoken

Some have the same present and past participle.

Present	Past	Past Participle
become	became	(has, have, had) become
come	came	(has, have, had) come
run	ran	(has, have, had) run

Some have the same past and past participle.

Present	Past	Past Participle
bring	brought	(has, have, had) brought
catch	caught	(has, have, had) caught
say	said	(has, have, had) said
teach	taught	(has, have, had) taught
think	thought	(has, have, had) thought

Skills Tryout

Name the past and past participle of each verb.

1. freeze   2. break   3. say   4. catch   5. become

Practice

A. Write the past and past participle of each verb.

    1. speak   **2.** think   **3.** teach   **4.** run   **5.** choose

B. Write the past or the past participle of the verb in parentheses ( ) to complete each sentence. Then write which principal part you used.

    6. Many English words have (come) from foreign languages.
    7. The word *typhoon* (come) from the Chinese word for "a great wind."
    8. Immigrants from Hamburg (teach) Americans about one food.
    9. This food (become) the American hamburger.
    10. Germans from Frankfurt (bring) frankfurters to America.
    11. Some experts have (say) that the word *mouse* comes from an early word for "steal."
    12. Long ago a Frenchman (think) a certain flower looked like a lion's tooth.
    13. He (speak) the French words *dent de lion.*
    14. Those words (become) *dandelion* in English.
    15. In England someone (choose) to call a flower "the day's eye."
    16. That flower has (become) the American daisy.
    17. The ancient Greeks (run) in a contest called an *agon.*
    18. If you have (run) a long way, you may know what agony is.
    19. Long ago a Greek runner (bring) news of a victory in battle from Marathon to Athens.
    20. Many runners have (break) records in today's marathons.

Application WRITING SENTENCES

Choose one irregular verb from each of the three groups on page 102. For each verb write one sentence using the past and one sentence using the past participle. You will write six sentences in all.

9 — Troublesome Verb Pairs

- Use the verb *can* to mean "to be able to do something." Use the verb *may* when you ask or give permission.
- Use the verb *let* to mean "to permit or allow." Use the verb *leave* to mean "to go away from" or "to allow to remain."

The verbs *can* and *may* do not mean the same thing. When asking or telling if someone is able to do something, use *can*.

> **Can** you come to dinner at our house on Friday?
> Yes, I **can** come.

When asking or giving permission, use *may*.

> **May** I have another piece of chicken?
> Yes, you **may** have some more.

People often confuse the verbs *let* and *leave*. When you mean "to permit or allow," use *let*.

> **Let** me help you clean up.   I cannot **let** you do that.

When you mean "to go away from" or "to allow to remain," use *leave*.

> We must **leave** the house soon.   **Leave** the book there.

Skills Tryout

Tell which verb in parentheses ( ) correctly completes each sentence.

1. You (can, may) serve dinner now.
2. (Can, May) you think of an interesting story to tell?
3. (Let, Leave) everyone have a chance to speak.
4. Please (let, leave) your napkin next to your plate.
5. (Can, May) I be excused?

Practice

A. Write each sentence. Use the correct verb in parentheses ( ).

1. You (can, may) make life more pleasant for everyone by improving your manners.
2. A camel (can, may) go a long way without water.
3. Don't (let, leave) others do all the work.
4. (Can, May) you find a way to help?
5. Did you (let, leave) your books on the chair?
6. (Can, May) I borrow your pen?
7. You (can, may) not borrow something without permission.
8. (Let, Leave) your room neat and clean.
9. Do you (let, leave) things in the proper place?
10. You (can, may) not open someone else's mail.

B. Write each sentence. Use the word *can, may, let,* or *leave* in place of the blank.

11. You _____ help others in many ways.
12. Do you _____ older people enter a door before you?
13. Don't _____ a door close in someone's face.
14. Never _____ litter in public places.
15. Don't _____ your dog run on the neighbor's lawn.
16. You _____ also practice good telephone manners.
17. Ask if you _____ take a message.
18. _____ clear messages for others.
19. _____ your messages be understood?
20. _____ you think of other ways to show good manners?

Application SPEAKING

Practice using *may* and *can* by asking a friend six questions. In three of the questions, use *may* to ask permission to do something. In the other three questions, use *can* to find out if the friend is able to do something.

—10— Troublesome Verb Pairs

> - Use the verb *teach* to mean "to instruct." Use the verb *learn* to mean "to gain understanding."
> - Use the verb *sit* to mean "to rest." Use the verb *set* to mean "to put or place something."

Some people make mistakes when using the verbs *teach* and *learn.* The verbs have different meanings. *Teach* means "to instruct" or "to show how something is done or what something means."

The Beckers <u>teach</u> their dogs many tricks.

Learn means "to gain understanding" or "to find out how something is done or what something means."

The dogs <u>learn</u> how to jump through hoops.

The verbs *sit* and *set* also have different meanings. *Sit* means "to rest" or "to stay."

The dogs <u>sit</u> in front of the hoops.

Set means "to put or place something."

The Beckers <u>set</u> the hoop on a high stand.

Skills Tryout

Tell which verb in parentheses ( ) correctly completes each sentence.

1. You can (teach, learn) an old dog new tricks.
2. Younger dogs (teach, learn) more quickly.
3. A dog should (sit, set) when its owner says so.
4. Many people (teach, learn) their dogs to heel and to stay.
5. You should try to (sit, set) aside thirty minutes a day for training your dog.

Practice

A. Write each sentence. Use the correct verb in parentheses (   ).

1. Any dog can (teach, learn) to walk beside its owner.
2. It is important to (teach, learn) a dog to heel.
3. A sharp snap on the leash will (teach, learn) a dog not to pull ahead.
4. A dog should (sit, set) when its trainer stops.
5. (Teach, Learn) the dog the correct sitting position.
6. Don't allow the dog to (sit, set) its paw on your foot.
7. Dogs (teach, learn) quickly when they are praised often.
8. (Sit, Set) a time limit for lessons.
9. Dogs (teach, learn) best with two short lessons a day.
10. Many fine books (teach, learn) people how to train dogs.

B. Write each sentence. Use the word *teach, learn, sit,* or *set* in place of the blank.

11. The dog-show judges _____ the trophies on the table.
12. A trainer will _____ a hurdle at its lowest level.
13. Another will _____ the planks for the long jump in place.
14. The people _____ quietly in the stands.
15. Trainers _____ dogs to ignore other dogs at shows.
16. Dogs must _____ this in order to perform well.
17. Trainers also _____ their dogs to walk in figure eights.
18. Dogs must _____ still for minutes at a time.
19. The trainer will _____ the trophy down so its winner can smell it.
20. A new dog owner can _____ many things at a dog show.

Application WRITING SENTENCES

Write six sentences that tell what you would like to teach a pet to do. Use the verbs *teach, learn, sit,* and *set* at least one time each.

11 — Prefixes

> ● A **prefix** is a letter or letters added to the beginning of a word. The prefix changes the meaning of the word.

Read the sentences below.

> Marie was <u>unable</u> to wait any longer. She <u>untied</u> the bow on the present. Then she <u>unwrapped</u> the box.

The underlined words begin with the prefix *un-*. A prefix is a letter or letters added to the beginning of a word. A prefix changes the meaning of the word it is added to. For example, *unable* means "not able." *Untied* means the opposite of *tied*, and *unwrapped* means the opposite of *wrapped*.

Some common prefixes and their meanings are listed below.

Prefix	Meaning	Examples
dis-	opposite of, away from	dislike, disobey
mis-	wrong, wrongly	mismatch, mistreat
un-	not, opposite of	unsure, uncover
re-	again, back	reuse, repay
pre-	before	preheat, prerecord
im-	not, opposite of	impolite, impatience
in-	not, opposite of	inexact, invisible

Skills Tryout

Identify the word with a prefix in each sentence. Tell what the word means.

1. Each year the Lees rediscover the joy of winter sports.
2. Marie sharpens and resharpens her figure skates.
3. Mother prepays the fees for the Winter Sports Festival.
4. Father and Don are always impatient to leave.
5. They must pack and unpack the car to fit everything.

Practice

A. Write the word with a prefix in each sentence. Then write what the word means.

1. Marie and Don dislike the car trip to the festival.
2. The roads are narrow and uneven.
3. At last they unload their equipment.
4. Marie feels insecure on her first downhill run.
5. She reapplies wax to her skis.
6. "Unbend your knees a little," Marie tells Don.
7. Don and Marie disappear down the slopes.
8. Minutes later they reappear on the chair lift.
9. At one point Don misguided his skis.
10. Next he unfolded himself from a snowdrift!

B. Write each sentence. Use a word with a prefix in place of the words in parentheses ( ).

11. Marie and Don watch the ski jumpers in (opposite of belief).
12. Such long jumps seem (not possible).
13. One wrong move could lead to (wrong fortune).
14. Bobsleds whizz by at (not believable) speed.
15. The speed skaters show (not usual) strength.
16. Iceboat captains (check again) their boats.
17. They have (planned before) their actions.
18. The starter has (wrongly placed) the starting gun.
19. Don and Marie skate (not hurriedly) to each boat.
20. After dinner they (tell again) the day's adventures.

Application USING LANGUAGE

Write six sentences about winter sports. Use a word with a prefix in each sentence. Use six different prefixes from this lesson to form the words.

Action Verbs and Linking Verbs   *pages 88–91*

A. Write the verb in each sentence. Then write *action* if it is an action verb or *linking* if it is a linking verb.

1. Scientists study about 250 kinds of sharks.
2. Only thirty kinds are dangerous to humans.
3. Some sharks become huge.
4. This book describes a twenty-five-foot white shark.
5. The tiny dwarf shark is only six inches long.
6. Sharks seem happiest in warm waters.
7. Usually nothing eats a shark except a bigger shark.
8. A shark's skin feels very rough.
9. Tiny sharp points cover the outside of most sharks.
10. Carpenters once used sharkskin for sandpaper.

Helping Verbs and Main Verbs   *pages 92–93*

B. Write the sentences below. Underline the helping verbs once and the main verbs twice.

11. Sharks will swallow almost anything.
12. Scientists have found cans and shoes in sharks' stomachs!
13. Sharks do not lay eggs like most fish.
14. Newborn sharks must protect themselves immediately.
15. A hungry mother shark may eat her babies.

Direct Objects   *pages 94–95*

C. Write the direct object in each sentence.

16. Usually sharks eat small fish.
17. Sharks can see their dinner from far away.
18. Their sharp ears hear very faint sounds.
19. Blood attracts sharks quickly.
20. They can smell tiny amounts in the ocean.

Grammar Review

Tenses of Verbs   *pages 96–97*

D. Write the verb in each sentence. Then write *present, past,* or *future* to show the tense of the verb.

21. The United States government used a computer during the 1890 census.
22. The mechanical computer counted the nation's population.
23. Today we use computers in business, science, and education.
24. Millions of Americans own personal computers.
25. Computers will play an even greater role in the future.

Irregular Verbs   *pages 100–103*

E. Write the three principal parts of the underlined verbs.

26. We <u>brought</u> a personal computer home.
27. I <u>write</u> my school reports on it.
28. My parents <u>run</u> their business with it.
29. The computer <u>taught</u> French to my sister.
30. After school we <u>take</u> turns on the computer.
31. We <u>give</u> answers to its questions.
32. Some computers <u>speak</u> with a funny voice.
33. They <u>come</u> with many exciting games.
34. Computers <u>know</u> a great deal.
35. They <u>have become</u> an important part of our lives.

Troublesome Verb Pairs   *pages 104–107*

F. Write each sentence. Use the correct verb in parentheses ( ).

36. My parents (let, leave) me use their computer.
37. I sometimes (sit, set) in front of it for hours.
38. Computers can (learn, teach) us many things.
39. It is hard for me to (let, leave) the computer alone.
40. (May, Can) I see your computer sometime soon?

See also Handbook pages 348–363.

Grammar Review

Writing with Verbs

● Use exact verbs to make your writing more interesting.

Read the sentences below.

1. Leon got out of bed at nine o'clock.
2. Leon jumped out of bed at nine o'clock.

These two sentences tell about the same incident. However, the second sentence is more specific than the first. Sentence 1 simply says that Leon *got* out of bed. Sentence 2 explains that he *jumped* out of bed. The exact verb *jumped* gives a much clearer picture of Leon's actions.

Read the sentence below. Notice how changing the verb creates a much different picture of Leon's actions.

Leon crawled out of bed at nine o'clock.

Look for opportunities to use exact verbs in your writing. An action verb can make the difference between dull and interesting writing.

Using Verbs Below is a list of verbs. What exact verbs could replace each one?

Select a verb from the list and write it on a piece of paper. Think of exact verbs that could replace it in a sentence. Write as many exact verbs as you can in two minutes.

make	want	put
work	take	get

How many exact verbs did you write? Think about how the meanings of your verbs are different from one another. Find a classmate who chose the same verb. What exact verbs did he or she write? Choose another verb from the list and start again. Had you realized how important verbs are in writing?

Replacing Verbs   Write each sentence. Replace the underlined word with a more exact verb.

EXAMPLE: Peter <u>cleaned</u> the house.
ANSWER: Peter dusted the house.

1. Rachel <u>was</u> in the annual Memorial Day parade.
2. Nicholas <u>had</u> six glasses of lemonade!
3. Louis Pasteur <u>found</u> the cure to many diseases.
4. Don't <u>use</u> your brother's bicycle without his permission.
5. I will <u>send</u> a letter to Sid about the boat trip.
6. The coach <u>said</u> to the girl not to be late for the game.

Using No Clues   Now replace verbs without using clues. Find the verb in each sentence. Think of a more exact verb that could replace it. Write the new sentence.

7. The rain fell all afternoon.
8. Sarah moved the pitcher away from the edge of the table.
9. People will one day go to the stars.
10. Judy shut the door to her room very quickly.
11. The mechanic checked the brakes of the automobile.
12. The wild animal ate the food on the picnic table.

Using the Thesaurus

Imagine that you just bought some items at a department store. Write four sentences about them. Find the entry for *buy* in the Thesaurus beginning on page 414. Choose four words that are synonyms for *buy*. Use them in your sentences.

Find the entry for *call* in the Thesaurus. Then use the synonyms listed to write a paragraph about someone who is calling for help. The person could be trapped in a burning building or locked in a closet. Try to use at least three synonyms for *call* in your paragraph.

12 Writing an Explanatory Paragraph

- An **explanatory paragraph** can inform someone how to make or do something.

One of the most useful kinds of paragraphs is a paragraph that explains how to make or do something. Here is a paragraph that explains how to make a vase from scrap materials.

It is easy to make a beautiful vase from a discarded bottle. First, gather the following: a wide-neck bottle, a box of paraffin, crayon stubs, and ornaments such as sequins and beads. Melt the paraffin over low heat. Then, add crayon stubs of the color you want, and stir until they are melted and mixed. Next, hold the bottle on its side and roll it in the paraffin. Coat the whole bottle. Repeat this procedure if you want to add layers of different colors. Finally, push ornaments into the warm paraffin while it is still soft.

Use the guidelines below to help you write an explanatory paragraph.

How to Write an Explanatory Paragraph

1. Begin with a topic sentence that tells what the paragraph will explain.
2. List any materials that will be needed.
3. Write step-by-step instructions. Use signal words, such as *first, second, next, after that, then,* and *last,* to help the reader understand the order of the steps.
4. Check that you have included all the necessary steps and that you have not included any unnecessary information.

Skills Tryout

Tell by answering the following questions how the example paragraph on page 114 follows the guidelines for an explanatory paragraph.

1. Which sentence in the paragraph follows the first guideline?
2. Which sentence follows the second guideline?
3. What signal words help show the order of the steps?
4. Should the paragraph have told what to put in the vase?

Practice

A. Write the following sentences as an explanatory paragraph. Write the topic sentence first. Then put the other sentences in the correct order.

1. Next, at a signal from the leader, each player throws a feather at the tree.
2. Each player begins by forming a circle with seven long feathers.
3. The player whose feather lands nearest the tree wins the round.
4. The following game is played in Africa.
5. Then a tree is chosen as the target.
6. After that, the game continues until all feathers have been thrown.

B. Study the pictures. Then write an explanatory paragraph that tells how to make a bowl from clay.

Application WRITING A PARAGRAPH

Write a paragraph that gives clear instructions on how to make or do something. You may use one of the following topics, or use one of your own ideas.

How to cook a ＿＿＿   How to start a ＿＿＿ collection
How to build a ＿＿＿   How to play a game of ＿＿＿

13 — Using the Telephone

> • When you write a telephone message, give correct and complete information.

The telephone is a powerful tool. Businesses depend on it, and our everyday lives are much easier because of it. In emergencies, the telephone can save lives. The word *DIALS* can help you use the telephone properly.

Dial all phone numbers carefully.
Identify yourself to the person who answers the telephone.
Ask politely for the person with whom you wish to speak.
Leave a message if the person you are calling is out.
Speak clearly and slowly when you leave a message.

A telephone message should contain the following information.

Date and time ⟶	*Dec. 10, 3:30 P.M.*
Person called ⟶	*Aunt Gina,*
Caller's name ⟶	*Lois Becker called.*
Message ⟶	*She can't meet you for lunch Tuesday.*
Caller's number ⟶	*Her office number is 555-3810.*
Message taker ⟶	*Ron*

The telephone directory is a useful tool, too. Follow these tips when using the white pages of your directory.

- Initials come before first names. *Wu, F* is before *Wu, Fred.*
- Abbreviations are listed as if they were spelled out. *Mt. Rose Clinic* would be alphabetized as *Mount Rose Clinic.*
- Names beginning with letters are the first listings in their alphabetical sections. *SA Sports* would begin the *S* section.
- When used as names, numbers are alphabetized as if they were spelled out. The name *10 Tailors* would be alphabetized as *Ten Tailors.*

Skills Tryout

Tell what is wrong with this telephone conversation.

Cara (answering the telephone): Hello?
Mike: Let me speak to Karen.
Cara: Karen isn't home.
Mike: Oh. Good-by.

Practice

A. Rewrite the following conversation so that Peter uses better telephone skills.

Peter: Hi, Maria?
Janice: No, this is Janice.
Peter: Is Maria there?
Janice: No, she isn't. May I ask who's calling?
Peter: Tell her that Peter can't be in the play. Good-by.

B. Rewrite the following message, filling in the missing information. You may make up any information you need.

> Suzie,
> Someone named Joe called.

Application LIFE SKILLS

Use your telephone directory and the tips on page 116 to answer the following questions.

a. In what section of the telephone directory would you find the listing for your favorite radio station?
b. Would *St. Ann's School* be listed after *Sainsbury, Wendy* or after *Srygly, Walter*?
c. Which listing would appear first, *Sanchez, Roberto* or *Sanchez, R*?
d. How would you find the listing for 20/20 Vision Center?
e. Where would you expect to find the listing for *H&H Typing*?

14 — Friendly Letters

> ● A friendly letter has five parts: the heading, greeting, body, closing, and signature.

Study the placement of the five parts of this letter.

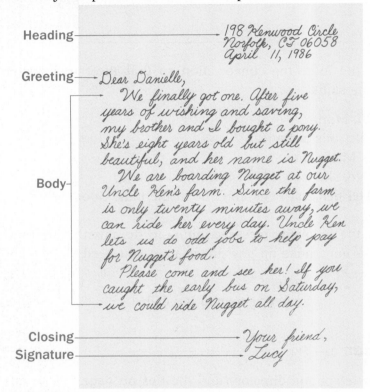

Heading —————————————— 198 Kenwood Circle
Norfolk, CT 06058
April 11, 1986

Greeting —— Dear Danielle,

Body ——— We finally got one. After five years of wishing and saving, my brother and I bought a pony. She's eight years old but still beautiful, and her name is Nugget.

We are boarding Nugget at our Uncle Ken's farm. Since the farm is only twenty minutes away, we can ride her every day. Uncle Ken lets us do odd jobs to help pay for Nugget's food.

Please come and see her! If you caught the early bus on Saturday, we could ride Nugget all day.

Closing ——————————— Your friend,
Signature ——————————— Lucy

Follow these rules when writing friendly letters.

- Include your address and the date in the heading. Place a comma between your city and state and between the day and year in the date.
- Capitalize the first word of the greeting. Place a comma after the greeting.
- Place a comma after the closing. Capitalize the first word of the closing.
- Indent each new paragraph.

Skills Tryout

Name these parts of a friendly letter.

1. The writer's address and the date
2. The writer's name
3. The writer's message

Practice

A. For each item, write *heading, greeting, body, closing,* or *signature.*

   1. Your cousin,
   2. 202 Ellis Avenue
      Brooklyn, NY 11201
      May 1, 1986
   3. Dear Aileen,
   4. I've caught a bad cold and won't be able to see the opening night of your play.
   5. *Joanne*

B. Write these items as if they were parts of letters. Punctuate and capitalize them correctly.

   6. january 11, 19___
   7. mount vernon, oh 43050
   8. dear kate
   9. Your Niece
  10. 611, maple avenue
  11. Dear dr. lewis
  12. chicago, il 60617
  13. 10 crestwood drive
  14. Dear Al And Betty
  15. best wishes

Application WRITING A FRIENDLY LETTER

Write a letter to inform a friend of something special that has happened to you recently. Include all five parts of a friendly letter. Then address an envelope for the letter. Refer to page 396 in the Young Writer's Handbook for the correct positions of envelope addresses.

15 — Business Letters

> ● When you write a business letter, make your message clear and brief.

Study the placement of the six parts of a business letter.

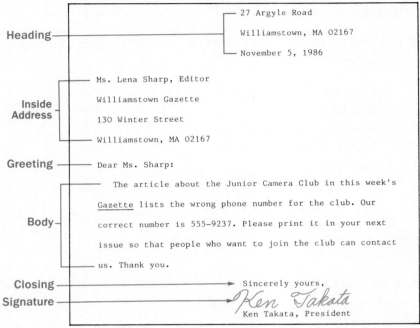

Heading
- 27 Argyle Road
- Williamstown, MA 02167
- November 5, 1986

Inside Address
- Ms. Lena Sharp, Editor
- Williamstown Gazette
- 130 Winter Street
- Williamstown, MA 02167

Greeting
- Dear Ms. Sharp:

Body
- The article about the Junior Camera Club in this week's *Gazette* lists the wrong phone number for the club. Our correct number is 555-9237. Please print it in your next issue so that people who want to join the club can contact us. Thank you.

Closing
- Sincerely yours,

Signature
- *Ken Takata*
- Ken Takata, President

Follow these rules when writing business letters.

- An inside address gives the name and address of the person or the company receiving the letter.
- The greeting is formal and is followed by a colon. If you do not know who will receive the letter, use the greeting *Dear Sir or Madam.*
- The body states the specific purpose for the letter. Facts are given in a brief and logical way.
- The closing is formal. Closings such as *Yours truly* and *Sincerely* are appropriate.
- In a typed business letter, the writer's name is typed four lines below the closing.

Skills Tryout

Tell what word or words complete each sentence.

1. A _____ appears after the greeting of a business letter.
2. The inside address is the address of _____.
3. Two appropriate closings for business letters are _____.

Practice

A. Write these items as if they were parts of a business letter. Punctuate and capitalize them correctly.

1. Dear sir or madam,
2. yours truly:
3. Mr. Peter Thyme; president
4. Dear dr. grillo—

5. northern lights company
   211 hilltop drive
   freeport me 04032
   june 12 1986

B. Write the following business letter in correct form. Then label each part of the letter.

102 Califon Road Calabasas, CA 91302 April 21, 1986 American Buckle Company 200 Industrial Way Bethesda MD 20014 Dear Sir or Madam On April 2, I ordered a Golden Eagle Belt Buckle, catalog number 135-GE. I enclosed a check for $12.50. Yesterday I received a Monkey's Claw Buckle instead. I am returning it and requesting that you fill my order correctly. Sincerely *Justin Esposito*

Application WRITING A BUSINESS LETTER

Newspapers are always looking for interesting topics for feature articles. Write a business letter to the managing editor of a local newspaper. Inform the editor of a special project or event in your school, town, or club that might make an interesting feature article. Include information such as telephone numbers, place, and time so that a reporter would be able to follow up on the project.

16 — Writing a Letter of Information

Writing Project

- In a **letter of information,** the writer tells about something of interest to the reader.

In lesson 14 you studied the form for writing a friendly letter. The form of the letter is important, but what you say is even more important to your reader. Your reader wants information—information about you and your activities. In this lesson you will use the five *W*'s to help you discover what you want to say. Then you will use that information in a letter you write to any person you choose.

1. Prewriting

▶ To whom would you like to write? Classmates and neighbors always appreciate letters. Cousins, aunts, uncles, and grandparents will welcome letters as well. Choose one person to whom you will write. That person is your audience.

► Your audience wants to know about you. What news do you have to share? Can you think of a topic for your letter? Here are some suggestions.

- Tell about your favorite club.
- Tell about a school music, drama, or science project.
- Tell about your visit to a museum, zoo, or park.
- Tell about an athletic event.
- Tell about a contest you entered.

Select a topic that will interest your audience, one that you will enjoy sharing with your reader.

► Write *Who? What? When? Where?* and *Why?* on a piece of paper. Answer those questions about your topic. Then look at the information you listed and select the items that will most interest your reader. Cross out any ideas that are not appropriate.

	Who?	Dad and I
		other people in the supermarket
	What?	entered a contest
		talked to a woman from the cereal company
		sampled a new breakfast cereal
		made up a name for it
	When?	last Saturday about 2:00
		on my cousin's birthday
		after we washed the car
	Where?	Livingston avenue
		at the supermarket
	Why?	because it was fun
		to win a trip to Disney World

2. Writing

▶ Write your letter as if you were speaking to your reader. How will you begin? Often, informative letters begin with a statement of purpose. For example, you might say "I cannot wait to tell you about a new club I joined." Your purpose for writing could be in the form of a question: "Did you know I entered a contest to win a trip to Disney World?"

After you explain why you are writing, give your reader a complete report. Tell *who, what, when, where,* and *why.*

3. Revising

▶ Read your letter aloud. Do you like the way it sounds? Do you want to make changes to improve it? The Revision Checklist will help you decide.

Revision Checklist
- Does my letter begin with a statement of purpose?
- Did I explain Who, What, When, Where, and Why?
- Did I give the information that will be most interesting to my reader?
- Does my letter sound friendly and natural, the way I talk?
- Did I take out unnecessary words?

Read the sample that follows. Notice how taking out unnecessary words improved the letter.

¶Did you know I ~~tried~~ *entered* a contest to win a ~~winning~~

trip to disney world? Last Saturday ~~over the~~

~~weekend~~ my dad and I ~~entered a contest when we~~

were in a supermarket. A breakfast *cereal* company ~~for~~

where

310 Woodland Avenue
Columbus, Ohio 43216
October 24, 1986

Dear Amanda,

   Did you know I entered a contest to win a trip to Disney World? Last Saturday my dad and I were in a supermarket where a breakfast cereal company was sponsoring a contest. Each contestant sampled the company's new product and wrote a catchy name for it on an entry blank.

   It might be unlucky for me to tell you the name I made up. The winner will be announced next month. Don't be surprised if you get a postcard from me—all the way from Disney World!

Your friend,
Lucy

▶ Revise your letter, using editing marks to make changes.

EDITING MARKS

——	cross out
∧	add
↷	move
≡	capital letter
/	small letter
¶	indent
◯	check spelling

4. Publishing

▶ As a courtesy to your reader, proofread your letter. Use the Proofreading Checklist in the Young Writer's Handbook on page 399. Make corrections with the editing marks.

▶ Address an envelope to your reader, using the form shown on page 396 of the Young Writer's Handbook. Then stamp it and mail it. Imagine how pleased your friend or relative will be to get your letter.

Writing Project

A Commemorative Stamp

A postage stamp that honors an important event, thing, or person is called a commemorative stamp. Design a commemorative stamp that illustrates a remarkable accomplishment that you have achieved or would like to achieve.

Use bright colors, bold outlines, and sharp contrasts to make the drawing stand out. Be sure to include the price on the stamp. You might also include your name or a label to help explain the illustration.

Science

By passing a beam of light through a prism, the scientist Sir Isaac Newton created a band of colors called a spectrum. Then, to explain how the colors relate to each other, Newton invented the color wheel. He painted the basic colors of the spectrum on the outside of the wheel. Next, he shaded in the colors as they met at the center. The wheel shows that equal parts of two opposite colors, such as green and red, form black. Unequal parts of opposite colors darken each other. The wheel also shows how two colors on the same side of the wheel can form other colors. For example, a blend of yellow and blue makes green.

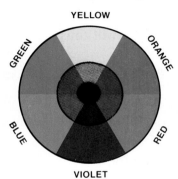

▶ Try it. Experiment with color by mixing paints. Using only the primary colors—red, blue, and yellow—create a shade such as maroon. Then write an explanatory paragraph that gives step-by-step instructions for recreating that shade.

Listeners and Speakers at Work Weather forecasters, or meteorologists, study changes in the weather. Then they inform the public about the expected changes. One way they communicate this information is by telephone.

▶ Look up the number of the weather forecast service in your telephone directory. Call and listen carefully to the forecaster. Then make up your own forecast. Tell it to the class.

Verbs   *pages 88–107*

A. Write each sentence. Draw one line under the linking verb. Draw two lines under the words that the verb connects.

1. This storm is a blizzard
2. The wind feels chilly.
3. These woods seem ghostly.
4. The hills are snowdrifts.

B. Write each sentence. Underline the helping verbs once and the main verbs twice.

5. We are building a treehouse in my yard.
6. Mr. Jander has been helping us all week long.
7. The treehouse does not have a roof yet.
8. We will finish it this Saturday.

C. Write the direct object in each sentence.

9. My uncle repairs shoes.
10. Bill chopped the firewood.
11. We washed the car.
12. Mr. Giles won a contest.

D. Write the past tense and future tense of each verb.

13. avoid   14. roll   15. remain   16. provide   17. include

E. Write the three principal parts of each verb. Use the helping verb *has* with each past participle.

18. grow   20. choose   22. memorize   24. carry
19. create   21. begin   23. do   25. finish

F. Write each sentence. Use the correct verb in parentheses ( ).

26. You (can, may) borrow my sleeping bag and pup tent.
27. Mr. Ricci will (learn, teach) the children a magic trick.
28. I like to (sit, set) in the crook of the apple tree.
29. Did Scott (let, leave) his library book at home?

Prefixes   *pages 108–109*

G. Write a word with a prefix for each pair of words.

30. play again
31. opposite of agree
32. not possible
33. plan before
34. not correct
35. inform wrongly
36. not steady
37. opposite of appear

Explanatory Paragraph   *pages 114–115*

H. Read the paragraph. Then answer the questions.

A dish garden is simple to make. First, find a glass bowl and put a layer of gravel in it. Next, spread soil on top of the gravel. Then place small plants in the soil. Finally, cover the bowl with a piece of glass fit to size.

38. Which sentence is the topic sentence?
39. What materials are used in a dish garden?
40. What signal words help show the order of the steps?

Letters   *pages 118–121*

I. Write these items as if they were parts of letters. Punctuate and capitalize them correctly.

41. dear maria
42. best wishes
43. march 16 1986
44. dear sir or madam
45. burbank ca 91503
46. ms. kim todd editor

J. Write *friendly letter*, *business letter*, or *both* for each statement below.

47. One of its parts is an inside address.
48. The first word of the closing is capitalized.
49. The greeting is formal and is followed by a colon.
50. The heading includes the writer's address.

See also Handbook pages 348–363, 391–393.

Checkpoint: Unit 3

Grammar
Pronouns

Composition
Narrating

The Pasture

I'm going out to clean the pasture spring;
I'll only stop to rake the leaves away
(And wait to watch the water clear, I may):
I sha'n't be gone long. — You come too.

I'm going out to fetch the little calf
That's standing by the mother. It's so young
It totters when she licks it with her tongue.
I sha'n't be gone long. — You come too.

—*Robert Frost*

1 Pronouns

> ● A **pronoun** takes the place of a noun or nouns.

Read this limerick about a robot named Artie. Notice that the word *he* takes the place of the name Artie four times.

> Our family's new robot is Artie.
> <u>He</u> is smart, helpful, neat, and quite hardy.
> <u>He</u> takes care of the folks,
> And <u>he</u> tells funny jokes.
> In fact, <u>he</u> is the life of the party!

Words that take the place of nouns are called pronouns. In the sentences below, the pronouns are shown in blue. The words they take the place of are shown in red.

Artie the Robot tells jokes.	He tells jokes.
Artie told the joke.	Artie told it.
Carrie polishes Artie's head.	Carrie polishes his head.

The chart below lists singular and plural pronouns.

Singular	Plural
I, me, my, mine	we, us, our, ours
you, your, yours	you, your, yours
he, she, it, him,	they, them, their, theirs
her, his, hers, its	

Skills Tryout

Name the pronouns in these sentences.

1. Robots are helpful, but they are expensive to build.
2. Robot builders call their science robotics.
3. It is a rapidly growing field.
4. Some robots already work in our factories and offices.
5. People find them fascinating.

Practice

A. Write each sentence. Underline the pronouns.

1. You may have seen the robot Silent Sam.
2. He directs traffic in many states.
3. The tall robot never tires of his work.
4. People cheerfully obey him.
5. Robots in factories do their jobs quickly and well.
6. They are connected to computers.
7. The computers direct them.
8. Robots will do many of our routine jobs in the future.
9. Mother thinks a robot could make her work easier.
10. Maybe it could help with my chores, too!

B. The second sentence in each pair contains a pronoun. Write the pronoun. Then write the noun that the pronoun takes the place of.

11. **a.** Hero of Alexandria described a robot long ago.
    b. He called the invention an automaton.
12. **a.** A Czech writer's play told about robots.
    b. His play was called *R.U.R.*
13. **a.** Robots became very popular during the 1920s.
    b. People saw them in movies and magazines.
14. **a.** A robot's appearance may be humanlike.
    b. Its size may be large or small.
15. **a.** Two Viking Landers were built for a spaceflight to Mars.
    b. They were very expensive robots.

Application WRITING SENTENCES

Robots will do many dangerous or routine jobs in our homes, offices, and factories in the future. Write six sentences that tell how you think robots might make life easier for people some day. Use a pronoun in each sentence.

2 Subject Pronouns

- The **subject pronouns** are *I, you, she, he, it, we,* and *they.*

You have learned that pronouns take the place of nouns. Some pronouns can be used as subjects of sentences. These pronouns are called subject pronouns. The subject pronouns are *I, you, she, he, it, we,* and *they.* Remember that the pronoun *I* is always capitalized.

Notice that any of the subject pronouns can be used as the subject of this sentence:

_____ **can make clay bowls.**

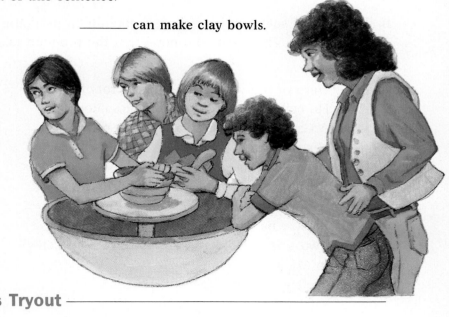

Skills Tryout

Name the subject pronoun in each sentence.

1. "Would you like to make a clay bowl?" asked Aunt Anna.
2. "I would love to," said Lucas.
3. "We can work together," said the boy's aunt.
4. She mixed water with some dry clay.
5. Then they rolled the clay into long coils.

Practice

A. Write each sentence. Underline the subject pronouns.

1. They set the coils on the table.
2. "I make the bowls from these coils," said Aunt Anna.
3. "First we must join the ends of the coils."
4. She showed Lucas how to do that.
5. Then he stacked the coils on top of each other.
6. They pressed the coils tightly together.
7. "Now it looks like a bowl!" said Lucas.
8. "You will make a good potter some day," said Aunt Anna.
9. "We will put the pot in the sun to dry."
10. "Later I will paint and bake the pot," said Lucas.

B. Each sentence contains two pronouns. Some are subject pronouns and some are not. Write the pronouns. Then circle *only* the subject pronouns.

11. They waited three days for their pot to dry.
12. At last it was ready for them to finish.
13. "First we coat our pot with a watery paint called slip," Aunt Anna told Lucas.
14. Then she asked him to polish the pot with a stone.
15. He rubbed and rubbed until his arm ached.
16. Next they used their paints to decorate the pot.
17. "May I paint an eagle and a snake on its sides?" Lucas asked Aunt Anna.
18. She nodded at him.
19. "You painted them very well," Aunt Anna said.
20. "Now we will bake the pot in my kiln."

Application WRITING SENTENCES

Write seven sentences about something you have made with an adult or a friend. Tell how you made it. Use a subject pronoun in at least four of your sentences.

3   Object Pronouns

- The **object pronouns** are *me, you, her, him, it, us,* and *them.*

You know that a pronoun can take the place of a noun used as the subject of a sentence. Pronouns can also take the place of nouns used as direct objects. These pronouns are called object pronouns.

Read the sentences below.

Jim spots an <u>owl</u>. Jim spots <u>it</u>.
The owl doesn't see <u>Jim</u>. The owl doesn't see <u>him</u>.

In the first sentence in each pair, the direct object is a noun. In the second sentence an object pronoun replaces the noun.

Object pronouns have different forms from subject pronouns. Here is a list of object pronouns: *me, you, her, him, it, us,* and *them.* Notice that *you* and *it* can be subject pronouns or object pronouns.

Skills Tryout

Name the object pronoun in each pair of sentences.

1. The Bird Watchers is a club. Jason will join it.
2. Club members look for birds. Members spot them all over.
3. Rita is the president. Jason asks her about the club.
4. Rita tells Jason about the club's next hike. She invites him to the hike.
5. Don wants to go, too. "Will Rita invite me?" he wonders.

Practice

A. Write the second sentence in each pair. Underline the object pronouns.

  1. The Bird Watchers go to the woods. Mrs. Lee takes them.
  2. A song sparrow sings happily. The children hear it.
  3. "Look at the sparrow," Rita says. "It doesn't see me."
  4. Mrs. Lee and Rita move closer. "Follow us," Rita says.
  5. The Bird Watchers see a cardinal. The bird startles them.
  6. Mrs. Lee walks toward a wren's nest. Rita follows her.
  7. A male wren is in the nest. Don watches him.
  8. The wren flies off. "The wren just saw you," Rita says.
  9. A woodpecker hammers on a tree. Jason watches it.
 10. Insects live in the tree. The woodpecker eats them.

B. The second sentence in each pair contains two pronouns. Write the pronouns. Then circle *only* the object pronouns.

EXAMPLE: The children continued the hike. They enjoyed it.
ANSWER: They, it

 11. A hummingbird flitted away. "I didn't see it!" Ann cried.
 12. "Don't worry," said Mrs. Lee. "We will spot it again."
 13. A goldfinch landed near the children. They all admired it.
 14. "These birds turn browner in winter," said Rita. "We can't spot them so easily then."
 15. A lark flew overhead. "It is watching us," said Rita.
 16. Don called to Rita. She followed him.
 17. "What bird is that?" asked Don. "Can you tell me?"
 18. "That is an owl," said Rita. "We have seen her before."
 19. "Do eagles live nearby?" asked Don. "I want to see them."
 20. "An eagle lives on that cliff," said Rita. "I have seen it."

Application WRITING SENTENCES

Write six sentences about birds you have seen. Use an object pronoun in at least three of your sentences.

4 — Possessive Pronouns

> ● A **possessive pronoun** shows ownership.

You know that possessive nouns show ownership. Pronouns can also show ownership. In the first stanza of "Cat," the poet uses the pronoun *her* in place of the possessive noun *cat's.*

Cat
The black cat yawns,
Opens <u>her</u> jaws,
Stretches <u>her</u> legs,
And shows <u>her</u> claws.
—*Mary Britton Miller*

Pronouns that show ownership are called possessive pronouns. A possessive pronoun never has an apostrophe. The possessive pronouns are listed below.

Used Before Nouns	Used Alone
my your his her its our their	mine yours his hers ours theirs

Notice that some possessive pronouns are used before nouns and others stand alone. *His* can be used in both ways.

I pet <u>my</u> cat.   She pets <u>hers</u>.

Skills Tryout

Name the possessive pronoun in each sentence.

1. Our neighborhood is having a cat show.
2. The brown tabby cat is mine.
3. Siamese cats are known for their blue eyes.
4. A cat uses its tail for balance.
5. Sal says the white Persian cat with long hair is his.

Practice

A. Write the possessive pronoun in each sentence. Then write *before* if it comes before a noun or *alone* if it stands alone.

1. Your cat has a tortoiseshell pattern.
2. Patches of brown, yellow, and black make up her coat.
3. Is the male calico cat yours?
4. His coat has large white patches.
5. Their short-haired cat is very soft.
6. The Rex cat is not ours.
7. Did you notice its curly hair?
8. Mrs. Pelton says the Manx cat is hers.
9. Its hind legs are long and muscular.
10. Our show was a great success.

B. Write each sentence. Use the correct pronoun in parentheses ( ).

11. Mrs. Day brought (her, hers) cat to the show.
12. The Burmese cat is (her, hers).
13. The Egyptians used (their, theirs) cats for hunting many years ago.
14. The first tame cats were probably (their, theirs).
15. This Russian Blue cat is (my, mine).
16. Russian Blues are known for (their, theirs) blue coats.
17. Which cat is (your, yours)?
18. Cats are clean, and (their, theirs) needs are simple.
19. My Dad and I think (our, ours) cats are graceful.
20. The cat that just won a prize is (our, ours).

Application WRITING SENTENCES

Some people love cats and think they are charming. Others dislike cats and feel they are too independent. Write six sentences that tell why you like or dislike cats. Use at least four possessive pronouns in your sentences.

Predicate Nominatives

> ● A **predicate nominative** is a noun or pronoun that follows a linking verb and renames or identifies the subject of the sentence.

A linking verb connects the subject of a sentence with a word in the predicate. Sometimes a linking verb connects the subject with a noun. That noun is called a **predicate noun**.

S   LV   PN

Jack was the clown at the party.

In the sentence above, the predicate noun is *clown. Clown* renames the subject of the sentence, *Jack.*

Sometimes a linking verb connects the subject with a pronoun. That pronoun is called a **predicate pronoun**.

S   LV   PP

The masked cowboy is   I.

In the sentence above, *I* is a predicate pronoun. It renames the subject of the sentence, *cowboy.* Only subject pronouns are used after linking verbs.

Predicate nouns and predicate pronouns are both predicate nominatives. A predicate nominative follows a linking verb and renames or identifies the subject of the sentence.

Skills Tryout

Name the predicate nominative in each sentence.

1. Don and Susan are the hosts of the costume party.
2. I am a cowboy without a horse.
3. That tall blackbird is Don.
4. The green frog was you!
5. The dessert is ice cream.

Practice

A. Write each sentence. Underline each predicate nominative.

   1. Each guest at the party was a mystery.
   2. The knight in armor is surely Freddy.
   3. Was Jake the bull?
   4. Marie is the ballerina by the stairs.
   5. The tall ghost by the piano isn't Judy.
   6. Yes, it is she!
   7. The twins are probably the horse.
   8. Is Marci the head of the horse?
   9. Charlie's costume was a spaceship.
  10. That garbage can by the door was the nose cone.

B. Write the predicate nominative in each sentence. Then write whether it is a predicate noun or a predicate pronoun.

  11. "The knight was I," said Freddy.
  12. "However, the bull was not Jake," Freddy added.
  13. "The bull was Susan!" said Don.
  14. "The horse was we," laughed the twins.
  15. "However, I was not the head of the horse," said Marci.
  16. This delicious punch is fresh cider.
  17. The food is a real feast.
  18. The two servers are ugly green monsters.
  19. The monsters were they.
  20. Our friends' party was a success.

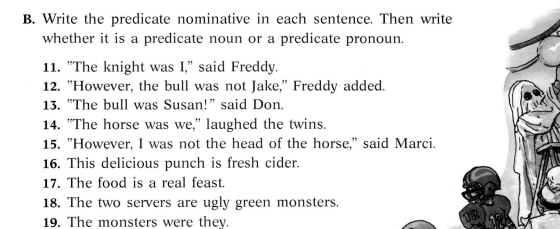

Application WRITING SENTENCES

Write six sentences about the costumes the children are wearing in the picture above. Use at least three predicate nominatives in your sentences.

6 — Using Pronouns Correctly

- Use a subject pronoun as the subject of a sentence.
- Use an object pronoun after an action verb.
- Use a subject pronoun after a linking verb.

Now that you have learned about subject and object pronouns, you will want to use them correctly. To help you decide which pronoun is correct in a sentence, ask yourself how the pronoun is used.

Always use a subject pronoun as the subject of a sentence. When using pronouns, it is polite to name yourself last.

Wrong: My brother and me visited Mexico's capital.
Right: My brother and I visited Mexico's capital.

Use an object pronoun as a direct object after an action verb.

Wrong: Some friends led Frank and she to Constitution Plaza.
Right: Some friends led Frank and her to Constitution Plaza.

Use a subject pronoun after a linking verb. Pronouns that follow linking verbs are predicate nominatives.

Wrong: The only people there were us.
Right: The only people there were we.

Skills Tryout

Tell which pronoun correctly completes each sentence. Then tell whether the pronoun is a subject or an object pronoun.

1. Benito told Frank and (I, me) about Mexico City.
2. Frank and (he, him) toured the National Palace.
3. Rosa and (I, me) went to the Aztec ruins.
4. I asked the other tourists and (she, her) about Montezuma.
5. That statue is (he, him)!

Practice

A. Write each sentence using the correct pronoun in parentheses ( ). Then write whether the pronoun you used is a subject or an object pronoun.

1. Rosa and (I, me) returned to the main square of the city.
2. Frank and Benito found Rosa and (I, me) there.
3. I told Benito and (he, him) about the ruins.
4. Then our friends and (we, us) boarded a bus.
5. The bus took (we, us) to Chapultepec Park.
6. Frank and (I, me) wanted to see the forest.
7. Benito and (she, her) wanted to visit the famous museum.
8. They met Frank and (I, me) by the bus.
9. Later we took Benito and (she, her) to dinner.
10. Then a plane flew other tourists and (we, us) to Acapulco.

B. Write the pronoun in parentheses ( ) that correctly completes each sentence. Then write whether the pronoun is a predicate nominative or a direct object.

11. The girl on the beach at Acapulco is (I, me).
12. The boy on water skis is (he, him).
13. Mother met Frank and (I, me) at Mérida.
14. I led Frank and (she, her) to the ancient city.
15. I photographed (they, them) in several places.
16. The tourists next to the pyramid are (they, them).
17. Later Mother drove some friends and (we, us) to Veracruz.
18. The riders in the back seat were Frank and (I, me).
19. Mexico's sights impressed my family and (I, me).
20. The friendly people delighted (we, us), too!

Application WRITING SENTENCES

Write eight sentences about a vacation you have taken or a place you would like to visit. Use four subject pronouns and four object pronouns in your sentences.

7 Contractions

> ● A **contraction** is a shortened form of two words.

You have learned when to use the subject pronouns *I, you, he, she, it, we,* and *they.* Sometimes these pronouns are combined with helping verbs such as *is, are, has, have, had,* and *would.* The combinations are called contractions. A contraction is a shortened form of two words.

Study how these contractions are formed:

I'm	(I am)	they've	(they have)
you're	(you are)	he's	(he is, he has)
she'll	(she will)	it's	(it is, it has)
we'll	(we shall, we will)	she'd	(she had, she would)

Notice that an apostrophe (') shows where a letter or letters have been left out.

Another group of contractions is formed with verbs and *not.* Examples of these contractions are listed below.

aren't	(are not)	haven't	(have not)
can't	(cannot)	isn't	(is not)
couldn't	(could not)	wasn't	(was not)
doesn't	(does not)	weren't	(were not)
hasn't	(has not)	won't	(will not)

In these contractions an apostrophe shows where the *o* has been left out of the word *not.* The *n't* is not part of the verb in these contractions.

Skills Tryout

Say the contraction for each pair of words.

1. was not　　**2.** it is　　**3.** we have　　**4.** I am　　**5.** will not

Practice

A. Write the contraction for each pair of words.

1. we are	**6.** we shall	**11.** is not
2. did not	**7.** you would	**12.** does not
3. it will	**8.** he is	**13.** you are
4. she has	**9.** I have	**14.** I will
5. cannot	**10.** they are	**15.** had not

B. Write the contraction in each sentence. Then write the words from which the contraction is formed.

16. January 1 hasn't always been New Year's Day.

17. It wasn't the beginning of the year for the Egyptians.

18. They wouldn't start their year until June.

19. The year didn't begin in January until Roman times.

20. The Romans weren't satisfied with existing calendars.

21. By the time of Julius Caesar, they'd developed a new calendar beginning in January.

22. The Roman calendar is much like the one we're using.

23. People used to think the old year couldn't leave easily.

24. So they'd drive it away by making loud noises.

25. Perhaps you've heard people making noise on New Year's Eve.

26. Don't forget to make your New Year's resolutions.

27. I haven't made any resolutions yet.

28. They're a good way to start a new year.

29. New Year's Day isn't just a holiday.

30. It's a new beginning.

Application WRITING SENTENCES

People celebrate the beginning of a new year in different ways. Some people have a party or a special meal. Many people make New Year's resolutions. Write seven sentences that tell how you celebrate New Year's Eve or New Year's Day. Use at least four contractions in your sentences.

Homophones and Homographs

> - **Homophones** are words that sound alike but have different meanings and spellings.
> - **Homographs** are words that are spelled alike but have different meanings and sometimes different pronunciations.

The contractions *it's*, *you're*, and *they're* are often confused with the possessive pronouns *its*, *your*, and *their*. The meanings of these words are given below.

it's—it is, it has	its—belonging to it
you're—you are	your—belonging to you
they're—they are	their—belonging to them

Words that sound alike but have different meanings and spellings are homophones. You may be familiar with other homophones such as *son* and *sun*, *buy* and *by*, and *tail* and *tale*.

Homographs are words that are spelled alike but have different meanings. For example, a band is something that encircles or ties together, but a band is also a group of musicians. The homographs below have different pronunciations.

bow (bō) a weapon; a looped knot   **bow** (bou) to bend the body
lead (led) a soft, heavy metal   **lead** (lēd) to show the way
wound (wünd) an injury   **wound** (wound) the past of *to wind*

Skills Tryout

Tell which homophones correctly complete the sentences.

1. The Outdoor Club went on (its, it's) first hike.
2. Jack had to (buy, by) a new (pair, pear) of boots.
3. We all thought we (wood, would) have fun.
4. We saw (too, two) rabbits under a tree.
5. (Their, They're) white (tails, tales) quickly disappeared.

Practice

A. Write each sentence below. Use the correct homophone in parentheses ( ).

1. Did you bring (your, you're) lunch?
2. We will eat (hear, here) by the (creak, creek).
3. (Your, You're) sitting in the (son, sun) too long.
4. (Ants, Aunts) got in the carrot cake I (made, maid).
5. I (threw, through) it in the trash can by the (road, rode).
6. After lunch we (heard, herd) a loud growl.
7. A (grate, great) big (bare, bear) appeared.
8. "(Its, It's) got a (peace, piece) of my cake," I shouted.
9. The huge animal dropped the cake (right, write) at our (feat, feet).
10. I (knew, new) my cake didn't taste good!

B. Write the correct pronunciation of the homograph in each sentence below.

11. Who will (led, lēd) the way to the campsite?
12. Hold the (bō, bou) steady before you release the arrow.
13. Father (wünd, wound) the clock before he went to bed.
14. This (led, lēd) pipe is too heavy to carry.
15. The nurse put a clean bandage on the (wünd, wound).

Application USING LANGUAGE

Use a pair of homophones from this list to describe each of the five items below.

| pale | dear | week | plane | our |
| deer | hour | pail | weak | plain |

a. a nice animal
b. a light-colored bucket
c. sixty minutes that belong to us
d. a flying machine that is not fancy
e. seven days that are not strong

Subject Pronouns *pages 132–135*

A. Write the pronouns in these sentences. Then circle the subject pronouns.

1. Did she leave her skis under the tree?
2. It fit neatly in my suitcase.
3. I try and try but can't catch her.
4. On his knees he watched the bees.
5. You play the piano very well.
6. They say Ray may play croquet.
7. We chased the rabbit away from our garden.
8. I feel quite trim next to him.
9. You won't see them until tomorrow.
10. We had a great time at the carnival!

Object Pronouns *pages 136–137*

B. Write only the object pronoun in each sentence.

11. Slim helped him to trim the limb.
12. I followed her to the store for more.
13. Gus and Russ saw us on the bus.
14. Lem helped them with the hen in the pen.
15. She did not give it to the cat on the mat.

Possessive Pronouns *pages 138–139*

C. Write the possessive pronouns in these sentences. Circle the possessive pronouns that come before a noun.

16. My tie is caught in the door, Lenore.
17. She likes to snooze while wearing her shoes.
18. He eats his pears but stares at theirs.
19. Is this line yours or mine?
20. The furs are hers, but the flowers are ours.

Predicate Nominatives   *pages 140–141*

D. Write each sentence. Underline each predicate nominative.

21. Our entry in the dog show was our poodle.
22. The best-groomed dog in the show was she.
23. The judges were experts on dogs.
24. Storm's prize was a small silver cup.
25. She is a great champion.

Using Pronouns Correctly   *pages 142–143*

E. Write the pronoun that correctly completes each sentence.

26. Anna and (I, me) visited the Washington Monument.
27. This is (we, us) standing next to it.
28. An elevator took Anna and (I, me) to the top.
29. Two guides told our friend Dan and (we, us) about the monument.
30. These women in uniform are (they, them).
31. Dan asked (they, them) about the height of the monument.
32. "It is 555 feet tall," a guide told the group and (he, him).
33. Anna and (he, him) took some photographs.
34. "I want to see some other monuments," Anna told (we, us).
35. Later a bus took Dan and (she, her) to the Lincoln Memorial.

Contractions   *pages 144–145*

F. Write the words from which each contraction is formed.

36. We'll visit the Jefferson Memorial later today.
37. I've always wanted to tour the White House.
38. We won't see the President there, though.
39. He's giving an important speech today.
40. We can visit the Capitol, but Congress isn't in session.

See also Handbook pages 364–369, 404–406.

Writing with Pronouns

> ● Use pronouns instead of repeating the same nouns too often.

Read the sentences below.

1. **Rosa and Carlos wonder if Rosa and Carlos should take Rosa's and Carlos's raincoats with Rosa and Carlos.**
2. **Rosa and Carlos wonder if they should take their raincoats with them.**

It is obvious which of these sentences is the better sentence. Sentence 1 repeats *Rosa and Carlos* so often that the sentence is clumsy and difficult to read. Sentence 2, however, uses the words *Rosa and Carlos* only once. They are replaced with pronouns in the remainder of the sentence. Now the sentence is much easier to understand.

Be careful not to overuse pronouns, however. It should always be clear to the reader what noun is replaced by a pronoun.

Using Pronouns In the first column of the chart below are five nouns. They are followed by places in the chart to put different pronouns that can replace those nouns in a sentence. Copy and complete the chart.

Noun	Subject Pronoun	Object Pronoun	Possessive Pronoun
Susan Ray			
ferry boat			
the magicians			
brother			
courage			

Now think of five more nouns. What pronouns would follow these nouns if they were on the chart?

Replacing Nouns Use pronouns to replace the underlined words in the sentences below. Write each new sentence.

EXAMPLE: Meg trained <u>Meg's</u> dog to play ball.
ANSWER: Meg trained her dog to play ball.

1. Dave's friend Claire told <u>Dave</u> about the test on Friday.
2. <u>Dave's</u> friend Claire told Dave about the test on Friday.
3. <u>Cynthia</u> went with the Gallagher twins to the track meet.
4. Cynthia went with <u>the Gallagher twins</u> to the track meet.
5. The train left the station without <u>Larry and me</u>.
6. <u>The train</u> left the station without Larry and me.
7. Victory means nothing without <u>honesty and fair play</u>.
8. <u>Victory</u> means nothing without honesty and fair play.
9. William and you will meet <u>my sister</u> tomorrow.
10. <u>William and you</u> will meet my sister tomorrow.

Pronouns in Paragraphs   Use pronouns to complete the paragraph below. Write the paragraph.

The ancient Greeks believed in gods. _____ called the king of the gods Zeus. _____ and _____ wife, Hera, lived with _____ children on Mount Olympus. _____ was the tallest mountain in the world. One day _____ daughter Artemis left Olympus to live in the forest, where _____ developed _____ skill as a hunter.

Using the Thesaurus

Write five sentences about jobs, but do not use the word *job*. Find the entry for *job* in the Thesaurus beginning on page 414. Use five different synonyms for *job* in your sentences. Then write your five sentences again. Change at least one of the nouns in each sentence to a pronoun. Here is an example.

Bob and Ann performed the task. They performed the task.

9 Writing a Narrative Paragraph

> - A **narrative paragraph** tells a story about events that happened to the writer or to someone else. The story may be real or imaginary.

People write for many reasons. One reason is to narrate, or to tell what happened. A narrative may tell about real or imaginary events. Diaries, ships' logs, minutes of a meeting, newspaper stories, novels, biographies, historical accounts, and letters telling about something that happened are all examples of narratives.

Even a single paragraph can tell a story. A narrative paragraph tells about a certain sequence of events. Most narrative paragraphs are organized in **time order.** That is, they tell about events in the order in which they happened. Words such as *first, second, next, then, after that,* and *at last* help make the time order of a paragraph clear to the reader.

The following narrative paragraph opens Scott O'Dell's *Island of the Blue Dolphins.* The storyteller is Karana, an American Indian girl who is the main character in the book. Notice how the underlined words help to make the time order clear.

> I remember the day the Aleut ship came to our island. <u>At first</u> it seemed like a small shell afloat on the sea. <u>Then</u> it grew larger and was a gull with folded wings. <u>At last</u> in the rising sun it became what it really was—a red ship with two red sails.

Like other kinds of paragraphs, a narrative paragraph should include important details. It should, however, omit anything that does not have a bearing on the story. Unnecessary details only confuse the reader.

Skills Tryout

Answer these questions about the narrative paragraph on the opposite page.

1. What event does the paragraph tell about?
2. How can you tell that the story is being told by one of the characters in it?
3. What did the ship look like at first?
4. What did the ship look like next?
5. What words were used to show time order?

Practice

A. Arrange these sentences in time order and write them as a paragraph.

1. Next she saw a small boat being lowered into the water with six men in it.
2. Then the men jumped out shouting.
3. First Karana saw a ship stop outside the cove.
4. In a short time the boat slid in to shore.
5. Immediately the men in the boat began rowing toward the island.

B. Choose one of these topics for a narrative paragraph. Write a topic sentence and list three supporting details.

6. A favorite memory
7. A special holiday
8. A hilarious happening
9. A stroke of luck
10. A thrilling experience

Application SPEAKING AND LISTENING

Tell a story to your classmates using time order words. You may tell about a real experience or about one that you make up. Try to limit your story to one paragraph in writing. Have your listeners write down the time order words you use.

10 — **Writing Quotations**

> ● Use **quotation marks** (" ") to show the exact words of a speaker.

When you write a quotation, you show the exact words of a speaker. Quotation marks indicate where the speaker's words begin and end. The first word of a quotation begins with a capital letter.

> "There is an exam today," said Tom testily.
> Tom said testily, "There is an exam today."

Notice that a comma separates the quotation from the speaker. The comma always comes before the quotation mark.

If a quotation is a question or an exclamation, use a question mark or an exclamation mark instead of a comma.

> "What was I supposed to buy?" Jean asked listlessly.
> "It is 110 degrees in the shade!" Sue shouted hotly.

Sometimes a quotation is divided. If a divided quotation is one sentence, use commas to separate the quotation from the speaker.

> "My bicycle tire," Pete remarked flatly, "needs air."

If a divided quotation is two sentences, use a period after the speaker. Capitalize the second sentence.

> "It is fun to go camping," Larry remarked good-naturedly.
> "The wilderness is so peaceful and beautiful."

When you quote a conversation, begin a new paragraph each time the speaker changes.

> "I'm cooking some of this delicious bacon for your lunch," said Pam's mother crisply.
> "Actually," replied Pam frankly, "I'd prefer a hot dog."

Skills Tryout

Tell where quotation marks and capital letters should be placed in these sentences.

1. The sherbet tastes awful, Dan complained icily.
2. Dan asked drily, may I have a glass of water?
3. I keep forgetting, said Dan darkly, to buy light bulbs.
4. Shall I inflate this balloon for you? Dan inquired airily. you look out of breath.
5. What, asked Dan tautly, is the past tense of *teach*?

Practice

A. Write the sentences. Add quotation marks and capital letters where needed.

1. I know a man, said Helen, who ran over himself.
2. Oh, no! exclaimed Ann. how did he do it?
3. First he asked me to run across the street and mail a letter for him, said Helen, but I couldn't.
4. What happened then? asked Ann eagerly.
5. He ran over himself, of course, giggled Helen.

B. Write the sentences. Add punctuation where needed. Start a new paragraph each time the speaker changes.

What makes it rain Johnny asked. Father replied I don't really know, son. Do you know asked Johnny how whales breathe? I'm afraid I don't know a thing about whales answered Father. Do my questions bother you, Dad Johnny asked. Of course not said Father. Asking questions is the best way to learn.

Application WRITING QUOTATIONS

Write one of your favorite jokes or riddles as a conversation between two or more people. Follow all the rules for punctuating, capitalizing, and indenting quotations.

Reading a Story

> ● In some stories a main character tells the story by speaking directly to the reader.

As you read this story by Isaac Asimov, notice how he uses the pronouns *I*, *me*, and *mine* to make it seem as though Larry is telling the story to you.

Ordinarily, Dad keeps his temper pretty well around the house, and he never loses it with me—almost never. I like to think it's because I'm a good kid, but he says it's because I'm smart enough to stay out of his way when he's mad.

I sure didn't stay out of his way this time. He swooped down on me, all red in the face, and snatched *The New York Times* right out from under my hand. "What do you think you're *doing*?" he said. "Don't you have any *brains*?"

I just stood there with my pencil in my hand. I wasn't doing *anything*.

I said, "What's the matter, Dad?" I was just plain astonished.

Mom was hurrying over, too. I guess she wanted to make sure her one and only son wasn't smashed beyond repair.

"What's the matter?" she asked. "What's he done?"

Dad stood there, getting even redder. It was as if he couldn't think what I had done. Then he said, "Doesn't he know better than to touch the paper? That's not our paper."

By that time I sort of got indignant. "Well, how am I supposed to know that, Dad?"

And Mom said, "How *is* he supposed to know? If that's something important, dear, you might have said so. You needn't have left it on the dining room table."

Dad looked as if he wanted to back down, but didn't know how. He said to me, "You didn't tear anything, throw anything away...."

I guess he had become so angry when he saw me at *The Times* that he didn't see what I was doing. "It's in perfect shape," I said.

He walked back and forth in the room, breathing hard, and we just watched him. I figured he must be on a hard case, and when a detective is on a difficult case, you can't blame him for breathing hard.

Then he stopped. He had worked it all out of his system, and he was himself again when he turned to me. "I'm sorry, Larry," he said. "I was wrong. It wasn't important. We have the paper microfilmed anyway.... I just can't make anything out of it."

Mom sat down and didn't say anything, because Dad isn't really supposed to talk about his cases at home. I knew that, but I just put a blank look on my face and said, "Out of what, Dad?" And I sat down, too.

Dad looked at us and *he* sat down and threw the paper back on the table. "Out of that. The paper."

I could tell he wanted to talk, so I kept quiet and let him.

After a while, he said, "There's a.... Well, never mind what there is, but it's pretty worrisome, and there's a code involved and we can't break it."

"That's not really your job, is it?" Mom asked. "You don't know anything about codes."

"There's something I might do."

I said, "All codes can be broken, can't they?"

"Some not as easy as others, Larry," he said. "Sometimes a code is based on a key word that changes every once in a while, maybe every day. That makes it hard, unless we can find what the key word is, or, better yet, what system they use to change the key word."

"How do you do that?" said Mom.

With a grim look on his face, Dad said, "One way is to pick up somebody's notebook."

"Surely no one would put it in a notebook for people to find," she said.

I butted in. "They would, Mom. You can't rely on remembering a complicated system, and you can't take chances on forgetting. Right, Dad?"

"Right," he said. "But no one has found a notebook or anything else, and that's it." The tone of his voice told me that was the end of the discussion. "Have you done your homework, Larry?"

"All except some of the geography." Then, to keep from being chased out of the room, I said, "What's *The New York Times* got to do with it?"

That took Dad's mind off the homework. "One of the men we had our eyes on was mugged last night. He managed to fight off the mugger, but he was hurt and we brought him to the hospital. That made it easy to search him very carefully without getting anyone suspicious and scaring them into changing their system or lying low. We got nowhere. No notebook."

"Maybe the mugger got away with ..." I said.

Dad shook his head. "We had a good man following him. He saw the whole thing. *But* the man being mugged had a *New*

York Times on him and he held onto it while he was fighting. I thought that was suspicious, so I had the paper microfilmed and brought it home. I thought there might be some system of picking out one of the words—in a headline on some particular page—last word in some particular column—who knows? Anyone can carry *The Times*. It's not like a notebook. There's nothing suspicious about it."

"How could you tell from the paper what the system was?" I said.

Dad shrugged. "I thought there might be a mark on it. He might look at the key word and just automatically, without even thinking, check it off. No use. There's not a word in the paper that's marked in any way."

I got excited, "Yes there are!"

Dad gave me that look I always get when he thinks I don't know what I'm talking about. "What do you mean?"

"That's what I was doing when you yelled and grabbed the paper," I said, showing him the pencil I was still holding. "I was doing the crossword puzzle. Don't you see, Dad, it was partly worked out. That's why I started on it, to finish it up."

Dad rubbed his nose. "We noticed that, but what makes you think that has any meaning? Lots of people work on crossword puzzles. It's natural enough."

"Sure, that's why it's a safe system. This one was worked out in the middle, Dad, just a little patch in the middle. No one just does a part in the middle. They start at the upper left corner, with number one."

"If it's a hard puzzle, you might not get a start till you reach the middle."

"It was an easy puzzle, Dad. One across was a three-letter word meaning 'presidential nickname' and that's got to be Ike or Abe, and one down.... Anyway, this guy just went straight to that part and didn't bother with anything else. Twenty-seven across was one of the words he worked out and the paper is for yesterday, which is the twenty-seventh of the month."

Dad waited a long while before answering. Then he said, "Coincidence."

"Maybe not," I said. *"The Times* crossword puzzle always has at least sixty numbers every day, twice as many on Sunday. Every day of the month has a number and for that day, the key word is the one in that number in the crossword puzzle. If there are two words, across and down, maybe you always take the across."

"Hmm," said Dad.

"How much simpler can it be? Anyone can remember that, and all you have to do is be able to work out crossword puzzles. You can get all kinds of words, long or short, even phrases, even foreign words."

Mom said, "What if a crossword puzzle happens to be too hard to work out just in the crucial spot?"

Now Dad got excited, "They could use each day's puzzle for the day after, and check with the solution to make sure." He had his coat on. "... except Sunday, for which the solution comes the next Sunday.... I hope the pencil you used made a different mark from his, Larry."

"He used a pen," I said.

... That wasn't all there was to the case, but they did break the code. Dad got a bonus and he put it in the bank toward my college education.

He said it was only fair.

About the Story

1. What events had already happened when Larry's father saw him holding *The New York Times*?
2. What important information did Larry's father give him about how some codes work?
3. What was unusual about the way the crossword puzzle had been worked out?
4. How was the key word determined?
5. How did Larry's knowledge of crossword puzzles help solve the case?

Activities

A. Suppose you were telling the story instead of Larry. You would use the pronoun *he* instead of *I*, *him* instead of *me*, and so on. Select a part of the story and read it to the class substituting the new pronouns. Which way of telling the story do you think is more effective? Why?

B. Since this story contains much conversation, it can easily be presented as a radio or TV play. Three students can read the conversation of Larry, his father, and his mother. A fourth student can read the comments Larry makes to the reader.

12 Writing a Book Report

- A **book report** tells what a book is about and gives an opinion of the book.

Read Maria's book report. Notice that the first paragraph gives the title and author of the book and gets the reader's interest. The second briefly tells what the book is about. The third gives an opinion of the book.

<u>A Wrinkle in Time</u>

by Madeleine L'Engle

"It was a dark and stormy night...." With this ordinary opening sentence, Madeleine L'Engle begins her novel <u>A Wrinkle in Time</u>. Before it is over, however, readers travel through space, go up against "IT," and meet the most extraordinary characters ever imagined.

The heroine, Meg Murray, must leave her home in America and travel through time and space in search of her father. Mr. Murray, a famous scientist, had disappeared while doing government research. With her brother, Charles Wallace, and her likable friend, Calvin O'Keefe, Meg bravely sets out on her dangerous and important mission.

This book is worthwhile for many reasons. The plot is filled with adventure. The characters are interesting and believable. Most important, the author presents thought-provoking ideas about time, space, and the universe!

Guidelines for Writing a Book Report

- Give the title and author of the book. Underline the title. Capitalize the first word, the last word, and all important words in the title.
- Describe the setting of the story—where and when it takes place.
- Briefly describe the major characters.
- Tell something about the plot, or what happens in the story, but don't give away the ending!
- Give your opinion of the book. Explain why you think the book is or is not interesting and worthwhile.

Skills Tryout

Tell which information should be included in a book report and which should not.

1. Many long quotations from the book to show the author's writing style
2. The title and author of the book
3. Brief descriptions of other books by the same author
4. The setting, characters, and plot of the book
5. A positive or negative opinion of the book

Practice

A. Write answers to these questions about the book report on page 162.

1. What words in the report are underlined? Why?
2. Who is the author of the book?
3. What information is given about the setting?
4. What characters are mentioned in the book report? Which one do you think is the main character?
5. What does the report tell about the plot? Write a sentence that tells what the story is about.
6. What is the book reporter's opinion of the book?
7. Does the report make you want to read the book? Why or why not?

B. Write a book report, using the guidelines on page 162. Choose a book that you are reading now or that you have recently completed.

Application ORAL REPORTING

Present your book report to the class. You may want to read a passage or two from the book, but remember not to give away the ending. Be familiar enough with your book report that you can look at your audience as you present it.

13 — Writing a Personal Narrative

Writing Project

> • A **personal narrative** is a story about a writer's own experiences.

Where can you find an idea for a story? Why not start with yourself? Write about something that has happened to you. This kind of a story is called a personal narrative because it is from the writer's own experience. Some of the world's best stories are personal narratives. They are especially convincing because they are true. In this lesson you will write a personal narrative and share it with classmates. You have already experienced your story—now enjoy telling it.

1. Prewriting

Artists sketch pictures to remember favorite scenes. Photographers take pictures for the same reason. Writers, however, take notes to help them remember names, dates, places, events, and feelings. The notebook a writer uses for this purpose is called a journal. A writer's journal is personal. It is for the writer's own use. It often becomes a valuable collection of anecdotes, observations, opinions, and feelings to use in future writings.

Here is a sample entry from a writer's journal.

> Thursday, Dec. 12
>
> Today I saw a little boy struggling with three leashes firmly attached to three wiggling, squirming dogs. One dog had run around the little boy's left leg. The largest dog, a red cocker spaniel, tugged as it tried to get away. The third dog looked like a Scotch terrier. It stood still, barking loudly and wagging its tail rapidly. This event reminded me of a time long ago when I owned three German shepherd pups.

▶ Begin your own writer's journal. During the next few days, write in your journal for ten minutes each day. (You can make a notebook by stapling sheets of paper together, if you wish.) Write about any subject that interests you. For example, you might write about a dog you saw that reminded you of your own pet; or you might write about a school project, an athletic event, a party—any number of things. Journal writing is writing you do for yourself. You need not share it unless you want to.

▶ Use your journal to help you find an unusual, humorous, or surprising topic for your personal narrative. Discuss possible topics with your classmates. Then select a topic you think will interest them.

▶ You have already learned about using time order when you tell a story. Now use time order to help you plan your personal narrative. Think about the experience you are going to write about. What happened first, second, third, and so on? List important details in time order like this:

1. I wanted a dog for my birthday.
2. On the morning of my birthday, my brother awakened me with a German shepherd puppy.
3. While I was petting him, the doorbell rang.
4. It was a telegram from Uncle Raymond in Michigan, saying he was sending me two puppies by airfreight.

Now you need to find a focus for your narrative. To do this, give your story a title. This is just a working title; you can change it later if you wish. "An Unexpected Birthday Present" is an example of a working title.

2. Writing

▶ Your prewriting discussions, your time-order listing, and the selection of your working title have helped you prepare for writing. Now, as you write your first draft, pretend you are telling your story to an interested listener who is waiting to hear each word. How will you begin? Use the words that are most natural for you. "I'll never forget the day ..." is one beginning. You could even begin with conversation: "Wake up, Christopher! Today is your birthday!"

Write your first draft as quickly as you can. The important thing is to get your ideas on paper.

3. Revising

▶ Share your first draft with a good listener. Ask your listener two things: "What do you like about my narrative?" "What would you like to know more about?"

Discuss the experience you have written about and talk about the changes you could make. Then ask your listener to work with you as you both use the Revision Checklist.

Revision Checklist
- Did I focus on a single incident?
- Did I tell what happened in time order?
- Did I use conversation in my story?
- Did I begin sentences in different ways?

Read the sample that follows. Notice how the paragraph was improved by using a variety of sentence beginnings.

A Triple Surprise
~~An Unexpected Birthday Present~~

¶ ~~My little brother yelled,~~ "Wake up, Christopher!" ~~He~~
screeched my little brother.
~~yelled again,~~ "Today is your birthday!" He tugged
,and then   patted
my blanket. He ⟨pated⟩ me on the back. Slowly I

A Triple Surprise

"Wake up, Christopher! Today is your birthday!" screeched my little brother. He tugged my blanket, and then he patted me on the back. Slowly I turned over. Suddenly a furry thing was scratching my chest and lapping my face. I opened my eyes to see a German shepherd pup, as plump as a teddy bear! "He's all yours!" my little brother announced. I stroked the pup's fur and felt so happy. More than anything else, I had wanted a dog for my birthday.

EDITING MARKS	
——	cross out
∧	add
↶	move
≡	capital letter
/	small letter
¶	indent
◯	check spelling

▶ Now use the editing marks to revise your narrative.

4. Publishing

▶ Before you share your writing, check it and make corrections. Use the Proofreading Checklist in the Young Writer's Handbook on page 399 as a guide. The editing marks will help you make corrections.

▶ Nearly everyone enjoys reading personal narratives. Make a class book that includes everyone's story and display the book in your classroom or library.

Writing Project

A Class Story Chart

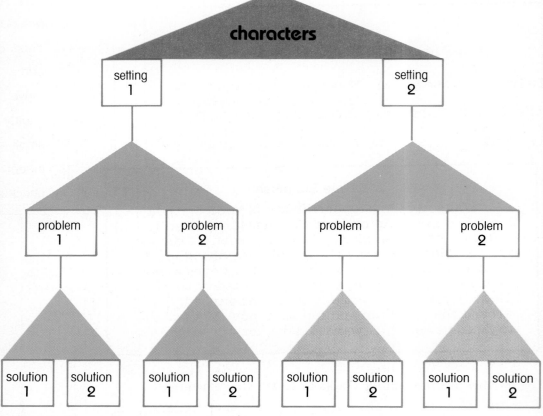

With your classmates make a story chart. Start with one set of characters. Then give two possible settings. For each setting add two problems. For each problem give two solutions. When you finish, you will have the skeletons of eight different stories.

Follow one story line. Write a story using one setting, one problem, and one solution from the chart. (The problem and solution will make up the plot of your story.) Add details to make the story more complete. If you wish, you can practice the art of storytelling by telling your completed story to the class.

Mathematics

In this unit you have studied narrative writing. A problem that tells a story is an example of narrative writing in mathematics. What you have learned about writing paragraphs in English can help you in mathematics. Following the steps below will make solving problems that are not all numbers easier.

▶ Try it. Use these steps to solve a story problem.

1. Read the entire problem once.
2. Look through the problem again to find the question. The question is like the topic sentence in a narrative paragraph. Decide what you are asked to find.
3. Tell the facts given in the problem. The facts are like supporting sentences.
4. Draw a picture or diagram of the problem if necessary.
5. Decide what operation is needed to solve the problem.
6. Work out the arithmetic.
7. Check the problem. Be sure your answer makes sense.

> Marci needed a winter coat. She went to Simpson's Department Store, which had advertised a pre-season sale. There she found two coats she liked. One was marked $150. The sale tag said, "Take 15% off." The other was marked $175. The tag said, "Take 25% off." Marci bought the less expensive coat. Which did she buy?

Listeners at Work When people want to borrow money to start a business, they often talk to a loan officer at a bank. The loan officer listens to their stories and decides whether or not the bank should lend the money.

▶ Imagine that you want to borrow money to start a business. Prepare the "story of your business" to tell a loan officer. Tell what you plan to do, and why your plan will succeed. Use time order words such as *first*, *then*, and *finally* in your story.

Pronouns   *pages 132–139, 142–143*

A. Write the pronoun in each sentence. Then write *subject* or *object* to show what kind of pronoun it is.

1. Donna and I play Ping-Pong every Saturday.
2. We are practicing for the school Ping-Pong championship.
3. Ted Ross sometimes coaches us in the mornings.
4. The students at school call him "The Ping-Pong Wizard."
5. He and Jay won the championship three years in a row.
6. Last year Cal and Liz Rose beat them by a few points.

B. Write each sentence. Use the correct pronoun in parentheses ( ).

7. Yesterday Mrs. Lee borrowed (our, ours) binoculars.
8. The book about bird-watching is probably (her, hers).
9. Where do bald eagles build (their, theirs) nests?
10. Are these photographs of eagles (your, yours)?

C. Write the pronoun that correctly completes each sentence.

11. Vera invited Paul and (me, I) to a clambake.
12. The loudest singers in the chorus are (they, them).
13. Ellen and (him, he) rode mules through the Grand Canyon.
14. The police officer directed (we, us) to the museum.

Predicate Nominatives   *pages 140–141*

D. Write each sentence. Underline each predicate nominative.

15. The concert was a success.
16. The band leader was she.
17. The drummers were they.
18. Ted was the guitarist.

Contractions   *pages 144–145*

E. Write the contraction for each pair of words.

19. will not
20. they have
21. it is
22. you are

Homophones *pages 146–147*

F. Write the correct homophone in parentheses ( ).

23. Please leave (your, you're) wet towels on the rack.
24. I (heard, herd) the rocking chair creak mysteriously.
25. My sister (red, read) the baby bedtime stories.
26. The river is swift when (its, it's) high.

Quotations *pages 154–155*

G. Write each sentence. Add quotation marks and capital letters where needed.

27. The plants, said Aunt Jean, should be watered.
28. Have you seen the watering can? asked Elaine.
29. Look in the closet, Aunt Joan called. it's on the shelf.
30. The shelf, replied Elaine, is empty.
31. Oh, my! exclaimed Aunt Joan. here it is, on the table.

Book Report *pages 162–163*

H. Write *yes* if the information should be included in a book report. Write *no* if it should not be included.

32. The title and author of the book
33. How many chapters the book contains

I. Write each book title correctly.

34. thimble summer   **35.** treasure island   **36.** a wrinkle in time

Narrative Paragraph *pages 152–153*

J. Write a topic sentence for a narrative paragraph about *an ideal day.* Then write four sentences that tell what happened. Write the sentences in correct time order.

See also Handbook pages 364–369, 404, 406, 408.

Sentences *pages 4–17*

A. Write the sentences using capital letters and correct end punctuation. After each sentence write *declarative, interrogative, imperative,* or *exclamatory.*

1. we are learning about bees
2. do all bees make honey
3. tell us about worker bees
4. how big that beehive is

B. Write each complete subject. Underline each simple subject.

5. Many visitors to New York have seen the Statue of Liberty.
6. This magnificent monument has become a national treasure.
7. The people of France presented the statue to our country.
8. Their gift marked 100 years of American independence.

C. Write each complete predicate. Underline each simple predicate.

9. Cactus plants grow in dry desert regions.
10. They absorb underground water through their long roots.
11. Their thick, hard stems prevent water loss.
12. Large cactus plants can live for two years without rain.

D. Write the subject of each sentence.

13. Get into the rowboat.
14. Did Dan bring some bait?
15. Hand me the net.
16. Did Meg catch a fish?

Commas *pages 18–19*

E. Write each sentence. Add commas where they are needed.

17. Mark Twain was born on November 30 1835 in Missouri.
18. Twain had careers as a journalist lecturer and author.
19. He wrote about steamboats curious boys and a jumping frog.
20. His home in Hartford Connecticut is now a museum.

Nouns   *pages 50–53, 58–61*

F. Write the nouns in each sentence. Then write whether each noun names a *person, place, thing,* or *idea.*

21. The Gibsons moved from the city to a farm.
22. The family wanted a chance to raise their own food.
23. A helpful farmer gave Mrs. Gibson some advice.
24. Now her garden contains ripe fruits and vegetables.

G. Write each underlined word. Then write whether it is a *common noun* or a *proper noun.*

25. Tracy has been telling us about her trip to Washington.
26. She rode a raft down the Columbia River.
27. Did you see Tracy's photographs of Seattle?
28. This city is located on the shore of Puget Sound.

H. Write the possessive form of each noun. Then write whether the noun is *singular* or *plural.*

29. windows   31. geese   33. Mr. Briggs   35. lamp
30. boss   32. marsh   34. oxen   36. giraffe

Capital Letters and Periods   *pages 54–57*

I. Write each sentence. Capitalize the proper nouns.

37. My new neighbor, carol nichols, is a dentist.
38. She moved to fremont city two months ago.
39. Her office is in the morris medical building.
40. I have an appointment with her on wednesday.

J. Write the word that each abbreviation stands for.

41. Jan.   42. Rev.   43. Tues.   44. La.

Verbs *pages 88–107*

K. Write each sentence. Draw one line under the linking verb. Draw two lines under the words that the verb connects.

45. Jeff is my friend.
46. You are very talented.
47. This banana looks ripe.
48. The bark feels rough.

L. Write each sentence. Underline the helping verbs once and the main verbs twice.

49. Our science class is learning about machines.
50. Machines have made many jobs easier.
51. You can lift heavy objects with a lever.
52. This log was split with a wedge.

M. Write the direct object in each sentence.

53. Claire cleaned her desk.
54. I play the clarinet.
55. Jason found my wallet.
56. We repaired the bicycles.

N. Write the past tense and future tense of each verb. Use *will* with the future tense.

57. need   **58.** promise   **59.** arrive   **60.** weigh   **61.** shout

O. Write the three principal parts of each verb. Use the helping verb *has* with each past participle.

62. talk   **64.** know   **66.** worry   **68.** break
63. catch   **65.** write   **67.** deliver **69.** drink

P. Write each sentence. Use the correct verb in parentheses ( ).

70. We will (learn, teach) a new game in gym class.
71. I (can, may) climb to the top of the mountain.
72. Please (sit, set) your sandwich on the table.
73. Did Trish (let, leave) her umbrella at home?

Pronouns   *pages 132–143*

Q. Write the pronoun in each sentence. Then write *subject* or *object* to show what kind of pronoun it is.

74. We are learning about rocks and minerals in school.
75. Mrs. Schwartz showed us a film about volcanic rock.
76. She brought some rocks to class, too.
77. Each student examined them with a magnifying glass.
78. The piece of granite interested me the most.
79. It contained flecks of three different minerals.

R. Write each sentence. Use the correct pronoun in parentheses ( ).

80. Peg and Joe brought (their, theirs) flippers to the beach.
81. Leslie's towel is just like (your, yours).
82. Tell Brenda to wear (her, hers) life jacket in the boat.
83. The yellow beach umbrella is (my, mine).

S. Write each sentence. Underline each predicate nominative.

84. My teammates are they.
85. The catcher is she.
86. The outfielders are we.
87. Our coach is he.

T. Write the pronoun that correctly completes each sentence.

88. The newest member of the outing club is (I, me).
89. Frank told (they, them) about the class play.
90. Leon and (I, me) are crossing guards at our school.
91. Theresa told (we, us) about the bake sale.

Contractions   *pages 144–145*

U. Write the contraction for each pair of words.

92. she is   93. have not   94. will not   95. I am

Grammar
Adjectives

Composition
Describing

I Wouldn't

There's a mouse house
In the hall wall
With a small door
By the hall floor
Where the fat cat
Sits all day,
Sits that way
All day
Every day
Just to say,
"Come out and play"
To the nice mice
In the mouse house
In the hall wall
With the small door
By the hall floor.

And do they
Come out and play
When the fat cat
Asks them to?

Well, would you?

—*John Ciardi*

1 — Adjectives

> ● An **adjective** describes a noun or pronoun.

The underlined words in the sentence describe the noun *plants*.

<u>Several</u> <u>unusual</u> plants catch their food!

Words that describe nouns are called adjectives. Adjectives often come before the nouns they describe. Sometimes, however, they follow the nouns they describe.

The Venus's-flytrap, <u>small</u> and <u>delicate</u>, traps insects.

Adjectives usually answer the question *What kind?* or *How many?* The chart lists examples of adjectives.

Adjectives					
What kind?	big	intelligent	blue	clean	heavy
How many?	one	two	several	few	many	all

The words *a*, *an*, and *the* are a special kind of adjective. They are called **articles**. Use *a* before a word that begins with a consonant sound. Use *an* before a word that begins with a vowel sound.

a plant   a hard shell   an unusual insect   an ant

Skills Tryout

Name the adjectives in these sentences. Include articles.

1. The interesting flytrap grows only in a few bogs.
2. The soil, damp and rich, lacks nitrogen.
3. Nitrogen is an important chemical for all plants.
4. A flytrap gets the necessary nitrogen from insects.
5. The curious plant traps and digests many insects.

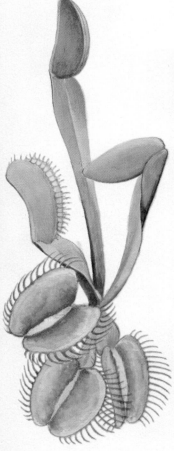

Practice

A. Write the adjectives in these sentences. Include articles.

1. The flowers, small and white, attract insects.
2. The plant lures hungry insects with a sweet liquid.
3. Each green leaf has two lobes.
4. The lobes have fine hairs on the inner surface.
5. Sharp bristles line the edges.
6. An unfortunate insect may land on a sensitive hair.
7. Then the two lobes close quickly.
8. The helpless insect cannot escape.
9. The plant uses a special liquid to digest the insect.
10. In a few days the clever little leaf will reopen.

B. Write each sentence. Use the correct article in parentheses (   ).

11. The pitcher plant is also (a, an) extraordinary plant.
12. It grows best in (a, an) damp place.
13. Each leaf forms (a, an) tube, or pitcher.
14. The leaves produce (a, an) sweet substance.
15. (A, An) insect may fly down a leaf after the juice.

C. Write each sentence. Underline the adjectives that tell *what kind* once and the adjectives that tell *how many* twice. Do not include articles.

16. Some bristly hairs at the top of the tube trap the insect.
17. Most insects cannot hang on to the slippery inner walls.
18. The tiny insect falls into a deep pit.
19. Here a special liquid digests the unlucky victim.
20. The peculiar plant is found in many states.

Application WRITING SENTENCES

Write eight sentences about a plant or tree. Use at least one adjective that tells *what kind* or *how many* in each sentence.

Proper Adjectives

> ● A **proper adjective** is formed from a proper noun.

Renaldo was looking for items in his home that had come from other countries. Here are some of the things he found.

jam from England   bacon from Canada   tea from China

The words *England*, *Canada*, and *China* are proper nouns. You know that proper nouns name particular persons, places, or things and that proper nouns are always capitalized.

Renaldo listed the items that he found like this:

Proper Nouns	Proper Adjectives
England	English (jam)
Canada	Canadian (bacon)
China	Chinese (tea)

An adjective formed from a proper noun is called a proper adjective. Like a proper noun, a proper adjective always begins with a capital letter.

The ending of a proper noun is usually changed to make a proper adjective. The endings *-ish*, *-an*, and *-ese* are often used to form proper adjectives.

Skills Tryout

Name the proper adjective in each sentence and tell how it should be capitalized.

1. Tablecloths of irish linen are very lovely.
2. This jacket is made of heavy scottish wool.
3. My sister plays spanish music on her guitar.
4. Our neighbors have just bought a swedish car.
5. They plan to visit some german castles on their vacation.

Practice

A. Write each proper adjective in the sentences correctly.

1. Many european countries are known for particular foods.
2. Have you ever eaten polish sausage?
3. Some people like norwegian sardines for a snack.
4. This portuguese cheese will be tasty in a salad.
5. Delicious austrian pastries are famous around the world.
6. This restaurant serves only american foods.
7. A popular item on the menu is alaskan crab.
8. A favorite for dessert is hawaiian pineapple.
9. In supermarkets you can often find australian lamb.
10. Sushi is a japanese dish made with raw fish.

B. Write each proper adjective correctly. Then write the proper noun from which it was formed.

EXAMPLE: This museum has a large collection of asian art.
ANSWER: Asian (Asia)

11. These bronze figures were made by an indian artist.
12. A special exhibit of persian rugs is now on display.
13. Have you seen the collection of russian coins?
14. Next month the museum will show a group of italian paintings from the Middle Ages.
15. The pottery in this case dates from roman times.
16. This ancient egyptian statue was carved from wood.
17. These african masks were worn in religious ceremonies.
18. Gold and silver were used to make this mexican jewelry.
19. A brazilian artist painted these scenes of common people.
20. These woolen blankets were made by bolivian weavers.

Application WRITING SENTENCES

Choose some items in your home, such as clothing, furniture, cars, or art. Write six sentences that tell where the items come from. Use a proper adjective in each sentence.

> ● A **predicate adjective** follows a linking verb and describes the subject of the sentence.

You have learned that a predicate nominative is a noun or pronoun that follows a linking verb and renames the subject of the sentence.

> Leif Ericsson was a famous Viking leader.

> The explorer in that painting is he.

Sometimes linking verbs are followed by adjectives.

> The Vikings were fearless in battle.

> Their long, slim boats looked very graceful.

In the sentences above, the adjectives *fearless* and *graceful* are predicate adjectives. A predicate adjective follows a linking verb and describes the subject of the sentence.

In the first sentence the adjective *fearless* follows the linking verb *were* and describes the noun *Vikings*. In the second sentence the adjective *graceful* follows the linking verb *looked* and describes the noun *boats*.

A list of common linking verbs appears on page 90. You may want to review them.

Skills Tryout

Name the predicate adjective in each sentence.

1. The seas around Scandinavia are very rough.
2. Viking ships were seaworthy.
3. The Vikings felt comfortable in their strong ships on long voyages.
4. Viking sailors seemed very adventurous at first.
5. Later they became quite warlike.

Practice

A. Write each sentence. Underline each predicate adjective.

1. The Vikings did not seem fierce at home.
2. Their agricultural society was fair to men and women.
3. The Vikings became skillful in carpentry and crafts.
4. However, fertile land was scarce.
5. Life in Scandinavia became difficult for many Vikings.
6. Their voyages were successful for many reasons.
7. All Viking sailors were equal in rank and training.
8. They seemed proud of their fine ships.
9. The sturdy sailors became familiar with Europe's coasts.
10. Their ability to sail without maps and compasses seems unbelievable today.

B. Write each sentence. Underline each predicate adjective once and each predicate nominative twice.

11. Many countries looked weak to the Vikings.
12. Viking traders soon became raiders.
13. England and Ireland were the sites of the first raids.
14. Towns in France, Italy, and Spain were victims, too.
15. Fear of the Vikings was common throughout Europe.
16. The Vikings became peaceful again after several hundred years.
17. Many Vikings were important explorers.
18. Eric the Red was the founder of a colony in Greenland.
19. The history of the Vikings is full of adventure.
20. Their influence on European history was great.

Application WRITING SENTENCES

Write six sentences using the adjectives below as predicate adjectives. You may want to write your sentences about the imaginary sea journey of a Viking sailor.

still   stormy   dangerous   courageous   strong   safe

4 — Demonstrative Adjectives

> ● A **demonstrative adjective** points out the noun it describes.

You have studied adjectives that answer the questions *What kind?* and *How many?* The underlined adjectives in the sentences answer the question *Which one?*

<u>This</u> month is Black History Month.
<u>That</u> display shows famous black Americans.
<u>These</u> books are by outstanding black authors.
<u>Those</u> filmstrips are about black scientists.

The words *this*, *that*, *these*, and *those* are often used as adjectives. They are called demonstrative adjectives, and they point out a specific person or thing.

This and *these* point out people or things nearby. *That* and *those* point out people or things farther away. *This* and *that* are used with singular nouns. *These* and *those* are used with plural nouns.

Sometimes *this*, *that*, *these*, and *those* are used alone in sentences. Then they are pronouns.

<u>This</u> is Black History Month.   <u>These</u> are by black authors.
<u>That</u> looks interesting.   <u>Those</u> are about scientists.

Skills Tryout

Name the demonstrative adjective in each sentence.

1. This book was written by Alex Haley.
2. In these chapters he traces his family's history.
3. The woman in that picture is Harriet Tubman.
4. She led those people to freedom from slavery.
5. This article tells how she helped 300 slaves to escape.

Practice

A. Write each sentence. Underline each demonstrative adjective.

1. These drawings are by the astronomer Benjamin Banneker.
2. Pages from his 1792 almanac appear in those books.
3. In this filmstrip we will see how Banneker taught himself astronomy and math.
4. He used those skills to help design our nation's capital.
5. Mary McLeod Bethune is the subject of this book.
6. With these students she began a college for black women.
7. That photo shows her with President Franklin D. Roosevelt.
8. Two of the greatest jazz musicians of this century were Louis Armstrong and Duke Ellington.
9. Some of their best recordings are on that tape.
10. The origins of jazz in America are traced in this book.

B. Write whether the underlined word is used as an *adjective* or a *pronoun*.

11. That is the great black leader Martin Luther King, Jr.
12. Some of his speeches are collected in this book.
13. The baseball player in this film is Jackie Robinson.
14. Those are his teammates on the Brooklyn Dodgers in 1947.
15. That was the first time a black played major-league ball.
16. Marian Anderson is one of the greatest singers this country has produced.
17. These are some very special recordings of hers.
18. That voice has thrilled millions all over the world.
19. This is a book about the scientist Dr. Charles Drew.
20. These pages tell how he set up the first blood bank.

Application WRITING SENTENCES

Write eight sentences about things found in your classroom. Include *this, that, these,* or *those* in each sentence. Use each word once as an adjective and once as a pronoun.

5 — Comparison of Adjectives

- Use the **comparative** form of an adjective to compare two persons, places, or things.
- Use the **superlative** form of an adjective to compare three or more persons, places, or things.

Notice the underlined adjectives in the sentences below.

1. Australia is a small continent.
2. Australia is smaller than Europe.
3. Australia is the smallest continent of all.

In sentence 1 the adjective *small* describes the continent of Australia.

In sentence 2 *smaller* compares Australia with Europe. *Smaller* is the comparative form of *small*. It is formed by adding *-er* to the adjective. The comparative form of an adjective is used to compare two persons, places, or things.

In sentence 3 *smallest* compares Australia with all the continents. *Smallest* is the superlative form of *small*. It is formed by adding *-est* to the adjective. The superlative form is used to compare three or more persons, places, or things.

Sometimes the spelling of an adjective is changed when *-er* or *-est* is added.

Drop final *e*	large	larger	largest
Change final *y* to *i*	funny	funnier	funniest
Double final consonant	big	bigger	biggest

Skills Tryout

Tell the comparative and superlative form of each adjective.

1. strong   2. happy   3. nice   4. sad   5. short

Practice

A. Write the comparative and superlative form of each adjective.

1. blue
2. risky
3. dull
4. thin
5. dark
6. fat
7. tall
8. wide
9. safe
10. cute
11. wealthy
12. hungry
13. clear
14. slow
15. wet

B. Write each sentence. Use the correct form of the adjective in parentheses ( ).

EXAMPLE: The continent of Asia is (big) than Africa.
ANSWER: The continent of Asia is bigger than Africa.

16. Asia is the (big) continent of all.
17. The (cold) continent is Antarctica.
18. The Atlantic Ocean is (deep) than the Indian Ocean.
19. The Pacific Ocean is the (deep) ocean on the earth.
20. It is also the (large) ocean.
21. The (high) mountain in North America is Mount McKinley in Alaska.
22. Asia's Mount Everest is (high) than Mount McKinley.
23. The (long) river in South America is the Amazon River.
24. It is (long) than North America's Mississippi River.
25. Lake Ontario is slightly (small) than Lake Erie.
26. Lake Ontario is the (small) of the five Great Lakes.
27. Europe has a (large) population than Africa.
28. The (low) point on the earth is the Dead Sea in Asia.
29. The Dead Sea is (low) than Death Valley in North America.
30. The Sahara is one of the (dry) spots on the earth.

Application WRITING SENTENCES

Use the comparative and superlative form of each adjective below in a sentence. You will write eight sentences in all.

tiny   sad   loose   sweet

6 — Comparison of Adjectives

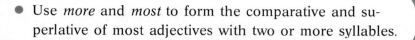

> • Use *more* and *most* to form the comparative and superlative of most adjectives with two or more syllables.

Read the sentences below. Notice how the adjective *important* forms its comparative and superlative.

> The space program is an <u>important</u> industry in Florida.
> Agriculture is a <u>more important</u> industry than space.
> Tourism is Florida's <u>most important</u> industry.

Most adjectives with two or more syllables do not form their comparative and superlative by adding *-er* and *-est*. Instead, they use the words *more* and *most*. *More* is used with an adjective to compare two persons, places, or things. *Most* is used to compare three or more persons, places, or things.

Never use *more* and the *-er* ending with the same adjective.

> **Wrong:** Florida is more bigger than England.
> **Right:** Florida is bigger than England.

Never use *most* and the *-est* ending with the same adjective.

> **Wrong:** The most beautifulest flowers grow in Florida.
> **Right:** The most beautiful flowers grow in Florida.

Some adjectives have special comparative and superlative forms. Learn the forms of the adjectives below.

Adjective	Comparative	Superlative
good	better	best
bad	worse	worst

Skills Tryout

Tell the comparative and superlative form of each adjective.

1. fabulous   2. strange   3. bad   4. serious   5. fine

Practice

A. Write the comparative and superlative form of each adjective.

    1. good   **2.** humorous   **3.** decent   **4.** radiant   **5.** brave

B. Write each sentence. Use the correct form of the adjective in parentheses ( ).

    6. Florida is the (southern) of the mainland states.
    7. Only Alaska has a (extensive) coastline than Florida.
    8. Florida's (popular) beach is Miami Beach.
    9. Many think Florida has the (good) climate of any state.
    10. Winters in Florida are (moderate) than elsewhere.
    11. Florida is one of America's (famous) resort states.
    12. Disney World, near Orlando, Florida, is one of the world's (extraordinary) amusement parks.
    13. Everglades National Park is the (large) tropical wilderness in the United States.
    14. Florida's southern swamplands are (fertile) than the northern lands.
    15. Farming is a (important) industry than fishing.
    16. Oranges are the state's (valuable) crop.
    17. Frost damage is a (bad) problem than hurricanes for orange growers.
    18. Florida is (populous) than forty-two other states.
    19. Cape Canaveral is a (frequent) launching site for missiles than Houston, Texas.
    20. In the United States, Lake Michigan is (big) than Florida's Lake Okeechobee.

Application WRITING SENTENCES

Write eight sentences comparing two or more persons or things. Use the comparative or superlative of each adjective.

fast	interesting	helpful	sharp
bad	difficult	unusual	wise

7 — Adjective Suffixes

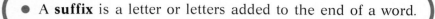

> • A **suffix** is a letter or letters added to the end of a word.

Notice the underlined adjectives in this poem.

> The dinosaurs were <u>greedy</u> beasts.
> All day they ate great <u>endless</u> feasts.
> They didn't stop at night. What for?
> The dinosaurs just dined some more!

The adjective *greedy* was formed by adding the suffix *-y* to the word *greed*. The adjective *endless* was formed by adding the suffix *-less* to the word *end*. A suffix is a letter or letters added to the end of a word to form a new word.

Some common suffixes and their meanings are listed below.

Suffix	Meaning	Examples
-able	worthy of, able to	likeable, changeable
-al	having to do with	educational, occasional
-ful	full of, having the qualities of	successful, playful
-ive	tending to	selective, responsive
-less	without, not having	homeless, careless
-ous	full of, having	courageous, glorious
-y	having, being like	dirty, funny

Skills Tryout

Name the adjective formed with a suffix in each sentence.

1. The allosaurus was a huge, fearless reptile.
2. This powerful animal was about thirty feet long.
3. Its mouth showed rows of shiny sharp teeth.
4. Each finger had a harmful talon, or claw.
5. The fierce and furious beast ruled its part of the world.

Practice

A. Write each sentence. Underline each adjective formed with a suffix. Then circle the suffix.

1. The stegosaurus was a remarkable dinosaur.
2. It had a rather comical appearance.
3. Its lengthy nose almost touched the ground.
4. This oppressive two-ton beast had a two-ounce brain!
5. A double row of bony plates ran down its back and tail.
6. The purpose of the plates remains debatable.
7. The name of this colorful creature means "roofed lizard."
8. The word *dinosaur* makes you think of frightful creatures.
9. The mysterious compsognathus, however, was no bigger than a chicken.
10. This small dinosaur enjoyed a diet of flavorful insects.

B. Write the adjective in each sentence formed with a suffix. Then write the word from which the adjective was formed.

11. *Tyrannosaurus rex*, which means "king tyrant," was the name of a mighty dinosaur.
12. This dinosaur had a huge, forceful body.
13. Because of its size it was not very speedy.
14. The giant had pointy, six-inch teeth.
15. The tyrannosaurus was not a likeable beast.
16. Many creatures were helpless against it.
17. The huge apatosaurus was a peaceful dinosaur.
18. The name of this agreeable beast means "unreal lizard."
19. The seventy-foot giant was quite harmless.
20. Its weak teeth could chew only pulpy plants.

Application USING LANGUAGE

Form adjectives from the words below using six different suffixes from this lesson. Use each adjective in a sentence.

danger   skill   notice   attract   thought   bump

Adjectives   *pages 178–179*

A. Write the adjectives in each sentence. Include articles.

1. Three smart beavers built a little round lodge there.
2. The long dam over there created a deep pond.
3. Beavers have large teeth and flat tails.
4. A mature beaver may weigh sixty pounds.
5. Beavers use small stones, short branches, and mud to build lodges.
6. The busy creatures sleep during the day and work at night.
7. They eat green plants in summer and dry bark in winter.
8. Beavers can stay underwater for fifteen minutes at a time.
9. Females give birth to small babies in late spring.
10. Both parents live with the young beavers in a lodge.

Proper Adjectives   *pages 180–181*

B. Write the proper adjective in each sentence correctly.

11. Last night we went out for chinese food.
12. Then we went downtown to an italian movie.
13. Fortunately there were english subtitles.
14. At home we ate danish pastries and drank milk.
15. Before bed I listened to a german opera.

Predicate Adjectives   *pages 182–183*

C. Write each sentence. Underline each predicate adjective.

16. At first the weather didn't look good for a picnic.
17. The day looked quite dreary.
18. Everyone felt rather unhappy about it.
19. Then suddenly the sky became bright.
20. The day seemed ideal for a picnic after all!

Demonstrative Adjectives *pages 184–185*

D. Write each sentence. Underline each demonstrative adjective.

21. These salmon swim upriver to lay their eggs.
22. We call this process spawning.
23. Many salmon will leap up that waterfall over there.
24. Those females will lay eggs in hollows in the streambed.
25. Baby fish like this one will hatch and swim back to sea.

Comparison of Adjectives *pages 186–189*

E. Write the comparative or superlative form of the adjective in parentheses ( ) to correctly complete each sentence.

26. This room is (large) than the first.
27. The little room in back is the (dark) of the three.
28. The wallpaper in this room is (beautiful) than that in the first.
29. The view from this window is (good) than from that one.
30. Your bedroom is (messy) than Jane's.
31. The leak in the kitchen is (bad) than the one in here.
32. This fireplace is (big) than the one upstairs.
33. The living room will be the (difficult) to paint.
34. This color is (cheerful) than that one.
35. Someday this will be the (good) house in town.

Adjective Suffixes *pages 190–191*

F. Write the adjective in each sentence formed with a suffix. Circle the suffix.

36. We had a perfectly dreadful evening at the Jones's.
37. The guests were rude and the food was tasteless.
38. Their dog's behavior was not at all predictable.
39. Suddenly the dangerous animal bit my leg.
40. I was lucky to get away with just a scratch.

See also Handbook pages 370–373, 407.

Grammar Review

Writing with Adjectives

> • Use adjectives to add detail to your writing.

Read the sentences below.

1. **Clouds floated over the lake.**
2. **Fluffy white clouds floated over the clear blue lake.**

These two sentences describe the same scene. However, the second sentence has much more detail. The noun *clouds* is described by the adjectives *fluffy* and *white*. The noun *lake* is described by the adjectives *clear* and *blue*. Sentence 1 just gives the basic facts. The adjectives in sentence 2 create a detailed, colorful picture.

The scene could be changed almost completely if different adjectives were used to describe it. Read the sentence below.

3. **Dark gray clouds floated over the lonely, misty lake.**

If the nouns you use do not add enough detail to your writing, use adjectives to describe them. Adjectives can really change the meaning of what you write. Adjectives create a pleasant scene in sentence 2 and a sad one in sentence 3.

Using Adjectives Below is a list of nouns that you might use in your own writing. Select one and write it on a piece of paper. Think of adjectives that might describe the noun in a sentence. See how many adjectives you can write in two minutes.

summer   highway   riddle   artist   explosion
     sunrise   celebration   animal   cave

How many adjectives did you list? Find a classmate who chose the same noun. Did he or she think of any adjectives that were not on your list? Do you have some that were not on your classmate's list? Choose a different noun and start again. You might form teams with one or more of your classmates.

Adding Adjectives   Read each sentence below. Think of adjectives that could describe the underlined nouns. Then write the sentence twice, adding a different adjective each time.

EXAMPLE: The piano player performed a melody.
ANSWER: The piano player performed a quiet melody.
            The piano player performed a beautiful melody.

1. The ship floated out of the harbor.
2. The sun was overhead as I worked in the backyard.
3. The fans watched the hockey game.
4. A raccoon pawed through our garbage can.
5. Sherlock Holmes was a detective in a group of stories.

Adjectives in Paragraphs   Use adjectives to complete the paragraph below. Write the paragraph.

A _____ fire started in a _____ cottage. A _____ crowd watched the _____ firefighters arrive and put the fire out. Suddenly there was a _____ cry from inside the cottage. A _____ boy rushed through the _____ door. He came out with a _____ baby in his arms. Everyone clapped for the _____ bravery shown by the boy.

Using the Thesaurus

Good and *bad* are two of the most overworked adjectives in writing. Find the entries for *good* and *bad* in the Thesaurus beginning on page 414. Then write three sentences using synonyms for *good* and three sentences using synonyms for *bad*.

Another overworked adjective is *great*. Imagine you have just been to a play and have liked it very much. You want to describe the performance of the main actor, but you do not want to use the word *great*. Using synonyms for *great* from the Thesaurus, write a paragraph describing the actor's performance.

8 Writing a Descriptive Paragraph

> • A **descriptive paragraph** creates a word picture.

Can you describe the person who took your bike? What does your lost dog look like? How will I recognize your house? What is your new neighbor like? Questions such as these call for descriptions.

The ability to describe things clearly, accurately, and vividly is important not only in school, but in everyday life. In order to give good descriptions, you need to be a careful observer. Train yourself to look for details. Think of yourself as a detective who sees the importance of little things—mud on a pair of shoes, a wisp of wool on a barbed-wire fence, a small scar above the left eyebrow, and so on. Being a good observer can help you to write a descriptive paragraph.

A descriptive paragraph creates a word picture. It often begins with a topic sentence that tells what will be described. The other sentences in the paragraph give details that help create a vivid picture for the reader. Details that appeal to the senses are especially effective. They help the reader see, smell, hear, taste, or feel what the writer is describing.

Read the descriptive paragraph below. Notice the use of details that appeal to the senses.

Topic Sentence →

Supporting Details →

At high noon the desert is a silent, sun-scorched wasteland. The only sound is the desert wind hissing through the dry mesquite bushes. A red-topped Gila woodpecker peeks out from its nest hole inside a towering cactus. In the gray shade of the same cactus, a small sidewinder rattlesnake lies in a slender *S*-shaped curve. All the desert creatures have sought shelter from the searing sun.

Skills Tryout

Answer these questions about the descriptive paragraph on the opposite page.

1. Does the second sentence appeal to the sense of sight or to the sense of hearing?
2. What sense does the third sentence appeal to?
3. What words suggest the feeling of heat?
4. What words describe size or shape?
5. Which sentence supports the statement "At high noon the desert is a *silent . . .* wasteland"?

Practice

A. Write a sentence to describe each of the following.

1. the shape and color of a pumpkin
2. sounds heard in the school gym
3. the smell of burning leaves
4. a taste you associate with summer
5. what you think an elephant's skin feels like

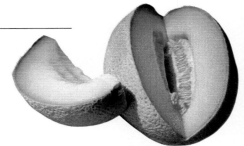

B. Write a detail sentence for each of these topic sentences.

6. It was an extremely hot July.
7. The lake is beautiful tonight.
8. Tantalizing smells mingled in the kitchen.
9. The trees were ablaze with the colors of autumn.
10. A strange sound awakened me from a deep sleep.

Application WRITING A PARAGRAPH

Choose one of the objects shown on this page and write a paragraph describing it. Begin with a topic sentence and add details that create a vivid word picture for the reader. Include details that appeal to at least one of the senses—sight, smell, hearing, taste, or touch.

Listening for the Main Idea and Descriptive Details

- When you listen to a description, identify the speaker's main idea.

A descriptive paragraph contains many details. However, it should also contain a main idea, or most important point. When you listen to a descriptive paragraph, try to identify its main idea. Once you have grasped the main idea, the details will be easier to remember.

Close your book and listen as your teacher reads the following paragraph. What do you think is its main idea?

In seconds the streets and yards were clear of people. The sky grew darker, and sudden gusts of wind blew leaves and scraps of paper all about. A blaze of lightning flashed, and a tearing sound shook the countryside. The first fat drops of rain began to hit the pavement. A powerful thunderstorm had struck!

The main idea of the paragraph above is stated in the topic sentence *A powerful thunderstorm had struck!* All the other sentences in the paragraph contain descriptive details. These details explain and support the main idea of the paragraph.

Suppose someone were to ask, "How do you know a powerful thunderstorm had struck?" Without looking back at the paragraph, name as many details as possible to answer the question.

Skills Tryout

Listen as your teacher reads this paragraph. Identify its main idea. Then tell three details that support the main idea of the paragraph.

The house had been deserted for a long time. Waist-high weeds grew up through cracks in the sidewalk. A bird made its nest in the mailbox. The front door and windows were all nailed shut.

Practice

A. Listen as your teacher reads this paragraph. Then write the main idea and three details that help explain it.

The jackrabbit has a very keen sense of smell. Its long, sensitive ears detect sounds from far off. The shape and location of its eyes let it see in many directions at once. Jackrabbits are well equipped to sense danger.

B. Listen as your teacher reads this paragraph. Then answer the questions that follow.

Most plant movement cannot be detected by people. Plant roots creep in all directions in search of water. Leaves and stems slowly bend and turn to get more light. Within a plant, sugar and other substances move constantly between root and blossom.

1. Why do the leaves and stems of plants move?
2. What movement takes place within a plant?
3. What is the main idea of the paragraph?

Application LISTENING

Listen to a radio or television commercial. Write a sentence that states the main idea. Then list three descriptive details given in the commercial.

10 — Using Space Order in Paragraphs

> ● **Space order** is one way to arrange details in a paragraph.

When you write, you organize your sentences into paragraphs. All the sentences in a paragraph work together to tell about one main idea. The details within a paragraph should be organized in a logical order. One way to organize the details in a paragraph is to list them in space order.

Space order is simply the way things are arranged in space. When you describe something in space order, you tell what it looks like from where you are. Using space order, you might describe something from left to right, from top to bottom, or from near to far. The details in the paragraph below are organized in bottom-to-top order.

We then recognized him at once. His red leather boots reached almost to his knees. Over his blue body suit he wore red trunks and a yellow belt. A large shield with the letter *S* appeared on his chest. Around the hero's neck hung a red cape. His handsome face had a strong chin and a straight nose. Superman's™ bright eyes glistened, and his dark hair shone in the light.

Some words and phrases often used to describe the location of things in space are listed below.

> above, below, next to, across from, beside, nearby, to the right, in back of, in the distance, alongside, farther away, over, under, on the left, closer, behind, opposite

Skills Tryout

Tell whether the space order of this paragraph is top-to-bottom, left-to-right, near-to-far, or front-to-back.

The mansion's grounds were lovely. Fine gardens surrounded the building. Beyond the gardens stretched acres of rolling lawns. In the far distance lay the forest.

Practice

A. Write the topic sentence. Then write the five detail sentences in left-to-right space order.

TOPIC SENTENCE: This mural shows events in Texas's history.

1. To the right of the Alamo, cowhands drive cattle and workers drill for oil.
2. On the far left an Indian village appears.
3. The Battle of the Alamo is shown in the center.
4. Spanish missionaries are beside the Indian village.
5. Modern day Dallas appears on the far right.

B. Use this diagram to write a paragraph that describes how ancient Roman roads were constructed. Organize the details in the paragraph in space order. You may wish to use some of the words from the box on the opposite page.

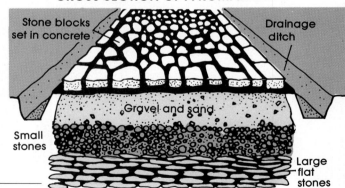

CROSS SECTION OF A ROMAN ROAD

Stone blocks set in concrete

Drainage ditch

Gravel and sand

Small stones

Large flat stones

Application WRITING A PARAGRAPH

Think of a place in your school or town that almost everyone in the class is familiar with. Then write a paragraph that describes this place clearly. Be sure to arrange the details in space order. When you are finished, read your paragraph aloud. See if your classmates can identify the place you have described.

11 — Interviewing

> ● An **interview** is a planned exchange of information.

At the Career Fair, each sixth grader is going to describe a different occupation. Patti plans to report on careers in law enforcement. She found some information in the library. To learn more, she scheduled an interview with Chief Dooley of the state police.

Asking questions is an excellent way to get to know people and to learn information firsthand. Unlike questions that occur in everyday conversations, however, interview questions should be carefully planned in advance. Each question should have a specific purpose. All the questions in an interview should deal with the topic under discussion.

Patti followed these guidelines for her interview.

Guidelines for Conducting an Interview

- Write or call to request an interview. Explain the purpose of the interview at this time.
- Prepare questions on your topic in advance. Begin your questions with the interviewing words *who, what, when, where, why,* and *how.*
- Listen carefully during the interview. If possible, tape-record the interview. Otherwise, take notes.
- Ask follow-up questions to clarify an answer or to explore a point. Be sure to keep to the topic, though.
- Thank the person for the interview.

Patti wrote her report immediately after the interview. That way the information was fresh in her mind. She learned many important facts through the interview. Seeing a typical police officer's workplace and equipment provided interesting details for the report, too.

Skills Tryout

Patti's interview topic was "Careers in Law Enforcement." Tell which questions below are appropriate for this topic.

1. How can a person prepare for a career in law enforcement?
2. How fast can police cars travel?
3. What is a police officer's typical day like?
4. Do you watch detective shows on TV?
5. What abilities and personal qualities are needed to do police work?

Practice

A. Choose a topic for an interview with each person below. Write the topic. Then write three questions you would ask each person about the topic.

1. your favorite musician
2. your state's governor
3. your school's principal
4. a race-car driver

B. Write the name of one well-known person you would like to interview. Then write at least four questions you would ask that person.

C. Interview someone in your school or neighborhood. Follow the guidelines on page 202. Be sure to take notes or tape-record the interview.

Application WRITING A PARAGRAPH

A written interview often begins with a description of the person being interviewed. This description serves as an introduction to readers of the interview. Write a descriptive paragraph about the person you interviewed in **Practice C.** Tell what the person looks like and describe where he or she lives or works. Include any other descriptive details, such as personality traits, that will let your readers know the person a little better.

12 — Writing a Character Sketch

> ● In a **character sketch** the writer uses facts and observations to describe a person.

Writing Project

In this unit you have sharpened your skills of observation and description. Now you will use those skills to describe someone you know. Your goal will be to write a character sketch that allows your reader to see your subject as a real person. When you have finished, you and your classmates will assemble the sketches in a "Who's Who" collection.

1. Prewriting

Select a subject for your character sketch. Choose a person you know and admire, someone you can interview in person. You might write about a classmate, another person in your school, a friend in the neighborhood, or a relative.

Authors often use a questionnaire, or question-and-answer sheet, to obtain information. Study this questionnaire that was prepared for a sixth-grade student.

CHARACTER SKETCH QUESTIONNAIRE

Name: _____

Address: _____

_____

Age: _____   Place of birth: _____

Favorite activity: _____

Favorite food: _____

Favorite book: _____

What do you want to do when you grow up? Why? _____

_____

What is the most enjoyable thing you have ever done?

_____

What place would you most like to visit? _____

Notice how the questions on the questionnaire encourage conversation. The author asks questions about activities, goals, and ambitions—subjects people like to talk about.

▶ Prepare your questionnaire. Make a list of possible questions. Then narrow the list to the best questions. Select your questions carefully. Remember, the questions for a classmate could be quite different from the questions you might ask your grandparents.

When you have chosen your questions, try them out. Try to answer the questions yourself. You will quickly discover whether or not your questions are clear. Then write your questionnaire neatly and make an appointment to interview the person you are going to write about.

▶ Conduct your interview, using the questionnaire as a base for conversation. On the questionnaire accurately record the information the person gives you. In addition, observe and listen. If you wish, take brief notes to help you remember details about the person's appearance, actions, and personality.

2. Writing

Your personal observations, the questionnaire, and the notes from the interview will help you describe your subject. They will provide the information you need to write a character sketch.

► In the first sentence of your character sketch, try to capture your reader's interest. There are several ways in which you can begin. Read the suggestions below.

Begin with an interesting response from your questionnaire.
Begin with a personal observation.
Begin by quoting the person you are writing about.

As you write your character sketch, you may not be able to use all of the information you have gathered. Be selective. Focus on a major topic, such as career goals or a favorite hobby.

3. Revising

► Share your writing with a good listener. As you and your listener discuss your character sketch, ask for suggestions that will help you make improvements. Consider your listener's suggestions. Use this Revision Checklist, too, as you review your first draft.

Revision Checklist
- **Will my first sentence capture my reader's interest?**
- **Did I focus on one major topic?**
- **Did I include facts and observations?**
- **Did I present my ideas in the best sequence?**

Read the sample that follows. Notice how moving a sentence improved the sequence of ideas.

The edited draft (handwritten marks):

꜡Deborah Conti does an excellent job as ~~reportor~~ *sixth-grade reporter* for the school newspaper. She would especially like to visit ~~australia~~. In the future ~~someday~~ she would like to be a newspaper reporter. ~~She would like to~~ travel to other ~~places~~ *and* ~~assinements~~ *countries assignments* on special ~~assinements~~. When

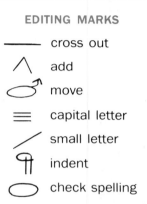

The revised draft:

Deborah Conti does an excellent job as sixth-grade reporter for the school newspaper. She would like to be a newspaper reporter someday and travel to other countries on special assignments. She would especially like to visit Australia. When Deborah walks briskly through the halls with her pencil and notepad, people know she is looking for a new story. Many of her readers think that Deborah is already on her way to achieving her future goal.

► Now revise your character sketch, using the editing marks.

EDITING MARKS

——	cross out
∧	add
⌿	move
≡	capital letter
/	small letter
꜡	indent
◯	check spelling

4. Publishing

► Proofread your character sketch before sharing it with the class. Use the Proofreading Checklist in the Young Writer's Handbook on page 399 and use the editing marks to make corrections.

► With your classmates make a "Who's Who" collection of character sketches. Illustrate your character sketch if you wish. Show your subject doing what he or she likes to do best. Display the collection in your classroom and in the library for others to enjoy.

Writing Project

A Coat of Arms

Long ago medieval knights carried colorful shields. The shields were decorated with designs called coats of arms. The symbols on a coat of arms described the knight's acts of courage and bravery.

You can design your own coat of arms. First sketch a large shield. Then divide the shield into four sections. In the upper left-hand section draw a picture of your favorite pet or a wild animal you especially like. In the upper right-hand section draw a picture that represents a sport or hobby you enjoy. In the lower left-hand section draw something that represents what you want to become. A scientist, a teacher, an artist? In the last section draw a picture of your favorite flower, tree, or fruit. Your completed coat of arms describes you.

Social Studies

In your social studies textbook, important information is often presented in photographs and illustrations. You can learn much if you train yourself to "read" these pictures. The skills you have developed in observing and describing will help you to do this.

▶ Try it. Use the suggestions given below to "read" this photograph. Then describe what you observed.

1. Just as paragraphs have main ideas, so do photographs. Ask yourself, "What is the main idea of the photograph? What does it show?" (Hint: Be sure to read the caption if there is one.)

2. The details in a photograph are like detail sentences in a paragraph. Look for details in the paragraph that give clues to people's lifestyles, customs, beliefs, and so on.

Writers at Work Police officers need to describe the scene of an accident and tell exactly what happened when they make out an accident report. To do this, they observe carefully, noting important details. They also interview the people involved as well as any witnesses.

▶ Pretend you are a police officer reporting on a minor traffic accident. First prepare five questions that you would ask each of the drivers involved in the accident. Then make up answers to the questions, and use the answers to write a paragraph describing the accident.

Adjectives   *pages 178–189*

A. Write the adjectives in each sentence. Include articles.

1. The sudden rainstorm woke Ellie from a deep sleep.
2. The heavy rain made a hollow sound on the roof.
3. She heard the faint rumble of distant thunder.
4. Lightning, sleek and bright, flashed across the sky.

B. Write each proper adjective in the sentences correctly.

5. Terry has a collection of indonesian puppets.
6. We admired the grace of the spanish dancers.
7. My uncle is proud of his fine swiss watch.
8. Sandy decorated the porch with pretty chinese lanterns.
9. Our music teacher showed us some african instruments.

C. Write each sentence. Underline each predicate adjective.

10. Our class play was very successful.
11. Abby and Fred were wonderful in the leading roles.
12. Rodney appeared quite timid as the cowardly lion.
13. The witch looked frightful in her black costume.
14. The whole audience seemed pleased with our performance.

D. Write each sentence. Underline each demonstrative adjective.

15. These musicians play at our community dances.
16. We hold the dances in that brick building.
17. This man plays both the fiddle and the banjo.
18. I do not know the names of those other instruments.

E. Write the comparative and superlative form of each adjective.

19. sharp	21. large	23. bad	25. expensive
20. dangerous	22. happy	24. fine	26. beautiful

Suffixes   *pages 190–191*

F. Write the adjective in each sentence formed with a suffix.

    27. The platypus is the only poisonous mammal in the world.
    28. It has heavy fur, a broad tail, and a rubbery bill.
    29. This toothless animal eats worms, insects, and crayfish.
    30. Its webfeet make the platypus a powerful swimmer.

Descriptive Paragraph   *pages 196–197*

G. Write a sentence to describe each of the following.

    31. sounds heard in a busy store
    32. smells of a day in early spring
    33. what the skin of fish feels like
    34. the shape and color of a head of lettuce

H. Decide whether each sentence below supports this main idea: *A stalled truck was blocking the busy intersection.* Write *yes* or *no* for each sentence.

    35. Horns, blared, honked by impatient drivers.
    36. Exhaust fumes from the backed-up traffic filled the air.
    37. Most of the automobiles were compact models.

Space Order   *pages 200–201*

I. Write the topic sentence. Then write the five detail sentences in left-to-right space order. Number the sentences from 1–5.

    Topic sentence: This is a painting of an old colonial town.

In the center stands a school building.
On the far right is the general store.
Beside the hat shop stands a tiny law office.
A bank can be seen next to the school building.
There is a hat shop on the far left.

See also Handbook pages 370–373.

Grammar
Adverbs

Composition
Researching

Swallows

The prairie wind blew harder than it could,
Even the spines of cactus trembled back,
I crouched in an arroyo clamping my hands
On my eyes the sand was stinging yellow black.

In a break of the black I let my lashes part,
Looked overhead and saw I was not alone,
I could almost reach through the roar and almost touch
A treadmill of swallows almost holding their own.

—*Thomas Hornsby Ferril*

1 Adverbs

- An **adverb** describes a verb, an adjective, or another adverb.

The underlined words in the following sentences are adverbs. They describe the verbs in the sentences. Adverbs answer the question *How? When? Where?* or *To what extent?*

How: Birds sing <u>sweetly</u> in the trees.
When: <u>Tomorrow</u> spring begins.
Where: Flowers will bloom <u>everywhere</u>.
To what extent: I can <u>hardly</u> wait!

An adverb can come before or after the verb it describes. It can also come between a helping verb and a main verb.

<u>Soon</u> warm days will arrive. Warm days will arrive <u>soon</u>.
Warm days will <u>soon</u> arrive.

An adverb can also describe an adjective. In this sentence the adverb *very* describes the adjective *beautiful.*

Spring is a <u>very</u> beautiful season.

An adverb can describe another adverb, too. In the sentence below, the adverb *quite* describes the adverb *early.*

The flowers are blooming <u>quite</u> early.

Skills Tryout

Name the adverb in each sentence.

1. The bees are buzzing busily.
2. The sun is shining warmly.
3. I'll plant my vegetable garden there.
4. Our spring cleaning is already finished.
5. I have almost forgotten winter!

Practice

A. Write each sentence. Underline each adverb.

1. The snows have melted now.
2. Streams quickly carry the water to the sea.
3. The alfalfa in the fields is growing rapidly.
4. Soon the apple trees in the orchard will blossom.
5. Baby ducks are swimming quietly in the pond.
6. Lambs run playfully in the meadow.
7. Yesterday a new colt was born.
8. We can see the colt later.
9. Some friends have started a baseball game nearby.
10. We always play baseball in the spring.

B. Write the adverb in each sentence. Then write *How, When, Where,* or *To what extent* to show which question the adverb answers.

EXAMPLE: We thoroughly enjoyed the game.
ANSWER: thoroughly (To what extent)

11. Today we will shear the sheep.
12. That ram will get away!
13. Father is fixing the plow here.
14. The fence in the pasture should be repaired immediately.
15. The chicken coop really needs paint.
16. Those sacks of seed go there.
17. The ditch is completely clogged with leaves.
18. The tractor is running poorly.
19. Soon we'll fertilize the fruit trees.
20. We'll be working constantly until summer!

Application WRITING SENTENCES

Write five sentences that tell what you like about spring. Use one of the following adverbs in each sentence.

really   finally   gently   quickly   very

2 — Adverb Location in Sentences

> ● An adverb that describes an adjective or another adverb usually comes directly before the word it describes.

You know that an adverb that describes a verb can appear almost anywhere in a sentence. An adverb that describes an adjective or another adverb, however, usually comes directly before the word it describes.

1. Jim Thorpe was an unbelievably fine athlete.

2. He won many events rather easily in the 1912 Olympics.

In the first sentence the adverb *unbelievably* describes the adjective *fine*. In the second sentence the adverb *rather* describes the adverb *easily*. Notice that *unbelievably* and *rather* could not appear anywhere else in the sentences without changing the meaning of the sentences.

Adverbs often end in *-ly*. Some common adverbs that do not end in *-ly* are shown below.

almost	ever	never	quite	still
already	here	not	seldom	there
also	just	often	so	too
always	maybe	perhaps	soon	very

Skills Tryout

Name the adverbs in the sentences.

1. Jim Thorpe excelled in very many sports.
2. He was a truly excellent football player.
3. This famous American Indian played baseball quite well.
4. He ran track-and-field events extremely quickly.
5. Thorpe was almost always a winner.

Practice

A. Write each sentence. Underline each adverb.

1. Jim Thorpe was an exceptionally athletic youngster.
2. He could run really fast.
3. Jim entered the Carlisle Indian School in Pennsylvania very soon after his nineteenth birthday.
4. Almost immediately he joined their football team.
5. Thorpe consistently led Carlisle to victories in football.
6. This small school often beat the best teams.
7. Jim played a truly important role in the 1912 Olympics.
8. He won the pentathlon contest effortlessly.
9. He did not stop there.
10. He won still more events in the decathlon.

B. Write the word that each underlined adverb describes. Then write whether the word is a verb, an adjective, or an adverb.

11. Jim Thorpe didn't keep his Olympic awards <u>too</u> long.
12. It was learned that he had <u>briefly</u> played baseball for money before the Olympics.
13. An <u>extremely</u> sad Jim Thorpe had to return his cherished Olympic medals.
14. Later he played professional football <u>remarkably</u> well.
15. His love of sports <u>never</u> ended.
16. His lost awards remained a <u>very</u> bitter memory, however.
17. Thorpe's family worked <u>hard</u> to have his awards returned.
18. In 1982 the family's efforts were <u>finally</u> successful.
19. Officials of the Olympics <u>not</u> only restored his medals.
20. They <u>also</u> restored his place in the record books.

Application WRITING SENTENCES

Write six sentences about an athlete you admire. Use two adverbs that describe adjectives and two adverbs that describe other adverbs in your sentences.

3 — Comparison of Adverbs

> • Use the comparative form of an adverb to compare two things.
>
> • Use the superlative form of an adverb to compare three or more things.

You have learned how to form the comparative and superlative of adjectives. Adverbs also have a comparative and a superlative form. The comparative is used to compare two things. The superlative is used to compare three or more things.

One-syllable adverbs usually add *-er* to form the comparative and *-est* to form the superlative.

I run <u>fast</u>.	(Adverb)
Richard runs <u>faster</u> than I.	(Comparative)
Ann runs the <u>fastest</u> of all.	(Superlative)

Most adverbs that end in *-ly* and adverbs with two or more syllables use *more* to form the comparative and *most* to form the superlative.

I run <u>rapidly</u>.	(Adverb)
Richard runs <u>more</u> <u>rapidly</u> than I.	(Comparative)
Ann runs the <u>most</u> <u>rapidly</u> of all.	(Superlative)

Some adverbs have special comparative and superlative forms.

Adverb	Comparative	Superlative
well	better	best
badly	worse	worst

Skills Tryout

Tell the comparative and superlative form of each adverb.

1. badly   2. willingly   3. hard   4. quickly   5. late

Practice

A. Write the comparative and superlative form of each adverb.

1. gently
2. hungrily
3. high
4. long
5. bravely

6. well
7. hopefully
8. sharply
9. loud
10. smoothly

B. Write each sentence. Use the correct form of the adverb in parentheses ( ).

11. This morning we got up (early) than usual to jog.
12. Ann ran the (gracefully) of all the joggers.
13. We jogged (quickly) today than yesterday.
14. Tomorrow we may run even (fast).
15. You use oxygen (rapidly) when running than when walking.
16. Therefore, you must breathe (deep) than usual.
17. Jan seems to breathe the (deep) of everyone.
18. She also runs the (fast) of all.
19. I always manage to run the (slow).
20. You should stretch your leg muscles (thoroughly) than that before running.
21. Beginners should run (slow) than experienced runners.
22. Joggers who practice hard run the (well).
23. You ran (well) this time than last time!
24. I run (comfortably) on grass than on roads.
25. Of all the different races, the marathon is the one for which runners train (seriously).

Application WRITING SENTENCES

Exercise is important for physical fitness. Write eight sentences about a type of exercise that you enjoy. It could be running, playing a sport, or doing some other kind of physical activity. Use the comparative or superlative form of an adverb in at least four of your sentences.

4 — Avoiding Double Negatives

> ● Some negative words, such as *not*, are adverbs. Avoid using two negative words in the same sentence.

A negative is a word that means "no." Some common negatives are *no, no one, not, none, never, nothing, nowhere*, and *nobody*. Contractions formed with *not* are also negatives.

Two negatives used in the same sentence are called a **double negative**. Double negatives should be avoided because they make the meaning of a sentence unclear.

> **WRONG:** Stacy can't never remember a joke.
> **RIGHT:** Stacy can never remember a joke.
> **RIGHT:** Stacy can't ever remember a joke.

Notice that a double negative can be corrected in different ways. In the third sentence above, an affirmative, or "yes" word, has been substituted for one of the negatives. This chart shows the affirmatives for other words.

Negative	Affirmative	Negative	Affirmative
no no one none	any, a, one anyone, someone all, some	nothing nowhere nobody	anything, something anywhere, somewhere anybody, somebody

Skills Tryout

Tell the word that makes each sentence negative.

1. What two things can you (ever, never) eat for breakfast?
2. You (can, can't) eat lunch or dinner for breakfast.
3. Why has (nobody, somebody) heard the joke about the bed?
4. (Anyone, No one) has made it up yet!
5. What is of (no, any) use until it is broken? (An egg)

Practice

A. Write each sentence. Use the word in parentheses ( ) that makes the sentence negative.

1. (Anybody, Nobody) knows the answers to all these riddles.
2. What falls often but (does, doesn't) ever get hurt? (Snow)
3. What room can (anyone, no one) enter? (A mushroom)
4. What table has (no, any) legs?
5. A multiplication table has (some, none).
6. What wears a cap but (has, hasn't) any head? (A bottle)
7. Why does an elephant (ever, never) forget?
8. It has (anything, nothing) to remember.
9. Why is there (no, any) sport noisier than tennis?
10. (Nobody, Anybody) can play it without raising a racket.

B. Write the word in parentheses that correctly completes each sentence. Avoid double negatives.

11. Why can't (no one, anyone) have a nose twelve inches long?
12. Then it wouldn't be (no, a) nose, but a foot!
13. What has a mouth but doesn't (never, ever) eat? (A river)
14. To what question can't (no one, anyone) answer yes?
15. You can't (never, ever) answer the question, "Are you asleep?" with a yes.
16. Why can't (no one, someone) with an empty stomach eat two peanuts?
17. After the first, the person's stomach isn't empty (no, any) more.
18. Why are some people like fences? They run around a lot but don't get (nowhere, anywhere).
19. I don't usually tell (no, any) jokes.
20. I can't (never, ever) remember the punch lines!

Application LISTENING

Listen for negatives in people's conversations. Write six sentences you hear that contain negatives. If any of the sentences contain double negatives, write them correctly.

5 ── Using Adjectives and Adverbs

- Use adjectives to describe nouns and pronouns.
- Use adverbs to describe verbs, adjectives, and other adverbs.

Which word would you use to complete each sentence?

1. Jeremy rides his bicycle very (careful, carefully).
2. Jeremy is very (careful, carefully) on his bicycle.

In the first sentence the adverb *carefully* is correct. It describes the verb *rides*. In the second sentence the correct word is *careful*. *Careful* is a predicate adjective that describes *Jeremy*. When you are not sure whether to use an adjective or an adverb, find the word being described.

The words *good* and *well* are often confused. *Good* is always an adjective. Use it to describe a noun or a pronoun.

A good rider is a safe rider.

Well is an adjective when it describes a noun or pronoun and means "healthy." It usually comes after a linking verb.

I didn't feel well during the trip.

Well is an adverb when it tells how something is done.

You ride that bicycle very well!

Skills Tryout

Tell which word correctly completes each sentence.

1. I want a new bicycle (bad, badly).
2. I don't feel (safe, safely) on my old one.
3. Unfortunately, bicycle accidents occur (regular, regularly).
4. Make sure your bicycle is running (smooth, smoothly).
5. Check it (thorough, thoroughly) before a long trip.

Practice

A. Write the word in parentheses ( ) that correctly completes each sentence.

1. Bikers should follow traffic laws (careful, carefully).
2. Don't ride too (rapid, rapidly) on busy streets.
3. Walk your bike (slow, slowly) through intersections.
4. Don't move (abrupt, abruptly) from lane to lane.
5. That worn tire looks (dangerous, dangerously) to me.
6. Bicycle lights let people see bikers (easy, easily).
7. Watch for cars that pull out (sudden, suddenly).
8. Ride (cautious, cautiously) on wet leaves.
9. Carry tools so you can fix your bicycle (quick, quickly).
10. Does that wheel feel (loose, loosely) to you?

B. Write each sentence. Use the word *good* or *well* in place of the blank. Then write whether the word is an adjective or an adverb.

EXAMPLE: It is not ____ to overload a bicycle.
ANSWER: It is not good to overload a bicycle. (adjective)

11. Don't ride a bicycle if you are not feeling ____.
12. It is ____ to give pedestrians the right of way.
13. Make sure your tires are in ____ condition.
14. Also make sure that your brakes are working ____.
15. A horn or bell is a ____ safety device.
16. Reflectors work ____ to make you more visible at night.
17. It is also a ____ idea to wear light-colored clothing.
18. You can have a ____ time riding a bicycle.
19. Bicycle riding is ____ exercise.
20. Exercise can help you stay ____.

Application WRITING SENTENCES

Write eight sentences that tell why you like to ride a bicycle. Use *good* or *well* in four of your sentences.

6 ── Context Clues

> ● A **context clue** helps you understand the meaning of an unfamiliar word.

When you read, you often come across new words. Sometimes the context, or words around a new word, will give clues to the word's meaning. Such clues are called context clues. The chart below shows different kinds of context clues.

Kinds of Clues	Examples
A *definition* of the new word	The king called his <u>vassals</u> together. *Vassals are loyal followers of a king or queen.*
Further information about the new word's meaning	The king's castle was *surrounded* by a <u>palisade</u> of logs *to prevent attacks.*
A *synonym*, or word with a similar meaning	The king gave each of his vassals a <u>fief</u>, or *estate.*
An *antonym*, or word with an opposite meaning	Vassals supported the king <u>zealously</u>, not *unwillingly.*

Skills Tryout

Tell whether each example gives a definition, further information, a synonym, or an antonym as a context clue for the underlined word.

1. War was <u>endemic</u>, not uncommon, in the Middle Ages.
2. Knights showed great <u>fealty</u>, or faithfulness, to their king or queen and to that ruler's children.
3. Each knight had a <u>squire</u> for a companion and servant.
4. The king met his vassals in the castle <u>keep</u>. The keep was a heavy stone building inside the castle's walls.
5. A deep <u>moat</u>, or ditch, surrounded the castle.

Practice

A. Write *definition, further information, synonym,* or *antonym* to name the context clue given for each underlined word.

1. A large courtyard, or <u>bailey</u>, surrounded the castle keep.
2. The <u>granary</u> and other storerooms were located there.
3. For protection there was a well-armed <u>garrison</u> of knights.
4. Knights practiced fighting with swords and <u>lances</u> on the bailey. A lance was a long pole with a sharp steel head.
5. Each knight had his own <u>escutcheon</u>, or coat of arms.
6. Living quarters in castles were <u>Spartan</u>, not comfortable.
7. The <u>solar</u>, however, was a comfortable room for the king.
8. The king and his family led an active, not <u>sedentary</u>, life.
9. They were rarely at home. Instead, they <u>migrated</u> from castle to castle.
10. The king's <u>steward</u> was responsible for running the castle.

B. Use the context to determine the meaning of the underlined words. Write the meaning.

11. A knight rode his <u>destrier</u> only in battle. A less valuable horse was ridden at other times.
12. A cloth <u>pennon</u> hung from the tip of the knight's lance, showing his coat of arms.
13. <u>Chain mail</u>, made up of thousands of tiny steel links, was much lighter than solid steel armor.
14. A <u>hauberk</u> made of chain mail protected a knight. It had a hood and sleeves, and it reached to the knees.
15. A knight armed with a heavy <u>martel</u> could smash through chain mail, however.

Application USING LANGUAGE

Use a dictionary to find the meaning of each word below. Then write a sentence containing a context clue for each word.

crossbow   catapult   siege   joust   knight-errant

Adverbs   *pages 214–215*

A. Write each sentence. Underline each adverb.

1. Yesterday, fire fighters fought a fire in an old building.
2. They could hardly see the roof through the smoke.
3. One high wall was swaying dangerously.
4. Police officers calmly controlled the crowd.
5. A person at an upper window suddenly cried, "Help!"

Adverb Location in Sentences   *pages 216–217*

B. Write the adverbs in the sentences. Then write the word each adverb describes.

6. Several fire fighters immediately got a large net.
7. Others soon joined them and held it very tightly.
8. They shouted loudly, "Jump down!"
9. The man jumped too far, but they caught him safely.
10. He was extremely upset but unharmed.

Comparison of Adverbs   *pages 218–219*

C. Write the correct form of the adverb in parentheses ( ) to complete each sentence.

11. Tim's vegetables are growing (well) than mine.
12. Perhaps he fertilized his soil (thoroughly) than I did.
13. He also works (hard) than I do.
14. Linda's garden, however, looks the (well) of the three.
15. Of all our crops, the peas will be ready (early).
16. The melons are growing the (slow) of all.
17. The squash are doing (badly) this year than last year, too.
18. My tomato plants produce (abundantly) than Tim's.
19. Our corn is selling (quickly) than our beans.
20. The weeds always grow (fast) than the vegetables!

Avoiding Double Negatives   *pages 220–221*

D. Rewrite each sentence avoiding double negatives.

21. Doesn't no one play with pogo sticks anymore?
22. Haven't you never bounced on one?
23. There isn't nothing that's more fun.
24. I can't find none in the stores these days.
25. As a child, I wouldn't go nowhere without my pogo stick.

Using Adjectives and Adverbs   *pages 222–223*

E. Write the word in parentheses ( ) that correctly completes each sentence. Write *adverb* or *adjective* to identify it.

26. Dad's new convertible looks (beautiful, beautifully).
27. The car performs (beautiful, beautifully), too.
28. Of course, he's (real, really) happy to own it.
29. The engine certainly runs (smooth, smoothly).
30. Someone polished the car very (good, well).
31. Anyone would feel (comfortable, comfortably) in it.
32. The seat covers fit (perfect, perfectly), too.
33. The instruments are arranged (beautiful, beautifully).
34. The radio and tape deck sound (good, well), don't they?
35. Dad drives the car very (careful, carefully).

Context Clues   *pages 224–225*

F. Write *definition, further information, synonym,* or *antonym* to tell what kind of context clue is given for each underlined word.

36. As the snake crossed the floor, I <u>quavered</u> with fear.
37. It was no <u>benign</u> snake but rather a very dangerous one!
38. It was a <u>diamondback</u>, a deadly rattlesnake.
39. Its <u>venom</u>, or poison, could kill me in seconds.
40. Luckily, it crept outside through a <u>crevice</u> in the wall.

See also Handbook pages 374–375, 407.

Writing with Adverbs

- Use adverbs to add detail to your writing.

Read the sentences below.

1. Cal waited for the bus.
2. Cal waited impatiently for the bus.

Both of these sentences tell what Cal did. He waited for the bus. However, only sentence 2 tells *how* Cal waited for the bus—impatiently. By including just one adverb, sentence 2 is a much more interesting sentence. The adverb *impatiently* adds a very important detail.

Another adverb could completely change the picture of Cal waiting for the bus. Read the sentence below. Notice how the adverb changes the meaning of the sentence.

3. Cal waited calmly for the bus.

Cal might also have waited *nervously* or *excitedly*. Different adverbs create different sentences.

Using Adverbs   Below is a list of verbs you might use in your own writing. Choose one and write it. How many adverbs can you think of that might describe that verb? Take two minutes to write as many adverbs as you can for your verb.

sink	defeat	start
hope	tease	imagine
chase	escape	examine

How many adverbs appear on your list? Find a classmate who chose the same verb and compare your lists.

Now select a different verb from the list. Then write any adverbs that might describe this new verb.

Adding Adverbs   Read each sentence below. Think of adverbs that could describe the underlined verb. Then write the sentence twice, adding a different adverb each time.

EXAMPLE: Lorraine <u>approached</u> the snake.
ANSWER: Lorraine approached the snake carefully.
               Lorraine approached the snake carelessly.

1. Harold <u>opened</u> the mysterious package.
2. The skater <u>moved</u> across the ice.
3. The guide dog <u>led</u> Randolph down the street.
4. The bird <u>sang</u> from a nearby pine tree.
5. Grabbing the rope, Mindy <u>climbed</u> to the mountaintop.

Adverbs in Paragraphs   Use adverbs to complete the paragraph below. Write the paragraph.

The spectators watched _____ as the new plane rolled _____ onto the runway. The engines rumbled _____. The plane traveled _____ and _____ down the pavement. _____ it leaped into the sky and _____ disappeared. The spectators began to move away _____. Then the plane _____ reappeared in the sky. Its silver color gleamed _____. Its journey had begun.

Using the Thesaurus

Imagine you have performed well in your favorite sport. You want to write a paragraph describing your performance. To avoid overusing the adverb *well,* turn to the Thesaurus beginning on page 414. Use synonyms for *well* to write your paragraph.

Find the entry for the verb *understand* in the Thesaurus. Write a sentence for each synonym you find for *understand.* Try to use a different adverb with the synonym in each sentence. You will write six sentences.

7 — Choosing a Topic

> • Choose a report topic that interests you. Then narrow the topic to fit the size of your report.

Choosing a suitable topic is the first step in writing a good report. Here are some guidelines that will help you do this.

- Choose a topic that interests you and that you want to know more about. Writing the report will then be easier. Your interest will also help make your report more interesting.
- Choose a topic that is suitable for your audience, your readers. Consider the general interests and knowledge of the audience.
- Choose a topic that is narrow enough for the size of your report.

Jason first chose *space* as his topic. He liked to read about space, and he knew it was a topic that would interest many of his readers. However, *space* is too broad a topic for a short report. In order to narrow the topic, Jason made this diagram.

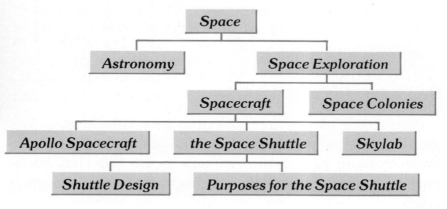

Jason finally decided on *purposes for the space shuttle* as his report topic. This topic was narrow enough to cover well in a three-paragraph report. However, it was not too narrow for his audience's knowledge and interests.

Skills Tryout

Tell which topic in each group is the narrowest.

1. coin collecting, hobbies, United States silver dollars
2. raising calves, agriculture, dairy farming
3. vegetables, foods, carrots
4. Saturn's ring, the solar system, planets
5. elementary school, kindergarten, education

Practice

A. Write the topics in each group in order from broadest to narrowest.

1. the backstroke, water sports, swimming
2. United States history, settling the West, the California gold rush
3. making cottage cheese, dairy products, cheeses
4. painting, art, oil painting
5. energy, solar power, solar heat collectors

B. Narrow each broad topic below to one that could be covered in a short report.

EXAMPLE: energy
ANSWER: new uses for windmills

6. sports
7. gardening
8. bicycles
9. TV shows
10. the ocean
11. famous athletes
12. airplanes
13. great artists
14. buildings
15. American government

Application USING STUDY SKILLS

Choose one of the broad topics in **Practice B**. Then make a diagram similar to the one on page 230 to narrow this topic step by step.

8 Using the Library

> • Books in a library are listed by title, author, and subject in a card catalog or computer listing.

The library is a storehouse of knowledge. No matter what topic you choose, you can learn more about it in the library. First, however, you need to know how to use the library.

Library books are divided into two main categories—fiction and nonfiction. Works of fiction, such as novels and short stories, are arranged alphabetically by the authors' last names. Nonfiction books give facts and are usually arranged numerically under the **Dewey Decimal System**. This system assigns a call number to each nonfiction book according to its subject. History books, for example, have numbers between 900 and 999.

To find the library books you want, use the card catalog or computer listing. These sources list every book in the library by title, author, and subject. Catalog cards are arranged alphabetically. Notice the information given on each kind of card.

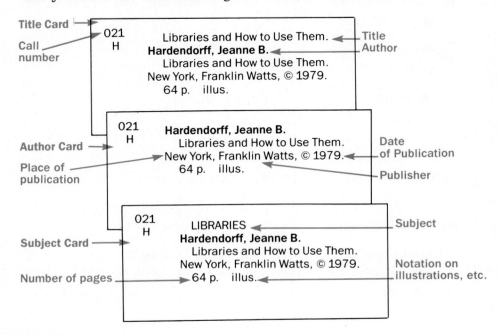

Skills Tryout

Use the catalog cards on page 232 to answer these questions.

1. What is the title of the book listed on the cards?
2. Who is the author of this book?
3. What is the book's call number?
4. In what year was the book published?
5. How many pages does the book have?

Practice

A. Write the word or words you would look up in the card catalog or computer listing to find the following items.

1. a book by Virginia Hamilton
2. the title of a book about figure skating
3. the call number of the book *The Reasons for Seasons*
4. the title of a book by Eleanor Estes
5. the call numbers of books about solar power

B. Write *title, author,* or *subject* to tell what kind of catalog card you would use to answer these questions.

6. What books by Scott O'Dell are in the library?
7. How many pages long is the book *Frozen Fire*?
8. Does the library have any books about opera?
9. Did the author of *Dragonwings* also write *The Summer of the Swan*?
10. What books for young readers has Ray Bradbury written?

Application USING STUDY SKILLS

Use the card catalog or computer listing in your library to answer the following questions. Write your answers.

a. What are the titles of two books by Robert Lawson?
b. What are the titles, authors, and call numbers of two non-fiction books on dogs. When was each one published?

Using an Encyclopedia

- Topics in an **encyclopedia** are arranged in alphabetical order.

An encyclopedia contains a great deal of information on a great many topics. Usually this information fills an entire set of books. Each book in an encyclopedia is called a volume.

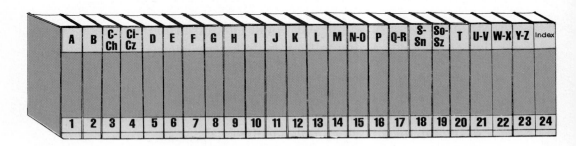

Look at the volumes of the encyclopedia above. The letter or letters on the spine of each volume tell you the beginning letters of the main topics in that volume. The topics are arranged in alphabetical order.

To find information in an encyclopedia, first determine the key word in the topic or in the question you want to answer. For example, *Florida* is the key word in the question *When did Florida become a state?* The letters on the encyclopedia's spine tell you that an article about Florida will be in Volume 7. Guide words at the top of each encyclopedia page will help you find the article you need. At the end of some encyclopedia articles, you will find cross-references. These are titles of other articles that give more information on the topic.

Notice that Volume 24 is labeled *Index.* The index lists all the topics in the encyclopedia in alphabetical order. It also gives the volume and page number where information on each topic can be found.

Skills Tryout

Identify the key words in these questions.

1. Do storks build nests on housetops?
2. What is the population of Ecuador?
3. Was Nathanael Greene an American general?

Practice

A. Write the key words in these questions.

1. Is Mount McKinley the highest peak in the United States?
2. What materials are used to make transistors?
3. Does Yale University have a medical school?
4. Is the vicuña a domestic animal?
5. Is quicksilver a metal?

B. Write the key words in the questions. Then write the numbers of the encyclopedia volumes in which you would look up the words. Use the illustration on page 234.

6. When did the Pueblo Indians build cliff houses?
7. What is the capital of Tennessee?
8. How are centrifuges used in hospitals?
9. Does a brig have two or three masts?
10. Did Charlie Chaplin compose music for his movies?
11. Which states make up the Corn Belt?
12. Do blueberries grow on vines?
13. Who wrote "The Star-Spangled Banner"?
14. Are chloroplasts found in the cells of all plants?
15. Did Hercules ever complete his twelve labors?

Application USING STUDY SKILLS

Choose a topic you want to know more about. Look up that topic in an encyclopedia index. List the volumes and page numbers where information on the topic can be found.

10 — Using Other Reference Materials

> ● **Atlases, almanacs, periodicals,** and the **Readers'
> Guide** are useful research tools.

The encyclopedia is the best place to begin research on almost any topic. If, however, you need the most up-to-date information on a subject, or if you need a detailed map, you will want to check other reference materials. Read the following descriptions of these materials. Then go to the library and become acquainted with them. Being familiar with these materials will enable you to quickly choose the research tool you need.

An atlas is a book of maps. Use it if you have a question about a place. Some maps show political boundaries. Some show physical features of the land. Others show roads, climate, or population.

An almanac is a book of interesting and useful facts from the past and present. Since it is published every year, it specializes in recent events and information. Here are just a few of the subjects an almanac covers: actors and actresses; aerospace; animals; telephone area codes and ZIP codes; this year's astronomy calendar; last year's important events; presidents, governors, mayors; laws; holidays; awards for books, films, music; United States history; sports.

Newspapers and magazines are periodicals. Use them to find the most current information. To find magazine articles on your topic, check the *Readers' Guide to Periodical Literature*. This is an index of articles from many magazines. The articles are listed alphabetically by subject and by the author's last name. The *Readers' Guide* tells you where to find the articles.

In addition, most libraries offer audiovisual materials, such as films, filmstrips, cassette tapes, records, videotapes, slides, and mounted pictures.

Skills Tryout

Tell what reference you would use to answer each question. Choose *atlas, almanac, periodical,* or *Readers' Guide.*

1. Who won last week's presidential election?
2. Where are Montana's national forests located?
3. Are there any recent magazine articles on sunspots?
4. Who was the fourth president of the United States?

Practice

Write the reference source you would use to answer each question. Choose *atlas, almanac, periodical,* or *Readers' Guide.*

1. Who is the mayor of Chicago?
2. What U.S. highway connects Houston and Dallas?
3. What recent magazines have articles on home computers?
4. What is the ZIP code for Wichita, Kansas?
5. What did the critics say about yesterday's TV special?
6. In what part of Alaska is Point Hope?
7. What is tomorrow's weather forecast?
8. Which issue of *Popular Science* discussed solar clocks?
9. In what year did the United States enter World War I?
10. What is the date of the next eclipse of the moon?
11. How large is California's Salton Sea?
12. Did Congress pass the new tax-cut bill?
13. What cities are on Florida's Tampa Bay?
14. Have any articles appeared recently about vitamin B_5?
15. On what day is Veterans Day celebrated?

Application LIFE SKILLS

Choose a foreign country you would like to visit. Use the almanac to prepare for a trip there. First see what facts it gives about the country. Next look under *Passport* to find out how to apply for one. Then look under *Customs, U.S.* to see what you can bring back without paying extra duty, or tax.

> ● The **title page, copyright page, table of contents,** and **index** give information about a book.

The main part of a book is called the body. However, books have other special parts that contain useful information. Study the descriptions of these parts below. Notice that some are in the front of a book and others are in the back.

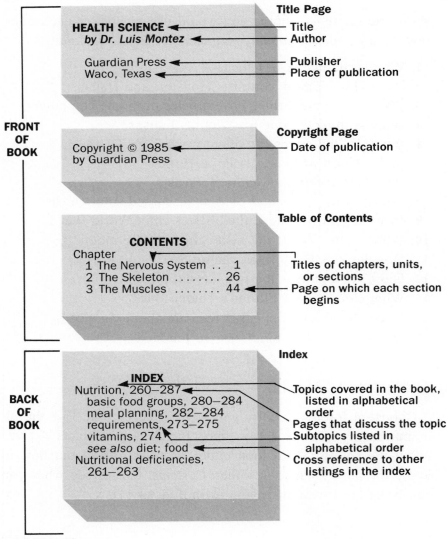

Title Page

HEALTH SCIENCE — Title
by Dr. Luis Montez — Author

Guardian Press — Publisher
Waco, Texas — Place of publication

Copyright Page

Copyright © 1985 — Date of publication
by Guardian Press

Table of Contents

CONTENTS
Chapter
  1 The Nervous System .. 1
  2 The Skeleton 26
  3 The Muscles 44

Titles of chapters, units, or sections
Page on which each section begins

Index

INDEX
Nutrition, 260–287
  basic food groups, 280–284
  meal planning, 282–284
  requirements, 273–275
  vitamins, 274
  see also diet; food
Nutritional deficiencies, 261–263

Topics covered in the book, listed in alphabetical order
Pages that discuss the topic
Subtopics listed in alphabetical order
Cross reference to other listings in the index

FRONT OF BOOK

BACK OF BOOK

Skills Tryout

Tell in what part of a book you would look to find the following information.

1. when the book was published
2. on what page Chapter 10 begins
3. whether the book has any information on the heart
4. the author of the book
5. the pages in the book that give information about vitamins

Practice

A. Write the part of a book in which you would look to answer each of these questions.

1. What company published the book?
2. Does the book have a chapter on nutrition?
3. Does the book tell who discovered how to prevent people from getting smallpox?
4. How up-to-date is the information in this book?
5. Which pages tell about the basic food groups?

B. Use the examples on page 238 to answer these questions.

6. On what page does the chapter "The Skeleton" begin?
7. Who wrote *Health Science*?
8. When was *Health Science* published?
9. On which pages would you find information on meal planning?
10. Under what other words in the index can you look to find information on nutrition?

Application   CRITICAL READING

Choose a nonfiction book from the library. Examine the parts of the book discussed in this lesson to get an overview of the book. Then write your opinion of the book's usefulness, based on what you learned from those parts of the book.

12 Taking Notes and Paraphrasing

- Use your own words when taking notes on what you read.

Carrie plans to write a report about alligators. In one library book, she found this background information.

Alligators hatch from eggs. During the dry season, a female alligator deposits twenty to fifty eggs in a three-foot-high mound of vegetation. The rotting vegetation warms the eggs, and after three months they are ready to hatch. Baby alligators are about nine inches long on hatching and grow about ten inches a year. At first they eat only insects. Later they catch fish and small animals.

To remember these facts, Carrie took notes. Notice that her notes follow the guidelines listed below.

Alligators hatch from eggs.
— Twenty to fifty eggs placed in a pile of vegetation.
— Eggs take 3 months to hatch.
— Babies are 9" long; grow 10" a year.
— Diet changes as they grow: insects-fish-animals.

The Big Book of Reptiles, Sylvia Woods, page 19.

How to Take Notes

- Write your notes on 3″ x 5″ index cards.
- State the main idea at the top of the card.
- List supporting details under it.
- Use key words or phrases or complete sentences.
- Do not copy information word for word. **Paraphrase,** or express the ideas you have read in your own words.
- Note the source in which you found the information—its title, author, and page numbers.

Skills Tryout

Restate each sentence in your own words.

1. Even day-old alligators are eager eaters.
2. Hunting insects is their main activity.
3. Newborn alligators follow their mother closely.
4. In a short time they are able to watch out for themselves.
5. Being eaten by a larger alligator is the most serious threat a young alligator faces.

Practice

A. Write these statements in your own words.

1. Marine turtles lead a peaceful existence in the sea.
2. In order to lay eggs, however, female turtles must struggle ashore.
3. The female scrapes away at the sand until her entire body is lying in a pit.
4. This activity usually takes place under cover of darkness.
5. After laying about one hundred eggs in the pit, the turtle fills it in and returns to the sea.

B. Read the paragraph below and take notes on it.

The time required for turtle eggs to hatch depends on the surrounding temperature. Usually it takes two to three months. The entire clutch, or group of eggs, hatch at once. Using their flippers, the babies scrape away at the sand until they lie just beneath the surface. They wait there until the temperature of the sand drops, indicating it is nighttime. Then they dig themselves free and hurry toward the sea.

Application USING STUDY SKILLS

Open your science or social studies textbook to the chapter you are currently studying. Use the rules on page 240 to take notes on one section of the chapter.

13 — Outlining

> ● An **outline** organizes material into main ideas and supporting ideas.

Mark plans to give a report on underground houses. To organize his notes, he made this outline.

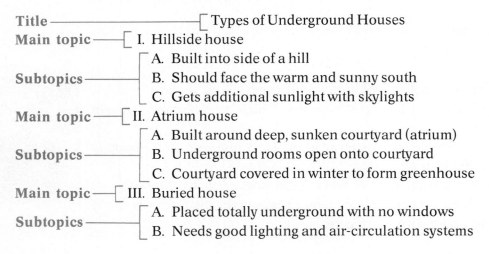

Title ——————————— Types of Underground Houses
Main topic —— I. Hillside house
Subtopics ——
　A. Built into side of a hill
　B. Should face the warm and sunny south
　C. Gets additional sunlight with skylights
Main topic —— II. Atrium house
Subtopics ——
　A. Built around deep, sunken courtyard (atrium)
　B. Underground rooms open onto courtyard
　C. Courtyard covered in winter to form greenhouse
Main topic —— III. Buried house
Subtopics ——
　A. Placed totally underground with no windows
　B. Needs good lighting and air-circulation systems

An outline is a simple and logical way to organize information before you write. Each main idea becomes a main topic of the outline. Main topics are indicated by Roman numerals. Each detail that supports a main idea becomes a subtopic. Subtopics are indicated by capital letters. These guidelines will help you write outlines.

How to Write an Outline

- Center the title of the outline at the top.
- Capitalize the first word of each topic or subtopic.
- Indent each subtopic.
- Place a period after each Roman numeral or letter.
- List at least two items under each element of the outline. That is, do not use a I. without a II. or an A. without a B.

Skills Tryout

Tell what words correctly complete each sentence.

1. A Roman numeral indicates a _____ in an outline.
2. A subtopic is indicated by a _____.
3. Each _____ is indented.
4. The first word of every topic and subtopic is _____.

Practice

A. Rewrite the outline below in the correct form. Then label each part *title, main topic,* or *subtopic.*

Advantages of an Underground House
I. economy
A. costs less to build
b. costs less to heat and cool
C. requires little maintenance
II. beauty and comfort
a. blends in with natural landscape
b. provides quieter, more private environment

B. Arrange the main topics and subtopics below into an outline entitled "Library Resources."

1. Title cards
2. Books in the library
3. The card catalog
4. Periodicals
5. Fiction
6. Author cards
7. Other major resources
8. Nonfiction
9. Nonprint materials
10. Subject cards

Application USING STUDY SKILLS

Read a short encyclopedia article on a topic that interests you. Arrange the main ideas and supporting ideas in outline form. Be sure to follow the guidelines on page 242 when writing your outline.

14 Giving Oral Reports

- Choose a topic appropriate for the audience.
- Outline your oral report on note cards.
- Use effective speaking techniques.

Oral reports and written reports are similar in many ways. For both you will need to choose an appropriate topic and do research. Careful note-taking and outlining are also necessary.

However, oral reports also differ from written reports. When you give an oral report, you face an audience directly. You must capture and hold this audience's attention. To do this, choose a topic that appeals to the interests and knowledge of your audience. Keep the audience's attention by presenting the report in a lively way. An amusing statement or unusual fact will make your report livelier. Charts and illustrations will add interest, too.

Since an oral report is spoken, there is no need to write it out word for word. Instead, outline the report on 3″ x 5″ note cards. Key words and phrases in the outline will remind you of the main ideas and details you want to tell about.

Look at the outline on the note cards below. Notice that the cards include directions to remind the speaker to show visual aids.

III. Heat, pressure, + gas cause volcanoes to erupt.
   A. Heat from core melts rocks in mantle.
     becomes steam.
     called magma.

II. Volcanoes are openings for Earth's surface.
   (Show chart w/cross section of Earth.)
   A. Earth's crust — 25 miles deep
     miles deep
     miles deep
     2 miles deep

I. Volcanoes inspire fear and awe.
   (Show photographs.)
   A. Mt. Vesuvius — 79 A.D. — Italy — buried city of Pompeii.

   B. Krakatoa — 1883 — East Indies — killed 36,000 people.

   C. Mt. St. Helens — 1980 — Washington State — caused $2.7 billion of damage!

Using your note cards, practice the oral report until you can give it smoothly and confidently. These rules will also help you.

- Speak loudly and clearly.
- Relax. Avoid nervous movements or laughter.
- Introduce the topic in an interesting way.
- Look directly at individuals in the audience.
- Follow your outline carefully.
- Conclude by summarizing your main points.

Skills Tryout

Tell whether each statement is true or false.

1. An oral report should be read word for word.
2. An oral report is outlined on note cards.
3. Charts and illustrations add interest to oral reports.

Practice

A. Choose and research a topic for an oral report. Organize your notes into an outline on 3″ x 5″ index cards. Find materials to illustrate your report.

B. Practice your oral report until you feel confident. Then, using the guidelines listed above, present the report to your class.

Application EVALUATING ORAL REPORTS

Make a checklist like the one below for each oral report you hear. Use it to rate the report and speaker.

Speaker: _____ Topic: _____	yes	no
Did the speaker		
get and hold audience's interest?		
speak loudly and clearly?		
organize information well?		
use illustrations?		

15 — Writing a Three-Paragraph Report

Writing Project

> • A **report** gives facts about a topic. It is based on research and is told in the writer's own words.

In school and perhaps later on in a job, you will be writing reports. People often ask for factual information, and writing a report is one way to present facts on a topic clearly and accurately. On the other hand, writing a report also helps you, the writer. You can learn a great deal about a topic that interests you. At the same time you can improve your research skills. Now you will have an opportunity to go through the steps of writing a three-paragraph report for your classmates to read.

1. Prewriting

▶ Before you write a report, you have some decisions to make. The first is: *What shall I write about?* To answer this question, ask yourself another: *What would I like to know more about?* Begin by thinking of general topics. Read the suggestions below and think of other topics with your classmates. Then choose one general topic for your report.

- computers
- a hobby or sport
- a foreign country
- health
- a famous person
- a historical event

Narrow your general topic by making a list of specific topics. Ask yourself these three questions about each specific topic and decide which topic you will write about.

Will my classmates be interested in this topic?
Can I tell about this topic in three paragraphs?
Can I find facts about it in books and periodicals?

▶ After you have a topic, you must decide what you will tell about it. What would you like to know about your topic? Write down questions you would like to find answers for.

▶ Begin your research with an encyclopedia. Does the encyclopedia article give facts that answer any of your questions? If so, take notes on 3″ x 5″ cards. Write the main idea at the top of the card and list interesting details under it. Be sure to use your own words when you take notes. Next locate books and use the *Readers' Guide to Periodical Literature* to locate magazine articles about your topic. Follow the same procedure to take notes as you read. Record each source you use—its title, author, and page numbers.

▶ Now use your notes to make an outline. Choose three of your main ideas, one for each paragraph in your report. Decide in what order you want to discuss them. Rewrite the main ideas as main topics in your outline, and label them *I*, *II*, and *III*. Then decide in what order you will present details telling about each of your main ideas. Write the details, or subtopics, below each main topic and label them *A*, *B*, *C*, and so on.

<u>Coin Collecting</u>
How can I start a coin collection?
What makes a coin valuable?
Which coins should I save?
How do I take care of the coins?
What are coin catalogs used for?

A coin's value is determined by three factors.
—condition
—demand
—scarcity

I. Starting a coin collection
   A. Check pocket change each day
   B. Check old clothes and furniture
   C. Buy rolls of coins from bank
   D. Save most valuable coins for each year
II. Determining value of coins
   A. Condition
   B. Scarcity
   C. Demand
III. Handling and storing coins
   A. Pick up by edges
   B. Do not clean
   C. Keep in envelopes or coin holders

2. Writing

▶Your report has been researched and well planned. Now follow your outline to write the first draft. Using the first main topic from your outline, write a topic sentence to begin the first paragraph. You might begin with a statement: "There are several ways to start your own coin collection." Your topic sentence might ask readers a question: "Have you ever thought about starting your own coin collection?" After you have written a topic sentence, add supporting sentences that give the facts you wrote as subtopics *A, B, C,* and so on.

Follow the same procedure to write the second and third paragraphs of your report. At the end of your report, list the sources you used. Then write an interesting and informative title.

3. Revising

▶Read your first draft aloud. Is it interesting? Is it clear? Ask another person to read it, too. See what suggestions your reader has as you discuss ways to improve your report. This checklist will also help you make revisions.

Revision Checklist

- Did I follow my outline?
- Does each paragraph begin with a topic sentence that states the main idea?
- Did I write supporting sentences for each topic sentence?
- Did I give facts in my own words?
- Did I add words that make my meaning clearer?

Read the sample report and notice how the first draft was improved by adding words that clarify the writer's meaning.

The easiest way to get started is to check your *pocket*
every day   *for coins*
change. Try looking in such places as old clothes or   *and*
furniture   *buy rolls of coins*
~~furnicher~~ or you can get them from banks, too.

You Can Be a Coin Collector

Have you ever thought about starting your own
coin collection? The easiest way to get started is to
check your pocket change every day. Try looking
for coins in old clothes and furniture. You can buy
rolls of coins from banks, too. From the coins you
collect, save the most valuable ones for each year.

A coin's value is determined by three factors—
its condition, its scarcity, and the demand for it.
Usually you can judge the condition of a coin. To
find out how rare a coin is and how much others
will pay for it, check a coin catalog in the library.

Special care must be taken in handling and
storing coins. Always pick them up by the edges and
touch them as little as possible. Never clean coins!
You may lessen their value. To protect your coins,
store each one in an envelope or in a coin holder.

▶ Now use the editing marks to make your revisions.

4. Publishing

▶ Proofread your report to be sure there are no errors. Use
the Proofreading Checklist in the Young Writer's Handbook
on page 399 and make corrections, using the editing marks.
Then hang your report on a classroom bulletin board and
invite your classmates to read it.

Writing Project

A Call Number Guide

A call number guide can help you become more familiar with the Dewey Decimal System. It will then be easier for you to locate nonfiction books in the library. Follow these directions for making a guide. (Your librarian can direct you to a source that shows the sections of the Dewey Decimal System.)

1. Divide a large sheet of poster board into forty-nine squares.
2. Place a call number, a heading, and a picture in each square. Use a picture from a magazine or draw your own.
3. Title the poster "Call Number Guide."
4. Place your poster where you and your classmates can see it and use it.

Science

As you prepared oral and written reports in this unit, you summarized information from various sources. That is, you selected the most important points and stated them in your own words. Summarizing can also be useful in other subjects. For example, in science you read material that contains many facts. How can you remember the important points from your reading? One of the best ways is to write a summary of it. Summarizing helps you find the main ideas in material that you read, and it aids in understanding and remembering it.

▶ Try it. Read this selection about the history of chemistry. Then summarize it. As you do, notice how summarizing forces you to think actively about what you read.

> **Early Times.** Long before chemistry became a science, people knew how to use various substances to make many things they needed. By the 2000's B.C., craftworkers of Egypt and Mesopotamia knew how to make weapons, tools, and ornaments from such metals as copper, gold, and silver. They made bronze by melting copper and tin together, and they prepared special substances to make glass beads and figures. Craftworkers also learned how to make perfume and wine. People could make these products because they could produce and control chemical changes. But they did not understand why these changes took place.

Writers at Work Chemists experiment with chemicals and then report their observations and conclusions.

▶ Try it. Do one of these experiments. Report what happens.

1. Mix vinegar and baking soda together.
2. Mix ¼ cup of salt, ¼ cup of water, ¼ cup of household bluing, and 1 tablespoon of ammonia. Pour over a charcoal briquette in a glass bowl. Observe it the next day.

Adverbs and Adjectives *pages 214–223*

A. Write each sentence. Underline each adverb.

1. Yesterday we took a trip to the aquarium.
2. We saw many types of fascinating ocean creatures there.
3. A large octopus moved slowly around the tank.
4. The sea urchins were completely covered with sharp spines.

B. Write the word each underlined adverb describes. Then write whether the word is a *verb*, an *adjective*, or an *adverb*.

5. The art classes <u>always</u> display their work at the library.
6. The most recent exhibit opened <u>there</u> last week.
7. Mr. Phillipi selected the drawings <u>very</u> carefully.
8. He is <u>quite</u> proud of his students' work.

C. Write the comparative and superlative form of each adverb.

9. smoothly	**11.** low	**13.** badly	**15.** sweetly
10. well	**12.** roughly	**14.** politely	**16.** late

D. Write the word in parentheses ( ) that correctly completes each sentence. Avoid double negatives.

17. Don't (ever, never) go swimming right after a meal.
18. Tim doesn't know (nothing, anything) about carpentry.
19. Why can't (someone, no one) answer the telephone?
20. My stomach isn't growling (no, any) more.

E. Write the word that correctly completes each sentence.

21. The orchestra played (magnificent, magnificently).
22. The musicians were in (good, well) form.
23. That violin solo was (beautiful, beautifully).
24. I listened (close, closely) to the chirping flute.
25. Everyone clapped (loud, loudly) at the end of the concert.

Context Clues   *pages 224–225*

F. Write *definition, further information, synonym,* or *antonym* to tell which kind of context clue is given for each underlined word.

26. Lee's <u>incredulous</u> look showed that he didn't believe us.
27. The desert is the natural <u>habitat</u>, or home, of the cactus.
28. The arrowhead that Maria found was <u>authentic</u>, not fake.
29. Zebras live on <u>savannahs</u>. Savannahs are grassy plains.

Library   *pages 232–233*

G. Write *title, author,* or *subject* to tell what kind of catalog card you would use to answer each question.

30. In what year was *The Secret Garden* published?
31. Does the library have any books about meteors?
32. What books by Charles Dickens are in the library?

Reference Materials   *pages 236–237*

H. Write whether you would choose an *atlas, almanac, periodical,* or *The Readers' Guide* to answer each question.

33. What countries share a border with Austria?
34. What happened at the President's press conference today?
35. What recent magazines have articles about space launches?
36. Who is the mayor of Atlanta, Georgia?

Reports   *pages 240–241*

I. In your own words, take notes on the encyclopedia entry below. Write the main idea. Then write a list of details.

CHAMELEON, a lizard known for changing its skin color. A chameleon is usually brown and gray-green. Its skin color is affected by sunlight, emotions, and temperature changes.

See also Handbook pages 374–377.

Sentences   *pages 10–15*

A. Write each complete subject. Underline each simple subject.

1. The new city library opened on Saturday afternoon.
2. The mayor delivered a speech on the library steps.
3. A local artist presented a sculpture for the front lawn.
4. Crowds of people attended the opening ceremony.

B. Write each complete predicate. Underline each simple predicate.

5. Gary is taking skating lessons at the community rink.
6. He enjoys skating more than any other sport.
7. Gary's lessons are difficult but fun.
8. His instructor has taught him some exciting jumps.

Nouns and Pronouns   *pages 50–53, 132–139*

C. Write the nouns in each sentence. Then write whether each noun names a *person, place, thing,* or *idea.*

9. A skydiver needs courage.
10. The bus drove into town.
11. My sister told the truth.
12. Lianne watered her plant.

D. Write whether each noun is *common* or *proper.*

13. holiday   14. Japan   15. cotton   16. April

E. Write the correct pronoun in parentheses ( ).

17. (My, Mine) family had a reunion last summer.
18. (We, Us) gathered at a nearby state park.
19. My mother introduced (I, me) to my cousin Daniel.
20. Uncle Thomas and (he, him) resemble my grandfather.
21. A newspaper reporter interviewed (we, us).
22. Other families have reunions like (our, ours).

Verbs *pages 92–93, 98–103*

F. Write each sentence. Underline the helping verbs once and the main verbs twice.

23. Bob may ride his bicycle. 25. You might enjoy this book.
24. The sun is shining today. 26. Kim does not know Janice.

G. Write the three principal parts of each verb. Use the helping verb *has* with each past participle.

27. say 28. choose 29. swim 30. walk

Adjectives and Adverbs *pages 182–189, 214–215, 218–219*

H. Write each sentence. Underline the demonstrative adjectives once. Underline the predicate adjectives twice.

31. This photograph album is full of old pictures.
32. My grandmother was young in these photographs.
33. In that snapshot she looks mischievous.
34. Grandfather Jonas seems serious in most of these pictures.

I. Write the comparative and superlative forms of each adjective.

35. neat 36. interesting 37. good 38. sturdy

J. Write the word each underlined adverb describes. Then write whether the word is a *verb*, an *adjective*, or an *adverb*.

39. Nathan slept <u>soundly</u> under several layers of covers.
40. <u>Quite</u> suddenly the alarm clock by his bed rang.
41. Nathan dreamed he was trapped inside a <u>very</u> large bell.
42. He stuffed a pillow over his ears and <u>loudly</u> groaned.

K. Write the comparative and superlative form of each adverb.

43. carefully 44. well 45. nicely 46. high

Grammar
Conjunctions and Prepositions

Composition
Reasoning

Shells

The bones of the sea
are on the shore,
shells
curled into the sand,
shells
caught in green weed hair.
All day I gather them
and there are always
more.

I take them home,
magic bones of the sea,
and when
I touch one,
then I hear
I taste
I smell the sea
again.

—*Lilian Moore*

1 Conjunctions

> ● A **conjunction** joins words or groups of words.

The words *and*, *but*, and *or* are conjunctions. In sentences these conjunctions can join nouns, pronouns, verbs, adjectives, or adverbs.

Examples of Conjunctions	
noun + noun	<u>Americans</u> <u>and</u> <u>Canadians</u> celebrate Arbor Day.
pronoun + pronoun	<u>She</u> <u>and</u> <u>I</u> always look forward to that holiday.
verb + verb	Schoolchildren <u>plant</u> <u>or</u> <u>tend</u> trees on Arbor Day.
adjective + adjective	Trees are both <u>beautiful</u> <u>and</u> <u>necessary</u>.
adverb + adverb	Young trees grow <u>slowly</u> <u>but</u> <u>surely</u>.

Conjunctions can also join groups of words.

People <u>have celebrated</u> <u>and</u> <u>will celebrate</u> Arbor Day for many years.
We planted <u>a maple tree</u> <u>and</u> <u>a red oak</u>.

Skills Tryout

Name the conjunction in each sentence.

1. Many states celebrate Arbor Day in March or April.
2. Some southern states and Hawaii celebrate it earlier.
3. Planting a tree is hard but satisfying work.
4. Arbor Day began and grew popular in Nebraska.
5. The once treeless but fertile prairies in Nebraska were called The Great American Desert.

Practice

A. Write each sentence. Underline each conjunction.

1. J. Sterling Morton spoke and wrote about the need for trees on the prairies of Nebraska.
2. He wanted every Nebraskan, young or old, to plant trees.
3. Eventually Nebraska's lawmakers introduced and passed a law making April 10, 1872, the first Arbor Day.
4. *Arbor* is a Latin word meaning "tree or shrub."
5. Prizes were given to persons and groups for planting trees.
6. A million or more trees were planted that first Arbor Day.
7. People were excited but uncertain about the trees.
8. Fortunately the trees lived and thrived!
9. By 1888 Nebraskans had planted 350 million trees and shrubs.
10. Other states and countries followed Nebraska's lead.

B. Write the conjunction in each sentence. Then write *nouns*, *pronouns*, *verbs*, *adjectives*, or *adverbs* to show what kind of words are joined.

11. More and more people now recognize the value of trees.
12. They appreciate and encourage planting trees.
13. Connecticut celebrates Arbor Day in spring and fall.
14. Some trees should be planted or transplanted only in fall.
15. This tree is small but healthy.
16. Birds live happily and well in trees.
17. Trees are important for them and us.
18. Trees provide people with food and lumber.
19. Can you think of a yard or park that needs a tree?
20. Why not plant and care for one this Arbor Day?

Application WRITING SENTENCES

Write six sentences about a holiday that you especially enjoy. Tell what you do on this holiday. Use the conjunctions *and*, *or*, and *but* at least once in your sentences.

2 — Prepositions

> ● A **preposition** relates a noun or pronoun to another word in the sentence.

In the sentence below, the underlined word is a preposition.

Europe is a continent <u>with a dense population.</u>

The preposition *with* relates the noun *population* to the word *continent*. The noun or pronoun that follows a preposition is the **object of the preposition**. In the sentence, *population* is the object of the preposition *with*.

A preposition, its object, and any words that describe the object make up a **prepositional phrase**. In the sentence above, the prepositional phrase is shaded in blue.

Forty Common Prepositions				
about	before	during	off	to
above	behind	for	on	toward
across	below	from	out	under
after	beneath	in	outside	until
against	beside	inside	over	up
along	beyond	into	past	upon
around	by	near	through	with
at	down	of	throughout	without

Skills Tryout

Name the prepositional phrase in each sentence.

1. Europe is a continent of large peninsulas.
2. Greece is located on the Balkan Peninsula.
3. Italy is a boot-shaped peninsula in the Mediterranean Sea.
4. Spain covers a large part of the Iberian Peninsula.
5. Norway shares a peninsula with Sweden.

Practice

A. Write each sentence. Underline each prepositional phrase.

1. Southern Europe's peninsulas are crossed by mountains.
2. The Pyrenees run along the Iberian Peninsula's base.
3. The Balkan Mountains cover much of the Balkan Peninsula.
4. The Alps stand at Italy's northern border.
5. The Alps rise more than 13,000 feet above sea level.
6. High in the Alps four important rivers begin.
7. The Rhine River flows north to the North Sea.
8. The Danube empties into the Black Sea.
9. The Rhone flows south through France.
10. The Po River flows east across northern Italy.

B. Write the prepositional phrase in each sentence. Underline the preposition once and the object of the preposition twice.

EXAMPLE: Forests once covered most of this continent.
ANSWER: of this continent

11. Europeans have changed their land greatly over the years.
12. They have drained swamps and cleared forests for farms.
13. Rich farmland can be found throughout Europe.
14. Much coal and iron ore lie beneath European soil.
15. Oil deposits can be found under the choppy North Sea.
16. Europeans have built great cities with their resources.
17. Ships travel across many nations using canals and rivers.
18. Fine roads and tunnels carry people past high mountains.
19. Large industries contribute to the European life-style.
20. Europe's universities are admired around the entire world.

Application WRITING SENTENCES

Write eight sentences about a real or imaginary country you would like to visit. Tell about the country's people, land, or climate. Use a prepositional phrase in each sentence. Underline the prepositional phrases.

3 Prepositional Phrases as Adjectives

> • A prepositional phrase that describes a noun or pronoun is an **adjective phrase**.

You know that an adjective describes a noun or pronoun by telling *What kind? How many?* or *Which one?* A prepositional phrase can also describe a noun or pronoun. Such prepositional phrases are called adjective phrases.

The same word can be described by an adjective or by an adjective phrase.

Adjective	Adjective Phrase
the <u>African</u> continent	the continent <u>of Africa</u>
a <u>desert</u> country	a country <u>in the desert</u>

Adjective phrases can describe nouns and pronouns in different parts of a sentence. Look at the sentences below. In sentence 1 the adjective phrase describes the subject. In sentence 2 it describes the predicate nominative. In sentence 3 it describes the direct object.

1. The people <u>of Africa</u> have many different life-styles.

2. Africa is a continent <u>with rich resources</u>.

3. Every African country has cities <u>with modern buildings</u>.

Skills Tryout

Name the adjective phrase in each sentence.

1. Africa has a great variety of wildlife.
2. Educational opportunities for Africans are increasing.
3. Africa is a continent of many different languages.
4. Occupations in agriculture are most common.
5. Some African countries have deposits of precious stones.

Practice

A. Write each sentence. Underline each adjective phrase.

1. The Sahara is the largest desert in the world.
2. This African desert is the size of the United States.
3. The other two thirds of the continent is a high plateau.
4. Much land on this plateau is savanna, or grassland.
5. Mountains with high peaks are also found there.
6. Mount Kilimanjaro is higher than any mountain in Europe.
7. Africa also has large forests with rainy climates.
8. The longest river in the world is Africa's Nile River.
9. The length of this river is more than 4,000 miles.
10. The Congo and the Niger are rivers with many waterfalls.

B. Write the adjective phrase in each sentence. Then write the noun the phrase describes.

EXAMPLE: Parts of Africa have valuable mineral deposits.
ANSWER: of Africa, Parts

11. Much soil in Africa is not rich.
12. The savannas, however, produce good harvests of grain.
13. Farmers on the savannas raise cattle and sheep.
14. Africans have cleared much land in the rain forests.
15. Forests throughout Africa produce coconuts and cacao.
16. Cacao is the main ingredient of chocolate.
17. Rubber for tires is another forest crop.
18. Africa also produces a large amount of coffee.
19. Sisal, a plant with strong fibers, grows well.
20. Sisal is used to make rope of all kinds.

Application WRITING SENTENCES

Using an encyclopedia or other reference book, write eight sentences about one country in Africa. Include information about the country's geography, resources, and people. Use at least four adjective phrases in your sentences.

4 — **Prepositional Phrases as Adverbs**

> ● A prepositional phrase that describes a verb, an adjective, or an adverb is an **adverb phrase**.

Prepositional phrases can work like adverbs in sentences.

1. Mr. Kelso planned his trip for weeks. (describes a verb)

2. He was ready by early June. (describes an adjective)

3. He returned late in July. (describes an adverb)

The underlined words in the sentences above are adverb phrases. In sentence 1 the phrase describes the verb *planned.* In sentence 2 it describes the adjective *ready.* In sentence 3 it describes the adverb *late.* Like adverbs, adverb phrases answer the questions *How? When? Where?* and *To what extent?*

Some words, such as *around, out, up, near,* and *by,* can be either prepositions or adverbs.

> Mr. Kelso traveled <u>around</u>. (adverb)
> Mr. Kelso traveled <u>around</u> Asia. (preposition)

If you aren't sure whether a word is an adverb or preposition, look at how it is used. A preposition begins a phrase and always has an object. An adverb does not have an object. It is used alone.

Skills Tryout

Name the adverb phrase in each sentence.

1. Asia's northernmost parts lie in the frozen Arctic.
2. Southern Asia ends near the equator.
3. Mr. Kelso flew to China first.
4. He arrived on a Tuesday.
5. He toured Peking, China's capital, with great interest.

Practice

A. Write each sentence. Underline each adverb phrase.

1. Forty-one countries are located in Asia.
2. Mr. Kelso could not go to all forty-one.
3. He did reach the Himalayas by July, though.
4. These mountains lie in central Asia.
5. Mount Everest, the world's highest mountain, is in the Himalayas.
6. The Indian peninsula stretches into the Indian Ocean.
7. Mr. Kelso toured India for several weeks.
8. He traveled down the Ganges River.
9. Many people live and farm along this river.
10. The Ganges flows into the Bay of Bengal.

B. Write the adverb phrase in each sentence. Then write the word the phrase describes.

11. Mr. Kelso also visited Indonesia on his trip.
12. The Indonesian islands lie near Malaysia.
13. They stretch along the equator.
14. Mr. Kelso was soon ready for more travel.
15. He reached Pakistan in a short time.
16. This rugged country lies in southwest Asia.
17. Finally, he flew over Iran and Iraq.
18. Even those countries are within Asia's boundaries.
19. Mr. Kelso is eager for his next trip.
20. Then he will travel early in the spring.

Application WRITING SENTENCES

Imagine that you are climbing Mount Everest, the highest mountain in the world. Write six sentences that tell about the difficulties you might encounter. Use at least three adverb phrases in your sentences.

5 Using Prepositional Phrases

> ● Use prepositional phrases carefully.

When you use a pronoun as the object of a preposition, always use an object pronoun. The object pronouns are *me, you, her, him, it, us,* and *them.* Be especially careful when the object of the preposition is made up of a noun and a pronoun.

> **My family flew to Australia with me.**
> **The Australians were friendly to my parents and me.**

People sometimes confuse the prepositions *between* and *among.* Use *between* when you refer to two persons or things. Use *among* when you refer to three or more persons or things.

> **We chose between Australia and New Zealand.**
> **We divided our time among four Australian cities.**

A prepositional phrase can be part of a sentence with **inverted word order**. In a sentence with inverted word order, the complete predicate comes before the complete subject. Notice the position of the prepositional phrases below.

Normal Word Order: Many sheep live in Australia.
Inverted Word Order: In Australia live many sheep.

Skills Tryout

Name the word that correctly completes each sentence.

1. There are many similarities (among, between) Australia, the United States, and Canada.
2. Mother went to Canberra with Father and (I, me).
3. Canberra is (among, between) Sydney and Melbourne.
4. The city will be interesting for you and (he, him).
5. The land (among, between) the Pacific Ocean and the Great Dividing Mountains gets the most rain in Australia.

Practice

A. Write the word in parentheses ( ) that correctly completes each sentence.

1. "Much of Australia was claimed by England in 1770," Mother explained to Father and (I, me).
2. "James Cook explored it," I said to Father and (she, her).
3. "The New South Wales region was named by (he, him)."
4. Father pointed out to (we, us) that the first Australian settlement was a prison colony.
5. England had sent (among, between) 160,000 and 170,000 convicts to the country by 1868.
6. There are many farms (among, between) Australia's coast and inland deserts.
7. Today Australia is (among, between) the world's four greatest producers of wheat and beef.
8. (Among, Between) all wool producers, it is ranked first.
9. Differences (among, between) city life and country life in Australia are relatively few.
10. Over half of the country's population is divided (among, between) the six state capitals.

B. Write each sentence with inverted word order in regular word order. Write each regular sentence in inverted order.

11. From the Latin word for "southern" comes the name *Australia*.
12. In Australia work many iron, bauxite, and nickel miners.
13. The Great Barrier Reef lies off the northeastern coast.
14. Kangaroos and bandicoots wander across the interior.
15. In rural areas live most of the Aborigines.

Application WRITING SENTENCES

Kangaroos and koala bears are two animals found in Australia. Write six sentences about either of these animals. Use *between* and *among* correctly in two of your sentences.

Parts of Speech Summary

> ● A **part of speech** tells how a word is used in a sentence.

The chart below shows the seven parts of speech you have learned. It also shows the eighth part—the **interjection**.

Part of Speech	Definition and Examples
1. noun	A noun names a person, place, thing, or idea. girl Chicago hat mercy
2. verb	A verb expresses action or being. run helps walked am become
3. pronoun	A pronoun takes the place of a noun or nouns. he her mine your them
4. adjective	An adjective describes a noun or pronoun. happy short twenty this
5. adverb	An adverb describes a verb, an adjective, or another adverb. happily now here
6. conjunction	A conjunction joins words or groups of words. and or but
7. preposition	A preposition relates a noun or pronoun to another word in the sentence. by on in
8. interjection	An interjection expresses feeling or emotion. Use an exclamation mark after an interjection. Hooray! Wow! Aha!

Skills Tryout

Name the interjection in each sentence.

1. Ugh! Look at this mess!
2. Whew! We're finally done!
3. Ouch! That's hot!
4. Ah! Here they are!

Practice

A. Write each interjection below.

    1. Oh! Look at these pictures of imaginary animals!
    2. Hooray! Here is a picture of a griffin.
    3. Aha! It's half lion, half eagle, and very beautiful!
    4. Eek! What's coming out of that fire?
    5. Wow! It is a phoenix, of course.

B. Two words are underlined in each sentence. Write the part of speech of each underlined word.

    EXAMPLE: The phoenix <u>rises</u> from its own <u>ashes</u>.
    ANSWER: verb, noun

    6. This <u>awful</u> <u>creature</u> is the Hydra.
    7. <u>It</u> had at least 100 <u>heads</u>.
    8. Many <u>heroes</u> tried to kill the <u>Hydra</u>.
    9. <u>They</u> <u>attempted</u> to cut off its heads.
    10. However, two new heads <u>quickly</u> <u>replaced</u> each lost head.
    11. The Leucrocotta was an imaginary animal <u>from</u> <u>India</u>.
    12. It had the tail <u>and</u> chest <u>of</u> a lion.
    13. <u>Ugh</u>! Its head looked like a <u>beaver's</u>, and its mouth went from ear to ear.
    14. People thought it could <u>imitate</u> the human <u>voice</u>.
    15. I'm <u>really</u> glad there aren't any around <u>now</u>!
    16. The unicorn <u>is</u> my favorite <u>imaginary</u> animal.
    17. It <u>looks</u> much like a <u>white</u> pony.
    18. However, it <u>has</u> a magical horn on <u>its</u> head.
    19. The black-and-white <u>horn</u> ends in a red <u>tip</u>.
    20. People <u>hunted</u> the unicorn <u>for</u> its magical horn.

Application WRITING SENTENCES

    Write eight sentences about a creature you would like to create. Tell what the creature would look like and what powers it would have. Use each of the eight parts of speech.

7 — Idioms

> ● An **idiom** is a combination of words that has a meaning different from the meaning of its separate words.

Have you ever heard the underlined idiom in this sentence?

Mike passed spelling <u>by the skin of his teeth</u>.

You know what the words *skin* and *teeth* mean. However, since teeth have no real skin on them, this idiom means "by very little" or "by hardly anything."

The underlined prepositional phrases in the paragraph below are idioms. How many are you familiar with?

Mike wished to do well in spelling, but the rules went <u>in one ear and out the other</u>. He knew <u>in his bones</u> he wouldn't do well, and it was getting <u>on his nerves</u>. Mike was <u>on his toes</u> in other subjects, but he started spelling <u>on the wrong foot</u>. Others could spell <u>without batting an eye</u>. He needed a dictionary <u>at his fingertips</u>.

An idiom does not have to be a prepositional phrase. It can be any combination of the different parts of speech. If you are unsure of the meaning of an idiom, use a dictionary.

Skills Tryout

Name the word or phrase from the list below that could be used in place of the underlined idiom in each sentence.

trouble   by very much   respected   be proud   energetic

1. Mike was ahead of his class in math <u>by a mile</u>.
2. Everyone <u>looked up to</u> him in science.
3. Mike could <u>hold his head high</u> in social studies, too.
4. In gym he was <u>a ball of fire</u>.
5. Only in spelling was he in <u>hot water</u>.

Practice

A. Write the word from the list below that could be used in place of the underlined idiom in each sentence.

great	help	nervousness	hope	difficult
read	worried	change	continued	completely

1. Mike was <u>shaken up</u> by his problems with spelling.
2. So he decided to <u>turn over a new leaf</u>.
3. Every night he <u>stuck his nose in</u> his spelling book.
4. It was <u>rough sledding</u> at first.
5. Week after week Mike <u>stuck with</u> his work.
6. At last there was <u>light at the end of the tunnel</u>.
7. In time his spelling problems disappeared <u>into thin air</u>.
8. He could even <u>lend a hand to</u> others.
9. Now during spelling tests Mike doesn't have any <u>butterflies in his stomach</u>.
10. Instead, he feels <u>like a million</u>.

B. Write the meaning of each idiom. Use a dictionary if you need help.

11. keep an eye on
12. hit the road
13. take the cake
14. hit the roof
15. out of this world
16. a shot in the dark
17. a change of heart
18. walk on air
19. be on pins and needles
20. run across an old friend

Application USING LANGUAGE

List six idioms that you use or hear often. Choose idioms that were not included in this lesson. Write a definition for each idiom. Then use each idiom in a sentence.

Conjunctions *pages 258–259*

A. Write the conjunction in each sentence. Then write *nouns,* *pronouns, verbs, adjectives,* or *adverbs* to show what kind of words are joined.

1. The room was large but comfortable.
2. The many guests talked and laughed loudly.
3. A small but lively fire blazed in the fireplace.
4. A dog and cat slept before the fire.
5. A woman at the piano played a piece by Bach or Mozart.
6. A huge stuffed marlin or sailfish was mounted on the wall.
7. Loudly and excitedly the host described his fishing trip with his friends.
8. It was thrilling for him and them.
9. Everyone had a chance to talk to the host sooner or later.
10. They all thanked him for the lovely and interesting party.

Prepositions *pages 260–261*

B. Write the prepositional phrase in each sentence. Underline the preposition once and the object of the preposition twice.

11. Walruses live in cold waters.
12. They usually travel in herds.
13. A walrus's tusks grow from its upper jaw.
14. The walrus defends itself with its tusks.
15. Walruses also have thick bristles above their upper jaw.
16. A walrus baby, or calf, rides on its mother's back.
17. When a mother first dives beneath the surface, a calf often sputters or chokes a bit.
18. However, it soon swims well under the frozen seas.
19. Walruses sometimes come to shore, but they prefer the sea.
20. The name *walrus* comes from a Dutch word that means "whale horse."

Prepositional Phrases as Adjectives and Adverbs *pages 262–265*

C. Write the prepositional phrase in each sentence. Then write *adjective* if it describes a noun or pronoun. Write *adverb* if it describes a verb, an adjective, or an adverb.

21. Tigers hunt with great patience.
22. A tiger will sometimes watch its prey for hours.
23. Tigers of all types are solitary creatures.
24. They rarely share their food with others.
25. They are also protective of their territory.
26. Tigers in frigid Siberia grow bushy coats.
27. The United States has banned the sale of tiger skins.
28. Many nations of the world have made tiger hunting illegal.
29. The tiger population increases in special preserves.
30. Tigers can roam there without fear.

Using Prepositional Phrases *pages 266–267*

D. Write the words that correctly complete the sentences.

31. I split the money (among, between) Matt and Eliot.
32. "You can't divide one banana (among, between) the whole class," I said to Mr. McGillicuddy and (he, him).
33. The ball is (among, between) the two oak trees.
34. I shared the popcorn with Susan and (they, them).
35. There was a fight (among, between) Sue and (she, her).

Interjections *pages 268–269*

E. Write the sentences. Punctuate the interjections correctly.

36. Bravo You passed the spelling test.
37. Ouch These shoes are too tight.
38. Whee This sled is really fun.
39. Whoops I didn't see that banana peel.
40. Eek What is that on your shoulder?

See also Handbook pages 378–379.

Grammar Review

Sentence Combining

- Sentences that describe the same thing can often be combined.

Grammar and Writing Workshop

Read the sentences below.

A. Dinosaurs roamed the earth millions of years ago.
B. The dinosaurs were <u>enormous</u>.
A + B. Enormous dinosaurs roamed the earth millions of years ago.

Both sentence **A** and sentence **B** tell something about dinosaurs. However, sentence **B** adds only the information that the dinosaurs are enormous. Sentence **A + B** tells everything that the two separate sentences did by adding the adjective *enormous*.

Now read these sentences.

C. Some dinosaurs devoured plants.
D. The dinosaurs devoured <u>constantly</u>.
C + D. Some dinosaurs constantly devoured plants.

Sentence **D** only tells *how* dinosaurs ate plants. This information can be combined with sentence **C** to make sentence **C + D**. Sentence **C + D** includes the adverb *constantly*.

Sometimes a prepositional phrase in one sentence may describe a word in another sentence.

E. Our local library has many exciting books.
F. The books are <u>about dinosaurs</u>.
E + F. Our local library has many exciting books about dinosaurs.

G. The books must be returned.
H. They must be returned <u>in two weeks</u>.
G + H. The books must be returned in two weeks.

Now combine the sentences on the next page. Use the underlined words the way they are used in the examples above.

Using Clues Combine the following sentences. Use the underlined clues the way they were used on page 274. Write each new sentence that results.

1. Scientists learn about dinosaurs by studying bones.
   The bones are <u>ancient</u>.
2. No one knows why the dinosaurs disappeared.
   The dinosaurs disappeared <u>suddenly</u>.
3. Perhaps the earth's climate changed.
   It changed <u>over a period of many years</u>.
4. The dinosaurs might have been destroyed by a meteor.
   The meteor was <u>from beyond our planet</u>.
5. Maria delivered a long speech.
   The speech was <u>about these amazing creatures</u>.
6. Many movies have been made.
   The movies are <u>about dinosaurs</u>.

Using No Clues Combine each pair of sentences without clues. Think how the sentences can be combined by adding adjectives, adverbs, or prepositional phrases to one sentence. Write the new sentence that results.

7. Two dinosaurs met on a vast plain.
   The dinosaurs were prehistoric.
8. The dinosaurs battled over a piece of food.
   They battled furiously.
9. The weaker dinosaur was defeated.
   It was defeated after many hours.
10. The dinosaur's body was buried.
    It was buried by a mudslide.
11. The bones can now be seen at an exhibit.
    The exhibit is in our neighborhood.
12. Many museums in the United States have wonderful exhibits.
    They are about dinosaurs.

8 — Writing Directions

> • When writing directions, be specific and use directional words.

> 9-14 C Palm Terrace
> Daytona Beach, FL 32018
> February 10, 1986
>
> Dear Patty,
>   I'm so glad you and your family will be able to visit us next month.
>   Getting to Palm Terrace is easy. Take Route 92 South from Jacksonville. Get off at the exit that says "Daytona Beach." Turn right onto Main Street at the first stoplight. Main Street will cross Peninsula Bridge. After you cross the bridge, turn left onto Peninsula Drive. Stay straight on Peninsula Drive for two miles. Then turn left onto Palm Terrace. Our building, number nine, is at the back of the apartment complex. You can park in front of the building. Go up to the fourteenth floor. Our apartment is at the end of the hall.
>
>   See you soon!
>
>   Your pen pal,
>   Dana

For directions to be understood and followed, they must be clearly written. Read the directions Dana wrote for her pen pal.

Follow these rules when writing directions.

- State the starting point at the beginning of the directions.
- Use directional words such as *south, right, left, across, straight, back, front, up,* and *end.*
- Include names of streets, bridges, and other landmarks.
- Give house or building numbers.

Skills Tryout

Write directions that tell Patty and her family how to get back to Route 92 from Dana's building on Palm Terrace.

Practice

A. Study the following map of Scranton, Pennsylvania. Then write directions that would help a person get from Center Theater on Center Avenue to Moses Taylor Hospital on Gibson Street.

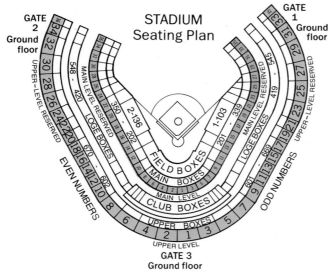

B. Write directions that tell how to get to your home from the nearest public library.

Application LIFE SKILLS

Study this seating plan of a baseball stadium. Then write directions that explain how to get from Gate 2 to Box 19 in the upper-level reserved section. You may make up information about stairs, souvenir stands, and food vendors. Remember to include directional words.

9 Recognizing Propaganda Techniques

> ● **Propaganda** is an organized effort to spread ideas about a person, product, or cause.

Propaganda is used to sway people's thinking. Advertisers often use it to persuade the public to buy certain products. Many political campaigners use propaganda to convince voters to choose certain candidates. Sometimes propaganda gives accurate information. Often it does not. Therefore, it is important that you recognize propaganda techniques in the advertisements and speeches you hear.

Here are three common propaganda techniques. Each appeals to people's emotions rather than to their ability to reason.

The **bandwagon** technique suggests that you will be happier if you "hop on the bandwagon" with everyone else. Propagandists who use this technique believe that people would rather go along with the group than think for themselves.

Nine out of ten people have switched to Zippy vitamins. Isn't it time you made the switch, too?

Another propaganda technique based on the idea that people do not think for themselves is the **testimonial**. In a testimonial, listeners are expected to accept the opinion of a famous person rather than to form their own opinions.

Screen star Gloria Wendel for Cloudcrest Airlines: "Cloudcrest is the only way to travel!"

Using **loaded words** such as *unwanted, dull, health,* and *vitality* is a propaganda technique that plays upon people's hopes and fears.

Is unwanted soap film leaving your hair dull and dirty-looking? Give your hair the look of health and vitality with Glimmer shampoo.

Skills Tryout

Name the propaganda technique used in each of these examples.

1. Candidate Nicolini is the best choice for the office of mayor. If you believe in honesty and justice, and if you want a better life for us all, vote for Nicolini.
2. Astronaut Flynn eats Wheato for breakfast every morning. "I eat Wheato because it tastes good," says Flynn. "I like its crunch and nutty flavor."
3. America's eyes are on Glowster, our nation's best-selling automobile. Join a nation of happy car owners. Buy Glowster!

Practice

A. Read the following statements. Then write the propaganda technique that is used in each.

1. Buy the watch most Americans prefer—Tock.
2. Famous race-car driver Dan Rono declares: "I think you should all test-drive the new Glowster."
3. Look great in Danka fashion jeans!
4. Join the ranks of educated consumers—buy Whirlit products.

B. Read the following campaign speech. Then list the loaded words in the speech.

A vote for our party is a vote for truth, honor, freedom, and all that is beautiful in our state. It is time for unfair, unwanted taxes and outdated ideas to be replaced by intelligent changes. We need courageous, honest leaders to give our state government a new vitality.

Application LISTENING

Listen for examples of the three propaganda techniques on television and radio. Repeat the examples in class. Then ask your listeners to name each technique.

10 — Making Analogies

> • An **analogy** is a statement that shows the relationship between two pairs of things or ideas.

The following statement is an analogy.

<u>Bright</u> is to <u>dull</u> as <u>wet</u> is to <u>dry</u>.

Analogies show relationships between things. Both ideas in the analogy above are opposites. However, analogies can show other kinds of relationships as well. Read this next analogy.

<u>Doe</u> is to <u>fawn</u> as <u>hen</u> is to <u>chick</u>.

The relationship between a doe and a fawn is the same as the relationship between a hen and a chick. Both are adult-and-child relationships.

Some analogies show relationships between those who act and their actions.

<u>Snake</u> is to <u>bite</u> as <u>bee</u> is to <u>sting</u>.

Here is an analogy about tools and their users.

<u>Wrench</u> is to <u>plumber</u> as <u>needle</u> is to <u>tailor</u>.

A wrench is a plumber's tool, and a needle is a tailor's tool.

As you can see from the examples above, analogies can reveal a wide variety of relationships.

Skills Tryout

Tell what word is missing in each of the analogies listed below. Then name the relationship that the analogy shows.

1. *Shovel* is to *dig* as *ax* is to _____.
2. *Edison* is to *light bulb* as *Bell* is to _____.
3. *Car* is to *steering wheel* as *bicycle* is to _____.

Practice

A. Write the following kinds of analogies.

   1. Write a worker-and-tool analogy.
      EXAMPLE: *Doctor* is to *stethoscope* as *dentist* is to *drill.*
   2. Write a part-and-whole analogy. Each pair of words should name part of an object and the object itself.
      EXAMPLE: *Finger* is to *hand* as *toe* is to *foot.*
   3. Write a mathematical analogy. Base it on a division fact.
      EXAMPLE: *Thirty-six* is to *nine* as *twenty* is to *five.*
   4. Write an example-and-category analogy. Each pair of words should name an example of a category and the category itself.
      EXAMPLE: *Beagle* is to *dog* as *tulip* is to *flower.*

B. Write the relationship shown in each of the following analogies. Choose from the relationships listed below.

   opposites   part-and-whole   tool-and-worker
       synonyms   child-and-adult   category-and-example

   5. *Quick* is to *rapid* as *small* is to *tiny.*
   6. *Kitten* is to *cat* as *puppy* is to *dog.*
   7. *Head* is to *bed* as *back* is to *chair.*
   8. *Brilliant* is to *dim* as *good* is to *bad.*
   9. *Insect* is to *beetle* as *reptile* is to *alligator.*
   10. *Spoon* is to *chef* as *paintbrush* is to *artist.*

Application COMPLETING ANALOGIES

Study the shape-and-shade analogies below. Then draw the fourth figure for each of the analogies. (Hint: In each analogy the only difference between the first figure and the second figure is that the second figure has been turned clockwise.)

   a. is to as is to _____.
   b. is to as is to _____.
   c. is to as is to _____.

11 — Making Common-Sense Decisions

> ● Making common-sense decisions requires you to evaluate a situation and use reasoning skills.

Sometimes you may find yourself in a situation where you must make a common-sense decision. You must decide what is the best thing to do. Read the situation described below.

Mary came to school early every morning to work in the school store. One day Joan saw Mary take three pens from the store counter and put them in her bag. When Mary saw Joan's surprised expression, she said, "I work every day before school starts. I've earned these pens."

Joan felt Mary was wrong to take the pens. She needed to decide what to do. First she evaluated the situation. She thought about the choices she had and the possible consequences of each choice. She could ignore what she had seen. She could tell Mary how she felt, or she could tell someone else what she had seen. Joan decided that the best thing to do was to tell Mary how she felt. She would try to convince her that taking the pens was wrong. Do you agree with Joan's decision?

Skills Tryout

Read the situation below and answer the questions that follow.

Steve and Richard were left alone in their grandmother's house while she went shopping. All of a sudden they discovered smoke coming from the basement. Richard pushed Steve out the front door. "No, we shouldn't leave the house!" yelled Steve. "We should try to put out the fire."

"It's too dangerous to stay," answered Richard. "We can call the fire department from the Smith's house next door."

1. Who was right, Steve or Richard? Explain your answer.
2. What would you have done in the same situation?

Practice

A. Read the three situations described below. Consider each problem carefully. Then write answers to the questions that follow. Include a reason for each answer.

   1. One day John stayed after school to work in the library. As he was leaving the building, the school doors locked behind him. John reached into his pocket and discovered that he did not have his bus pass with him. He did not even have enough money to call home. What should John have done?
   2. Judy wanted to play the leading role in the class play. She practiced reading her lines and had even memorized a part of the play. The day before tryouts, a new student was assigned to Judy's class. The new student had taken drama lessons and dancing lessons. Judy decided she did not have a chance for the leading role. She told her teacher to take her name off the tryout list. Do you agree with Judy's decision? What do you think Judy should have done?
   3. Sally and Bill are responsible class members. They take turns feeding the animals in the science room and cleaning their cages. One day they accidentally left some cage doors open. One white rabbit, two field mice, and a snake escaped from their cages and disappeared in the classroom. Sally and Bill did not know what to do. What should they have done?

B. List three problems you have faced that required you to make a common-sense decision.

Application USING THINKING SKILLS

Choose one of the problems you listed in **Practice B.** Write a paragraph that explains the problem. Tell what you decided to do and why you made that decision.

12 — Writing a Cause-and-Effect Paragraph

Writing Project

> • A **cause-and-effect paragraph** explains why something happens by telling the results of an action.

An action often causes something else to happen. The action has an effect, or result. Think about the effect, for example, of each action listed below. As you do this, you will be finding cause-and-effect relationships.

> Ice cubes are left in the warm sun.
> A bicycle tire is punctured.
> Yellow and blue paints are mixed together.

Recognizing and understanding cause-and-effect relationships are important reasoning skills. In this lesson you will choose a cause-and-effect relationship and write a paragraph about it. When you have finished, you may read your paragraph to the class and ask your classmates to identify the cause and the effects you wrote about.

1. Prewriting

How will you find a topic for a cause-and-effect paragraph? Here are two examples of cause and effect to start you thinking.

Cause: Jerry practiced the piano for two hours every day.

Effects: Jerry plays very well, and music is the most important thing in his life.

Cause: Last summer Libby mowed lawns in her neighborhood.

Effects: Libby earned her own money and became friends with many of her neighbors.

► Have you had similar experiences? Think of cause-and-effect situations in your own life. Discuss them with your classmates and try to identify both the cause and the effects. After your discussion, choose one cause-and-effect situation as the topic for your paragraph. You may write about the results of your own actions or of the actions of another person.

► Once you have selected a topic, make a chart like the example. It shows how to develop your topic. Begin by listing the cause and the effects of the situation you are going to write about. Then add important details that explain what happened and why it happened.

Cause	Details
Jerry practiced the piano for two hours every day.	He got up early. He gave up soccer and TV.
Effects	**Details**
Jerry plays the piano well. Music is the most important thing in his life.	He performed in a concert. He formed a musical group. He composes music.

2. Writing

► Use your chart as you write your first draft. How will you begin? You could explain the cause first and then give the effects. You could also start with the effects. If you begin this way tell what happened and then tell why it happened. As you add important details, use cause-and-effect signal words, like those in the box. These words will help your reader recognize cause-and-effect relationships.

> Cause-and-effect *signal words* because as since so as a result therefore thus due to consequently

3. Revising

▶ Read your paragraph to yourself to hear how it will sound to others. Is your language clear and easy to understand? Then read your paragraph to someone else and ask your listener to identify the cause and effects. Also ask for suggestions on how to improve your paragraph. Working with your listener, use this checklist as a guide for making changes.

Revision Checklist

- Does my topic sentence state either a cause or an effect?
- Does my paragraph make the cause-and-effect relationship clear?
- Did I use cause-and-effect signal words?
- Did I avoid overusing the same words?

Read the sample and notice how it was revised to avoid overusing the same words.

Jerry practiced ~~the piano~~ for two hours every day. ~~Every day~~ he got up early and even ~~He~~ gave up soccer and television so he could ~~have~~ devote more time ~~for~~ to his ~~practice and~~ training. as a result of his ~~practicing every day,~~ discipline and drill, Jerry now plays the piano very well. in fact, music

Jerry practiced the piano for two hours every day. For months he got up early and even gave up soccer and television so he could devote more time to his training. As a result of his discipline and drill, Jerry now plays the piano very well. In fact, music has become the most important thing in Jerry's life. In addition to composing original pieces, Jerry has formed his own musical group and recently performed in a concert.

▶ Did you decide how you can improve your cause-and-effect paragraph? Use the editing marks to make your revisions.

4. Publishing

▶ Proofread your paragraph before publishing it. Use the Proofreading Checklist in the Young Writer's Handbook on page 399 and use the editing marks to make corrections.

▶ Read your paragraph to the class and ask them to identify the cause and the effects you wrote about. Then ask the class to think of other possible effects of the cause in your paragraph. Have classmates suggest what else might have happened in the same situation.

EDITING MARKS	
——	cross out
∧	add
∽	move
=	capital letter
/	small letter
¶	indent
◯	check spelling

Writing Project

A Puzzle Potpourri

Create puzzles that emphasize likenesses and differences.

1. Make a category puzzle. List four animals or things that share a physical characteristic. Then include in the list one animal or thing that does not have that characteristic. Ask: "Which is least like the others?"

elephant   boa constrictor
water buffalo   dog   giraffe

2. Make a sequence puzzle. List numbers or letters in a regular pattern. Break the pattern with one number or one letter. Ask: "Which number (or letter) does not belong in the sequence?"

2 4 8 16 30 32 64 128 285

3. Make a design puzzle. Draw four designs that have one characteristic in common. Then include one design that does not have the characteristic. Ask: "Which one is least like the other four?"

4. Make an alphabet puzzle. Select four letters that have one common characteristic. Then add a letter that does not have that characteristic. Ask: "Which letter is least like the others?"

D   B   L   P   R

Computers

Computer programs are based on reasoning. A kind of map called a **flowchart** shows the step-by-step directions in a computer program.

The shape drawn around each step in a flowchart shows what kind of step it is. A rectangle is drawn around statements that tell exactly what to do. A diamond shows a step in which a choice must be made. An oval shape is used for *Start* and *End*.

▶ Try it. Read the following flowchart. Begin at *Start*. Then follow the arrows. When you get to a diamond, read the question. Then choose the arrow for *Yes* or the arrow for *No*.

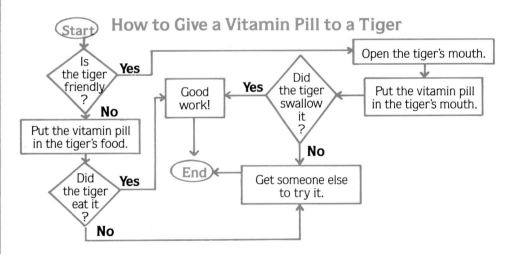

How to Give a Vitamin Pill to a Tiger

Writers at Work   A computer programmer writes flowcharts in order to map out the steps involved in solving a problem.

▶ Write a flowchart that shows the steps involved in solving a problem. Use one of the following problems or use an idea of your own.

How to open a combination lock   How to catch a fish
How to put out a fire   How to fix a flat tire

Conjunctions, Prepositions, and Interjections   *pages 258–269*

A. Write each sentence. Underline each conjunction.

1. Carpentry is a difficult but rewarding hobby.
2. A good carpenter must work slowly and carefully.
3. Jessica designed and built this oak trunk.
4. She will store blankets or clothes in it.

B. Write each prepositional phrase. Underline the preposition once and the object of the preposition twice.

5. We cheered for our team.
6. Rick laughed at my joke.
7. Katie dove into the pool.
8. I like this book of poems.

C. Write each prepositional phrase. Write *adjective* if it describes a noun. Write *adverb* if it describes a verb, an adjective, or an adverb.

9. The valley looked peaceful in the sunset.
10. A small family of squirrels nestled together.
11. Two red-winged hawks soared smoothly with the wind.
12. Long shadows touched the trees by the river.

D. Write the word that correctly completes each sentence.

13. I hung the hammock (among, between) two trees.
14. Grandfather went with Pat and (I, me) on a fishing trip.
15. Four boys shared the peanuts (among, between) themselves.
16. The teacher repeated the directions for (we, us).

E. Write each sentence. Punctuate the interjections correctly.

17. Aha I knew my gloves were in this drawer.
18. Wow That hot-air balloon is landing right in our yard.
19. Ouch The thorns on this rose are sharp.
20. Hooray We are going to a movie tonight.

Checkpoint: Unit 7

Idioms   *pages 270–271*

F. Write the word or phrase from the list that could be used in place of the underlined idiom in each sentence.

> hurry   cheaply   clumsy

21. When it comes to threading a needle, I'm <u>all thumbs</u>.
22. The shopkeeper sold me this compass <u>for a song</u>.
23. <u>Step on it</u>, or you'll miss the first inning of the game.

Directions   *pages 276–277*

G. The directions below are not written clearly. Rewrite each sentence, being specific and using directional words.

24. Be sure to turn at the next corner.
25. You will be on a narrow street.
26. Deliver this package to a green house on Fry Road.

Propaganda Techniques   *pages 278–279*

H. Write *bandwagon, loaded words,* or *testimonial* to show the propaganda technique used in each statement.

27. Three out of five kids ride Glide-O bikes. Shouldn't you?
28. Actress Pat Jenkins says: "Lift Soap keeps me feeling fresh."
29. Treat your family to healthy, flavorful Carrot Twists.

Analogies   *pages 280–281*

I. Write the relationship shown in each analogy. Choose from the relationships listed below.

> category-and-example   opposites   part-and-whole

30. *Branch* is to *tree* as *petal* is to *flower*.
31. *Strange* is to *normal* as *noise* is to *silence*.
32. *Fruit* is to *watermelon* as *vegetable* is to *onion*.

See also Handbook pages 378–381.

Grammar
Sentences

Composition
Creating

Summer Rain

The sky is
scrubbed
of every smudge of
cloud.

The sidewalk is a
slate
that's quickly
dry.

Light
dazzles
like
a washed
window pane,

and
I

breathe
the freshly laundered
air
of after-rain.

—*Lilian Moore*

1 — Compound Subjects and Compound Predicates

- A **compound subject** is two or more simple subjects that have the same verb.
- A **compound predicate** is two or more verbs that have the same subject.

You know that the simple subject is the main word in the complete subject and that the simple predicate is the main word or words in the complete predicate. The simple subject is shown in blue and the simple predicate in green.

A strong <mark>wind</mark> suddenly <mark>blew</mark> through town.

Some sentences have more than one simple subject. Two or more simple subjects that have the same verb are called a compound subject. A conjunction such as *and* or *or* usually joins the simple subjects.

A <mark>storm</mark> or <mark>tornado</mark> was on the way!

Some sentences have more than one simple predicate. Two or more verbs that have the same subject are called a compound predicate. A compound predicate is sometimes called a compound verb.

Thunder <mark>rumbled,</mark> <mark>roared,</mark> and <mark>echoed</mark> through the valley.

Skills Tryout

Name the compound subject or predicate in each sentence.

1. Dust and leaves sailed overhead.
2. The wind rose and blew harder.
3. Heavy raindrops fell and splashed on the sidewalk.
4. Men, women, and children scurried for shelter.
5. Jan and her mother closed their doors and windows.

Practice

A. Write the compound subject or predicate in each sentence.

1. The clouds opened and released the rain.
2. The gutters and roads filled with water.
3. Paper, wood, and other rubbish floated by.
4. Cars moved slowly or stalled in flooded areas.
5. Emergency workers gathered and helped motorists.
6. Lightning bolts struck and split many trees.
7. Broken trunks and branches fell onto nearby cars.
8. Many orchards and fields were damaged by the winds.
9. Flooded basements and broken windows were common.
10. At last the clouds passed and revealed the sun again.

B. Write each sentence. Underline each compound subject once and each compound predicate twice. If a sentence has no compounds, write *no compound.*

11. This book explains the formation of clouds.
12. Moist air rises from the ground and becomes cooler.
13. The cooler air cannot hold all its water vapor.
14. The vapor condenses and forms clouds.
15. Water droplets in a cloud may form larger droplets.
16. Rain, sleet, or snow falls to the earth.
17. Animals and plants use this water.
18. The water flows into streams and refills lakes.
19. *Cumulus* and *cirrus* are the names of two kinds of clouds.
20. Nimbus clouds are dark rain clouds.

Application WRITING SENTENCES

Some clouds are fluffy white masses. Others are dark threatening sheets. Write eight sentences about different kinds of clouds you have seen. Tell what they reminded you of or how they made you feel. Use at least two compound subjects and two compound predicates in your sentences. Underline each compound subject once and each compound predicate twice.

2 — Compound Sentences

> ● A **compound sentence** consists of two or more simple sentences.

The sentences you have studied so far have been simple sentences. A simple sentence expresses one complete thought and has a subject and a predicate.

The United States celebrates Mother's Day.

A compound sentence consists of two or more simple sentences. In the following compound sentences, pairs of simple sentences are joined by the conjunctions *and, or,* and *but.* Notice that a comma is placed before the conjunction.

We celebrate Mother's Day, and others do, too.
People visit their mothers, or they send cards.
Mother's Day is in May, but Father's Day is in June.

Do not confuse a compound sentence with a simple sentence that has a compound subject or predicate.

Compound Sentence: Anna Jarvis campaigned for a nationwide Mother's Day in 1907, and the idea became popular.
Compound Predicate: Anna Jarvis planned and organized Mother's Day celebrations.

Skills Tryout

Tell whether each sentence is simple or compound.

1. West Virginia celebrated the first Mother's Day in 1910.
2. President Woodrow Wilson made Mother's Day a national observance.
3. He signed a bill in 1914, and Mother's Day became official.
4. Children gave flowers on this day, or they made gifts.
5. Father's Day began in 1910, but it did not become official until 1972.

Practice

A. Write *simple* or *compound* for each sentence.

1. The ancient Romans honored mother goddesses in spring.
2. On Parentalia the Romans remembered dead relatives.
3. The English once honored mothers on Mothering Sunday, but the holiday died out in the 1800s.
4. Children baked cakes, or they did household chores.
5. Mother's Day was a big success in the United States, and other nations soon imitated it.
6. Sonora Dodd of Spokane, Washington, liked Mother's Day, but she wanted a Father's Day, too.
7. Spokane celebrated the first Father's Day in 1910.
8. Mother's Day is the second Sunday in May.
9. America celebrates Father's Day on the third Sunday in June.
10. You can give your father a gift, or you can just thank him.

B. Write *compound sentence, compound subject*, or *compound predicate* for each sentence.

11. Mom slept late on Mother's Day and had breakfast in bed.
12. Aaron cleaned the house, and I bought red carnations.
13. Dad made dinner, but he burned it badly.
14. So we went out to dinner and had a great Mother's Day.
15. Aaron and I bought Dad a shirt for Father's Day.
16. Mom picked red roses, and Dad sneezed a lot.
17. Dad got a polka dot tie, but he returned it.
18. Mom, Aaron, and I took Dad on a picnic.
19. Dad swam and played tennis with Mom.
20. Then it started to rain, and we all went home.

Application WRITING SENTENCES

Write six sentences about Mother's Day or Father's Day. Write at least two compound sentences and two simple sentences with compound subjects or predicates.

3 Subject-Verb Agreement

> ● The subject of a sentence must agree with its verb.

Like nouns and pronouns, verbs have singular and plural forms. The singular form must be used with a singular subject and the plural form with a plural subject. When the correct verb form is used in a sentence, the subject and verb are said to agree. Study the chart below.

Subject-Verb Agreement

1. Singular nouns and the pronouns *he, she,* and *it* use a present tense verb ending in *-s* or *-es.*
    Sandra Day O'Connor <u>sits</u> on the Supreme Court.
    She <u>searches</u> for justice.

2. Plural nouns and the pronouns *I, you, we,* and *they* use a present tense verb not ending in *-s* or *-es.*
    Nine judges <u>sit</u> on the Supreme Court.
    They <u>search</u> for justice.

The verb *be* has special forms you must learn.

Subject	Forms of *Be*	Examples
1. The pronoun *I*	uses *am* or *was.*	I <u>am</u> a judge.
2. Singular nouns and the pronouns *she, he,* and *it*	use *is* or *was.*	She <u>is</u> a judge.
3. Plural nouns and the pronouns *we, you,* and *they*	use *are* or *were.*	They <u>were</u> judges.

Skills Tryout

Tell the forms of *be* that agree with each subject.

1. you	**3.** I	**5.** courts	**7.** we	**9.** truth
2. law	**4.** she	**6.** judge	**8.** it	**10.** men

Practice

A. Write the two forms of *be* that agree with each subject.

1. he   **3.** judges   **5.** people   **7.** rule   **9.** girls
2. they   **4.** court   **6.** laws   **8.** books   **10.** man

B. This story about Sandra Day O'Connor is written in the present tense. Write the form of the verb in parentheses ( ) that correctly completes each sentence.

11. Sandra Day (grows, grow) up in Arizona in the 1930s.
12. She (works, work) on her parents' ranch.
13. Sandra (finishes, finish) college and law school in only five years.
14. No law firms (gives, give) her a job, though.
15. They (refuses, refuse) to hire women lawyers.
16. Sandra (marries, marry) John O'Connor and raises a family.
17. Later she (decides, decide) to enter politics.
18. The voters (elects, elect) her state senator in Arizona.
19. The people (learns, learn) what a good worker she is.
20. Next, the governor (makes, make) her a judge.
21. As a judge she (is, are) always fair.
22. In 1981 President Reagan (chooses, choose) Sandra Day O'Connor for the Supreme Court.
23. The Supreme Court (is, are) the highest court in the land.
24. Sandra Day O'Connor (feels, feel) proud to be the first woman Supreme Court judge.
25. Her court decisions (affects, affect) the nation's future.

Application WRITING SENTENCES

Sandra Day O'Connor was the first woman to become a judge on the Supreme Court. Write eight sentences that tell what it might be like to be the first to do something. Write your sentences in the present tense. Make sure the subject and verb of each sentence agree. To form the present singular of a verb that ends in a consonant and *y*, change the *y* to *i* and add *-es*.

4 — Subject-Verb Agreement

- Compound subjects joined by *and* use the plural form of the verb.
- Compound subjects joined by *or, either/or,* or *neither/nor* sometimes use the singular form of the verb and sometimes the plural.

You know that a compound subject is two or more simple subjects that have the same verb. When the parts of a compound subject are joined by *and*, the verb is always plural.

> Honey and fruit <u>contain</u> sugar.
> Breads, potatoes, and cereals <u>contain</u> starches.
> Cheese and eggs <u>contain</u> protein.

When *or, either/or,* or *neither/nor* join the parts of a compound subject, the verb is sometimes singular and sometimes plural. Use a singular verb when both parts of the subject are singular and a plural verb when both parts are plural.

> Fish or meat also <u>provides</u> protein.
> Vegetable oils or nuts <u>provide</u> necessary fats.

When one part of a compound subject is singular and one part plural, the verb agrees with the nearer subject.

> Neither sugar nor starches <u>provide</u> much iron.
> Neither starches nor sugar <u>provides</u> much iron.

Skills Tryout

Name the verb that correctly completes each sentence.

1. Bacon, butter, and margarine (provides, provide) fat.
2. Either milk or milk products (supplies, supply) calcium.
3. Neither chocolate nor butter (contains, contain) much iron.
4. Seafoods or iodized salt (is, are) a good source of iodine.
5. Sugar and starches (is, are) carbohydrates.

Practice

A. Write the verb that correctly completes each sentence.

1. Starches and sugar (is, are) prime sources of energy.
2. Neither body growth nor body repair (takes, take) place without proteins.
3. Fish or meats (provides, provide) complete proteins.
4. Neither beans nor cereal (gives, give) complete proteins.
5. Calcium, phosphorus, and iron (is, are) minerals.
6. Green vegetables or meat (furnishes, furnish) iron.
7. Anemia and other diseases (comes, come) from lack of it.
8. Neither blood nor muscles (stays, stay) healthy without adequate phosphorus.
9. Strong teeth and bones (requires, require) calcium.
10. Cheese or fish (is, are) a good source of phosphorus.

B. Write each sentence. Use the correct present tense form of the verb in parentheses ( ). Then write whether the verb is singular or plural.

11. Poor vision or rough skin (result) from lack of vitamin A.
12. Carrots or butter (provide) this vitamin.
13. Thiamine and niacin (belong) to the vitamin B group.
14. Neither good physical health nor good mental health (seem) possible without them.
15. Meat or beans (provide) most B vitamins.
16. Some vegetables and citrus fruit (furnish) vitamin C.
17. Either tomatoes or oranges (be) a good source.
18. Unhealthy gums or scurvy (result) from no vitamin C.
19. Egg yolks and fortified milk (furnish) us with vitamin D.
20. Strong bones and teeth (need) vitamin D.

Application WRITING SENTENCES

Write eight sentences about the foods you eat. Use *and, or, either/or,* and *neither/nor* to connect compound subjects in four of your sentences.

5 — Sentence Errors

> - A **sentence fragment** is a group of words that does not express a complete thought.
> - A **run-on sentence** is two or more sentences not separated by correct punctuation or connecting words.

You know that a sentence has a subject and a predicate and expresses a complete thought. A group of words that does not express a complete thought is called a sentence fragment. You can correct a fragment by adding words to make it a complete thought.

Fragment: Marched for hours.
Complete Sentence: The band marched for hours.

A run-on sentence strings sentences together incorrectly. The following are run-on sentences.

People enjoyed the parade they cheered loudly.
People enjoyed the parade, they cheered loudly.

You can correct a run-on sentence by separating each thought into a sentence of its own. Or you can use a comma and a conjunction between each thought. You can also correct a run-on sentence by using a compound subject or predicate.

People enjoyed the parade. They cheered loudly.
People enjoyed the parade, and they cheered loudly.
People enjoyed the parade and cheered loudly.

Skills Tryout

Tell whether each group of words is a sentence or a fragment. Add words to each fragment to make a sentence.

1. Waved in the breeze.
2. Lisa marched in step.
3. Soldiers in fine uniforms.
4. The mayor was there.
5. Her shiny trumpet.
6. With their heads high.

Practice

A. Write *sentence* or *fragment* for each group of words. Add words to each fragment to make a sentence. Then write the sentences.

1. At the War Memorial.
2. Carried large bouquets.
3. They applauded loudly.
4. A wonderful Memorial Day.
5. Fourteen soldiers saluted.
6. Gave stirring speeches.

B. Correct these run-on sentences. Rewrite each run-on sentence as two separate sentences, as a compound sentence, or as a sentence with a compound predicate.

EXAMPLE: Most states observe Memorial Day on the last Monday in May, many cities have parades.

ANSWER: Most states observe Memorial Day on the last Monday in May. Many cities have parades.

7. The holiday began in 1866 the people of Waterloo, New York, first observed it.
8. People decorated the graves of soldiers with flowers they placed flags on the graves.
9. The nation honored its heroes it recalled their bravery.
10. Now we celebrate Memorial Day we remember our freedoms.
11. Flag Day is another patriotic holiday, it is June 14.
12. Congress authorized the first American flag in 1777 the first Flag Day was in 1877.
13. People display their flag they think about its importance.
14. Schools hold Flag Day programs students learn about the flag.
15. The stripes on the American flag stand for the original thirteen colonies there is a star for each state.

Application LISTENING

Write three complete sentences and three sentence fragments. Read them aloud. Have your listeners identify the fragments and tell how they can be corrected.

6 — Using Commas

- Use a comma after *yes, no,* or *well* at the beginning of a sentence.
- Use a comma to set off the name of a person spoken to.
- Use a comma to separate a last name from a first name of a person when the last name is written first.

In Unit 1 you learned that commas separate certain words or word groups within a sentence. The following chart explains three other ways in which commas help make your writing clearer.

Explanation	Examples
1. When words such as *yes, no,* or *well* introduce a sentence, use a comma after them.	Yes, I like to tell jokes. No, I didn't know about the joke-telling contest. Well, why don't we sign up?
2. The name of a person directly spoken to is set off by commas in a sentence.	Harry, whose business is always looking up? The answer to that joke, Lois, is *an astronomer.* Do you know any jokes, Ben?
3. When a last name must be written first, use a comma after the last name.	Cheng, Harry Smith, Roger Velez, Lois

Skills Tryout

Tell where commas belong in these sentences.

1. What worker finds almost everything dull Roger?
2. Well the obvious answer is *a knife sharpener* Harry.
3. Yes that's the answer Lois.
4. Ben do you know why the weather forecaster lost her job?
5. Yes Harry the climate didn't agree with her!

Practice

Write each sentence, adding commas where needed.

1. Lois have you heard the joke about the ceiling?
2. No I haven't Ben.
3. Well it's over your head anyway!
4. Do you know Ben who always whistles while they work?
5. Could it be the police officers who direct traffic Lois?
6. Yes you guessed it.
7. Did you know Mrs. Velez that Columbus was never more than three miles from land?
8. No Harry I didn't know that.
9. Well he was, but the direction of the land was straight down!
10. Did ships like Columbus's sink often Lois?
11. No a ship like Columbus's could only sink once.
12. Harry how many feet are in a yard?
13. Well it depends Ben on how many people are standing in the yard at the time.
14. My family had five guests for dinner last night Ben.
15. Well Lois my family had steak and potatoes!

Application FILLING OUT FORMS

Peter Lee, Mary Carlson, Allen Bacci, Clarence Green, and Karen Krinski signed up to perform in a talent contest. Copy the form shown below. Then enter their names on the form. Enter your name on the form, too.

Talent Contest Sign-Up Form

Name (List last name first.)

1. _____   4. _____
2. _____   5. _____
3. _____   6. _____

---

7 — **Word Connotations**

> • **Connotation** is the positive or negative meaning associated with a word.

Stan described his summer vacation.

Another <u>dull</u> vacation at our <u>shack</u> in the mountains! Dad <u>lazes around</u> the lake all day. Mom buys <u>cheap old-fashioned fur-niture</u>, and Marie <u>shows off</u> her swan dive.

Stan's brother Dan described the same vacation.

Another <u>peaceful</u> vacation at our <u>cabin</u> in the mountains! Dad <u>relaxes at</u> the lake all day. Mom buys <u>inexpensive antiques</u>, and Marie <u>performs</u> her swan dive.

Look at the underlined words in the descriptions. Stan and Dan have used words with similar meanings. However, it is clear that Dan is having a good time and Stan is not.

Words with similar meanings can suggest different feelings and reactions. Connotation is the positive or negative meaning associated with a word. For example, *cheap* has a negative connotation, and *inexpensive* has a positive one.

It is important to be aware of the connotations of the words you use. A thesaurus can help you find words with the exact meaning you intend.

Skills Tryout

Tell which word in parentheses ( ) has a positive connotation.

1. Dan feels (brave, reckless) and will raft down the river.
2. Stan has to (slave, work) around the cabin.
3. Marie exercises all summer to stay (slender, skinny).
4. We all wear (casual, sloppy) clothing.
5. Mom and Dad (argued, debated) about what to eat for lunch.

Practice

A. Write each sentence. Use the word in parentheses ( ) that has the more positive connotation.

1. Dana is (firm, stubborn) when it comes to her summer plans.
2. She will be camping in some (unpopulated, desolate) areas of the state.
3. Dave has some (smart, crafty) ideas for making money this summer.
4. One (scheme, plan) is to sell baseballs that light up when it becomes dark.
5. Gretchen will put on more of her (comical, silly) plays.
6. She plans to perform for a (group, mob) of young children.
7. Paul will be (traveling, drifting) around at the shore.
8. Anna will be working with her home computer in her usual (businesslike, cold) manner.
9. Jason is (asking, pestering) his parents for a new ten-speed bicycle.
10. Karen will read more (weird, imaginative) science fiction.

B. Write the word in each pair that has a negative connotation.

11. thrifty/stingy
12. smirk/grin
13. confident/cocky
14. tall/lanky
15. youthful/childish

16. ambitious/pushy
17. odor/fragrance
18. economize/scrimp
19. nosy/curious
20. expensive/overpriced

Application USING LANGUAGE

Write six sentences that tell what you plan to do this summer. Use a word with a positive connotation in each sentence. Underline the word with the positive connotation. Then, for each of the six underlined words, write a synonym that has a negative connotation.

Compound Subjects and Compound Predicates

pages 294–295

A. Write the compound subject or compound predicate in each sentence.

1. Vast herds of bison once roamed and grazed on the plains.
2. The Plains Indians needed and valued these animals.
3. Their food, clothing, and shelter came from the bison.
4. European settlers and the railroads destroyed the bison.
5. Millions and millions were slaughtered wastefully.

Compound Sentences   *pages 296–297*

B. Write *simple* or *compound* for each sentence.

6. Bison are often called buffalo, but true buffalo live in Asia and Africa.
7. Bison have fourteen pairs of ribs, and buffalo have thirteen.
8. A bison has a larger head than a buffalo.
9. Bison eat grass and chew on twigs.
10. The United States protects bison, and Canada does, too.

Subject-Verb Agreement   *pages 298–301*

C. Write the verb that correctly completes each sentence.

11. Marta and Juan (studies, study) astronomy.
12. The planets and stars (is, are) fascinating to them.
13. Neither Marta nor Juan (owns, own) a telescope.
14. Venus and Earth (is, are) similar in size.
15. Neither their temperatures nor atmospheres (is, are) alike.
16. Evening Star and Morning Star (is, are) names for Venus.
17. Probably neither animals nor plant life (is, are) found there.
18. Only the sun or the moon (appears, appear) brighter.
19. Fine dust or sharp rocks (covers, cover) its surface.
20. Both Mercury and Pluto (is, are) smaller than Earth is.

Sentence Errors   *pages 302–303*

D. Add words to each sentence fragment to make a sentence. Rewrite each run-on sentence as a compound sentence.

21. In the park many people.
22. Joggers ran around the lake children flew kites.
23. A big white dog under a tree.
24. A batter hit a home run the crowd cheered wildly.
25. Enjoyed the park so much.

Using Commas   *pages 304–305*

E. Write each sentence, adding commas where needed.

26. Ava the banana-eating contest starts in two minutes.
27. Yes there is still time Brad to sign up.
28. No this is the first contest of its kind Ella.
29. Well you've got to enter if you want to win.
30. Yes Charles the contest has officially begun!
31. No I wouldn't eat the peels Josh.
32. No Ted I only count twenty peels beside your plate.
33. Don't feel too bad about losing Brad.
34. Yes you would feel better Ava if you had eaten less.
35. Well maybe this contest wasn't such a good idea!

Word Connotations   *pages 306–307*

F. Write each sentence. Use the word in parentheses ( ) that has the more positive connotation.

36. Ellen enjoys reading (romantic, mushy) stories.
37. That's a very (flashy, colorful) dress you're wearing.
38. You're looking (scrawnier, slimmer) than ever, Mae.
39. He was (ignorant, unaware) of many local customs.
40. This soup certainly has a (bland, mild) taste, Frank.

See also Handbook pages 382–389, 403, 405.

Sentence Combining

> ● Sentences with ideas that go together can be combined.

Read the following sentences.

Grammar and Writing Workshop

    A. Our class is performing a full-length play.
    B. I'm going to be acting in it. (, and)
**A + B. Our class is performing a full-length play, and I'm going
      to be acting in it.**

Sentence B provides an additional idea that belongs with the idea in sentence A. Since the two sentences have equally important ideas, they can be combined by adding a comma and the word *and*. Sentence A + B gives the same information that sentence A and sentence B did separately. However, the relationship of the ideas in the two shorter sentences is made clearer by combining them into one compound sentence.

The two sentences below can also be combined into one compound sentence. However, the idea in sentence C contrasts with the idea in sentence D. Combining the two sentences with a comma and the word *but* shows this contrast better.

    C. We want to do a play by Shakespeare.
    D. We cannot decide on the right one. (, but)
**C + D. We want to do a play by Shakespeare, but we cannot
      decide on the right one.**

Sometimes two sentences give two possible choices. Such sentences can be combined with a comma and the word *or*. Study sentence E + F below.

    E. Diane will direct the play.
    F. An outside professional will be hired. (, or)
**E. + F. Diane will direct the play, or an
      outside professional will be hired.**

Using Clues   Combine each pair of sentences below. Use the clues in parentheses ( ) the way they were used on page 310. Write each new sentence that results.

1. *Romeo and Juliet* will be presented in May.
   Luis will be playing the part of Romeo. (, **and**)
2. We have not cast the part of Juliet.
   We are not in any hurry. (, **and**)
3. Luis has never been in a play by Shakespeare before.
   He speaks his lines clearly and confidently. (, **but**)
4. Buy your tickets as soon as possible.
   The best seats will be taken. (, **or**)
5. There will be a picnic for the cast at Greenwood Park.
   There will be a rainy-day party at Diane's house. (, **or**)
6. Diane thinks the whole school will attend.
   There should be enough seats for everyone. (, **but**)

Using No Clues   Combine each pair of sentences without clues. Think how the ideas in each pair of sentences go together. Then use a comma and the words *and, but,* or *or* to join the sentences. Write each new sentence that results.

7. William Shakespeare wrote his plays 400 years ago.
   Actors and audiences still admire them today.
8. Shakespeare also wrote poems.
   They are not as famous as his plays.
9. Romeo and Juliet love one another.
   Young people can identify with them.
10. They devise a plan to escape.
    Their plan does not succeed.
11. Romeo and Juliet die in the last scene.
    Their deaths end the feud between their families.
12. People must learn to live together peacefully.
    They will destroy themselves.

8 — **Reading Imaginative Poetry**

> ● Poems may view familiar things in a new way.

Poetry can help you see familiar things in a new way by making unusual comparisons or by looking at things from a different point of view. Poetry can show you what might be, and what could never be. Poetry frees the imagination.

As you read each of the poems that follow, think about how the poet has used imagination.

1. Fog

The fog comes
on little cat feet.

It sits looking
over harbor and city
on silent haunches
and then moves on.
—*Carl Sandburg*

2. Water

The world turns softly
Not to spill its lakes and rivers.
The water is held in its arms
And the sky is held in the water.
What is water,
That pours silver,
And can hold the sky?
—*Hilda Conkling*

3. Steam Shovel

The dinosaurs are not all dead.
I saw one raise its iron head
To watch me walking down the road
Beyond our house today.
Its jaws were dripping with a load
Of earth and grass that it had cropped.
It must have heard me where I stopped,
Snorted white steam my way,
And stretched its long neck out to see,
And chewed, and grinned quite amiably.
—*Charles Malam*

4. Southbound on the Freeway

A tourist came in from Orbitville,
parked in the air, and said:

The creatures of this star
are made of metal and glass.

Through the transparent parts
you can see their guts.

Their feet are round and roll
on diagrams or long

measuring tapes, dark
with white lines.

They have four eyes.
The two in back are red.

Sometimes you can see a five-eyed
one, with a red eye turning

on the top of his head.
He must be special—

the others respect him
and go slow

when he passes, winding
among them from behind.

They all hiss as they glide
like inches, down the marked

tapes. Those soft shapes,
shadowy inside

the hard bodies—are they
their guts or their brains?

—*May Swenson*

About the Poems

1. Which poems make comparisons? What is being compared?
2. In poem 2 what is meant by "...the sky is held in the water"?
3. In poem 4 identify the following.
   - **a.** "creatures ... of metal and glass"
   - **b.** "the transparent parts"
   - **c.** "diagrams or long measuring tapes"
   - **d.** "feet"
   - **e.** "eyes"
   - **f.** "five-eyed one"

Activities

A. Illustrate one of the poems in the lesson. As a caption for your drawing, write a quotation from the poem.

B. Read aloud from a dictionary the definitions of *fog, steam shovel,* and *automobile.* Then read poems 1, 3, and 4. Discuss differences between the descriptions of the dictionary and the poets.

C. Describe a common object as it might be viewed by a Martian or by a pet dog or cat. Write your description as a poem if you wish. See if others can guess what you are describing.

9 — Listening for Sounds in Poetry

> ● Sounds of poetry include **rhyme, rhythm, repetition, alliteration,** and **onomatopoeia.**

Poetry makes special use of the sounds of language. Here are some of the "sound effects" that set poetry apart.

Words that rhyme end with the same sound: *light, night, fright.*

Rhythm is a pattern created by accented and unaccented syllables: *HOW do you LIKE to go UP in a SWING....*

Repetition is the repeating of words or groups of words: *Clippety, clippety, clippety, clop.*

Alliteration is the repetition of the same sound at the beginning of words: *One misty, moisty, morning....*

Onomatopoeia is the use of words that imitate sounds: *meow, bow-wow, snarl, growl, screech, drip, hiss, squeak.*

Listen for the sounds of poetry in these poems as you read them aloud.

1. Onomatopoeia

The rusty spigot
sputters,
utters
a splutter,
spatters a smattering of drops,
gashes wider;
slash,
splatters,
scatters,
spurts,
finally stops sputtering
and plash!
gushes rushes splashes
clear water dashes.

—*Eve Merriam*

2. The Loon

A lonely lake, a lonely shore,
A lone pine leaning on the moon;
All night the water-beating wings
Of a solitary loon.

With mournful wail from dusk to dawn
He gibbered at the taunting stars—
A hermit-soul gone raving mad,
And beating at his bars.

—*Lew Sarett*

3. The Bells
I

Hear the sledges with the bells–
  Silver bells!
What a world of merriment their melody foretells!
  How they tinkle, tinkle, tinkle,
   In the icy air of night!
  While the stars that oversprinkle
  All the heavens, seem to twinkle
   With a crystalline delight;
  Keeping time, time, time,
  In a sort of Runic rhyme,
To the tintinnabulation that so musically wells
  From the bells, bells, bells, bells,
   Bells, bells, bells–
From the jingling and the tinkling of the bells....
                —*Edgar Allan Poe*

About the Poems

1. Give examples of rhyme from poems 2 and 3.
2. Which poem has the strongest repeated rhythm?
3. Which poem has many repeated words? What are they?
4. Which poem uses many words that begin with the sound of *s*? Which uses many words that begin with the sound of *l*?
5. Give examples of onomatopoeia from each poem.

Activities

A. Reread the poems aloud, trying in "Onomatopoeia" to imitate the sounds of the spigot, in "The Loon" to sound mournful and lonely, and in "The Bells" to emphasize the rhythm.
B. Choose your favorite letter of the alphabet. Write a sentence in which almost every word begins with that letter.
C. Write a sentence or a poem to illustrate rhyme, rhythm, repetition, alliteration, or onomatopoeia. Ask others to identify which of those it illustrates.
D. Choose another poem that emphasizes the sounds of language and share it with the class.

10 Using Figures of Speech

> ● **Figures of speech** are expressions used to create an image, or "word picture."

Writers use figures of speech to create word pictures that are fresh and vivid. Most figures of speech are comparisons. They create a fresh, strong impression by comparing things that in most respects are quite different. The two most commonly used figures of speech are the simile and the metaphor.

A **simile** is a comparison that uses the word *like* or *as*.

> The wheat rippled <u>like</u> a golden lake.
> The veil was <u>as</u> sheer <u>as</u> a cobweb.

A **metaphor** is a comparison that does not use the word *like* or *as*. A metaphor says or implies that one thing *is* something else.

> The wheat <u>is</u> a golden lake, rippling in the wind.
> The moon <u>is</u> the night's lantern.

The first simile and the first metaphor above illustrate the difference between these two figures of speech. Notice that the simile says that the wheat is *like* a golden lake, while the metaphor states that the wheat *is* a golden lake.

Skills Tryout

Identify each of the sentences below as either a simile or a metaphor. Then tell how you made your decision.

1. His lies were as transparent as soap bubbles.
2. The windmills are like giant sunflowers.
3. All the world's a stage.
4. The lights on the bridge are a diamond necklace.
5. They squawked at each other like quarreling bluejays.

Practice

A. Identify each of the following by writing *simile* or *metaphor*.

1. The crackling fire sounded like someone crumpling a bag of potato chips.
2. The sun is a golden chariot blazing across the sky.
3. You are the sunshine of my life.
4. Raymond is as pesky as a mosquito.
5. A new year is like a sheet of blank paper.

B. Change each of these similes into a metaphor.

6. The glaring headlights were like dragons' eyes.
7. The helicopter is like a huge horsefly hovering above.
8. Raindrops are like commas, punctuating the windshield.
9. The clouds were like streaks of dust in the sky.
10. The oil looked like a layer of pearl on the water.

C. Complete each sentence to make a simile or metaphor.

11. The storm was _____.
12. Time is like a _____.
13. The dandelion seeds were _____.
14. The hum of night insects was as _____ as a _____.
15. A daffodil is a _____.

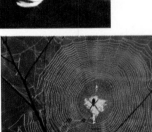

Application WRITING SIMILES AND METAPHORS

Use your imagination, and think of original similes and metaphors. Write a sentence with a simile that uses the word *like*, a sentence with a simile that uses the word *as*, and a sentence that contains a metaphor. If you need help in getting started, look at objects around you for inspiration. Or think of the world of nature—plants; animals; weather; objects in the sky, in the sea, or on earth.

11 — Writing a Poem

> ● A poet may use imagination, sounds of language, and figures of speech to express personal memories in a **poem**.

As the school year comes to a close, think about the many things that have happened. What special memories do you have of this year? In this lesson you will create a poem to capture those memories and reflect upon them. To save those memories, you and your classmates will make a scrapbook with your poems and other keepsakes from the school year.

1. Prewriting

▶ Start gathering ideas for a poem by talking with your classmates about days you want to always remember. On the chalkboard, list memorable days of the school year.

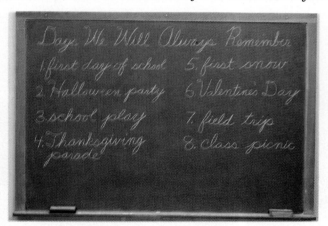

Days We Will Always Remember
1. first day of school   5. first snow
2. Halloween party   6. Valentine's Day
3. school play   7. field trip
4. Thanksgiving   8. class picnic
   parade

▶ Next recall details about the special days you have listed. Write an ending for each memory starter below.

> I remember …
> The most amazing thing was …
> On the first day of school I thought …
> The biggest surprise came …

►Discuss memories of the school year with your class-mates. Listen and take notes on important details. Then use the chalkboard list, your memory-starter sentences, and your discussion notes to help you select the topic of your poem.

►To find special words and phrases for your poem, try re-calling sense impressions. Think back to your memorable day. What did you see, hear, smell, taste, and feel? Jot down words and phrases as they come to you.

2. Writing

How will you begin your poem? Perhaps you already have an idea. If not, here are some possibilities to consider.

- Repeat an opening phrase.

> I remember . . . polished floors,
>   clean desks, the smell of
>   new books.
>
> I remember . . . a kind teacher
>   with sparkling eyes
>   and a warm smile.

- Begin each line with the same kind of word (such as "ing" verbs).

> Shuffling through sleet and snow,
> Clutching my books,
> Tugging at my scarf,
> Bracing myself against the wind.

- Begin with a key idea and build on it.

> Some things never change:
>   Each autumn turns the leaves to gold,
>   Each new day erases the old.

►Write the first draft of your poem using any pattern that seems best for your ideas.

3. Revising

▶ Revise your poem with a classmate. Take turns reading your first drafts aloud. Listen to the sounds of the words. Are they pleasing? Ask your classmate to tell you what your poem is about. Discuss what you intended to say. Use the Revision Checklist and talk about the changes you could make.

Revision Checklist

- Does my poem have a pattern?
- Did I include the most appropriate details?
- Did I use rhythm, rhyme, alliteration, or figures of speech?
- Did I choose descriptive words and phrases carefully?

Read the sample below. Notice how choosing more exact descriptive words and phrases strengthened the poem.

I remember:
  Looking for a good *~~friend~~* (*my best friend*),
  Getting lost in big, new *long, unfamiliar* hallways,
  ~~Clean~~ *Polished* pine floors that shined *gleamed like a new penny*,

I remember:
  Looking for my best friend,
  Getting lost in long, unfamiliar hallways,
  Polished pine floors that gleamed like a new penny,
  The spicy smells of wax and window cleaner,
  The crack of purple bindings as we opened
    our new math books,
  Feeling excited and happy at the same time.
I'll never forget
  that first day of school.

► Use the editing marks to make revisions in your poem. Each time you make a change, read your poem aloud to hear the way it sounds.

4. Publishing

► Use the Proofreading Checklist in the Young Writer's Handbook on page 399 to help you check and proofread your poem. Use the editing marks to make corrections. Remember, however, that a poem is different from a paragraph. It is not necessary to indent the first line of your poem, nor do you have to use punctuation marks and capital letters as you would in a paragraph.

► Illustrate your poems and put them into a class scrapbook. Add photographs, awards, newspaper clippings, programs from school events, and other keepsakes. Share your scrapbook with other classes and copy your favorite poems to take home.

EDITING MARKS	
——	cross out
∧	add
⤳	move
≡	capital letter
/	small letter
¶	indent
◯	check spelling

Writing Project

A Greeting Card

Dear Lisa,

Ten times a day
I hear our friends say
They all are blue
Because they miss you.

Until you come back,
We'll be out of whack.
So don't say "ah-choo."
Get rid of your flu!

Love,
Alison

Get Well Soon

You can design and make a personal greeting card that says exactly what you want to say. First, choose the occasion for the card. You might want to send a birthday or holiday greeting. Or you might want to send a message to someone who is not feeling well or to a friend who has moved away. For your message write a short poem that expresses your feelings.

To make your card, fold a large sheet of paper in half, then in half again. Or fold a long sheet of paper over and under accordian-style. Write your message on the inside of the card. Use your best handwriting or some fancy lettering. Draw a picture or design with colored pencils or markers to decorate the front of your card.

Music

A ballad is a poem intended to be sung. Usually a ballad tells a story about some dramatic incident. The story is told in a direct and simple way, often through dialogue. Early ballads were passed on orally. The verses of a ballad are four lines long. The second and fourth lines usually rhyme.

▶ Try it. Read these verses from "Streets of Laredo." Look for the qualities that make it a ballad. Notice that the third verse of the ballad is missing. Write your own version of what you think the missing verse might be.

> **Streets of Laredo**
> As I walked out in the streets of Laredo,
> As I walked out in Laredo one day,
> I spied a young cowboy wrapped up in white linen,
> Wrapped up in white linen and cold as the clay.
>
> "I see by your outfit that you are a cowboy,"
> These words he said as I boldly walked by;
> "Come listen to me and I'll tell my sad story.
> I'm shot in the chest and I'm sure I will die.
> . . . .
> "Go run to the spring for a cup of cold water
> To cool down my fever," the young cowboy said.
> But when I returned, his poor soul had departed,
> And I wept when I saw the young cowboy was dead.

Writers at Work   People who write song lyrics are really poets. Some listen to a piece of music and then write lyrics. Others write lyrics and have a composer set them to music.

▶ Take a familiar melody, such as "Home on the Range" or "Happy Birthday to You." Write your own lyrics for the melody.

Sentences   *pages 294–303*

A. Write the compound subject or predicate in each sentence.

1. Whales, seals, and manatees are all sea mammals.
2. Most seals swim and feed near the shoreline.
3. Female whales and their babies stay close together.
4. Manatees live alone or form small family groups.

B. Write *simple* or *compound* for each sentence.

5. Safra and Ben planned a trip to their grandmother's house.
6. Grandmother Levin lives far away, but she enjoys visitors.
7. Ben packed his suitcase, and Safra prepared a bag lunch.
8. They arrived at Grandmother Levin's after a long bus ride.

C. Write the verb that correctly completes each sentence.

9. A famous region in Florida (is, are) the Everglades.
10. This swampy area (contain, contains) a variety of animals.
11. Engineers (drain, drains) part of the swamp for farming.
12. Either vegetables or sugar cane (grow, grows) well there.

D. Add words to each fragment to make a sentence. Rewrite each run-on sentence as a compound sentence.

13. The polar bear in the zoo.
14. Cars may drive over the bridge trucks are too heavy.
15. The scientists discovered a star they named it Stella.
16. Arranged in a circle on the floor.

Commas   *pages 304–305*

E. Write each sentence, adding commas where needed.

17. Jake are you ready yet?
18. No I need more time.
19. Please Jake hurry.
20. Yes we will be late.

Word Connotations   *pages 306–307*

F. Write the word in each pair with the negative connotation.

21. artificial/fake
22. pushy/ambitious
23. brave/foolhardy
24. sloppy/casual
25. cheap/inexpensive
26. generous/extravagant

Figures of Speech   *pages 316–317*

G. Change each of these similes into a metaphor.

27. The sidewalk at noontime was like a hot griddle.
28. The donkey's bray was like a sour bugle note.
29. The excited students were like chattering sparrows.
30. The wriggling child was like an eel.
31. The roar of the traffic was like nonstop thunder.

Poetry   *pages 312–315*

H. Read the poem. Then answer the questions.

> A cold wind whistles its lonely way
> Down city streets
> And the sky grows gray.
> In the alleys dry leaves scuffle;
> Ragged pieces of paper ruffle,
> Till gently swirling flakes of white
> Create within the city night
> A silent sweep of snow.

32. What three pairs of rhyming words are in the poem?
33. What is one example of onomatopoeia from the poem?
34. Which line from the poem uses three words that begin with the sound of *s*?

I. 35. Write two sentences that illustrate alliteration.

See also Handbook pages 382–389, 403, 405.

Sentences   *pages 6–9, 16–17, 294–295, 298–301*

A. Write the sentences using capital letters and correct end punctuation. After each sentence write *declarative, interrogative, imperative,* or *exclamatory.*

1. we like woodworking class
2. use the saw carefully
3. did you make this bench
4. what a good job you did

B. Write the subject of each sentence.

5. Meet me at the concert.
6. Will Beth be there tonight?
7. Does Joe have a ticket?
8. Save a seat for Todd.

C. Write the compound subject or predicate in each sentence.

9. Swimming and reading are my favorite hobbies.
10. My friend Dale builds and flies model airplanes.
11. Tennis, football, and puzzles keep Roy very busy.
12. Arnie collects and trades foreign stamps.

D. Write the verb that correctly completes each sentence.

13. My friends and I (make, makes) special lunches together.
14. All the recipes (come, comes) from foreign countries.
15. Stella (bake, bakes) stollen, a delicious German bread.
16. Either Rick or Lisa (bring, brings) the dessert.
17. Neither the soup nor the sauces (taste, tastes) too spicy.

Commas   *pages 18–19, 304–305*

E. Write each sentence, adding commas where needed.

18. Look Helen at this beautiful patchwork quilt.
19. Yes my grandmother sewed it together by hand.
20. She used pieces of blue yellow and green cloth.
21. Well your grandmother is very talented.

Nouns *pages 52–53, 58–59*

F. Write the plural form of each noun.

   22. duty   **23.** rodeo   **24.** wife   **25.** moose   **26.** stable

G. Write each noun below. Then write whether it is a *common noun* or a *proper noun*.

   27. Charles Lindbergh became a national hero in 1927.
   28. He flew a plane across the Atlantic Ocean in 33½ hours.
   29. His journey began in New York and ended in Paris.
   30. Crowds cheered him upon his return.

Apostrophes *pages 60–61*

H. Write the possessive form of each noun. Then write whether the noun is *singular* or *plural*.

   31. closets   **32.** children   **33.** rake   **34.** bus   **35.** colony

Pronouns *pages 132–141*

I. Write each sentence. Use the correct pronoun in parentheses ( ).

   36. Ann's snacks are always tastier than (my, mine).
   37. Will you give (he, him) some of these crackers?
   38. The cheese sandwiches are (their, theirs) favorites.
   39. Tony offered (we, us) a whole package of raisins.
   40. (They, Them) were a healthy and delicious dessert.

J. Write each sentence. Underline each predicate nominative.

   41. The contestants in the spelling bee were they.
   42. One of the scorekeepers was I.
   43. The teacher in charge of the spelling bee was he.
   44. The best speller in our school is she.

Cumulative Review

Verbs   *pages 92–97*

K. Write each sentence. Underline the helping verbs once and the main verbs twice.

45. The state of Hawaii is located in the Pacific Ocean.
46. Hawaii did not become our fiftieth state until 1959.
47. The islands of Hawaii were formed by volcanoes.
48. Two of these volcanoes have erupted in recent years.

L. Write the direct object in each sentence.

49. Last summer Grace spent her vacation in London.
50. A helpful tour guide provided a map of the city.
51. One day Grace saw the guards at Buckingham Palace.
52. At Trafalgar Square she fed some pigeons.

M. Write the past and future tense of each verb. Use *will* with the future tense.

53. borrow   54. refuse   55. decide   56. practice   57. taste

Adjectives   *pages 182–185*

N. Write each sentence. Underline the predicate adjective.

58. Stephen felt weak after the bicycle race.
59. The last two miles of the race were difficult.
60. The other bicyclists seemed very fast.
61. Stephen was proud of his silver trophy.

O. Write each sentence. Underline each demonstrative adjective.

62. Tina is reading that book about glassblowing.
63. Did Mary show you how to weave this blanket?
64. Jerry and Kim made these mobiles for us.
65. Will you sell those clay pots at the crafts fair?

Adjectives and Adverbs   *pages 214–215, 222–223*

P. Write the word each underlined adverb describes. Then write whether the word is a *verb*, an *adjective*, or an *adverb*.

66. Our harbor tour was a <u>very</u> exciting event.
67. Porpoises played <u>remarkably</u> close to our ship.
68. A pair of them leaped <u>gracefully</u> into the air.
69. Seagulls <u>noisily</u> called for crusts of bread.
70. The jellyfish we saw were <u>surprisingly</u> large.
71. The wonderful trip ended much <u>too</u> soon.

Q. Write the word in parentheses ( ) that correctly completes each sentence.

72. Chang felt (nervous, nervously) before his speech.
73. We listened (close, closely) to his remarks.
74. Chang spoke (confident, confidently) to his audience.
75. All of us thought Chang's speech was (good, well).

Conjunctions and Prepositions   *pages 258–265*

R. Write each sentence. Underline each conjunction.

76. Vinnie and his brother work at a Shetland pony farm.
77. They are always busy grooming or exercising the ponies.
78. Shetland ponies are small but sturdy.
79. Both children and adults can ride these animals.

S. Write each prepositional phrase. Write *adjective* if it describes a noun. Write *adverb* if it describes a verb, an adjective, or an adverb.

80. Our volleyball team won the first game of the tournament.
81. Friends and relatives cheered us from the stands.
82. The players on the other team were skillful and quick.

Acknowledgments continued from page ii

Row, Publishers, Inc. Page 212: Poem "Swallows" from *Words for Denver and Other Poems* by Thomas Hornsby Ferrill. Copyright © 1964, 1966 by Thomas Hornsby Ferrill. Reprinted by permission of William Morrow & Company. Page 251: Excerpt from *The World Book Encyclopedia.* Copyright © 1983 World Book, Inc. Pages 256, 292: Poems "Shells" and "Summer Rain" from *I Thought I Heard the City* by Lilian Moore. Text copyrighted © 1969 by Lilian Moore. Reprinted by permission of Atheneum Publishers. Page 312: Poem "Fog" from *Chicago Poems* by Carl Sandburg. Copyright 1916 by Holt, Rinehart and Winston, Inc. Copyright © 1944 by Carl Sandburg. Reprinted by permission of Harcourt Brace Jovanovich, Inc. Poem "Water" from *Poems by a Little Girl* by Hilda Conkling. F. Stokes Co., 1920; J.B. Lippincott, 1949. Reprinted by permission of the author. Poem "Steam Shovel" from *Upper Pasture* by Charles Malam. Copyright © 1930, © 1958 by Charles Malam. Reprinted by permission of Holt, Rinehart and Winston, Publishers. Page 313: Poem "Southbound on the Freeway" from *New & Selected Things Taking Place* by May Swenson. Copyright © 1963 by May Swenson. By permission of Little, Brown and Company in association with the Atlantic Monthly Press. Page 314: Poem "Onomatopoeia" from *It Doesn't Always Have to Rhyme* by Eve Merriam. Copyright © 1964 by Eve Merriam. Reprinted by permission of the author. Poem "The Loon" from *Many Many Moons* by Lew Sarett. Reprinted by permission of Lloyd Sarett Stockdale.

SCHOOL ADVISORY PANEL

CLASSROOM TEACHERS

Levels 5 and 6
Louise Carson, Sunset Elementary School, Issaquah, Washington; Judy Dawson, North Run Elementary School, Birch Run, Michigan; Doug Dillon, Madoux Elementary School, Cincinnati, Ohio; Ronnie Fassberg, Bluefield Elementary School, Spring Valley, New York; James Knox, Thomasboro Elementary School, Charlotte, North Carolina; John Manalili, Sachem Central School District, Holbrook, New York; Laima Stede, Taft School, Ferndale, Michigan; Carolyn Wilson, New Monmouth School, Middletown, New Jersey

SPECIAL CONSULTANTS

Betty Gould, Patchogue, New York; Barbara Todd, Los Angeles, California
Teacher Focus Group, New Jersey Public and Parochial Schools: Marie Antieri, Phyllis Mordente Farese, Constance B. Fenner, Maureen Fulop, Carole Guild, Linda Larner, Eileen C. Molloy, Annette Rauscher, Eileen St. André, Barbara M. Silvernale, Barbara Verian
Thesaurus Lessons Consultant: Rosemary Cooke, Southern Boulevard School, Chatham Township, New Jersey

Contributors to the Teacher's Edition: James J. Alvino, gifted notes; Nancy S. Bley, learning disabled notes; Claudia Campbell, translation of Parent Letters into Spanish; Contemporary Perspectives, Inc., marginal notes, Reinforcement Masters, and Practice Masters; Rita M. Deyoe-Chiullán, English as a Second Language notes; Anthony D. Fredericks, Parent Letters; National Evaluation Systems, Inc., tests; Rita Steinglass, Unit Sparkler language games.

Review and Practice Handbooks

Grammar Handbook

Sentences	332
Subjects and Predicates	336
Nouns	340
Singular and Plural Nouns	344
Verbs	348
Tenses of Verbs	352
Irregular Verbs	356
Irregular Verbs	360
Troublesome Verb Pairs	362
Pronouns	364
Using Pronouns	368
Adjectives	370
Adverbs	374
Conjunctions, Prepositions, and Interjections	378
Compound Subjects and Compound Predicates	382
Compound Sentences	384
Subject-Verb Agreement	386
Sentence Errors	388

Young Writer's Handbook

Paragraphs	390
Writing Forms: Friendly Letters	391
Writing Forms: Thank-You Notes and Invitations	392
Writing Forms: Business Letters	393
Writing Forms: Outlines	394
Writing Forms: Book Reports	395
Addressing Letters: Envelopes	396
Addressing Letters: State Abbreviations	397
Editing Marks	398
Proofreading Checklist	399
Capitalization	400
Punctuation	403
The 10 Most Useful Spelling Rules	407
100 Spelling Demons	409
Handwriting Models	411
7 Tips for Taking Tests	413

Sentences

sentence

- A **sentence** is a group of words that expresses a complete thought.   *page 4*

  George had a dream about unidentified flying objects.

declarative
sentence

- A **declarative sentence** makes a statement and ends with a period (.).   *pages 6 and 8*

  The library has a rare-book collection.

interrogative
sentence

- An **interrogative sentence** asks a question and ends with a question mark (?).   *pages 6 and 8*

  Where is the nearest fire station?

imperative
sentence

- An **imperative sentence** gives a command or makes a request. It ends with a period (.).   *pages 6 and 8*

  Speak clearly into the microphone.

exclamatory
sentence

- An **exclamatory sentence** expresses strong feeling and ends with an exclamation mark (!).   *pages 6 and 8*

  What an incredible view this is!

MORE PRACTICE 1   Sentences

Write *sentence* or *not a sentence* for each group of words.

1. The sun always sets in the west.
2. Filling out job applications.
3. The police officer received a medal for bravery.
4. A monthly pass to the swimming pool costs four dollars.
5. Owner of a beautiful Irish setter puppy.
6. The lifeguard blew the whistle at closing time.
7. An extremely sore throat and headache.
8. Wrote three definitions for the same word.
9. Ms. Jones sat in the first row of the theater.
10. Seventeen boys and nineteen girls on the stage.

MORE PRACTICE 2   Sentences

A. Add words to make each group of words a sentence. Try to make a proverb, or wise saying. Then write the sentence.

1. A stitch in time ＿＿.
2. ＿＿ gathers no moss.
3. ＿＿ is worth two in the bush.
4. All work and no play ＿＿.
5. ＿＿ spoil the broth.
6. The early bird ＿＿.
7. ＿＿ heals all wounds.
8. ＿＿ is not gold.

B. Write each sentence. After each sentence write *declarative, interrogative, imperative,* or *exclamatory.*

9. Is Pedro coming over for dinner?
10. They were delighted to get my post card in the mail.
11. I can't believe I ate the whole thing!
12. Turn out all the lights when you leave.
13. What a ridiculous excuse that was!
14. Do you have change for a dollar?
15. Be home by seven o'clock at the latest.
16. Who brought the delicious chicken salad to the picnic?
17. The last slice of pizza is for Jan.

C. Write the sentences using capital letters and end punctuation correctly.

18. wait for Sue Ellen near the front entrance to the shopping mall
19. what time does the express bus come by
20. what exciting news they brought
21. would you like to share a bag of peanuts with me
22. the newspaper article was about personal computers
23. look up the vocabulary words in the dictionary
24. how friendly he is
25. we spent nearly two hours waiting in line to see the movie

MORE PRACTICE 3   Sentences

A. Write which kind of sentence each of the following is. Then tell the purpose of each sentence.

EXAMPLE: The student carried a portable radio.
ANSWER: declarative (makes a statement)

1. You can't be serious!
2. When did you first notice the rash on your arm?
3. The weeds in our vegetable garden multiply quickly.
4. Water the plants on Tuesdays and Fridays, please.
5. Ms. Williams is the chief pharmacist at a large city hospital.
6. Where did Geraldo Cepeda attend law school?
7. I smell something burning!
8. Include a self-addressed stamped envelope with your letter.
9. The canoe tipped over in the middle of the lake.
10. Who is your favorite author?

B. Write the sentences using capital letters and correct end punctuation. After each sentence write *declarative, interrogative, imperative,* or *exclamatory.*

11. she fell asleep in the middle of the movie
12. send in fourteen labels for a free calendar with Boris the cat
13. what a scary movie that was
14. help me carry this box of books to the basement
15. what does your family like to do on weekends
16. how foolish I was to yell
17. my brother and my sister take turns doing the ironing
18. have you ever tried to eat with chopsticks before
19. my family often has toasted muffins or bagels at breakfast
20. what are you wearing to the costume party next week
21. what an amazing trick it was
22. sign your name on the dotted line
23. how much does that bag of cat food weigh
24. dolphins are extremely intelligent mammals
25. bring along your umbrella in case of rain

MORE PRACTICE 4 Sentences

A. Write each sentence. After each sentence write *declarative, interrogative, imperative,* or *exclamatory.*

1. That is the most ridiculous excuse I have ever heard!
2. Have you heard the riddle about the elephant with a bad memory?
3. Write the correct date on the chalkboard.
4. What is the average daily temperature in Fairbanks, Alaska?
5. It can't be time to leave already!
6. The pilot contacted the control tower for further instructions.
7. Tell Rhoda about the plans for the car wash.
8. I worked for hours on yesterday's math assignment.

B. Write which kind of sentence each of the following is. Then tell the purpose of each sentence.

9. I won first prize!
10. Dr. Morris checked my vision.
11. Who left the stove on?
12. Show Lisa the photographs.
13. Has Glen arrived yet?
14. Dad fell asleep in the chair.
15. Wait for me after school.
16. We won the big game!
17. Marty broke his arm again.
18. Close the window, please.
19. Your haircut looks terrific!
20. My sister made dinner.

C. Write the sentences using capital letters and correct end punctuation. After each sentence write *declarative, interrogative, imperative,* or *exclamatory.*

21. what an unusual ending for a story that was
22. stretch your muscles before you start jogging
23. we rehearsed the play for four weeks
24. will the parade be cancelled if it rains
25. what a close call we had
26. the snow melted today
27. remind me to return my overdue library books
28. my mother usually rides her bicycle to work
29. did you look under the bed for your other shoe
30. guess how many points the winning team scored

complete subject

● The **complete subject** is all the words in the subject part of a sentence. The subject part names someone or something. *page 10*

> A herd of antelope grazed peacefully near the river.

complete predicate

● The **complete predicate** is all the words in the predicate part of a sentence. The predicate part tells what the subject is or does. *page 10*

> A herd of antelope grazed peacefully near the river.

simple subject

● The **simple subject** is the main word in the complete subject. *page 12*

> A flock of wild geese flew over the frozen lake.

simple predicate

● The **simple predicate,** or verb, is the main word or words in the complete predicate. *page 14*

> A flock of wild geese flew over the frozen lake.

subject in interrogative sentence

● Change an interrogative sentence into a declarative sentence to find the subject. *page 16*

> Has Robin left already? Robin has left already.

subject in imperative sentence

● *You* (understood) is the subject of an imperative sentence. *page 16*

> (You) Pass me the mustard and the mayonnaise.

MORE PRACTICE 1 Subjects and Predicates

Write the complete subject of each sentence.

1. Mrs. Rossi ordered an omelet.
2. The sleepy kitten yawned.
3. The boy in the back stood up.
4. Walruses have tusks.
5. Everyone waited for Marty.
6. A pound of butter will be enough.
7. Two parakeets shared the cage.
8. The dirty cups are in the sink.

A. Write each sentence. Underline the complete subject once. Underline the complete predicate twice.

    1. This rubber tree plant needs more sunlight.
    2. Houston is in the southern part of Texas.
    3. We climbed to the top of the Washington Monument.
    4. Her sprained ankle swelled during the night.
    5. The new mayor won the election by a narrow margin.
    6. My sister is allergic to synthetic fibers.
    7. Senator Robinson gave a speech in the state senate.
    8. Uncle Timothy works for the largest computer company in the country.
    9. The curious squirrel approached our picnic table.
  10. The Thanksgiving Day parade featured wonderful floats and balloons.

B. Write the simple subject of each sentence.

  11. Electronic games fascinate many children and adults.
  12. The lazy mule refused to move one single inch.
  13. Mrs. Grant presented her first photography exhibit in March.
  14. The officer warned us about jaywalking.
  15. Her flight is scheduled to arrive at four o'clock.
  16. Joel accidently hit the ball through a window.
  17. A portion of the bridge collapsed during the storm.
  18. The fresh bread smells absolutely delicious.

C. Write the simple predicate, or verb, of each sentence.

  19. Baja California is a long, thin peninsula.
  20. The helicopter landed near the Pennsylvania Turnpike.
  21. The Strand Theater is showing two science-fiction thrillers.
  22. The bus will leave right after the game.
  23. Many of us watched the rocket launch on television.
  24. The latest copy of your favorite magazine has arrived in the mail.
  25. I bumped my head on the open cabinet door in the kitchen.

MORE PRACTICE 3 Subjects and Predicates _____

A. Write each sentence. Underline the complete subject once and the simple subject twice.

1. A chameleon can blend in with the colors around it.
2. The busy secretary wrote a memo in shorthand.
3. Aunt Eliza served fresh figs for dessert last night.
4. The captain of the team accepted the trophy proudly.
5. He filled the glass with juice.
6. A large tortoise crawled on the beach.
7. That white house has been vacant for months.
8. Two frisky kittens unraveled a skein of yarn.
9. Dr. Winters wrote a prescription for Kenny.

B. Write each sentence. Underline the complete predicate once and the simple predicate twice.

10. The frightened puppy was hiding under the bed.
11. Her ten-speed bicycle has two flat tires.
12. My cousin collects flags from foreign countries.
13. Joseph has invited several friends to his house.
14. Three of us ordered a large pepperoni pizza.
15. I will patch the bicycle tire by Friday.
16. A tremendous avalanche of snow buried the cabins.
17. The old Mayes Hotel burned to the ground last week.

C. Write the subject of each sentence.

18. Did Samantha finish her science report?
19. Help me with this jigsaw puzzle.
20. Is John absent from school today?
21. Has the teacher seen this note already?
22. Does your sister go to the University of Maryland?
23. Think of a number between one and twenty.
24. Add some more onions and carrots to the stew.
25. Will the bus stop at Fourth Street and Heatherton?

MORE PRACTICE 4 Subjects and Predicates _____

A. Write each sentence. Underline the complete subject once and the simple subject twice.

   1. A gentle breeze blew the papers off the desk.
   2. Jody rode a unicycle in the parade.
   3. My father sent a recipe to an international cooking contest.
   4. These hot peppers are burning my tongue and throat.
   5. My brother knit a sweater for the dog.
   6. Cynthia Leonard ordered two scoops of banana mint ice cream.
   7. Few people voted in the last city election.
   8. Eli Whitney invented the cotton gin.

B. Write each sentence. Underline the complete predicate once and the simple predicate twice.

   9. Most runners stretch their legs before each race.
  10. I shampooed the carpet in the living room.
  11. The baby listened carefully to the music box.
  12. The kitten's eyes opened for the first time on Wednesday.
  13. The batter has hit three home runs this week.
  14. The rice is cooking in our shiny new saucepan.
  15. Lisa carries a toothbrush in her backpack.
  16. The show will begin in exactly ten minutes.
  17. We are planning a special assembly for the last day of school.

C. Write the subject of each sentence. Then write whether the sentence is interrogative or imperative.

  18. Will the bus stop here within the next hour?
  19. Take the last blueberry muffin.
  20. Ask Dr. Kendall about the test results.
  21. Is your aunt enjoying her vacation in Montana?
  22. Has the cafeteria run out of ketchup again?
  23. Choose your favorite flavor for dessert.
  24. Is the temperature very cold at Mirror Lake?
  25. Play a game of backgammon with me before dinner.

Nouns

noun • A **noun** names a person, place, thing, or idea. *page 50*

> <u>Stephanie</u> went to the <u>planetarium</u>.
>
> The <u>show</u> was a huge <u>success</u>.

common noun • A **common noun** is the general name of a person, place, or thing. *page 52*

> The <u>mayor</u> visited our <u>school</u>.

proper noun • A **proper noun** names a particular person, place, or thing.
page 52

> <u>Dr. Judith Kerr</u> lives in <u>Dallas</u>.

possessive noun • A **possessive noun** shows ownership. *page 60*

> The <u>teacher's</u> car stalled.
> <u>Jess's</u> cat ran away from home.
> Many <u>writers'</u> books are published.
> The storm changed some <u>people's</u> plans.

MORE PRACTICE 1   Nouns _____

Write the nouns in these sentences.

1. Leo read about a goose that lays golden eggs.
2. My grandparents traveled across the country by train.
3. Joan solved the mystery of the empty lunchbox.
4. Both tires on my bicycle need more air.
5. The movers hoisted a heavy piano through the window.
6. The lawyer asked the judge for a short recess.
7. Mrs. McMahon has a job with a huge company in the Southwest.
8. My cousin peeled two pounds of potatoes.
9. Christopher Columbus sailed to North America with three tiny ships.
10. Our team of runners set a new record in the race.

MORE PRACTICE 2 Nouns

A. Write the nouns in these sentences. Then write whether each noun names a person, place, thing, or idea.

EXAMPLE: Greg Simpson read another magazine.
ANSWER: Greg Simpson (person), magazine (thing)

1. The conductor on the train punched my ticket.
2. The shop sold beautiful furniture.
3. Dr. Green took my appendix out during an operation.
4. Her waterproof jacket has a broken zipper.
5. A geologist predicted the earthquake in Alaska.
6. The lawyer presented the information to the judge.
7. The source of this river is beyond that mountain.
8. Pablo worked on his report at the library.

B. Write each underlined word. Then write whether it is a *common noun* or a *proper noun*.

9. My older sister has a roommate from France.
10. The desserts are delicious at Pie in the Sky Cafe.
11. On Tuesday Jake attended a lecture at Lincoln High School.
12. Marty has hiked through the Grand Canyon several times.
13. The stoplight at Carlton Boulevard and Central Avenue was repaired last week.
14. Dr. Joan Gold works at San Leandro General Hospital.
15. My cat Clarabelle refuses to eat tuna.

C. Write the possessive noun in each sentence. Then write whether it is *singular* or *plural.*

16. Someone washed the windows of Mr. Jones's car.
17. The players' uniforms were muddy after the first three minutes of the game.
18. Do foxes' eyes glow in the dark?
19. The city's libraries are closed on most holidays.
20. The children's department is on the second floor of the store.

MORE PRACTICE 3 Nouns

A. Write each sentence. Draw one line under each common noun and two lines under each proper noun.

1. Everglades National Park is a swampy area in Florida.
2. The students presented a special program on Columbus Day.
3. Governor Dixie Lee Ray lived in the state of Washington.
4. The magician asked Charlene to be an assistant on Sunday.
5. The Golden Gate Bridge goes from San Francisco to Marin County.
6. Bob Wallinsky works for Montreal Central Bank.

B. Write the possessive noun in each sentence. Then write whether it is *singular* or *plural.*

7. The women's drill team marched in the parade.
8. The ponies' hooves on the wooden bridge sounded like thunder.
9. The company's employees have been planning a picnic.
10. The little boy gripped his father's hand tightly.
11. Several passengers' suitcases were put on the wrong airplane.
12. Her grandchildren's pictures hung on the wall.
13. Jess's jokes always make me laugh.
14. We arrived after the movie's opening scene.
15. Were any Presidents' children married in the White House?
16. These knives' blades need sharpening.
17. Raymond hooked a child's shoe when he went fishing!
18. The babies' crying kept everyone in the nursery busy.

C. Write the nouns in these sentences. Then write whether each noun names a person, place, thing, or idea.

19. The judge announced the decision of the jury.
20. My uncle served a baked apple with cinnamon and cream.
21. The visitor enjoyed the view of the bay.
22. The crystal of my watch has a tiny crack.
23. Each vote expresses an opinion in an election.
24. The timid deer disappeared into the forest.
25. The zoo in our city has a new panda.

A. Write the possessive form of each noun.

1. deer
2. Dr. Martinez
3. gentlemen
4. nurses
5. teacher
6. mosquito
7. friends
8. dress
9. Chris
10. people
11. baby
12. schools
13. parties
14. church
15. witnesses

B. Write each sentence. Draw one line under each common noun and two lines under each proper noun.

16. The Colorado River is a border between California and Arizona.
17. The Statue of Liberty was a gift from the people of France.
18. Dr. David Stein is a professor of music at Northwestern University.
19. My sister was born on April Fools' Day.
20. A herd of camels crossed the sandy desert in Egypt.
21. The tournament will take place at Sunnyvale School on Saturday.
22. The mayor traveled to Memphis for a conference.
23. February is the shortest month of the year.

C. Write the possessive noun in each sentence. Then write whether it is *singular* or *plural.*

24. The telephone's sudden ringing woke us at midnight.
25. Texas's largest city is not the capital of the state.
26. My relatives' homes are in five different parts of the country.
27. The jury listened carefully to the witness's story.
28. Several classes' schedules were interrupted by the fire drill.
29. Goldilocks was an unwelcome guest in the bears' house.
30. The boss's announcement surprised many of the workers.
31. The store is having a sale on men's clothing this week.
32. Several doctors' offices are on the fourteenth floor.
33. The taxi stopped at the employees' entrance.
34. The teakettle's whistle reminded me to turn off the stove.
35. The monkeys' antics amused the spectators.

Singular and Plural Nouns

singular noun

- A **singular noun** names one person, place, thing, or idea. *page 58*

plural noun

- A **plural noun** names more than one person, place, thing, or idea. *page 58*

> The <u>kitten</u> stretches.   The <u>puppies</u> bark.

spelling

plural nouns

- Add *-s* to form the plural of most nouns.

- Add *-es* to form the plural of nouns that end in *s*, *x*, *ch*, or *sh*.

cup, cup<u>s</u>	witness, witnes<u>ses</u>	brush, brush<u>es</u>
plate, plate<u>s</u>	box, box<u>es</u>	bunch, bunch<u>es</u>

- If a noun ends in a consonant and *y*, change the *y* to *i* and add *-es* to form the plural.

- If a noun ends in a vowel and *y*, add *-s* to form the plural.

> cher<u>ry</u>, cher<u>ries</u>   trol<u>ley</u>, trol<u>leys</u>

- If a noun ends in a single *f* or *fe*, usually change the *f* to *v* and add *-s* or *-es* to form the plural.

> kni<u>fe</u>, kni<u>ves</u>   shel<u>f</u>, shel<u>ves</u>

- If a word ends in a vowel and *o*, add *-s;* in a consonant and *o*, add *-s* or *-es*. Some words that end in *o* have two correct plurals.

> rad<u>io</u>, rad<u>ios</u>   volca<u>no</u>, volca<u>nos</u> **or** volca<u>noes</u>

- Some singular nouns change their spelling to form the plural.

> child, children   man, men   tooth, teeth

- Some nouns have the same form for the singular and plural.

> moose, moose   deer, deer   sheep, sheep

MORE PRACTICE 1   Singular and Plural Nouns _____

A. Write the plural form of each noun below.

1. bunch	9. volcano	17. valley
2. tax	10. thief	18. dress
3. man	11. family	19. scarf
4. strawberry	12. peach	20. worry
5. sheep	13. tooth	21. motto
6. business	14. wish	22. eyelash
7. grandchild	15. day	23. rash
8. shoe	16. supply	24. sky

B. Write each sentence using the plural forms of the nouns in parentheses ( ).

25. Becky's (hobby) include raising (guppy).
26. The (dog) help the (rancher) herd (sheep).
27. Student (helper) from two (class) painted the new (shelf) in the school library.
28. The congressional (representative) voted to raise (tax).
29. It is very painful when (particle) of dust or (eyelash) get under contact (lens).
30. The (alley) behind the (house) and apartment (building) in some (neighborhood) are quite narrow.
31. The dentist cleaned my (tooth) and gave me two new (toothbrush).
32. I counted the (splash) from the (rock) we skipped at the lake.
33. The (harvester) filled (dozen) of large (box) with crisp red and yellow (apple).
34. Some (clown) work at (rodeo).
35. She bought three (dress) at (sale).
36. I love to read (story) about explorers' (journey).
37. There are active (volcano) in the Hawaiian (Island).
38. My parents and I saw many (calf) and (lamb) at the county fair.
39. The (man) wore (tuxedo) at my cousin's wedding.
40. Many (family) enjoy outdoor (activity).

A. Write the plural form of each noun below.

1. branch	**8.** woman	**15.** church
2. cherry	**9.** fox	**16.** donkey
3. foot	**10.** company	**17.** beach
4. toy	**11.** tornado	**18.** squash
5. mattress	**12.** dish	**19.** pony
6. calf	**13.** deer	**20.** guess
7. rodeo	**14.** knife	**21.** turkey

B. Write each sentence using the plural forms of the nouns in parentheses ( ).

22. The (contestant) each made three (guess) at the number of (penny) in the jar.

23. Many (song) tell us to forget our (care).

24. The (officer) finally caught the (thief) who had robbed six small (business) in three (week).

25. It has been suggested that (child) and (adult) get their (tooth) cleaned every six (month).

26. Morse code uses a system of (dot) and (dash) to send (message).

27. Many (tourist) in San Francisco enjoy riding on the old (trolley).

28. Several of his (relative) have (farm) where they raise (turkey), (goose), and (chicken).

29. Neither of my (parent) could remember where they had put the (key) to the car.

30. Grandma Moses painted many (picture) in her (seventy).

31. Bruce brought delicious (sandwich) made with (slice) of cheese, (onion), and alfalfa (sprout).

32. Several (tornado) caused damage to three (county).

33. The food (server) carried (tray) to the (guest).

34. All the (bed) have lumpy (mattress).

35. We took (turn) making (wish) as we threw the shiny (coin) into the wishing well.

GRAMMAR HANDBOOK

MORE PRACTICE 3   Singular and Plural Nouns _____

A. Write the plural form of each noun below.

1. party	**10.** sandwich	**19.** wife
2. patio	**11.** radio	**20.** trolley
3. box	**12.** gentleman	**21.** child
4. muscle	**13.** witness	**22.** success
5. crash	**14.** country	**23.** grocery
6. moose	**15.** tray	**24.** inch
7. key	**16.** birch	**25.** shelf
8. reply	**17.** loss	**26.** stone
9. dash	**18.** branch	**27.** eagle

B. Write each sentence using the plural form of the nouns in parentheses (   ).

28. This season our basketball team had an equal number of (loss) and (victory).

29. My (grandparent) raised (blueberry), (radish), and many (variety) of (bean).

30. They made (jelly) from fresh (strawberry) and (peach).

31. The (traveler) blew (kiss) to their (family) as the ship pulled away from the dock.

32. The (branch) of these (plant) grew more than three (inch) last week after I gave them (vitamin).

33. I like corduroy (jacket) with (patch) on the (elbow).

34. How many (bag) of (grocery) can you carry?

35. The (member) of the jury listened carefully to the (attorney) and the (witness).

36. (Donkey) carried (basket) of (cherry) to sell at the marketplace during the summer months.

37. The band (member) sold (box) of sugarless (candy) to raise money for new (uniform).

38. On hot (day) I drink ten (glass) of water.

39. They picked (bunch) of ripe (grape) from the (vine).

40. The (child) heard several (radio) playing different (station).

Verbs

verb ● A **verb** expresses action or being. *page 88*

> An officer <u>directs</u> traffic.   The drivers <u>are</u> patient.

linking verb ● A **linking verb** connects the subject with a word or words in the predicate. *page 90*

> Katrina <u>is</u> a dancer.   He <u>appears</u> nervous.
> We <u>are</u> hungry.   These lemons <u>taste</u> sour.

helping verb ● A **helping verb** works with the main verb to express action or being. *page 92*

> They <u>are</u> <u>leaving</u> now.   Julia <u>has</u> not <u>called</u> yet.
> Dale and Burt <u>should</u> <u>have</u> <u>arrived</u> by now.

direct object ● The **direct object** receives the action of the verb. *page 94*

> Lisa brushed her <u>hair.</u>   We called <u>Francine.</u>

MORE PRACTICE 1 Verbs

A. Write the sentences. Underline each verb.

1. Each student recites a poem from memory in this class.
2. Gerald changes the radio station too often.
3. Matt is a part-time clerk at Supershop Market.
4. The pilot landed the jumbo jet safely in the storm.
5. We have weekly discussion meetings with all our teachers.

B. Write the verb in each sentence. Then write *action verb* or *state-of-being verb* after each verb.

6. She is the leader of the school safety patrol.
7. The drawbridge crosses the Chicago River near the docks.
8. Red Riding Hood visits her grandmother often.
9. I am an amateur photographer.
10. These Italian sausages are extremely spicy!

MORE PRACTICE 2   Verbs

A. Write each sentence. Draw one line under the linking verb. Draw two lines under the words that the verb connects.

EXAMPLE: This chili is delicious!
ANSWER: This <u>chili</u> <u>is</u> <u>delicious</u>!

1. This wool sweater feels scratchy.
2. The heavy box was a gift for Josef's cousin.
3. Sometimes our cat appears unfriendly to strangers.
4. Rachel is the youngest child in her family.
5. The rapids of the Wagonwheel River are treacherous for canoes and rafts during the autumn months.
6. The ducks in the pond near the civic center are mallards.
7. Grant looks nervous about something.
8. The players' uniforms were muddy after the first three minutes of the game.

B. Write the sentences below. Underline the helping verbs once and the main verbs twice.

9. The stubborn donkey has not moved an inch.
10. We have been writing letters to our congressional representatives.
11. Geologists are studying active volcanoes around the world.
12. I was not thinking very clearly yesterday.
13. The sun will set in exactly eighteen minutes.
14. Lightning had damaged the transmitting towers on the station roof.
15. They were not marching in step with the music.

C. Write the direct object in each sentence.

16. My family usually eats dinner at six o'clock sharp.
17. Pauline has saved enough money for a new ten-speed bicycle.
18. I love the smell of fresh pine trees in the forest.
19. Noriko Tanaka designed the unusual fountain in the botanical garden.
20. The tired driver drank two large mugs of hot coffee.

MORE PRACTICE 3 Verbs

A. Write the verbs in the sentences. Then write *MV* if the sentence has a main verb but no helping verb. Write *HV + MV* if the sentence has both a helping verb and a main verb.

EXAMPLE: The rocket has entered the earth's atmosphere.
ANSWER: has entered (HV + MV)

1. The Scouts are marching in the Fourth of July parade this year.
2. Three new films opened during the past weekend.
3. The Walk-A-Thon course will cover twenty kilometers around town.
4. The kitten has not wanted any food or water all day.
5. Our school chorus has been practicing for weeks for a spring concert in the park.
6. You should wait for Sharon near the front lobby of the theater.
7. They planned a surprise dinner for their grandparents' fortieth wedding anniversary.
8. Their house is being painted next week.

B. Write the direct object in each sentence.

9. The soldiers saluted the visiting general during inspection.
10. The graduates are presenting a new flag to the school.
11. Doris and Frank heard an echo from deep within the canyon.
12. Astronomers have discovered several new stars in recent years.
13. Our teacher always assigns fascinating topics for reports.
14. The clown wore bright red suspenders with plaid pants.
15. I pried the lid off the jar of peanut butter carefully.

C. Write the verb in each sentence. Then write *action verb* or *state-of-being verb* after each verb.

16. During the drought last summer our water supply was low.
17. The ranchers herded the cattle from the open range to the corral.
18. A signal light flashed from a lighthouse on the rocky shore.
19. The leaders of the group were mountain climbers.
20. A thesaurus is an extremely helpful reference book.

A. Write the sentences. Underline each action verb once and each direct object twice.

1. That candidate needs a snappy slogan for the campaign.
2. The cooking class baked twelve loaves of banana nut bread.
3. Your visit brightened my stay in the hospital.
4. Their garden yielded a generous harvest of vegetables.
5. The computer has lost some important data again.
6. The movers hoisted the heavy piano through a window upstairs.
7. Someone has sprayed green paint all over the sidewalk.
8. The children carved a jack-o-lantern with a mischievous grin.

B. Write the verbs in the sentences. Then write *MV* if the sentence has a main verb but no helping verb. Write *HV* + *MV* if the sentence has both a helping verb and a main verb.

9. Leslie added a black eyepatch and bright green scarf to the pirate costume.
10. The letter was delivered to the wrong address.
11. The detectives searched for clues at the scene of the crime.
12. I am learning some words in Portuguese from my new next-door neighbors.
13. The coach will announce the starting lineup for tomorrow's game at our practice after school.
14. We must finish the assignment before lunchtime.
15. Monster movies terrify many adults and children.
16. The largest corporation in our state might move its main office to Tulsa, Oklahoma.

C. Write each sentence. Draw one line under the linking verb. Draw two lines under the words that the verb connects.

17. Our new puppy is a collie.
18. You looked angry last night.
19. This milk tastes sour.
20. I am a good speller.

Tenses of Verbs

tense ● The **tense** of a verb shows time.   *page 96*

> **Present:** We <u>recycle</u> glass bottles.
> **Past:**   Karen <u>collected</u> newspapers.
> **Future:**   George <u>will</u> <u>save</u> aluminum cans.

principal
parts ● The **principal parts** are the basic forms of a verb. They include the present, the past, and the past participle.   *page 98*

Present	Past	Past Participle
arrive	arrived	(has, have, had) arrived
play	played	(has, have, had) played
worry	worried	(has, have, had) worried
plan	planned	(has, have, had) planned

MORE PRACTICE 1 Tenses of Verbs _____

A. Write the underlined verbs from the sentences below. Then write *present tense, past tense,* or *future tense* after each verb.

1. This advertisement <u>compares</u> two brands of detergent.
2. The fire <u>occurred</u> in a vacant house on Grant Street.
3. Our friendship <u>will</u> <u>last</u> a lifetime.
4. The reporter <u>interviewed</u> each candidate before the debate.
5. I <u>will</u> <u>feel</u> relief after my dentist's appointment.
6. Jean <u>climbed</u> the ladder to the roof.
7. We <u>wash</u> the dishes immediately after dinner in my house.
8. Millions of viewers <u>watched</u> the space launch on television.

B. Write the present, past, and past participle of each verb. Use the helping verb *has* with each past participle.

9. clean	12. reply	15. hurry	18. move
10. mail	13. stir	16. replace	19. satisfy
11. drop	14. apply	17. greet	20. grin

GRAMMAR HANDBOOK

MORE PRACTICE 2   Tenses of Verbs _____

A. Write the verb in each sentence. Then write *present tense, past tense,* or *future tense* after the verb.

1. Many athletes will train for the Olympic games.
2. Anna jogs at least five mornings a week regardless of weather.
3. Your paycheck will arrive in tomorrow's mail.
4. The helicopter reported the traffic jam to the news station.
5. The fire engines responded to several false alarms last week.
6. Sometimes the early bird catches the worm.
7. The officer warned us about jaywalking.
8. The judges will announce the winners in five minutes.
9. That company will replace worn parts for the lifetime of the appliance.
10. Greg polished the car with a new kind of wax.
11. Aunt Esther replies immediately to each of my letters.
12. The ushers distribute programs at every concert.
13. Paul mixed a batch of cookie dough.
14. I will present my oral report next Friday afternoon.
15. The art museum closes early on Thursdays.
16. In the cartoon the ostrich buried its head in the sand.
17. Ms. Graham will schedule a meeting with your parents on Thursday.

B. Write the past tense and future tense of each verb below. Use *will* with the future tense.

18. bloom	**21.** flip	**24.** count	**27.** destroy
19. wax	**22.** hurry	**25.** thank	**28.** laugh
20. wait	**23.** crash	**26.** bury	**29.** fascinate

C. Write the three principal parts of each verb. Use the helping verb *has* with each past participle.

30. inspect	**34.** slam	**38.** print	**42.** copy
31. terrify	**35.** reach	**39.** smell	**43.** use
32. explain	**36.** occupy	**40.** shatter	**44.** organize
33. whistle	**37.** spray	**41.** grip	**45.** supply

MORE PRACTICE 3 Tenses of Verbs

A. Write the past tense and future tense of each verb below. Use *will* with the future tense.

1. need	**5.** qualify	**9.** sniff	**13.** snap
2. contain	**6.** relax	**10.** suspect	**14.** create
3. add	**7.** shop	**11.** testify	**15.** prevent
4. respond	**8.** groan	**12.** grab	**16.** grin

B. Write the verb in each sentence. Then write *present, past,* or *past participle* to show which principal part of the verb was used.

17. A glass of orange juice satisified my craving for something sweet.
18. Every morning the teacher writes a daily schedule on the board.
19. The janitor has replaced several light bulbs in the cafeteria.
20. The ambulance raced to the scene of the accident.
21. Francine had carried enough extra food on the hike for me.
22. The ice cream has melted all over the kitchen counter.
23. Michael earned enough money last week for a new pair of skates.
24. Several new films have opened in local theaters recently.
25. The governor had changed the date of the press conference.
26. Tommy switches the radio station too often.
27. Scientists have studied the structure of cells for many years.
28. I received an invitation to a surprise birthday party for Ed.
29. The cafeteria has served macaroni and cheese twice this week.
30. You owe me two dollars for the movie ticket.
31. Mrs. Rogers tripped on the icy steps in front of her house.
32. The police have stopped all traffic on the bridge during the storm.
33. Dr. Tamaya had removed the cast from Glen's arm a week ago.

C. Write the three principal parts of each verb. Use the helping verb *has* with each past participle.

34. remain	**37.** unwrap	**40.** live	**43.** charge
35. love	**38.** marry	**41.** exchange	**44.** train
36. spy	**39.** attach	**42.** trap	**45.** identify

MORE PRACTICE 4　Tenses of Verbs

A. Write the verb in each sentence. Then write *present tense, past tense,* or *future tense* after the verb.

1. The moon blocked the sun's light during the eclipse.
2. The congressional representatives will attend a special session.
3. Many pilots contact the control tower for landing instructions.
4. The zookeeper tossed fish to the hungry dolphins.
5. The rain will affect our plans for the class picnic.
6. The teacher postponed the science test until Wednesday.
7. The security guards at the shopping mall use walkie-talkies.
8. The lifeguards will demonstrate lifesaving techniques.
9. Several people know the combination to my gym locker.
10. Dr. Ramirez attended a huge medical convention in Atlanta during the second week of December.
11. Those sunglasses shield her sensitive eyes from glare.
12. Many countries will send athletes to the next Olympic games.

B. Write the verb in each sentence. Then write *present, past,* or *past participle* to show which principal part of the verb was used.

13. The jury has decided in favor of the defendant.
14. We tossed a salad of lettuce, tomatoes, celery, and carrots with vinegar and oil.
15. Gail burned a hole in the shirt with a hot iron.
16. The basketball players hoped for an easy victory.
17. The water in the saucepan had boiled for three minutes.
18. Our teachers arrange some fascinating field trips for us.
19. My sister has applied to three different law schools.
20. Many people plant trees and flowers on Arbor Day.
21. I wrapped the anniversary gift with silver paper and red ribbon.
22. The team captain accepted the beautiful trophy proudly.
23. Someone has borrowed my thesaurus without permission again.
24. The weeds in the vegetable garden multiply too quickly.
25. We have completed more than half of the school year already.

Irregular Verbs

● **Irregular verbs** do not form the past and past participle by adding *-ed.*   *page 100*

Present	Past	Past Participle
begin	began	(has, have, had) begun
blow	blew	(has, have, had) blown
do	did	(has, have, had) done
drink	drank	(has, have, had) drunk
eat	ate	(has, have, had) eaten
fly	flew	(has, have, had) flown
give	gave	(has, have, had) given
go	went	(has, have, had) gone
grow	grew	(has, have, had) grown
know	knew	(has, have, had) known
ring	rang	(has, have, had) rung
sing	sang	(has, have, had) sung
swim	swam	(has, have, had) swum
take	took	(has, have, had) taken
throw	threw	(has, have, had) thrown
write	wrote	(has, have, had) written

The verb be

Present: I am   (he, she, it) is   (we, you, they) are
Past: (I, he, she, it) was   (we, you, they) were
Past participle: been

The verb have

Present: (I, you, we, they) have   (he, she, it) has
Past: (I, you, he, she, it, we, they) had
Past participle: had

MORE PRACTICE 1   Irregular Verbs _____

A. Write the three principal parts of the verbs below.

    1. blow   **3.** fly   **5.** know   **7.** throw
    2. drink   **4.** go   **6.** ring   **8.** swim

B. Write each sentence using the past or the past participle of the verb in parentheses ( ).

  9. A powerful wind has (blow) an entire tree across the road.
 10. The sales clerk (give) me the wrong change from a dollar.
 11. My feet have (grow) at least two sizes in a year.
 12. The ferry ride from San Francisco to Sausalito (take) about thirty minutes.
 13. Juanita and Leslie have (know) each other since kindergarten.
 14. I (throw) several coins into the wishing well at the park.
 15. Connie had (do) all of the math problems already.
 16. Someone has (write) all over the playground walls with green spray paint.
 17. The teakettle (begin) to whistle when the water boiled.
 18. We (eat) in the patio at the Garden Spot Cafe.
 19. The pilot (fly) from Seattle to Las Vegas with a broken light on the airplane's wing.
 20. Karen and Nick have (swim) in several races this summer.
 21. On hot summer afternoons I have (drink) five or six glasses of water in a row.
 22. That is absolutely the best idea you have (have) in a long time.
 23. The three bears wanted to know who had (be) in their house.
 24. The telephone (ring) at least thirteen times before anyone answered.
 25. We have (begin) to learn about multiplying fractions in school.
 26. They (have) the wrong key to the locker.
 27. George has (sing) on television twice.
 28. The magazine article has (give) me a better understanding of home computers.
 29. Occasionally a pigeon has (fly) into the gym through an open window.
 30. Ken has (be) in the hospital with pneumonia.

MORE PRACTICE 2   Irregular Verbs _____

A. Write the three principal parts of the verbs below.

  1. begin   3. eat   5. grow   7. write
  2. do   4. give   6. sing   8. take

B. Write each sentence using the past or the past participle of the verb in parentheses ( ).

  9. The kindergarten children (grow) vines from sweet potato plants.
 10. Mr. Wallace's store has (give) some free toys to the children's hospital in our town.
 11. Nobody (know) the solution to the puzzle.
 12. Ronald (do) the laundry before his parents came home from work.
 13. She (write) a letter to her uncle in Ecuador.
 14. We (take) our sick poodle to the veterinarian on Tuesday.
 15. The breeze through the open window (blow) the door shut with a loud bang.
 16. Jeremy has (go) to mail some letters.
 17. The pitcher has (throw) eight strikes in a row.
 18. The workers had (begin) digging the ditch before Sunday's storm.
 19. The team members (do) their best, but they still lost the game.
 20. Dad has (take) several classes in Japanese cooking.
 21. The bells in the Town Hall have (ring) every fifteen minutes for over one hundred years.
 22. Someone has (eat) my lunch by mistake!
 23. She has (fly) by herself across the ocean several times.
 24. The team captain had (know) the coach's plan before the game.
 25. We (swim) towards the raft in the middle of the lake.
 26. Laura had (be) asleep for an hour when the telephone rang.
 27. We (have) the toughest exam ever in school yesterday.
 28. A famous entertainer (sing) the national anthem before the football game.
 29. The alarm clock had (ring), but Betsy slept through it.
 30. Who (drink) the can of apple juice that was on the top shelf of the refrigerator?

A. Write each sentence using the past or the past participle of the verb in parentheses ( ).

   1. Craig has (take) the overdue books back to the library.

   2. We (begin) working before Sally arrived.

   3. The lifeguard dived in the pool and (swim) towards the struggling swimmer.

   4. Mr. Wilson has (give) us his secret chili recipe.

   5. Someone has (drink) from my glass of milk by mistake.

   6. Maria has (grow) taller than her mother in the past year.

   7. Ms. Kuroda (go) to her piano lesson on Thursday.

   8. Mike has (know) how to roller-skate for several years.

   9. Susan (throw) away the discount coupon without knowing it.

10. The dog (eat) my book report!

11. The wild ducks (fly) south in search of warmer temperatures.

12. She has (write) the directions on the chalkboard.

13. When the hot water heater was broken, I (take) a cold shower.

14. Jason and Richard have (go) to the corner market for more milk.

15. Someone has (ring) the doorbell and left a package there.

16. No one (know) what language the space creature was speaking.

17. The show had (begin) fifteen minutes later than scheduled.

18. She has (have) a terrible case of laryngitis for two weeks.

19. Mary had (be) our first choice for class president.

20. The shivering child (drink) a mug of hot cocoa.

21. I have (grow) to like many different vegetables this year.

22. Your invitation (go) to the wrong address.

23. Pablo (give) me half of his chicken salad sandwich.

24. We (sing) songs around the campfire for hours.

B. Write the three principal parts of the verbs below.

25. write	**29.** swim	**33.** take	**37.** ring
26. eat	**30.** go	**34.** drink	**38.** throw
27. grow	**31.** sing	**35.** blow	**39.** give
28. fly	**32.** begin	**36.** know	**40.** do

Irregular Verbs

irregular verbs   ● Some irregular verbs follow a pattern in the way they are
formed.   *page 102*

Present	Past	Past Participle
break	broke	(has, have, had) broken
choose	chose	(has, have, had) chosen
freeze	froze	(has, have, had) frozen
speak	spoke	(has, have, had) spoken
become	became	(has, have, had) become
come	came	(has, have, had) come
run	ran	(has, have, had) run
bring	brought	(has, have, had) brought
catch	caught	(has, have, had) caught
say	said	(has, have, had) said
teach	taught	(has, have, had) taught
think	thought	(has, have, had) thought

MORE PRACTICE 1   Irregular Verbs _____

A. Write the past and past participle of each verb.

1. think	**4.** speak	**7.** become	**10.** teach
2. catch	**5.** freeze	**8.** say	**11.** come
3. run	**6.** break	**9.** bring	**12.** break

B. Write the past or the past participle of the verb in parentheses ( ) to
complete each sentence. Then write which principal part you used.

13. The substitute teacher (teach) us an interesting new method of adding
fractions.

14. I am afraid that our new puppy has (break) your favorite glass vase.

15. In spite of her arthritis, my Aunt Maryann (run) in several marathons
last year.

MORE PRACTICE 2 Irregular Verbs _____

A. Write the past or the past participle of the verb in parentheses ( ) to complete each sentence. Then write which principal part you used.

1. The coach has (choose) the starting team for Friday's game.
2. All day long I (think) today was Wednesday instead of Tuesday.
3. An enormous truck had (run) out of fuel on the highway.
4. The milk (freeze) because the refrigerator temperature was too low.
5. The mayor (speak) at a press conference concerning the tax increase.
6. My older cousin has (become) the first female player on the Rockets.
7. Who (bring) the delicious potato salad to the picnic?
8. Jerome (come) over to watch a program about whales with me.
9. Helen had (catch) a bad cold during the last rainstorm.
10. Aunt Lydia (say) she would visit us during the holidays.
11. Calvin (break) his leg in a skiing accident last winter.
12. Gloria has (teach) some of her friends how to play chess.
13. No one had (think) to bring a can opener on the camping trip.
14. What famous person has (say), "The early bird catches the worm!"?
15. Sam and Dave have (bring) their guitars to school today.
16. The janitor had (come) to repair the leaking faucet.
17. A senator had (speak) to the committee about air pollution.
18. Who (choose) this strange color of paint?
19. Usually the skating pond has (freeze) over by the middle of January.
20. Carlos (become) impatient after waiting an hour for the bus.
21. The water (run) over the top of the bathtub.
22. Everyone (bring) a different dish to the pot-luck supper.
23. We each (choose) our favorite flavor for dessert.
24. Mrs. Morris has (catch) several large fish from the pier.
25. A special-delivery letter (come) for you this morning.
26. Everyone (think) Louise's poster would win first prize.

B. Write the past and past participle of each verb.

27. break	**30.** bring	**33.** come
28. freeze	**31.** teach	**34.** run
29. say	**32.** become	**35.** think

Troublesome Verb Pairs

**the verbs
can and may**

● Use the verb *can* to mean "to be able to do something." Use the verb *may* to mean "to ask or give permission."   *page 104*

> **Can** you stand on your head?   **May** I watch?

**the verbs
let and leave**

● Use the verb *let* to mean "to permit or allow." Use the verb *leave* to mean "to go away from" or "to allow to remain."   *page 104*

> **Let** me have a turn.   Please **leave** the door open.

**the verbs
teach and learn**

● Use the verb *teach* to mean "to instruct." Use the verb *learn* to mean "to gain understanding."   *page 106*

> The lifeguards **teach** water-safety classes.
> We **learn** about artificial respiration.

**the verbs
sit and set**

● Use the verb *sit* to mean "to rest." Use the verb *set* to mean "to put or place something."   *page 106*

> It is fun to **sit** around the campfire.
> They **set** the tent up near the lake.

MORE PRACTICE 1   Troublesome Verb Pairs _____

Write each sentence. Use the correct verb in parentheses ( ).

1. We always (sit, set) and rest a while after exercising.
2. His parents seldom (leave, let) him stay out late.
3. In this book the chief detective (can, may) solve any mystery.
4. You (can, may) watch television when all your homework is finished.
5. Some music students (learn, teach) to play several instruments.
6. Please (leave, let) the window open until the smoke disappears.
7. Regina and Eloise always (sit, set) together at lunchtime.
8. Can you (learn, teach) me how to play backgammon?
9. The carpenter (sit, set) the saw down carefully.
10. If we (leave, let) our coats here, no one will take our seats.

MORE PRACTICE 2 Troublesome Verb Pairs _____

A. Write each sentence. Use the correct verb in parentheses ( ).

1. Where did the messenger (sit, set) the note from the principal?
2. Karen's older sister and brother (learn, teach) us all the new dances.
3. In Japan, children and adults usually (sit, set) their shoes outside the door and wear slippers in the house.
4. Will you (let, leave) me help you plan the surprise party?
5. My baby brother (can, may) drink from a cup already.
6. Some people say you can't (teach, learn) an old dog new tricks, but I disagree.
7. Please (leave, let) at least one slice of pumpkin bread for Dad.
8. My cousin (can, may) turn cartwheels using just one hand!
9. At the Moroccan restaurant, people (sit, set) on big pillows on the floor while eating.
10. You (may, can) help yourself to a piece of fruit from the refrigerator if you are still hungry.

B. Write each sentence. Use the word *can, may, let,* or *leave* in place of the blank.

11. It isn't a good idea to ___ your bicycle outside overnight.
12. You ___ choose your favorite color.
13. I appreciate it when people ___ me make my own decisions.
14. Martin ___ climb a rope faster than anyone else in my class.
15. Be sure to turn out all the lights when you ___.

C. Write each sentence. Use the word *teach, learn, sit,* or *set* in place of the blank.

16. Where did Eleanor ___ to make clay pots?
17. My mother forgot where she ___ the keys to the car.
18. Robbie and I like to ___ in the front row.
19. They will ___ us how to type next year.
20. It is uncomfortable to ___ on hard wooden bleachers.

Pronouns

pronoun
- A **pronoun** takes the place of a noun or nouns. *page 132*

  The <u>dogs</u> chased a <u>car</u>.   <u>They</u> chased <u>it</u>.

subject pronoun
- The **subject pronouns** are *I, you, she, he, it, we,* and *they.* *page 134*

  <u>Dolores</u> raised her hand.   <u>She</u> raised her hand.

object pronoun
- The **object pronouns** are *me, you, her, him, it, us,* and *them.* *page 136*

  Don gave the <u>book</u> to <u>Rick</u>.   Don gave <u>it</u> to <u>him</u>.

possessive pronoun
- A **possessive pronoun** shows ownership. *page 138*

  <u>Dr. Kern's</u> office is closed.   <u>His</u> office is closed.
  The jacket is <u>Rita's</u>.   The jacket is <u>hers</u>.

predicate nominative
- A **predicate nominative** is a noun or pronoun that follows a linking verb and renames or identifies the subject of the sentence. *page 140*

  George was the <u>winner</u>.   The winner was <u>he</u>.

MORE PRACTICE 1 Pronouns _____

Write each sentence. Underline the pronouns.

1. Jennifer came to our house for dinner on Saturday.
2. They were caught in a sudden cloudburst without their umbrellas.
3. Jan and I waved to Aunt Hilda from the window of the airplane.
4. The bottle of grape juice in the refrigerator is mine and not yours.
5. The magic slipper fit her perfectly.
6. Would you prefer potato salad or cole slaw with your sandwich?
7. The boss's announcement surprised us a great deal.
8. Mr. Roberts gave me a ride to school in his new car.

GRAMMAR HANDBOOK

MORE PRACTICE 2   Pronouns

A. Write each sentence. Underline the subject pronouns.

1. We saved some money by purchasing the giant economy size.
2. I could not possibly eat another bite.
3. You really ought to see the new adventure movie at the Embassy.
4. Finally he concluded the report with some startling facts.
5. She could hear an echo from deep within the canyon.
6. They traveled by bicycle all around the state last year.
7. It fell off the wall during the earthquake and shattered.
8. Tina and I wore the same costume to the Halloween party.

B. Write the second sentence in each pair. Underline the object pronoun.

9. George woke up quite suddenly. The ringing of the alarm clock startled him.
10. James and Ellie helped at the Special Olympics. The mayor thanked them.
11. I ate lunch in the park yesterday. A noisy blue jay scolded me.
12. Danny called Rita. Danny told her about the plans for the party.
13. Mr. Graham forgot his lunch. The man left it on the kitchen table.
14. Ray and I went to the movies. The first film bored us.
15. My family is eating dinner now. I will call you later.

C. Write the possessive pronoun in each sentence.

16. The teacher thought hers was the best story.
17. The kitten licked its sore paw.
18. I can't remember the combination to my locker.
19. Have Marcy and Rich finished their assignments already?
20. On Saturday we are having our class picnic at Lincoln Park.
21. Your house could certainly use a new coat of paint.
22. The bicycle with the red flag is his.
23. Why does Bonnie have such a sad look on her face?
24. This lunch isn't nearly as appetizing as yours.
25. The digital watch that Joey found is mine.

MORE PRACTICE 3 Pronouns _____

A. Write each sentence. Underline each predicate nominative.

1. That brilliant red bird is a cardinal.
2. The first prize was a free dinner at Caruso's.
3. The last car in line is a taxicab.
4. The first person in line was I.
5. The woman was a complete stranger.
6. Our math teacher this week is a substitute.
7. The coach's first choice was you.
8. The telephone caller on Sunday was she.
9. Nan and I are cousins.
10. The most talented musician in the show was he.

B. Each sentence contains two pronouns. Some are subject pronouns and some are not. Write the pronouns. Then underline *only* the subject pronouns.

11. She is a teacher at our school.
12. Usually we wait for them at the corner.
13. Sometimes you make me laugh.
14. He burned a hole in his favorite shirt with a hot iron.
15. They remembered to bring extra blankets with them.
16. Actually it was not your fault.
17. I forgot the dictionary was yours.

C. The second sentence in each pair contains two pronouns. Write the pronouns. Then underline *only* the object pronouns.

18. The students gave a play. They presented it to the kindergarten.
19. Derek wrote to Angela. She answered him immediately.
20. Pedro and I talked to the clerk. He told us about home computers.
21. My sister did not see the bee. Its sting hurt her.
22. Dr. West called. She wants you to stop by the office.
23. Les and Greg walked by. I called them by name.
24. I called Mark on the phone. He told me about the plans.
25. The cat was cold and hungry. I fed it in our kitchen.

MORE PRACTICE 4 Pronouns

A. The second sentence in each pair contains a pronoun. Write the pronoun. Then write the noun or nouns that the pronoun takes the place of.

1. Eddie went to the library. He studied for several hours.
2. My parents exercise regularly. Sometimes they jog along Main Street.
3. The monkey was quite hungry. It ate three bananas.
4. Samantha found someone's wallet. The person thanked her.
5. Dave came over for dinner. Mother invites him often.
6. The family traveled to Tucson. We rode on a bus overnight.
7. The governor gave a speech in City Hall. She spoke about pollution.
8. The coach gave instructions. Mr. Green wrote them on a chalkboard.
9. The pharmacist filled a prescription. It was for Dolores.

B. Write each sentence. Use the correct pronoun in parentheses ( ).

10. (Her, Hers) jacket has a broken zipper.
11. Jeff said (your, yours) was the highest score on the exam.
12. (Our, Ours) bus always seems to run late in bad weather.
13. I loaned (my, mine) stopwatch to Edgar for the track meet.
14. (Their, Theirs) is the largest house on the block.
15. I like (her, hers) better than the other drawing.
16. Dad agrees with (your, yours) suggestion.
17. (My, Mine) is the bicycle with the green sticker on the back wheel.
18. Have you seen (your, yours) grandparents recently?
19. I hope (our, ours) is the winning ticket.

C. Write the predicate nominative in each sentence. Then write whether it is a predicate noun or a predicate pronoun.

20. My all-time favorite food is pizza!
21. The guest of honor at the banquet will be you.
22. A handshake from the mayor was his only reward.
23. The mysterious strangers were they.
24. The fastest runner on the team is Janice.
25. The new secretary of the Drama Club is I.

Using Pronouns

subject pronoun • Use a subject pronoun as the subject of a sentence. *page 142*

> **She** practiced the piano for over an hour.

object pronoun • Use an object pronoun after an action verb. *page 142*

> **Gavin told us about the hurricane in Florida.**

pronoun after a linking verb • Use a subject pronoun after a linking verb. *page 142*

> **The winner of the contest was he.**

MORE PRACTICE 1   Using Pronouns _____

A. Write each sentence using the correct pronoun in parentheses ( ). Then write whether the pronoun you used is a subject or an object pronoun.

1. George's uncle drove (him, he) to the library after school.
2. Margarita and (I, me) shared some popcorn at the movies.
3. The coach warned (us, we) about the other team's strategy.
4. We have not seen (her, she) for nearly six months.
5. (They, Them) volunteered to clean the cabinets in the science lab.
6. (She, Her) prepared dinner for the entire family and three guests.
7. (My cousins and I, I and my cousins) write to each other often.
8. The tour guide showed Lisa and (we, us) around the art museum.

B. Write the pronoun in parentheses ( ) that correctly completes each sentence. Then write whether the pronoun is a predicate nominative or a direct object.

9. The only people at the restaurant were (we, us).
10. This morning's storm caught (we, us) by surprise.
11. The new governor of our state is (she, her).
12. Dr. Lawrence appointed (me, I) to the committee.
13. The detectives at the scene of the crime were (they, them).
14. The attorney advised (they, them) of their legal rights.
15. Loud music bothers (him, he).

MORE PRACTICE 2 Using Pronouns

A. Write each sentence using the correct pronoun in parentheses ( ). Then write whether the pronoun you used is a subject or an object pronoun.

1. You and (I, me) should work together on a project for the school's science fair.
2. Geraldine's noisy upstairs neighbors disturbed (her, she) during the entire evening.
3. The judges selected (him, he) for "Most Improved Player of the Year" trophy.
4. Mr. Rodriguez asked (Jonathan and me, me and Jonathan) about the lost briefcase.
5. The other team members and (I, me) practice daily.
6. (He, Him) collects aluminum cans and glass bottles for recycling.
7. Dr. Kensington reminded (I, me) about my dental appointment.
8. Kathryn and (we, us) ride the express bus to school every day.
9. Yolanda and (she, her) are my closest friends.
10. The nurse told (they, them) about emergency first-aid procedures.

B. Write the pronoun in parentheses ( ) that correctly completes each sentence. Then write whether the pronoun is a predicate nominative or a direct object.

11. My parents took (us, we) to a delicatessen for supper.
12. The only injured person in the accident was (he, him).
13. Reggie saw Wayne and (me, I) on our way to the basketball game in the gym.
14. The most popular musicians these days are (they, them).
15. The one on the far left in the top row of the class photograph is (me, I).
16. Some of the volunteers at the Special Olympics this year will be (us, we).
17. The most reliable assistant is usually (he, him).
18. The visiting professor confused (we, us) with all the difficult words in the lecture.
19. Joanna's poodle followed (her, she) to school yesterday.
20. The youngest senator in the state is (she, her).

Adjectives

adjective
- An **adjective** describes a noun or pronoun. *page 178*
Adjectives answer the question *What kind?* or *How many?*
The articles *a, an,* and *the* are a special kind of adjective.

> Twelve <u>red</u> roses arrived in <u>a</u> <u>thin</u> box.
> <u>Several</u> students did <u>an</u> <u>excellent</u> job in <u>the</u> play.

proper adjective
- A **proper adjective** is formed from a proper noun. *page 180*

> <u>Spanish</u> border   <u>Canadian</u> railroad   <u>Japanese</u> flag

predicate adjective
- A **predicate adjective** follows a linking verb and describes the subject of the sentence. *page 182*

> The trip was <u>pleasant</u>.
> Jack felt <u>angry</u>.

demonstrative adjective
- A **demonstrative adjective** points out the noun it describes. *page 184*

> <u>This</u> toast is burnt.   Try one of <u>these</u> muffins.
> <u>That</u> hat is mine.   <u>Those</u> students were late.

comparative form of adjectives
- Use the **comparative** form of an adjective to compare two persons, places, or things. *page 186*

> A grapefruit is <u>sweeter</u> than a lemon.

superlative form of adjectives
- Use the **superlative** form of an adjective to compare three or more persons, places, or things. *page 186*

> An orange is the <u>sweetest</u> of the three citrus fruits.

comparison of adjectives using more and most
- Use *more* and *most* to form the comparative and superlative of most adjectives with two or more syllables. *page 188*

> Strawberry is a <u>more popular</u> flavor than pistachio.
> Vanilla is the <u>most popular</u> flavor of all.

GRAMMAR HANDBOOK

MORE PRACTICE 1   Adjectives

A. Write the adjectives in these sentences. Include articles.

1. Juan lost two quarters in the machine.
2. A flock of wild ducks flew over the lake.
3. The recipe calls for an egg and several cups of heavy cream.
4. Many candidates, eager and hopeful, give speeches before elections.
5. The new mall has beautiful fountains and colorful gardens.

B. Write each sentence. Underline the adjectives that tell *what kind* once and the adjectives that tell *how many* twice. Do not include articles.

6. We wrote an original play to present at a special assembly.
7. Ellen lives on a busy street near several schools.
8. Few people expressed strong opinions about the important issue.
9. Greg read thirty pages of a new mystery.
10. The skier, cold and weary, drank two mugs of hot cocoa.
11. The curious squirrel approached some picnickers.
12. The crowd, noisy and happy, cheered for their favorite team.

C. Write each sentence. Use the correct article in parentheses ( ).

13. She ate (a, an) omelet.
14. I lost (a, an) dollar.
15. It was (a, an) easy test.
16. He wrote (a, an) short note.
17. That is (a, an) silly question!
18. Who wants (a, an) glass of juice?
19. Hank wants to be (a, an) author.
20. This is (a, an) old sweater.

D. Write each proper adjective correctly. Then write the proper noun from which it was formed.

EXAMPLE: They skied in the austrian mountains.
ANSWER: Austrian, Austria

21. We have a german clock in our living room.
22. The italian ambassador gave a speech on television.
23. She sang a lovely song about smiling irish eyes.
24. Dawn owns a beautiful burmese cat.
25. We saw a huge dragon in the chinese New Year's parade.

MORE PRACTICE 2 Adjectives

A. Write each sentence. Underline each predicate adjective.

1. These chili peppers are hot!
2. Jacob felt sorry about the misunderstanding.
3. The house on the corner of Elm and Spruce was vacant for at least six months.
4. The ending of the new space thriller at the Strand Theater is unusual.
5. Crystal Bay is popular with swimmers and sailors.
6. The motorist appeared calm after the accident on the highway.

B. Write each sentence. Underline each predicate adjective once and each predicate nominative twice.

7. Applesauce tastes delicious on potato pancakes.
8. Will Watson is the perfect choice for class treasurer.
9. Her grandmother's diamond earrings are valuable.
10. Carla's parents were happy with her report card.
11. Our new puppy is a miniature poodle.
12. Their plans for the summer vacation are indefinite.
13. Hans Christian Andersen was a famous writer of children's stories.
14. The narrow road to Lookout Point is treacherous in foggy weather.

C. Write each sentence. Underline each demonstrative adjective.

15. These boots need polish.
16. That rose smells lovely.
17. Steve wrote this poem for you.
18. Try one of these muffins.
19. This radio uses batteries.
20. I heard that riddle already.

D. Write whether the underlined word is used as an *adjective* or a *pronoun*.

21. That is the most ridiculous story I have ever heard!
22. Those cheerleaders certainly have a lot of energy.
23. This soup is too salty to eat.
24. Nothing is left from Joe's birthday cake but these crumbs.
25. Everyone thinks that is a terrific picture.

MORE PRACTICE 3 Adjectives

A. Write the comparative and superlative form of each adjective.

1. expensive	8. easy	15. powerful
2. good	9. thin	16. wet
3. strange	10. difficult	17. terrible
4. graceful	11. brave	18. noisy
5. hot	12. bad	19. dangerous
6. witty	13. chilly	20. grateful
7. nervous	14. considerate	21. crispy

B. Write each sentence. Use the correct form of the adjective in parentheses ( ).

EXAMPLE: Silver is (valuable) than copper.
ANSWER: Silver is more valuable than copper.

22. A diamond is the (hard) of all minerals.
23. Incredible Edibles serves the (good) cherry cheesecake in town!
24. The Rocket is the (exciting) ride in the whole amusement park.
25. I am (old) than my brother Norman.
26. This is the (bad) sore throat I have ever had.
27. Last December was the (snowy) month in fifty years.
28. The average temperature in Phoenix is (hot) than in Albuquerque.
29. Do you know anyone who is (irritable) before breakfast than after?
30. The team played a (bad) game this week than last week.
31. The governor gave the (important) speech of her career.
32. I like banana mint (good) than coconut ice cream.
33. My hair is (curly) than Aunt Lily's.
34. This jigsaw puzzle is (difficult) than the last one we tried.
35. Wanda is (thin) now than she was last year.
36. Buttons the Clown is the (comical) character in the whole circus.
37. A Whammoburger from Gordo's is the (large) hamburger I've ever seen.
38. Gail's watch is (accurate) than mine.
39. Fresh garlic has a (strong) aroma than garlic powder.
40. In stories the owl is often considered the (wise) of all birds.

Adverbs

adverb
- An **adverb** describes a verb, an adjective, or another adverb. *page 214*

> The rain stopped quite suddenly.
> An incredibly beautiful rainbow appeared.

- An adverb that describes an adjective or another adverb usually comes directly before the word it describes. *page 216*

> Extremely humid days pass rather slowly.

comparison of adverbs
- Use the comparative form of an adverb to compare two things. *page 218*

- Use the superlative form of an adverb to compare three or more things. *page 218*

> I arrived late. Dan arrived later than I. The twins arrived the latest of any of us.

> Jan cheered loudly. Ray cheered more loudly than Jan. Kelly cheered the most loudly of all.

negative words
- Some negative words, such as *not*, are adverbs. Avoid using two negative words in the same sentence. *page 220*

> Debra never eats sugar.
> Debra does not ever eat sugar.
> Debra doesn't ever eat sugar.

using adjectives and adverbs
- Use adjectives to describe nouns and pronouns. *page 222*

> Steve is a slow worker. He does a good job.
> Healthy children feel well.

- Use adverbs to describe verbs, adjectives, and other adverbs. *page 222*

> The game went quickly. The team played well.

MORE PRACTICE 1 Adverbs

A. Write each sentence. Underline each adverb.

1. Everyone listened intently to the candidate's speech.
2. Seth gazed up at the Milky Way for a long time.
3. They hiked to the top of Diablo Mountain today.
4. The April snowstorm was completely unexpected.
5. An enormous blimp floated overhead during the football game.
6. These blueberry muffins taste rather stale.
7. The baby slept peacefully through the entire commotion.
8. The express bus passes here without stopping on weekends.

B. Write the adverb in each sentence. Then write *How, When, Where,* or *To what extent* to show which question the adverb answers.

EXAMPLE: The gas tank was completely empty.
ANSWER: completely (To what extent)

9. Ms. Lewis always wears a gardenia in her hair.
10. The butterfly floated gently from flower to flower.
11. Winter temperatures in Alaska can be quite low.
12. Yesterday an unexpected cloudburst soaked the garden.
13. In the event of rain the graduation will be held indoors.
14. Sometimes I forget my own telephone number.
15. The dancer leaped gracefully across the stage.

C. Write the word that each underlined adverb describes. Then write whether the word is a verb, an adjective, or an adverb.

16. The twins' personalities are <u>certainly</u> different.
17. We looked <u>everywhere</u> for Margaret's missing lunchbox.
18. Don't you think Northfield Junior High School's team played <u>rather</u> badly during the third quarter?
19. I <u>never</u> won a prize in a contest before.
20. Everyone in our class thought the test on multiplying fractions was <u>incredibly</u> difficult.

MORE PRACTICE 2 Adverbs _____

A. Write the comparative and superlative form of each adverb.

1. high	**6.** carefully	**11.** hard
2. busily	**7.** fast	**12.** brightly
3. badly	**8.** long	**13.** straight
4. quietly	**9.** happily	**14.** soft
5. patiently	**10.** well	**15.** cheerfully

B. Write each sentence. Use the correct form of the adverb in parentheses ( ).

16. Foods spoil (quickly) at room temperaure than in the refrigerator.
17. Walter spoke the (clearly) of all the speakers at the assembly.
18. Carla left for school (early) than Sandra did this morning.
19. Snap-Pop Popcorn pops (fast) than Crunch-Munch Popcorn.
20. Kate writes the (carefully) of anyone in our class.
21. Our car rides (smoothly) since its tune-up.
22. Of all the days in the week I sleep the (late) on Saturday.
23. Joe did (well) on this week's spelling test than on last week's.
24. Panhandle Drive curves the (dangerously) of any road in the county.
25. Alan cried the (loud) of all the babies in the nursery.

C. Write each sentence. Use the word in parentheses ( ) that makes the sentence negative.

26. She will (never, ever) try that stunt again!
27. I (have, haven't) seen David's new digital watch yet.
28. (Nobody, Anybody) from my class is performing in the talent show.
29. The weather has (something, nothing) to do with her sour mood.
30. There is (some, no) reason to miss any questions on this exam.
31. (Anyone, No one) can finish knitting an afghan in one week.
32. I (can, can't) help to decorate the gym for the dance.
33. (One, None) of the contestants could spell that word correctly.
34. He (does, doesn't) look anything like his picture.
35. The driver could remember (anything, nothing) after the accident.

MORE PRACTICE 3 Adverbs

A. Write the word in parentheses ( ) that correctly completes each sentence. Avoid double negatives.

1. You have not (ever, never) tasted anything as marvelous as this!
2. They haven't made (any, no) predictions about the election results.
3. Everyone was delighted when there (was, wasn't) no homework assigned.
4. I can't find my bus pass (nowhere, anywhere).
5. We haven't found (none, any) of the hidden clues yet.
6. She couldn't think of (anything, nothing) to say.

B. Write the word in parentheses ( ) that correctly completes each sentence.

7. The hailstorm began quite (sudden, suddenly) on Wednesday.
8. The clerks at Good Value Hardware Store are always (courteous, courteously) to customers.
9. The junior orchestra played (good, well) at the spring concert.
10. The veterinarian was (patient, patiently) with the terrified cat.
11. The police officer spoke (gentle, gently) to the crying child.
12. We saw a (good, well) movie on Saturday afternoon.
13. Don't gulp your food so (quick, quickly).
14. Their story is (strange, strangely) but true.
15. Jennifer gave me an (honest, honestly) answer.
16. We walked (careful, carefully) along the side of the road.

C. Write each sentence. Use the word *good* or *well* in place of the blank. Then write whether the word is an adjective or an adverb.

EXAMPLE: We could not see ____ in the fog.
ANSWER: We could not see well in the fog. (adverb)

17. Most people in town think the Chicken Coop Cafe is a ____ restaurant.
18. Stephen Becker did ____ in the chess tournament.
19. The weather is usually ____ in San Diego.
20. A balanced diet will help you feel ____.

Conjunctions, Prepositions, and Interjections

conjunction

- A **conjunction** joins words or groups of words. *page 258*

  Call a friend <u>or</u> nearby neighbor in an emergency.

preposition

- A **preposition** relates a noun or pronoun to another word in the sentence. *page 260*

object of the preposition

- The noun or pronoun that follows a preposition is the **object of the preposition.** *page 260*

  The bowl was full <u>of</u> fresh <u>fruit</u>.   Give an apple <u>to</u> <u>me</u>.

prepositional phrases as adjectives

- A prepositional phrase that describes a noun or pronoun is an **adjective phrase.** *page 262*

  Joe drank a glass <u>of cold water.</u>

prepositional phrases as adverbs

- A prepositional phrase that describes a verb, an adjective, or an adverb is an **adverb phrase.** *page 264*

  I was hungry <u>after dinner.</u>   I looked <u>for more food.</u>

using prepositional phrases

- Use an object pronoun as the object of a preposition. *page 266*

  Sonya told the riddle <u>to Lauren and me.</u>

- Use the prepositions *between* and *among* correctly. *page 266*

  I sat <u>between</u> Sue and Dan.   Choose <u>among</u> these five books.

- A prepositional phrase can be part of a sentence with inverted word order. In a sentence with inverted word order, the complete predicate comes before the complete subject.

  <u>In Lake Lucifer swim</u> many fish.

interjection

- An **interjection** expresses strong feeling or emotion and is followed by an exclamation mark (**!**). *page 268*

  Hooray!   Wow!   Oh!   Gee!

GRAMMAR HANDBOOK

MORE PRACTICE 1 Conjunctions, Prepositions, and Interjections_____

A. Write each sentence. Underline each conjunction.

1. The horses in the corral kicked and snorted.
2. I would like an apple or some blueberries.
3. Joanna Marshall and I are in the same gymnastics class.
4. It is silly to worry about the past or the future.
5. These green chili peppers are spicy but tasty.
6. Many musicians practice every day or every other day.
7. The soldier wore a hat and a clean, starched uniform.
8. The hike to Lake Arguello was tiring but enjoyable.
9. Kelly wants to be a veterinarian or marine biologist.
10. Many enthusiastic collectors save and trade foreign stamps.
11. He or I usually arrive at school before the teacher.
12. The skaters, cold and weary, drank mugs of steaming cider.

B. Write the prepositional phrase in each sentence. Underline the preposition once and the object of the preposition twice.

EXAMPLE: Annie read a fascinating article about blue whales.
ANSWER: about blue whales

13. We peered nervously into the dark, dreary cave.
14. The necklace was made of sparkling diamonds.
15. My cousin had written to her congressional representative.
16. The play is a comedy about a very large family.
17. The pharmacist prepared a prescription for me.
18. My mischievous puppy was hiding under Dad's bed.
19. The careless driver headed toward another car.
20. Is that your lunchbox beside my backpack?
21. The food server brought our sandwiches to the table.
22. I watched the game with Sandy's binoculars.
23. Inside the box were twelve beautiful roses.
24. The cowhand leaned against the wooden gate.
25. I sent a special-delivery letter to her.

MORE PRACTICE 2 Conjunctions, Prepositions and Interjections

A. Write the conjunction in each sentence. Then write *nouns, pronouns, verbs, adjectives,* or *adverbs* to show what kind of words are joined.

1. Adults and children enjoy a day at the zoo.
2. The tickets will cost four or five dollars.
3. The winner of the race felt weak but happy.
4. The dog waited patiently and quietly for its owner.
5. Janet washed and ironed her favorite shirt for the party.
6. She or I will call you with all the important information.
7. It was a dark and stormy night.
8. My grandparents write or call us nearly every week.

B. Write the adjective phrase in each sentence. Then write the noun the phrase describes.

EXAMPLE: The donkey carried two baskets of fresh fruit.
ANSWER: of fresh fruit, baskets

9. A letter for Jennifer arrived today.
10. The glasses in the dishwasher need to be washed again.
11. I bought a long-sleeved sweatshirt with a hood.
12. The dog chewed a pair of my slippers.
13. A popular writer from Connecticut wrote this story.
14. My grandmother always drinks strong tea with lemon and honey.

C. Write the adverb phrase in each sentence. Then write the word the phrase describes.

15. Kevin Stevens hurried out the employees' entrance.
16. The frisky colt trotted beside its mother.
17. We walked around the entire lake.
18. Mr. Reynolds was angry at the impolite sales clerk.
19. We are moving early in September.
20. Everyone felt good after the math test.

MORE PRACTICE 3 Conjunctions, Prepositions and
Interjections

A. Write the word in parentheses ( ) that correctly completes each sentence.

1. The last kilometer of the hike up Pinetop Peak was extremely difficult for (we, us).
2. I bought a ticket to the exhibit at the planetarium for my brother and (I, me).
3. Lou spotted a turkey (among, between) the geese, chickens, and ducks at the poultry ranch.
4. Patricia waited nearly an hour for (he, him) near the front entrance of the botanical garden.
5. You can find the cottage cheese in the dairy section of the store (among, between) the yogurt and the milk.
6. Teresa showed the photographs to (they, them) before class.
7. The prize money was divided (among, between) the five winners.
8. The magician said, "Stand (among, between) this table and that chair."
9. I'll save a place for you and (he, him) in the cafeteria at lunch.
10. I could not decide (among, between) chocolate and vanilla.

B. Write each sentence with inverted word order in regular word order. Write each regular sentence in inverted order.

11. Around the track jogged several athletes.
12. The graceful swans swam across the pond.
13. Off the desk disappeared her new crayons.
14. In our neighborhood stands a vacant office building.
15. Three fragile eggs lay in the nest.
16. Under the bush hid a very tiny frightened kitten.

C. Write the interjection in each sentence.

17. Ah! That cool breeze feels so refreshing.
18. Gosh! Do you smell something burning?
19. Ouch! I bumped my head on the cabinet door.
20. Golly! I lost my lunch money somewhere!

Compound Subjects and Compound Predicates

compound subject
- A **compound subject** is two or more simple subjects that have the same verb. *page 294*

<u>Adults</u> and <u>children</u> enjoy a circus performance.

compound predicate
- A **compound predicate** is two or more verbs that have the same subject. *page 294*

Danielle <u>washed</u> and <u>waxed</u> the family car.

MORE PRACTICE 1 Compound Subjects and Compound Predicates

A. Write the compound subject or predicate in each sentence.

1. Books, records, and magazines are available at the public library.
2. Swimmers and boaters enjoy Canyon Lake all year round.
3. Garlic powder and onion flakes add flavor to many different foods.
4. Esteban sealed the envelopes and mailed the letters immediately.
5. The rooster crowed and strutted around the barnyard.
6. Tulips or daffodils will make a lovely arrangement for the table.
7. I swept the floors and vacuumed the rugs on Saturday.
8. The energetic lumberjack split logs and stacked firewood behind the house.

B. Write each sentence. Underline each compound subject once and each compound predicate twice. If a sentence does not have a compound subject or predicate, write *no compound*.

9. The poultry farmer raised chickens and turkeys.
10. The fawn stood on wobbly legs and followed its mother.
11. Taxicabs and buses moved down the avenue.
12. She remembered the story and told every detail to me.
13. The climate of the tropics is hot and rainy.
14. Grapefruit, oranges, and lemons grow in Florida and Arizona.
15. An apple or a glass of juice will satisfy my hunger until dinner.

MORE PRACTICE 2 Compound Subjects and Compound Predicates_____

A. Write the compound subject or predicate in each sentence.

1. Rosalind or Louisa will handle the lights at the talent show.
2. Two bicycles, a red wagon, and a pair of roller skates lay on the grass in the front yard.
3. The road crew leveled and paved a new section of the highway.
4. Lightning bolts and crashing thunder came before the heavy rains.
5. The kitten jumped off the bed and hid under it.
6. The enthusiastic crowd cheered wildly, clapped their hands, and waved banners for the home team.
7. Sand in your food or a painful sunburn may be an unpleasant part of a day at the beach.
8. Edward washed and dried all the dishes after dinner last night.
9. A collie pup and two young terriers caught our attention at the show.
10. Alicia and I split a jumbo bag of popcorn at the movies.

B. Write each sentence. Underline each compound subject once and each compound predicate twice. If a sentence does not have a compound subject or predicate, write *no compound.*

11. The sleepy baby yawned in the crib.
12. A police officer stood in the middle of the busy intersection and directed traffic.
13. Martin carried two heavy suitcases and a canvas bag on his trip.
14. Sylvester Graham and the Earl of Sandwich invented two popular food items.
15. The doctor removed the plaster cast from Maria's arm on Tuesday.
16. Jane toasted a bagel, spread cream cheese on it, and ate it in three quick bites for breakfast.
17. The judge and the jury listened carefully to the witness.
18. My cousins called from Indiana and told us the exciting news.
19. The impatient teenager and the nervous driving instructor looked at each other.
20. Lester dropped two letters and a post card into the mailbox.

Compound Sentences

compound sentence ● A **compound sentence** consists of two or more simple sentences. *page 296*

Andrew waited in the rain for an hour, but the bus never arrived.

MORE PRACTICE 1 Compound Sentences _____

A. Write *simple* or *compound* for each sentence.

1. We washed the family car, and the storm began within an hour.
2. My parents barbecued hot dogs and hamburgers at the Fourth of July picnic.
3. Jill prepared a very special dinner for Dad's birthday.
4. Willie hesitated for a moment, and then he dived off the raft into the icy water.
5. I always have scrambled eggs for breakfast, but Jenny prefers oatmeal with cinnamon and raisins.
6. The attorney asked the judge for a ten-minute recess.
7. On Thursdays the cafeteria serves tacos, or sometimes the main dish is stew.
8. No one spelled the last word correctly on this week's spelling quiz.

B. Write *compound sentence, compound subject,* or *compound predicate* for each sentence.

9. A state senator or the governor will speak at the graduation ceremony in June.
10. My grandfather loves to cook, and he often enters contests with his original recipes.
11. The thief grabbed the money and ran for the door.
12. Sandy made a mushroom omelet, and I shared it with her for lunch.
13. Benjamin wrote down the address and promptly lost the paper.
14. The puppy whined at the door, but no one was home.
15. Twinkling stars and several planets appeared in the night sky.

MORE PRACTICE 2 Compound Sentences _____

A. Write *simple* or *compound* for each sentence.

1. You can pay for the tickets now, or you can pay for them on the night of the performance.
2. Katie turned on her favorite show, but a special news broadcast interrupted it.
3. A squirrel scampered across the yard and ran up the side of a tree.
4. We called the florist with our order, and Ralph carried the plant home on his bicycle.
5. Nearly two thousand people attend Central High School!
6. Our class visited the modern art museum, and the tour guide showed us many different kinds of paintings and statues.
7. Aunt Esther or Uncle Jack will drive you to the airport on Sunday.
8. The hot-water heater was out of order, but Josh took a shower anyway.
9. I woke up at midnight, and I could not fall asleep again for hours.
10. They carved a grinning jack-o-lantern and set it on the front porch.

B. Write *compound sentence*, *compound subject*, or *compound predicate* for each sentence.

11. Barry had a serious case of the flu and missed nearly a week of school in December.
12. Finish your homework before dinner, or you will miss the TV special about sharks.
13. The telephone rang suddenly and startled me.
14. Dr. Brewer or Dr. Fujita will clean your teeth on Wednesday.
15. Ellen will bring fruit salad, or she will make cole slaw for the pot-luck dinner.
16. We wanted to play soccer after school, but the unexpected storm changed our plans.
17. Gerry found a wallet and took it to the police station immediately.
18. Mumps, measles, and chickenpox are usually considered childhood diseases.
19. Stacy entered the contest, but she has not heard any results yet.
20. Llamas, deer, and a baby elephant approached us at the children's zoo.

Subject-Verb Agreement

subject-verb
agreement

- The subject of a sentence must agree with its verb. *page 298*

> (The dog, He, She, It) <u>waits</u> near the door.
> (The dogs, I, You, We, They) <u>wait</u> near the door.
>
> I <u>am</u> happy.   I <u>was</u> happy.
> (The bus, He, She, It) <u>is</u> late.
> (The bus, He, She, It) <u>was</u> late.
> (Those people, We, You, They) <u>are</u> busy.
> (Those people, We, You, They) <u>were</u> busy.

- Compound subjects joined by *and* use the plural form of the verb. *page 300*

> Tulips and daffodils <u>bloom</u> in the spring.

- Compound subjects joined by *or, either/or,* or *neither/nor* sometimes use the singular form of the verb and sometimes the plural. *page 300*

> Usually Stephen or Jill <u>arrives</u> early.
> Either apples or peaches <u>make</u> great pies.
> Neither a chicken nor turkeys <u>fly</u>.
> Neither lemons nor a pickle <u>tastes</u> sweet.

MORE PRACTICE 1 Subject-Verb Agreement

Write the form of the verb in parentheses ( ) that correctly completes each sentence.

1. My kitten (curl, curls) up in a ball at the foot of the bed.
2. Joanna (was, were) an assistant at the magic show on Saturday.
3. Neither my tape recorder nor my flashlight (need, needs) new batteries.
4. He (is, are) the fastest runner in the school.
5. These artificial jewels (look, looks) quite genuine.
6. The newspapers (was, were) on the front porch.
7. Either Amanda or her sisters (know, knows) the bus schedule.
8. I (am, is) the oldest child in the family.

MORE PRACTICE 2   Subject-Verb Agreement

A. Write the two forms of *be* that agree with each subject below.

   1. she   **3.** children   **5.** we   **7.** they

   2. I   **4.** you   **6.** grandfather   **8.** it

B. Write the form of the verb in parentheses ( ) that correctly completes each sentence.

   9. Jacques and Patricia (live, lives) across the street from me.

  10. Either John Adams or Thomas Jefferson (was, were) the second President of the United States.

  11. Roasted almonds or raisins (make, makes) a healthful snack.

  12. Jennifer and I (was, were) partners at the tennis tournament.

  13. Neither bicycle riders nor skaters (use, uses) the sidewalk at Golden Gate Park.

  14. Usually some monkeys or a parrot (attract, attracts) my attention at the zoo.

  15. Neither celery nor a cucumber (contain, contains) many calories.

  16. A brisk walk or a bike ride (provide, provides) excellent aerobic exercise.

  17. The crossing guard or a teacher (walk, walks) the kindergarten children across the street.

C. Write each sentence. Use the correct present tense form of the verb in parentheses ( ).

  18. Mushrooms or an onion (taste, tastes) delicious in an omelet.

  19. She and I (am, are) both allergic to certain foods.

  20. Either a rabbit or raccoons (chew, chews) the young lettuce plants in our garden.

  21. Nora's birthday and my birthday (come, comes) on the same day.

  22. A cold or a sore throat (keeps, keep) Jan out of school occasionally.

  23. Either strawberries or a cantaloupe (is, are) a good source of vitamin C.

  24. Neither Aunt Elena nor Dad's other sisters (live, lives) nearby.

  25. Judith, Patty, and Susan (help, helps) the librarian at school.

GRAMMAR HANDBOOK

Sentence Errors

sentence
fragment

● A **sentence fragment** is a group of words that does not
express a complete thought. *page 302*

> Fragment: Spaghetti with tomato sauce.
> Complete Sentence: The chef prepared spaghetti with
> tomato sauce.

run-on
sentence

● A **run-on sentence** is two or more sentences not separated
by correct punctuation or connecting words. *page 302*

> Greg has a new job he delivers newspapers.

MORE PRACTICE 1 Sentence Errors _____

A. Write *sentence* or *fragment* for each group of words. Then add words to
each fragment to make a sentence. Write the sentence.

1. A Navajo architect designed several new buildings in our city.
2. The main characters of the story.
3. Ms. Garcia and another student teacher.
4. This cereal contains bran flakes and oats.
5. Was hiding under the bed.
6. The new baby demanded a lot of attention.

B. Correct these run-on sentences. Rewrite each run-on sentence as two
separate sentences, as a compound sentence, or as a sentence with a
compound predicate.

7. The telephone rang at least thirty times no one answered it.
8. Never use an electric appliance with wet hands you might get a bad
   shock.
9. Heavy rains fell during the sudden storm a beautiful double rainbow
   appeared afterwards.
10. We wanted to know the names of all the countries of Europe we looked
    in an atlas.

GRAMMAR HANDBOOK

A. Write *sentence* or *fragment* for each group of words. Then add words to each fragment to make a sentence. Write the sentence.

1. Compares two popular brands of dog food.
2. An epidemic of measles.
3. They use a microwave oven in the kitchen.
4. Dr. Salk discovered a vaccine for polio.
5. Applesauce with cinnamon.
6. Tastes too salty.
7. I had a terrible headache after the concert.
8. He takes several vitamin capsules at each meal.
9. Cynthia Lucas and Roberta Carrasco.
10. The cafeteria has run out of mayonnaise again.

B. Correct these run-on sentences. Rewrite each run-on sentence as two separate sentences, as a compound sentence, or as a sentence with a compound predicate.

11. The pilot flew over the International Date Line it was her very first flight.
12. Dolores babysits every weekend she is saving money for a ten-speed bicycle.
13. Many of my friends like mystery stories I prefer science fiction.
14. Dr. Wilson's office called me twice I still forgot about my dental appointment on Tuesday.
15. Tony and she were looking forward to playing tennis the weather had an unexpected effect on their plans.
16. The alarm clock rang at six o'clock my sister Jennifer slept right through it.
17. We can go to the matinee on Saturday afternoon there is another show scheduled for Saturday night.
18. Someone left the water running the bathtub overflowed!
19. We traveled by train to Seattle the trip took over twelve hours.
20. He threw the ball toward the dog it just sat there and watched without moving an inch.

Paragraphs

paragraph
- A **paragraph** is a group of sentences that tell about one main idea. *page 32*

topic sentence
- The **topic sentence** states the main idea of a paragraph. *page 34*

supporting sentences
- **Supporting sentences** develop the main idea. *page 34*
- The first word of a paragraph is indented.

Indent ——— A spider can tell when an insect touches its web. When the
Topic sentence — insect touches one strand of the web, it makes the strand vibrate.
Since all the strands are connected, the vibrations travel to every
Supporting sentences — part of the web. If the spider is anywhere on the web, it can feel
the vibrations.

PRACTICE

A. Write a topic sentence for each of these topics.

1. why you watch (don't watch) a certain TV program
2. a product that someone should invent
3. what you hope to be doing ten years from now
4. your favorite season of the year
5. a famous person whom you admire

B. Read the supporting details below. Then write a topic sentence for them.

The center of a campsite should be free of trees and shrubs.
A campsite should have trees to the west and north for protection.
A campsite should be higher than the land around it.

C. Choose one of the topic sentences you wrote for **Practice A** above. Then write a paragraph, using that topic sentence as your first sentence. Make sure that the other sentences in your paragraph are supporting sentences that develop the main idea. Indent the first sentence of your paragraph.

YOUNG WRITER'S HANDBOOK

Writing Forms: Friendly Letters

- A **friendly letter** has five parts: the heading, greeting, body, closing, and signature. *page 118*

  friendly letter

- The **heading** shows the address of the writer and the date. Proper nouns are capitalized. A comma is used between the city and the state and between the date and the year.

  heading

- The first word of the **greeting** is capitalized as well as the proper noun. The greeting is followed by a comma.

  greeting

- The **closing** is followed by a comma. Only the first word in the closing is capitalized.

  closing

- The **signature** is below the closing.

  signature

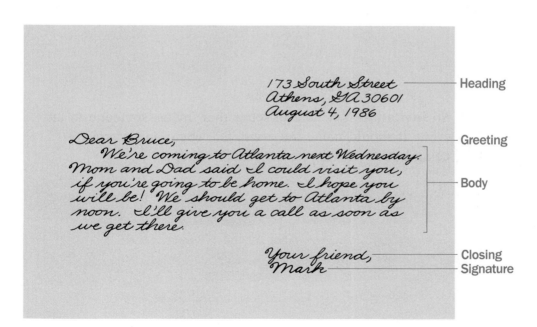

173 South Street
Athens, GA 30601
August 4, 1986 —————— Heading

Dear Bruce, —————— Greeting
We're coming to Atlanta next Wednesday.
Mom and Dad said I could visit you,
if you're going to be home. I hope you
will be! We should get to Atlanta by   — Body
noon. I'll give you a call as soon as
we get there.

Your friend, —————— Closing
Mark —————— Signature

PRACTICE

Following the form shown above, write a friendly letter to a friend or relative. Tell news that will interest the person you are writing to. Use the form shown on page 396 of this Young Writer's Handbook to address the envelope.

Writing Forms: Thank-You Notes and Invitations

thank-you note

● A **thank-you note** is a short letter of thanks for a gift or favor. It follows the form of a friendly letter.

158 Oak Street
Baker, OR 97814
August 14, 1986

Dear Grandma,
Thank you so much for the record album! How did you know that Stop-and-Go Traffic is my favorite rock group? The next time you visit us, I'll play the records for you. You'll be a Stop-and-Go fan too!

Love,
Kathy

invitation

● An **invitation** is a note or letter that invites someone to an event. It should name the event, tell where and when it is being held, and tell who sent the invitation.

Please come to *our class play*
Place: *Room 6B, Washington School*
Date: *Friday, November 3*
Time: *10:00 to 10:45 A.M.*
Given by: *Mrs. Schmidt's class*

PRACTICE

Write a thank-you note or invitation. It can be about a real or made-up gift or event. Follow the examples shown above if you wish.

Writing Forms: Business Letters

- A **business letter** has six parts: the heading, inside address, greeting, body, closing, and signature. *page 120*

  business letter

- When you write a business letter, make your message clear and brief. *page 120*

- The **heading** gives the writer's address and the date.

  heading

- The **inside address** gives the name and address of the person or company to whom the letter is sent.

  inside address

- In a business letter, the **greeting** is followed by a colon.

  greeting

- Only the first word in the **closing** is capitalized. Acceptable closings include: *Respectfully, Yours truly, Sincerely.*

  closing

- If the letter is typed, the writer's name is typed four lines below the closing under the writer's **signature.**

  signature

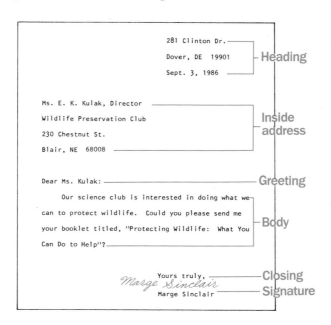

PRACTICE

Write a business letter to a real or made-up company or organization.

Writing Forms: Outlines

outline
- An **outline** organizes information into main ideas and supporting ideas. *page 242*

- Each main idea is listed as a main topic in an outline, and each supporting idea is listed as a subtopic.

main topic
- A **main topic** is numbered with a Roman numeral, followed by a period. The first word begins with a capital letter.

subtopic
- A **subtopic** is listed under its main topic and is indented. Each subtopic is labeled with a capital letter, followed by a period. The first word begins with a capital letter.

title
- The **title** is centered at the top of the outline.

- At least two items must be listed under each element of the outline. That is, a **I** must not be used unless there is a **II**. An **A** must not be used unless there is a **B**.

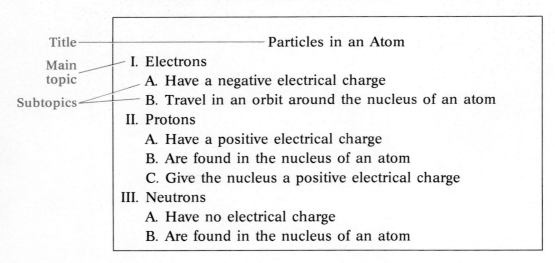

Title — Particles in an Atom

Main topic — I. Electrons

Subtopics —
    A. Have a negative electrical charge
    B. Travel in an orbit around the nucleus of an atom

II. Protons
    A. Have a positive electrical charge
    B. Are found in the nucleus of an atom
    C. Give the nucleus a positive electrical charge

III. Neutrons
    A. Have no electrical charge
    B. Are found in the nucleus of an atom

PRACTICE

Making an outline helps you organize and remember material you read. An outline is very useful when you need to review for a test. Try it. Choose a lesson in this book or part of a chapter in a social studies or science book. Outline it. Use the chapter's headings and subheadings as a guide.

Writing Forms: Book Reports

- A **book report** tells what a book is about and gives an opinion of the book.   *page 162*

book report

- A **book title** is underlined.

book title

Study this book report form. It shows what kind of information to include in a book report.

Title *Mr. Revere and I*

Author *Robert Lawson*

Setting *Boston in Colonial times*

Main Characters *Scheherazade, Paul Revere, and Sam Adams. Scheherazade is Paul Revere's horse. Her nickname is Sherry.*

What the book is about *This is the story of Paul Revere's famous ride, but it is told by Paul Revere's horse, Sherry. Sherry had been a British cavalry horse. Sam Adams rescued her from a glue factory and gave her to Paul Revere. Sherry soon knew all about the Revere family and the Sons of Liberty. She felt that Paul Revere was her dear friend. She also felt that she made Paul Revere famous.*

Your opinion *This was a funny book. It also taught me a lot about Colonial times and the Revolutionary War.*

PRACTICE

Copy the book report form shown above. Use it to write a report about a book you enjoyed and would recommend to the class.

YOUNG WRITER'S HANDBOOK

Addressing Letters: Envelopes

- When you address an envelope, you write the return address and the receiver's address.

return address
- Write your name and address in the upper left-hand corner. This is the **return address.** It shows where to return the letter if it cannot be delivered.

receiver's address
- In the center of the envelope, write the **receiver's address.** This is the name and address of the person who will receive the letter. For business letters, the receiver's address is an exact copy of the inside address.

state abbreviations
- You may use an abbreviation for the name of a state. See the chart on the next page. It lists the abbreviations approved by the Postal Service.

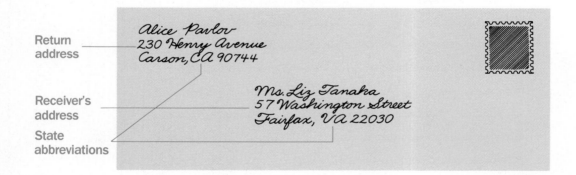

Return address

Alice Pavlov
230 Henry Avenue
Carson, CA 90744

Receiver's address

Ms. Liz Tanaka
57 Washington Street
Fairfax, VA 22030

State abbreviations

PRACTICE

Using a ruler, draw three envelopes like the sample above. Then address each one, using the information given below.

1. *Return address:* Walt Jamison   93 Fox St.   Oxford, NC 27565
   Receiver's address: Mr. Fred Bosch   30 Green Lane   York, PA 17405
2. *Return address:* Leslie Pruce   12 Elm St.   Warwick, NY 10990
   Receiver's address: Mrs. Edna Wright   78 Sunset Dr.   Stanhope, NJ 07874
3. *Return address:* Pedro Sanchez   222 Penn St.   Cody, WY 82414
   Receiver's address: Mr. Justin Mendel   9 Ranch Ave.   El Paso, TX 79910

Addressing Letters: State Abbreviations

- Use these abbreviations of state names when you write addresses. Notice that periods are not used in the abbreviations.

Alabama	**AL**	Maine	**ME**	Oregon	**OR**
Alaska	**AK**	Maryland	**MD**	Pennsylvania	**PA**
Arizona	**AZ**	Massachusetts	**MA**	Rhode Island	**RI**
Arkansas	**AR**	Michigan	**MI**	South Carolina	**SC**
California	**CA**	Minnesota	**MN**	South Dakota	**SD**
Colorado	**CO**	Mississippi	**MS**	Tennessee	**TN**
Connecticut	**CT**	Missouri	**MO**	Texas	**TX**
Delaware	**DE**	Montana	**MT**	Utah	**UT**
Florida	**FL**	Nebraska	**NE**	Vermont	**VT**
Georgia	**GA**	Nevada	**NV**	Virginia	**VA**
Hawaii	**HI**	New Hampshire	**NH**	Washington	**WA**
Idaho	**ID**	New Jersey	**NJ**	West Virginia	**WV**
Illinois	**IL**	New Mexico	**NM**	Wisconsin	**WI**
Indiana	**IN**	New York	**NY**	Wyoming	**WY**
Iowa	**IA**	North Carolina	**NC**	***	
Kansas	**KS**	North Dakota	**ND**	District of	
Kentucky	**KY**	Ohio	**OH**	Columbia	**DC**
Louisiana	**LA**	Oklahoma	**OK**		

PRACTICE

Write the abbreviations for each of these state names.

1. Hawaii
2. Montana
3. Texas
4. Tennessee
5. Wisconsin
6. New Hampshire
7. Kentucky
8. Kansas
9. Idaho
10. Illinois
11. Oregon
12. Oklahoma
13. Florida
14. Georgia
15. Virginia

Editing Marks

● Use editing marks to make changes when you revise and proofread your writing.

Mark	Meaning	Example
——	cross out	No one pitches ~~more~~ better than Lee.
		No one pitches better than Lee.
∧	add	*beagle* That∧puppy is the one I want.
		That beagle puppy is the one I want.
⤴	move	As I listened to the speech now and then, (my mind wandered.)
		As I listened to the speech, my mind wandered now and then.
≡	capital letter	The waters of lake michigan were icy.
		The waters of Lake Michigan were icy.
/	small letter	The River overflowed its banks.
		The river overflowed its banks.
¶	indent	¶ The Smithsonian Institution has twelve museums. Eleven are in Washington, D.C., and one is in New York City.
		The Smithsonian Institution has twelve museums. Eleven are in Washington, D.C., and one is in New York City.
⬭	check spelling	*surprise* What a wonderful (suprise)!
		What a wonderful surprise!

YOUNG WRITER'S HANDBOOK

Proofreading Checklist

When you write something for others to read, be considerate of your audience. Proofread your paper for errors. If you find a mistake, correct it neatly, using the editing marks. The proofreading checklist below will help you find errors. Copy the checklist if you wish. Notice that the writer has checked *No* for questions **1** and **5.** The checks help the writer notice what kind of errors he or she is making.

When you proofread, it is generally a good idea to check for one thing at a time. For example, first check for spelling errors. It is easier to spot these if you start at the end of your composition and move to the beginning. Check each word separately, looking only for spelling errors. Next check for sentence sense, and so on.

Questions	YES	NO
1. Did I spell each word correctly?		✓
2. Does each sentence make sense? Does it have a subject and a predicate?	✓	
3. Did I indent the first word of each paragraph?	✓	
4. Did I begin each sentence with a capital letter and end it with the correct punctuation mark?	✓	
5. Did I use capital letters correctly?		✓
6. Did I choose the best words?	✓	

Capitalization

- A **proper noun** always begins with a capital letter. *page 54*

persons and pets
- Capitalize the names of persons and pets.

> Doris John Paul Jones
> the Browns Lassie

titles and initials
- Capitalize titles, such as *Miss* or *Mr.*, and initials.

> Miss Maria L. Starr Mr. Jeff A. Turnbull
> President John Quincy Adams

place names
- Capitalize important words in the names of particular places and things.

> Broad Street New York City Oklahoma
> Lake Erie Statue of Liberty Mount Everest

special groups
- Capitalize the names of nationalities, languages, clubs, organizations, and business firms.

> Sterling Co. German Garden Club of America

calendar words
- Capitalize the names of months, days, holidays and special days.

> January Friday Labor Day Halloween

pronoun I
- The pronoun *I* is always capitalized.

> After I finish my homework, I'll play softball.

book title
- Capitalize the first word, last word, and all important words in the title of a book.

> A Wrinkle in Time

title of story, poem, or report
- Capitalize the first word, last word, and all important words in the title of a story, poem, or report.

> "The Rains of Spring" (poem) "A Web of Sunny Air" (story)

PRACTICE 1 Capitalization

A. Write each name correctly.

1. mr. eric p. dorsi
2. ms. anita r. marino
3. spotty
4. dr. i. t. chen
5. general robert e. lee

6. king richard III
7. miss cleo y. jefferson
8. mrs. stephanie wasko
9. judge ruth ann sayers
10. mayor carlos o. torez

B. Write each address. Use capital letters correctly.

11. mr. harold p. irwin
    210 monroe ave.
    chico, california 95926

12. ms. alicia t. carazo
    58 glenn road
    sitka, alaska 99835

13. dr. stephan d. gault
    37 preston st.
    alton, illinois 62002

14. miss sonia y. lanz
    16 fern drive
    sparks, nevada 89431

C. Write each sentence. Use capital letters correctly.

15. The company is located at 593 fairfax st., bartow, florida.
16. The okefenokee swamp is the largest freshwater swamp in america.
17. The great salt lake in utah is saltier than the ocean.
18. In acadia national park in maine, the mountains meet the sea.
19. The wind is very strong on top of mount washington in new hampshire.

D. Write each sentence. Use capital letters correctly.

20. James bought english cloth and irish lace.
21. The armco tool company is advertising for workers.
22. Some words in english have come from latin, greek, french, german, spanish, italian, and dutch.
23. The model railroad club of eastham meets once a month.
24. We wrote to the american kennel club for information about collies.
25. The far east trading company imports japanese, chinese, korean, and indian jewelry.

PRACTICE 2   Capitalization

A. Write these days and dates. Use capital letters correctly.

1. tuesday, april 1
2. memorial day
3. thursday, february 4
4. groundhog day
5. saturday, december 5

6. thursday, september 11
7. armed forces day
8. columbus day
9. wednesday, august 8
10. veterans day

B. Write each sentence. Use capital letters correctly.

11. Every friday afternoon, i work out at the gym.
12. On sunday, july 28, i'm leaving for Dallas.
13. Is halloween on monday or tuesday this year?
14. Yes, i'll be marching in the parade on independence day.
15. Since tomorrow is washington's birthday, i think i'd better go to the bank today.

C. Write each sentence. Use capital letters correctly.

16. Yes, i'd recommend the book the case of the silver egg.
17. Since i like science fiction i enjoyed reading the donkey planet.
18. When i've finished reading little house on the prairie, i'm going to read on the banks of plum creek.
19. The book i am now reading is the house of sixty fathers.
20. Tomorrow i must return secret of the emerald star to the library.

D. Write each sentence. Use capital letters correctly.

21. Our class dramatized the story "stone soup."
22. The poem "the city of falling leaves" was written by Amy Lowell.
23. Have you read Shelley's report, "the skeletal system"?
24. The story "the silver skates" comes from Holland.
25. My brother's favorite poem is "excuse us, animals in the zoo."
26. Hans Christian Andersen wrote the famous story, "the emperor's new clothes."
27. Jo interviewed zoo keepers for her report, "feeding zoo animals."

Punctuation

- Use a **comma** after *yes, no,* or *well* at the beginning of a sentence. *page 304*

        Yes, that is my signature.
        No, I've never been to Boston.

- Use a **comma** to set off the name of a person spoken to. *page 304*

        Ray, is this your pen?
        Your question, Terry, is a good one.

- Use a **comma** to separate the last name and the first name of a person when the last name is written first. *page 304*

        Bingham, Andrea   Danzig, Louis

- Use a **comma** to separate words in a series. *page 18*

        The daffodils, tulips, and crocuses are in bloom.

- Use a **comma** to separate the date and the year.

        Christopher Columbus sighted land on October 12, 1492.

- Use a **comma** to separate the name of a city from a state or country.

        Jean was born in Columbus, Ohio.

- If a two-word place name or a date is within a sentence, use a comma both before and after the name of the state (or country) and before and after the year.

        On January 3, 1959, Alaska became the forty-ninth state.
        We flew to Atlanta, Georgia, last weekend.

- Use a **comma** before the conjunction in a compound sentence.

        On Monday it rained, and on Tuesday it snowed.
        We went to the amusement park, but it was closed.
        Use honey as a sweetener, or use molasses.

- In a quotation, use a **comma** to separate the quotation from the speaker. The comma comes before the quotation marks.

    Carla said, "The streets are very icy."

Sometimes a quotation is divided. If a divided quotation is one sentence, commas separate the quotation from the speaker.

    "The new movie in town," said Sheila, "is hilarious!"

apostrophe
- Use an **apostrophe** to show where a letter or letters have been left out in a contraction.

    you + have = you've   does + not = doesn't

quotation marks
- Use **quotation marks** to show the exact words of a speaker. *page 154*

    "I'm trying out for the swimming team," said Joyce.

- Use **quotation marks** before and after the title of a story, poem, article, or report when you write about it.

    You will enjoy this story, "The Lion's Whiskers."

underlining
- **Underline** the title of a book, magazine, newspaper, or movie.

    Freedom Train (book)   **Denver Post** (newspaper)

colon
- Use a **colon** after the greeting in a business letter.

    Dear Ms. Sharp: Dear Sir or Madam:

- Use a **colon** between an hour and minutes.

    6:35 A.M.   12:24 P.M.

period with abbreviations
- Many abbreviations begin with a capital letter and end with a **period**. *page 56*

    Read the chart of common abbreviations at the top of the next page. Notice that each abbreviation begins with a capital letter and ends with a period.

Rev. = Reverend	Dr. = Doctor		Gov. = Governor
Mr. = Mister (a man)	Mrs. = a married woman		
Ms. = a woman (*Miss* is a title for an unmarried woman.)			

St. = Street	Rd. = Road	Ave. = Avenue	La. = Lane
Dr. = Drive	Pl. = Place	Blvd. = Boulevard	

Sun.	Mon.	Tues.	Wed.	Thurs.	Fri.	Sat.

Jan.	Feb.	Mar.	Apr.	Aug.	Sept.	Oct.
Nov.	Dec.	(Other months are not abbreviated.)				

A.M. = *ante meridiem* (Latin for *before noon*)
P.M. = *post meridiem* (Latin for *after noon*)

PRACTICE 1 Punctuation

A. Write each sentence. Use commas correctly.

1. No I didn't order ten boxes of cookies.
2. The phone call is for you Wendy.
3. Well I suppose I could visit her tomorrow night.
4. Mark have you finished your homework yet?
5. I am not sure Jean where I put your keys.

B. Write each sentence. Use commas correctly.

6. Joe wrote his name on the form, last name first: Walker Joseph.
7. Today we had rain sleet ice and snow.
8. We must move the chairs tables and benches to the side of the room.
9. The batter swung the bat hit the ball and ran to first base.
10. Beat the eggs add the dry ingredients and mix well.

C. Write these place names and dates. Use commas correctly.

11. March 9 1895
12. Detroit Michigan
13. Paris France
14. October 29 1954
15. Minneapolis Minnesota
16. November 30 1642

PRACTICE 2   Punctuation

A. Write these sentences. Use commas correctly.

1. Mr. Harris was born in Macon Georgia on October 5 1943.
2. There was a major flood in Johnstown Pennsylvania on both May 31 1889 and on July 19 1977.
3. On January 5 1841 the family left Jackson Wyoming and headed toward Independence Missouri.
4. The ship left Boston Massachusetts on May 3 1775.

B. Write these sentences. Use commas and quotation marks correctly.

5. Brian said Puppies are cute but they are a lot of trouble.
6. I may buy a ranch house or I may stay in my apartment he replied.
7. Jamie stated The sun rose at 6:32 A.M. and it will set at 5:32 P.M.
8. The key to the mystery she explained lies in this ancient map.
9. He said The water may taste all right but it is polluted.

C. Write the contraction for each pair of words.

10. were not   11. it is   12. we will   13. have not   14. I am

D. Write these titles. Use quotation marks and underlining correctly.

15. Tulsa World (newspaper)
16. Journey Outside (book)
17. A Song of Greatness (poem)
18. A Night at the Opera (movie)
19. The Basic Food Groups (report)
20. The Nightingale (story)
21. Trains at Night (poem)
22. Caddie Woodlawn (book)
23. Zorro Rides Again (movie)
24. The Wild Swans (story)

E. Write these times with numerals. Use colons correctly.

25. four fifty-three A.M.   26. one fifteen P.M.   27. six nineteen A.M.

F. Write the abbreviation for each of the following.

28. November   30. Tuesday   32. before noon   34. Doctor
29. Reverend   31. Road   33. Governor   35. Avenue

The 10 Most Useful Spelling Rules

1. <u>If a word ends in *e*</u>, drop the *e* when you add a suffix that begins with a vowel.

    save + ing = saving   late + er = later

    Keep the *e* when you add a suffix that begins with a consonant.

    safe + ty = safety   peace + ful = peaceful

2. <u>If a word ends in a vowel and *y*</u>, keep the *y* when you add a suffix.

    delay + s = delays   annoy + ed = annoyed

3. <u>If a word ends in a consonant and *y*</u>, keep the *y* when you add a suffix that begins with *i.*

    apply + ing = applying   baby + ish = babyish

    Change the *y* to *i* when you add a suffix that does not begin with *i.*

    beauty + ful = beautiful   factory + es = factories

4. <u>If a one-syllable word ends in one vowel and one consonant</u>, double the final consonant when you add a suffix that begins with a vowel.

    stop + ing = stopping   repel + ing = repelling

5. <u>When you choose between *ie* and *ei*</u>, usually choose *ie*.

    field   shriek   friend

    Choose *ei* after *c* or for the long *a* sound.

    receive   deceit   ceiling
    neighbor   weigh   beige

    (Exceptions: *leisure, seize, neither, weird.*)

6. The suffix *-s* can be added to most nouns and verbs. If the word ends in *s*, *ss*, *sh*, *ch*, *x*, or *zz*, add *es*.

gas	gases	hiss	hisses
push	pushes	match	matches
fox	foxes	buzz	buzzes

7. If a word ends in a single *f* or *fe*, usually change the *f* to a *v* when you add *-s* or *-es*.

calf	calves	elf	elves
knife	knives	wife	wives

8. The letter *q* is always followed by the letter *u* in English words.

question   quarrel   equal

The letter *v* is always followed by another letter; it is never the last letter in a word.

love   have   give

9. Add an apostrophe and *s* ('s) to a singular noun to show possession, but do not add them to a pronoun. Special pronouns show possession.

doctor's	spider's	Mary's
his	hers	its
ours	yours	theirs

10. Use an apostrophe (') in a contraction to show where a letter or letters have been left out.

is + not = isn't	I + am = I'm
we + are = we're	it + is = it's
you + will = you'll	they + have = they've

100 Spelling Demons

1. ache	31. exaggerate
2. again	32. experience
3. aisle	33. February
4. all right	34. foreign
5. always	35. forty
6. among	36. friend
7. answer	37. governor
8. anything	38. grammar
9. assignment	39. guess
10. been	40. handkerchief
11. beginning	41. hear
12. believe	42. heard
13. break	43. height
14. business	44. here
15. busy	45. imagine
16. calendar	46. interested
17. children	47. it's
18. color	48. knew
19. coming	49. know
20. committee	50. knowledge
21. cough	51. laid
22. could	52. library
23. country	53. loose
24. different	54. lose
25. doctor	55. many
26. done	56. meant
27. early	57. minute
28. easy	58. much
29. especially	59. necessary
30. every	60. neighbor

61. often	81. they
62. once	82. though
63. opposite	83. threw
64. piece	84. through
65. pretty	85. tired
66. raise	86. together
67. receive	87. too
68. said	88. truly
69. separate	89. Tuesday
70. shoes	90. two
71. since	91. unusual
72. some	92. very
73. sometime	93. Wednesday
74. stationary	94. where
75. sugar	95. whether
76. sure	96. woman
77. surprise	97. women
78. their	98. would
79. there	99. writing
80. therefore	100. you're

PRACTICE

Write the following spelling words in alphabetical order. Then write a sentence for each word. When you have finished, you can use your sentences to give a spelling test. Work with a partner. Say each demon word clearly. Then read the sentence for that word.

1. stationary	7. women
2. grammar	8. exaggerate
3. committee	9. especially
4. always	10. foreign
5. surprise	11. receive
6. though	12. opposite

Handwriting Models

a b c d e f g h i
j k l m n o p q r
s t u v w x y z

Circle letters

a b d o p q

Double-curved letter

s

Slant-line letters

k v w x y z

Curved letters

c e f h m n r u

Straight-line letters

b d h i k l t

Below-the-line letters

g j p q y

A B C D E F G H I
J K L M N O P Q R
S T U V W X Y Z

Handwriting Models

a b c d e f g h i

j k l m n o p q r

s t u v w x y z

Upward-loop letters

b e f

h k l

Rounded letters

m n v

x y z

Oval letters

a c d

g o q

Pointed letters

i j p r

s t u w

A B C D E F G H I

J K L M N O P Q R

S T U V W X Y Z

Used with permission from Zaner-Bloser *Handwriting: Basic Skills and Application*. Copyright © 1984, Zaner-Bloser, Inc., Columbus, Ohio.

7 Tips for Taking Tests

1. Be prepared. Have several sharp pencils and an eraser.

2. Read or listen to the directions carefully. Be sure you know what you are to do and where and how you are to mark your answers.

   > Match the synonyms in columns A and B.
   > Circle the correct answer.
   > Cross out the wrong number.
   > Fill in the circle next to the correct answer.

3. Answer the easy questions first. Quickly read all the questions on the page. Then go back to the beginning and answer the questions you are sure you know. Put a light check mark next to those you are not sure of or don't know.

4. Next try to answer the questions you are not sure you know. You may have a choice of answers. If so, narrow your choice. First eliminate all the answers you know are wrong. Try to narrow your selection to two answers. Then mark the answer you think is right.

5. Answer the hardest questions last. If you can't answer a question at all, don't waste time worrying about it. Skip the question and go on to the next. (Sometimes a percentage of wrong answers is subtracted from the number of correct answers.)

6. Plan your time. Don't spend too much time on just one question. Check your watch or a clock from time to time as you take the test. If you spend too much time on one part of the test, you won't have time to finish the rest. You will also need to save some time to check your answers.

7. Check your answers when you have finished. Make sure you have marked your answers correctly. Unless you're sure you made a mistake, you probably should not change an answer.

Thesaurus

What Is a Thesaurus?

In a thesaurus, entry words are listed in alphabetical order. Under each entry word, synonyms and antonyms are shown.

Below is part of a thesaurus entry from this book.

Entry word → **right** (adj) — **1** agreeing with what is just, lawful, or good. It is <u>right</u> to help others who are in need. **2** conforming to facts or truth; correct; true. My watch does not have the <u>right</u> time.

Synonym → *correct* — free from faults or mistakes; right; true. Most of the class had <u>correct</u> answers on the quiz.

Antonym → ANTONYM: erroneous

An entry word appears in dark type: **right**
The synonyms appear in italic type: *correct*
The antonyms appear in blue type: erroneous

How to Use the Thesaurus Index

To find a word, use the Thesaurus Index. An entry word is shown this way:

right (adj) 429

A synonym is followed by its entry word. The example below means "To find *correct*, look under the entry for **right**, which begins on page 429."

correct **right** (adj) 429

An antonym is followed by its entry word. The example below means "To find erroneous, look under the entry for **right**, which begins on page 429."

erroneous **right** (adj) 429

A cross-reference (marked "See also") lists an entry that gives additional synonyms, related words, and antonyms.

right (adj) 429
See also **true** (adj) 431

To learn more about a thesaurus, turn to the lesson "Using a Thesaurus" on page 30.

A

abandon (v) keep (v) 425
abhor enjoy (v) 422
abhor like (v) 426
absence need (n) 427
abundance need (n) 427
abundant enough (adj) 422
accomplish do (v) 421
accurate right (adj) 429
achieve win (v) 432
acquire buy (v) 420
acquire take (v) 430
acquire win (v) 432
activity rest (n) 428
adequacy need (n) 427
admire enjoy (v) 422
admire like (v) 426
adore enjoy (v) 422
affirm say (v) 429
affluence need (n) 427
afraid (adj) 420
aid help (v) 424
ample enough (adj) 422
amusing funny (adj) 423
ancient (adj) new (adj) 427
answer (v) 420
antique (adj) new (adj) 427
anxious afraid (adj) 420
appreciate enjoy (v) 422
appreciate like (v) 426
apprehend understand (v) 431
arrive go (v) 423
artificial true (adj) 431
ask answer (v) 420
assist help (v) 424
astonishing wonderful (adj) 433
auction (v) buy (v) 420
authentic true (adj) 431
average (adj) wonderful
  (adj) 433
awful bad (adj) 420
awful (adj) good (adj) 423

B

bad (adj) 420
  See also wrong (adj) 433
bad (adj) good (adj) 423
badly well (adv) 432
beginning (n) end (n) 421
behold see (v) 429
beneficial bad (adj) 420
big (adj) 420
  See also great (adj) 423
big (adj) small (adj) 430
blaring loud (adj) 426
block (v) help (v) 424
boisterous quiet (adj) 428
bold afraid (adj) 420
border end (n) 421
brave (adj) afraid (adj) 420
build make (v) 427
buy (v) 420

C

call (v) 421
calm (adj) 421
calm (n) noise (n) 427
certain true (adj) 431
chat talk (v) 431
cherish like (v) 426
chilly hot (adj) 425
chore job (n) 425
clamor noise (n) 427
clamorous quiet (adj) 428
clarify explain (v) 422
clatter noise (n) 427
coarse fine (adj) 422
coarse (adj) sleek (adj) 430
come go (v) 423
comical funny (adj) 423
commencement end (n) 421
commendable fine (adj) 422
common (adj) wonderful
  (adj) 433
communicate talk (v) 431

compel make (v) 427
competently well (adv) 432
complete do (v) 421
comprehend know (v) 426
comprehend understand
  (v) 431
conceive think (v) 431
concept idea (n) 425
conclusion end (n) 421
confiscate take (v) 430
confuse explain (v) 422
conserve keep (v) 425
conserve (v) use (v) 432
considerable big (adj) 420
considerate good (adj) 423
construct make (v) 427
contemplate think (v) 431
converse talk (v) 431
cool (adj) hot (adj) 425
correct right (adj) 429
correct true (adj) 431
correct (adj) wrong
  (adj) 433
courageous afraid (adj) 420
crawl (v) run (v) 429
create make (v) 427
creep (v) run (v) 429
cry call (v) 421
current new (adj) 427

D

deafening loud (adj) 426
decent right (adj) 429
declare say (v) 429
decline (v) grow (v) 424
decrease (v) grow (v) 424
deficiency need (n) 427
deliberate think (v) 431
delicate fine (adj) 422
demolish make (v) 427
demonstrate explain (v) 422
deplete use (v) 432

THESAURUS **415**

deposit **put** (v) 428
describe **explain** (v) 422
despise **enjoy** (v) 422
destroy make (v) 427
detest like (v) 426
detest enjoy (v) 422
develop **grow** (v) 424
diminish grow (v) 424
diminutive (adj) big (adj) 420
din **noise** (n) 427
discard (v) keep (v) 425
discourage help (v) 424
discuss **talk** (v) 431
dislike (v) enjoy (v) 422
dislike (v) like (v) 426
disquiet (n) rest (n) 428
disregard (v) look (v) 426
disregard (v) see (v) 429
distinguish **see** (v) 429
district **place** (n) 428
do (v) 421
See also **make** (v) 427
dull (adj) sleek (adj) 430
dwindle grow (v) 424

E

earn **win** (v) 432
earsplitting **loud** (adj) 426
eavesdrop **hear** (v) 424
edge **end** (n) 421
employ **use** (v) 432
encourage **help** (v) 424
end (n) 421
endure **have** (v) 424
enjoy (v) 422
enjoy **like** (v) 426
enormous **big** (adj) 420
enormous small (adj) 430
enough (adj) 422
erroneous right (adj) 429
ethical wrong (adj) 433
examine **look** (v) 426
excellent bad (adj) 420
excess (n) need (n) 427
excitement rest (n) 428
exercise **use** (v) 432

exhaust **use** (v) 432
exit **go** (v) 423
expand **grow** (v) 424
experience **have** (v) 424
explain (v) 422
explain **answer** (v) 420
express **say** (v) 429
extraordinary **wonderful** (adj) 433

F

factual **true** (adj) 431
fail (v) win (v) 432
fall (v) win (v) 432
false (adj) true (adj) 431
fathom **understand** (v) 431
fearful **afraid** (adj) 420
fearless **afraid** (adj) 420
fictitious **true** (adj) 431
fierce **calm** (adj) 421
finale **end** (n) 421
fine (adj) 422
See also **good** (adj) 423
fine (adj) bad (adj) 420
fine **well** (adv) 432
finish **do** (v) 421
fledgling **new** (adj) 427
flop (v) win (v) 432
flourish **grow** (v) 424
forfeit (v) win (v) 432
free (v) keep (v) 425
freezing hot (adj) 425
fresh **new** (adj) 427
frightened **afraid** (adj) 420
frigid hot (adj) 425
frustrate help (v) 424
function **work** (v) 433
funny (adj) 423

G

gaze **look** (v) 426
gentle (adj) loud (adj) 426
get buy (v) 420
gigantic **big** (adj) 420
give (v) take (v) 430
glassy **sleek** (adj) 430
gleaming **sleek** (adj) 430

glossy **sleek** (adj) 430
go (v) 423
good (adj) 423
See also **fine** (adj) 422
good (adj) bad (adj) 420
grasp **know** (v) 426
grasp **take** (v) 430
grasp **understand** (v) 431
grave (adj) funny (adj) 423
great (adj) 423
See also **big** (adj) 420
great (adj) small (adj) 430
grow (v) 424

H

halt (v) go (v) 423
harmful **bad** (adj) 420
hate (v) enjoy (v) 422
hate (v) like (v) 426
have (v) 424
hear (v) 424
heed **hear** (v) 424
help (v) 424
hilarious **funny** (adj) 422
hinder help (v) 424
historical **true** (adj) 431
holler **call** (v) 421
honest **good** (adj) 423
hot (adj) 425
hubbub **noise** (n) 427
huge **big** (adj) 420
humorous **funny** (adj) 423
hurry **run** (v) 429

I

icy **hot** (adj) 425
idea (n) 425
ignore look (v) 426
ignore see (v) 429
illegal **wrong** (adj) 433
illustrate **explain** (v) 422
illustrious **great** (adj) 423
imagine **think** (v) 431
immense small (adj) 430
impart **say** (v) 429
imperfectly well (adv) 432

impression **idea** (n) 425
improper good (adj) 423
improper right (adj) 429
inaccurate **true** (adj) 431
inaccurate **wrong** (adj) 433
inadequate enough (adj) 422
inadequately well (adv) 432
inappropriate **wrong** (adj) 433
inaudible **quiet** (adj) 428
inconsequential great (adj) 423
inconsiderable great (adj) 423
incorrect true (adj) 431
incorrect **wrong** (adj) 433
increase **grow** (v) 424
inferior fine (adj) 422
inquire answer (v) 420
insignificant great (adj) 423
insignificant **small** (adj) 430
insufficient enough (adj) 422
interpret explain (v) 422
interrogate answer (v) 420
intonation **sound** (n) 430

J
job (n) 425
jog **run** (v) 429
judge **hear** (v) 424
justify **explain** (v) 422

K
keep (v) 425
know (v) 426
know **understand** (v) 431

L
labor **work** (v) 433
lack (v) have (v) 424
lack **need** (n) 427
large **big** (adj) 420
large (adj) small (adj) 430
leave **go** (v) 423
leisure rest (n) 428
letup **rest** (n) 428
like (v) 426
listen **hear** (v) 424

little (adj) big (adj) 420
loathe enjoy (v) 422
loathe like (v) 426
location **place** (n) 428
look (v) 426
    See also **see** (v) 429
loquacious quiet (adj) 428
lose keep (v) 425
lose win (v) 432
loud (adj) 426
love **enjoy** (v) 422
low (adj) loud (adj) 426
ludicrous **funny** (adj) 423
lustrous **sleek** (adj) 430

M
magnificent **great** (adj) 423
maintain **keep** (v) 425
make (v) 427
    See also **do** (v) 421
mammoth **great** (adj) 423
manipulate **use** (v) 432
manufacture **make** (v) 427
market (v) buy (v) 420
marvelous **wonderful** (adj) 433
mature **grow** (v) 424
meager enough (adj) 422
mediocre wonderful (adj) 433
melancholy (adj) funny (adj) 423
mellow (adj) loud (adj) 426
mention **say** (v) 429
microscopic **big** (adj) 420
microscopic **small** (adj) 430
miniature (adj) big (adj) 420
miniature **small** (adj) 430
minimal **enough** (adj) 422
minor **small** (adj) 430
mischievous bad (adj) 420
miss (v) look (v) 426
misinterpret explain (v) 422
misunderstand understand (v) 431
modern **new** (adj) 427
monotone **sound** (n) 430

mournful funny (adj) 423
move **go** (v) 423

N
necessity **need** (n) 427
need (n) 427
need (v) have (v) 424
new (adj) 427
noise (n) 427
    See also **sound** (n) 430
noise **sound** (n) 430
noiseless **quiet** (adj) 428
noisy **loud** (adj) 426
noisy quiet (adj) 428
notice **see** (v) 429
notion **idea** (n) 425
novel **new** (adj) 427

O
obscure (v) explain (v) 422
observe **look** (v) 426
obstruct **help** (v) 424
obtain **buy** (v) 420
occupation **job** (n) 425
old (adj) **new** (adj) 427
operate **work** (v) 433
opinion **idea** (n) 425
oppose **help** (v) 424
ordinary (adj) wonderful (adj) 433
outdated **new** (adj) 427
outmoded **new** (adj) 427
outstanding **great** (adj) 423
overlook (v) look (v) 426
overlook (v) see (v) 429
own **have** (v) 424

P
peaceful **calm** (adj) 421
peek **look** (v) 426
perceive **hear** (v) 424
perceive **know** (v) 426
perform **do** (v) 421
perform **work** (v) 433
petrified **afraid** (adj) 420
pitch **sound** (n) 430
place (n) 428
place **put** (v) 428

placid **calm** (adj) 421
play (v) work (v) 433
plenty **enough** (adj) 422
poor bad (adj) 420
poor fine (adj) 422
poorly well (adv) 432
position **job** (n) 425
position **put** (n) 428
possess **have** (v) 424
possess **keep** (v) 425
powdery **fine** (adj) 422
precise **right** (adj) 429
prefer **like** (v) 426
preserve (v) use (v) 432
pressure **make** (v) 427
prevail **win** (v) 432
prevent **keep** (v) 425
procure **buy** (v) 420
procure **take** (v) 430
produce **do** (v) 421
profession **job** (n) 425
proficient **good** (adj) 423
proficiently **well** (adv) 432
progress **go** (v) 423
proper **right** (adj) 429
proper (adj) wrong (adj) 433
pulverized **fine** (adj) 422
purchase **buy** (v) 420
put (v) 428

Q

query (v) answer (v) 420
question (v) answer (v) 420
quiet (adj) 428
quiet **calm** (adj) 421
quiet (adj) loud (adj) 426
quiet (n) noise (n) 427
quiet (n) sound (n) 430
quiz (v) answer (v) 420

R

race **run** (v) 429
racket **noise** (n) 427
raging **calm** (adj) 421
real **true** (adj) 431
realize **know** (v) 426
realize **understand** (v) 431

reap **win** (v) 432
reason **think** (v) 431
recent **new** (adj) 427
recess **rest** (n) 428
recognize **know** (v) 426
refute **answer** (v) 420
region **place** (n) 428
relaxation **rest** (n) 428
release (v) keep (v) 425
relinquish keep (v) 425
relinquish take (v) 430
relish **enjoy** (v) 422
remain **go** (v) 423
remarkable **wonderful**
   (adj) 433
reply **answer** (v) 420
report **talk** (v) 431
repose **rest** (n) 428
requirement **need** (n) 427
rescue **help** (v) 424
reserved **quiet** (adj) 428
residence **place** (n) 428
respite **rest** (n) 428
respond **answer** (v) 420
respond **say** (v) 429
rest (n) 428
rest **put** (v) 428
restlessness rest (n) 428
restrain **keep** (v) 425
retain **have** (v) 424
retort **answer** (v) 420
return (v) take (v) 430
reverberation **sound** (n) 430
right (adj) 429
   See also **true** (adj) 431
right (adj) wrong (adj) 433
rough (adj) calm (adj) 421
rough (adj) fine (adj) 422
rough (adj) sleek (adj) 431
ruckus **noise** (n) 427
ruin (v) make (v) 427
run (v) 429

S

satisfactorily **well** (adv) 432
satisfactory bad (adj) 420

save (v) use (v) 432
savor **enjoy** (v) 422
say (v) 429
   See also **talk** (v) 431
scamper **run** (v) 429
scant (adj) enough
   (adj) 422
scorching **hot** (adj) 425
scream **call** (v) 421
see (v) 429
   See also **look** (v) 426
seize **take** (v) 430
sell (v) buy (v) 420
serene **calm** (adj) 421
serious funny (adj) 423
set **put** (v) 428
shiny **sleek** (adj) 430
shortage **need** (n) 427
shriek **call** (v) 421
shrink (v) grow (v) 424
significant small (adj) 430
silence (n) noise (n) 427
silence (n) sound (n) 430
silent **quiet** (adj) 428
silky **sleek** (adj) 430
site **place** (n) 428
situate **put** (v) 428
sizable **big** (adj) 420
sizzling **hot** (adj) 425
skillful **good** (adj) 423
skillfully **well** (adv) 432
skimpy **enough** (adj) 422
sleek (adj) 430
slender **fine** (adj) 422
slight **small** (adj) 430
small (adj) 430
small (adj) big (adj) 420
small (adj) great (adj) 423
sober **funny** (adj) 423
soft (adj) loud (adj) 426
soft **quiet** (adj) 428
solemn **funny** (adj) 423
solve **answer** (v) 420
sound (n) 430
   See also **noise** (n) 427
speak **talk** (v) 431

THESAURUS

splendid **fine** (adj) 422
spoiled **bad** (adj) 420
spread **grow** (v) 424
sprint **run** (v) 429
stale (adj) **new** (adj) 427
stare **look** (v) 426
start (n) **end** (n) 421
stay (v) **go** (v) 423
steaming **hot** (adj) 425
still **calm** (adj) 421
stop (v) **go** (v) 423
store **keep** (v) 425
stormy **calm** (adj) 421
stroll (v) **run** (v) 429
subdued **loud** (adj) 426
substantial **enough**
    (adj) 422
successfully **well** (adv) 432
sufficient **enough** (adj) 422
suitable **wrong** (adj) 433
superb **wonderful** (adj) 433
superior **bad** (adj) 420
superior **good** (adj) 423
support **help** (v) 424
suppose **think** (v) 431
surrender (v) **take** (v) 430
sweltering **hot** (adj) 425

T

take (v) 430
talk (v) 431
    See also **say** (v) 429
task **job** (n) 425
teeny **small** (adj) 430
termination **end** (n) 421
terrific **wonderful** (adj) 433
terrified **afraid** (adj) 420
territory **place** (n) 428
theory **idea** (n) 425
thick **fine** (adj) 422
think (v) 431
thought **idea** (n) 425
thunderous **loud** (adj) 426

tick **work** (v) 433
tiny **big** (adj) 420
tiny **great** (adj) 423
toil (n) **rest** (n) 428
toil **work** (v) 433
tone **sound** (n) 430
torrid **hot** (adj) 425
toxic **bad** (adj) 420
tranquil **calm** (adj) 421
tranquility **noise** (n) 427
transport **take** (v) 430
travel **go** (v) 423
treasure **like** (v) 426
tremendous **great** (adj) 423
triumph **win** (v) 432
tropical **hot** (adj) 425
trot **run** (v) 429
true (adj) 431
    See also **right** (adj) 429
true **right** (adj) 429
true (adj) **wrong** (adj) 433
try **hear** (v) 424
turbulent **calm** (adj) 421

U

unacceptably **well** (adv) 432
unafraid **afraid** (adj) 420
undergo **have** (v) 424
understand (v) 431
understand **know** (v) 426
unethical **right** (adj) 429
unethical **wrong** (adj) 433
unfair **right** (adj) 429
unfinished **fine** (adj) 422
uninteresting **wonderful**
    (adj) 433
unsatisfactorily **well**
    (adv) 432
unsatisfactory **right**
    (adj) 429
unskilled **good** (adj) 423
unsuitable **wrong** (adj) 433
untrue **true** (adj) 431

unvoiced **quiet** (adj) 428
use (v) 432
usual (adj) **wonderful**
    (adj) 433
utilize **use** (v) 432

V

valiant (adj) **afraid**
    (adj) 420
vast **great** (adj) 423
vend **buy** (v) 420
verbose **quiet** (adj) 428
view **see** (v) 429
visualize **see** (v) 429
vociferous **loud** (adj) 426

W

walk (v) **run** (v) 429
wane **grow** (adj) 424
want (v) **have** (v) 424
watch **look** (v) 426
wealth **need** (n) 427
well (adv) 432
wild (adj) **calm** (adj) 421
win (v) 432
windup **end** (n) 421
withdraw **go** (v) 423
witness **see** (v) 429
witty **funny** (adj) 423
wonderful (adj) 433
work (v) 433
work **job** (n) 425
work (n) **rest** (n) 428
worthless **good** (adj) 423
worthwhile **good** (adj) 423
wreck (v) **make** (v) 427
wrong (adj) 433
    See also **bad** (adj) 420
wrong (adj) **good** (adj) 423
wrong (adj) **right** (adj) 429

Y

yell **call** (v) 421

THESAURUS

THESAURUS

A

afraid (adj)—feeling fear; alarmed; frightened. Were you afraid of the dark when you were small?

anxious—uneasy because of fears or thoughts of what may happen; worried. Daniel was anxious about the first day of school.

fearful—causing fear; terrible; feeling fear; frightened. The fearful person approached the old house with caution.

frightened—afraid; filled with fright. The frightened mouse raced across the ground.

petrified—paralyzed by great fear. The petrified rabbit stayed perfectly still as we ran by.

terrified—suddenly filled with a very great and paralyzing fear. The terrified individual would not move from his chair until all the thunder and lightning had ceased.

ANTONYMS: bold, brave (adj), courageous, fearless, unafraid, valiant (adj)

answer (v)—**1** to respond to; to write with or speak in response to. Will you please answer these questions right away? **2** to find the solution to. I answered all of the questions on the test correctly.

explain—to tell the meaning of; to make plain or clear; to tell how to. Juan explained how to work out the math problem.

refute—to show an opinion to be incorrect or false; to prove wrong. Can you refute the statement that our school needs a new gymnasium?

reply—to answer by words or action; to respond. I have already replied to the letter that I received yesterday morning.

respond—to reply in words; to answer; to act in answer; to react. I responded to the favorable comment by smiling.

retort—to say in a sharp or quick reply. "I won't go," he retorted.

solve—to find the answer to; to clear up. The detective solved the mystery.

ANTONYMS: ask, inquire, interrogate, query (v), question (v), quiz (v)

B

bad (adj)—not good; not as it ought to be; causing harm; troublesome. The bad weather prevented us from going outdoors.

harmful—causing pain, damage, or loss. Because it causes rust, salt can be harmful to automobiles.

mischievous—showing conduct that causes annoyance; naughty. The mischievous children enjoyed playing jokes on one another.

poor—not good in quality; not satisfactory. This jacket is in poor condition.

spoiled—bad or unfit for use; decayed. I hope you will not drink the spoiled milk.

toxic—very harmful to health; poisonous. The water in this stream is toxic.

awful [informal]—very bad or otherwise unusual. It is just awful to be ill with the flu.

See also *wrong* (adj).

ANTONYMS: beneficial, excellent, fine (adj), good (adj), satisfactory, superior

big (adj)—great in size or amount; large. That hat is much too big for me.

considerable—in large quantity; much; not a little. If you are still hungry, there is a considerable amount of soup left.

enormous—very large; huge; immense; gigantic. David has an enormous appetite for buttered rolls.

gigantic—of, like, or having to do with a giant; enormous; colossal; huge. During the storm gigantic waves crashed against the cliffs.

huge—very large; unusually large in bulk, dimension, or size; extremely large in number or quantity. Many huge elephants were in the circus parade this morning.

large—of more than the usual amount, number, or size; great; big. Please hand me the large cardboard box that is in the garage.

sizable—fairly large. There is a sizable amount of paperwork on your desk.

See also *great* (adj).

ANTONYMS: diminutive (adj), little (adj), microscopic, miniature (adj), small (adj), tiny

buy (v)—**1** to gain ownership of something by the payment of money. I bought this suit on sale in the department store.

acquire—to get by one's own actions or efforts. The museum recently acquired a rare piece of sculpture.

get—to obtain possession of. Let's go to the cafeteria and get our lunch.

obtain—to get or attain, usually through planned action. I <u>obtained</u> the tickets to the concert months ago.

procure—to get or obtain; to acquire. The broker <u>procured</u> many shares of stock.

purchase—to obtain through the payment of money. They <u>purchased</u> a piano for their living room.

ANTONYMS: auction (v), market (v), sell (v), vend

C

call (v)—to say, especially in a loud voice; to cry out or shout. When I <u>call</u> your name, please raise your hand.

cry—to call loudly; to shout. Did someone just <u>cry</u> for help?

scream—to make a loud, piercing cry. Some people <u>screamed</u> while riding the roller coaster at the amusement park.

shriek—to make a shrill or high-pitched sound. As the train approached the station, the whistle <u>shrieked</u>.

yell—to cry out with a loud, strong sound. The children in the playground are <u>yelling</u>.

holler [informal]—to shout or cry loudly. I <u>holler</u> for my dog when he runs away from me.

calm (adj)—not stormy or windy; not stirred up; not excited; peaceful. On that pleasant morning the sea was <u>calm</u>.

peaceful—full of peace; calm; quiet. On a <u>peaceful</u> evening I can hear the gentle, rhythmic chirping of crickets.

placid—pleasantly peaceful or calm; quiet. A <u>placid</u> brook meanders among the rolling hills of that farm.

quiet—moving very little; calm; still. The class was <u>quiet</u> while the test was in progress.

serene—calm; peaceful; untroubled. His <u>serene</u> smile showed that he was happy.

still—without noise; quiet; unruffled or undisturbed; free from waves, violent winds, or the like. Prior to the thunderstorm the air was absolutely <u>still</u>.

tranquil—peaceful; calm; quiet; free from agitation or disturbance; placid. I spent a <u>tranquil</u> day in the park sketching some trees.

ANTONYMS: fierce, raging, rough (adj), stormy, turbulent, wild (adj)

D

do (v)—to carry through to completion any work or action; to finish; to perform; to carry out; to make. Rena <u>did</u> all of the work efficiently.

accomplish—to succeed in completing; to carry out or perform a plan or undertaking. What did you <u>accomplish</u> today?

complete—to get done; to end; to finish. She <u>completed</u> her paper after doing research.

finish—to bring an action, work, or anything else to an end; to reach the end of; to complete. Janice <u>finished</u> the race ahead of all the other runners.

perform—to do; to go through and finish; to accomplish. My brother <u>performed</u> well in the school play.

produce—to bring into existence by effort or labor; to create; to make from various materials. That factory <u>produces</u> light bulbs.

See also *make* (v).

E

end (n)—**1** the last part; the conclusion. Their house is at the <u>end</u> of the street. **2** The part where a thing begins or where it stops. Hold the two <u>ends</u> of the string with your left hand.

border—the side, boundary, or edge of anything; a line that separates one country, state, or town from another; a frontier. You must show your passport when you cross the <u>border</u> between some countries.

conclusion—the final part; the end; the close. Before I could read the <u>conclusion</u> of this novel, I fell asleep.

edge—the place or line where something ends; the part farthest from the middle; the side. I cautiously looked over the <u>edge</u> of the rim of the Grand Canyon.

finale—the last part of a play or a piece of music. The <u>finale</u> of Tchaikovsky's "1812 Overture," which includes the sounds of bells and cannon, is very exciting.

termination—the act of ending or the fact of being ended; the end. With the <u>termination</u> of the contract with the builder all construction on the skyscraper ceased.

end *(continued)*

THESAURUS

THESAURUS

windup [informal]—an end, conclusion, or finish. At the windup of the festivities, everyone cheered.
ANTONYMS: beginning (n), commencement, start (n)

enjoy (v)—to use or have with joy; to be happy with. I enjoy bowling very much.
admire—to regard with wonder, approval, and pleasure; to feel satisfaction or delight in. I admire the astronauts for their courage.
appreciate—to think highly of; to recognize the quality or worth of; to value. Do you appreciate the good things that come your way?
love—to take great pleasure in; to like very much. I love to ride my bicycle in the park.
relish—to take delight or pleasure in; to like the taste of. Kevin relished every moment of his first day in New York City.
savor—to enjoy the taste or smell of; to appreciate by taste or smell. I savored every bite of the food in the Japanese restaurant.
adore [informal]—to like very much. Because she adores horses, Pamela works at the stable whenever she can.
ANTONYMS: abhor, despise, detest, dislike (v), hate (v), loathe

enough (adj)—as much as wanted or needed; sufficient. There is enough fried chicken for everyone to enjoy.
abundant—very plentiful; more than enough. An abundant harvest is the goal in every farmer's mind.
ample—large in degree or kind; more than enough; as much as is needed; sufficient. There is an ample supply of pencils.
minimal—least possible; very small. The tropical storm continued to intensify until it attained minimal hurricane force winds.
plenty—abundant; plentiful; enough. Four tomatoes will be plenty.
substantial—important; large; ample. The workers received a substantial increase in salary.
sufficient—as much as is needed; enough. Without sufficient rainfall corn withers.
ANTONYMS: inadequate, insufficient, meager, scant (adj), skimpy

explain (v)—to tell how to do; to make plain or clear; to tell the meaning of; to give reasons for. I will explain how to get there.

clarify—to make clearer; to explain. Please clarify what you mean by that statement.
demonstrate—to show clearly; to explain by carrying out experiments or by showing and explaining samples; to show how something is done. My uncle demonstrated how to make a delicious cheese sauce.
describe—to tell in words how a person acts, feels, or looks, or how a thing, a place, or an event looks or happened; to write or tell about. Betty described her new outfit.
illustrate—to explain or make clear by examples, stories, or comparisons. By using a chart, she illustrated the facts she was presenting.
interpret—to explain the meaning of; to bring out the meaning of a dramatic work, music, or other written material. How would you interpret the meaning of that poem?
justify—to give a good reason for; to show to be right or just. Can you justify spending all that money for a pair of gloves?
ANTONYMS: confuse, misinterpret, obscure (v)

F

fine (adj)—**1** of a very high quality; excellent; good. The city art museum contains a fine collection of paintings. **2** very small or thin. That piece of thread is so fine that it is nearly invisible. **3** not heavy or coarse; delicate. The fine sand on this beach is extremely smooth to the touch.
commendable—deserving approval or praise; praiseworthy. Everyone who helped make the scenery did a commendable job.
delicate—of fine weave, make, or quality; easily torn; thin. Please handle that delicate crystal vase carefully.
powdery—of powder or dust; in the form of powder; dusty. Is powdery snow best for skiing?
pulverized—having been ground into powder or dust; like powder or dust. Is pulverized limestone good for lawns?
slender—thin and long; not big around; slim. I think that the slender tree is a poplar.
splendid—glorious; brilliant; magnificent, grand. The splendid light in the artist's studio is just right for painting.

See also *good* (adj).

ANTONYMS: coarse, inferior, poor, rough (adj), thick, unfinished

funny (adj)—causing laughter; amusing; comical. My sister likes to make <u>funny</u> faces.

amusing—causing smiles or laughter; entertaining. You must tell that <u>amusing</u> story.

comical—funny; amusing. We enjoyed the <u>comical</u> antics of the clowns.

hilarious—very merry; noisily happy; mirthful. Everyone had a <u>hilarious</u> time at Johnny's birthday party.

humorous—full of humor; having an amusing quality; funny. That book contains many <u>humorous</u> stories.

ludicrous—absurd, or not logical or true, but amusing; causing derisive laughter. The little boy and the Great Dane make a <u>ludicrous</u> pair.

witty—full of wit or the ability to perceive quickly and to express cleverly ideas that are striking, unusual, and amusing; amusing and clever. One character in the play continually made <u>witty</u> remarks.

ANTONYMS: grave (adj), melancholy (adj), mournful, serious, sober, solemn

G

go (v)—to move along; to proceed; to move away; to leave. Tomorrow I will <u>go</u> to the shopping mall with my friends.

exit—to go out; to leave. You should <u>exit</u> quickly and quietly during a fire drill.

leave—to go away; to depart. Our cousins <u>left</u> shortly after dinner because they had a long ride home.

move—to pass from one position or place to another; to change position or place. Please <u>move</u> that chair closer to the table.

progress—to advance; to move forward; to go ahead. The long freight train <u>progressed</u> slowly toward its destination.

travel—to go from one place to another; to journey. My neighbors <u>travel</u> to distant places whenever they are on vacation.

withdraw—to go away; to leave. Is it true that the leading lady <u>withdrew</u> from the play?

ANTONYMS: arrive, come, halt (v), remain, stay (v), stop (v)

good (adj)—**1** having high quality; superior; excellent. The food at this restaurant certainly is <u>good</u>. **2** as it ought to be; right; proper; desirable. It was <u>good</u> of you to visit your ailing friend. **3** clever, skillful. Obviously, a <u>good</u> artist painted that picture.

considerate—thoughtful of others and their feelings. It was <u>considerate</u> of you to call me when I was sick.

honest—not cheating, lying, or stealing; fair and upright; truthful. An <u>honest</u> person returned the necklace I had lost in school.

proficient—advanced in any science, art, or subject; skilled. Many of the students in my class are <u>proficient</u> in spelling.

skillful—having skill or ability; expert. The <u>skillful</u> carpenter quickly replaced the broken porch step.

superior—above the average; excellent; higher in amount, degree, or quality; better. I find the hamburgers at this restaurant <u>superior</u> to all others I have tasted.

worthwhile—worth attention, effort, or time; having real merit or value. The trip to the historical site was a <u>worthwhile</u> one.

See also *fine* (adj).

ANTONYMS: awful (adj), bad (adj), improper, unskilled, worthless, wrong (adj)

great (adj)—**1** large in amount, size, or number; more than usual. The <u>great</u> ship moved silently and majestically into the harbor. **2** important; famous; high in rank. While on our tour of one of the motion picture studios in Hollywood, we saw a <u>great</u> actor.

illustrious—very famous; outstanding; renowned. The <u>illustrious</u> painter greeted all who came to see the exhibit of his works.

magnificent—noble; impressive; extraordinarily fine; superb. The <u>magnificent</u> trees of Sequoia National Park are incredible to behold.

mammoth—gigantic; huge. A <u>mammoth</u> power shovel was used to dig the trench.

outstanding—standing out from others; important; well-known. Jack is an <u>outstanding</u> tennis player.

tremendous—very great; immense; enormous. That <u>tremendous</u> bridge is over one hundred years old.

great *(continued)*

vast—of great area; of immense extent; tremendous. The continent of Asia is vast.
See also *big* (adj).
ANTONYMS: inconsequential, inconsiderable, insignificant, small (adj), tiny

grow (v)—to become bigger by taking in food; to develop toward full age or size; to thrive; to increase. I have grown very much during the past year.
develop—to come into activity or being; to grow; to change in character through successive periods; to evolve; to become bigger or better. Carl developed strong leg muscles through bicycle riding.
expand—to increase in size; to make grow larger; to enlarge. A balloon expands when you blow into it.
flourish—to develop or grow with vigor; to do well; to be prosperous; to thrive. The marigolds are flourishing in the garden.
increase—to become greater; to advance in quality, power, or success; to become more numerous; to multiply. I will increase the amount of water in this lemonade.
mature—to come to full growth; to ripen. Tomatoes that mature before they are picked taste best.
spread—to cover a large or larger area; to expand; to extend or grow outward from a center or trunk. The ivy is spreading over the entire stone wall.
ANTONYMS: decline (v), decrease (v), diminish, dwindle, shrink (v), wane

H

have (v)—**1** to hold in one's possession or in one's keeping; to possess. We have two horses in the barn. **2** to experience. We had a wonderful time during our trip to the zoo.
endure—to put up with; to tolerate; to experience. Chris endured a toothache for most of the day.
experience—to feel; to meet with; to live through. You haven't experienced sledding until you have gone down the giant hill near the tennis courts.
own—to have or hold as property; to possess. That family owns two automobiles.
possess—to have a knowledge, attribute, or

skill; to have as property. Do you possess the skills needed to do this job?
retain—to continue to hold or have; to keep. She retains much of what she studies.
undergo—to go through; to experience. Will you undergo the minor surgery tomorrow?
ANTONYMS: lack (v), need (v), want (v)

hear (v)—**1** to take in a sound or sounds through the ear; to listen to. I heard my favorite song on the radio this morning. **2** to give a chance to be heard; to give a formal hearing to, as a judge does. The judge will hear the case on Tuesday.
eavesdrop—to listen to talk that one is not supposed to hear; to listen secretly to a private conversation. My sister sometimes eavesdrops on my conversations.
heed—to give careful attention to; to take notice of; to mind. Drivers must heed all traffic signals in order to drive safely.
judge—to hear and decide a case in a court of law. That case will be judged next week.
listen—to try to hear; to attend with the ears in order to hear; to pay attention. Please listen carefully to what I am about to say.
perceive—to be aware of through the senses; to hear. I barely perceive the chirping of birds somewhere in the distance.
try—to investigate in a court of law. The defendant was tried and found innocent.

help (v)—to give or do what is useful or needed; to relieve someone in trouble or distress; to assist; to aid. Tim helped me change the flat tire.
aid—to give support to; to assist. My friends aided me when I fell off my bicycle.
assist—to help someone either when in need or when doing something; to give aid to. I assisted the teacher by handing out the homework papers.
encourage—to give courage, hope, or confidence to; to urge on; to support. My teammates encourage me before every game.
rescue—to save from capture, danger, or harm; to free. During the snowstorm the stranded motorists were rescued by the state police.
support—to give courage, strength, or confidence to; to keep up; to supply with the necessities of life; to provide for. When I

was ill my neighbors supported me by cooking all of my meals.
ANTONYMS: block (v), discourage, frustrate, hinder, obstruct, oppose

hot (adj)—having a temperature that is relatively high. This coffee is too hot to drink.
scorching—that burns slightly; burning; withering. The scorching sun made it difficult to stay on the playground for long.
sizzling—very hot; burning up with intense heat. The sizzling steaks looked appetizing while they were cooking on the grill.
steaming—emitting steam or vapor; very hot. I would like another steaming bowl of soup.
sweltering—oppressively hot; unbearably hot. On sweltering summer days I like to go swimming.
torrid—parched with heat; scorching. What animals live in the torrid desert climate?
tropical—like the climate of the tropics; very hot; burning. In this tropical weather I really enjoy something cold to drink.
ANTONYMS: chilly, cool (adj), freezing, frigid, icy

I

idea (n)—a notion or picture of anything in the mind; a mental image; any result of mental activity; a thought. I have a great idea for a report topic.
concept—an idea or general notion. The concept of transportation takes form in various conveyances, such as automobiles.
impression—an idea or notion. My first impression is that this subject will be difficult.
notion—an understanding; an idea; an opinion; a belief. I have a notion to go shopping.
opinion—belief not so strong as knowledge; judgment; what one thinks. Can you support your opinion with facts?
theory—an explanation based on reasoning and observation, especially one that has been confirmed and tested as a general principle explaining many related facts; an explanation based on thought. The research scientist has developed a new theory.
thought—what a person thinks; a notion; an idea. Many thoughts about the excellent show we saw continue to occupy my mind.

J

job (n)—a piece of work; anything one has to do; work done for pay; employment. My mother has a job with an advertising firm.
chore—a small task; an odd job; a disagreeable or difficult thing to do. I do not mind doing chores around the house.
occupation—the work that a person does regularly or to earn a living; employment; trade. Have you ever thought about what occupation you might want to pursue?
position—a job; employment. Her position in that company is an important one.
profession—an occupation requiring special education, such as law or medicine; any occupation by which a person earns a living. To become a member of the medical profession, a person must study for many years.
task—work assigned or found to be necessary; a duty; work to be done. The task of scrubbing the floor is not pleasant.
work—effort in making or doing something; something to do; employment; occupation. Some outdoor work, such as the repairing of downed power lines, must be done even in inclement weather.

K

keep (v)—**1** to have for a long time; to continue to hold; to have and not let go of. May I keep any seashells I find while at the beach? **2** to hold back; to prevent. The high fence around the playground keeps children from running into the street.
conserve—to keep from loss or from being used up; to preserve. Please conserve water during the drought.
maintain—to keep up; to keep; to preserve. I will maintain the lawn this year by mowing it frequently.
possess—to own; to have as belonging to one; to maintain or keep. My friend possesses many pieces of antique furniture.
prevent—to stop or keep from. The workers prevented people from walking in the wet cement of the new sidewalk.
restrain—to keep in check; to hold back; to keep within limits. Please restrain your dog from chasing my cat.

keep *(continued)*

THESAURUS

store—to stock or supply; to put away for later use. Do squirrels <u>store</u> acorns?
ANTONYMS: abandon (v), discard (v), free (v), lose, release (v), relinquish

know (v)—**1** to have understanding of the facts of. I <u>know</u> many of the poems in that book. **2** to be acquainted with. Do you <u>know</u> our neighbors, the Logans?
comprehend—to understand the nature or meaning of something. Do you <u>comprehend</u> that difficult mathematical concept?
grasp—to lay hold of with the mind; to understand. Donny instantly <u>grasped</u> the meaning of what I was saying about the riddle.
perceive—to be aware of through the senses; to feel, hear, see, smell, or taste; to take in with the mind. She <u>perceived</u> that they wanted to have a private conversation.
realize—to be fully aware of; to understand clearly. I <u>realized</u> later that I had left my purse under my seat in class.
recognize—to be aware of someone or something previously known. While out shopping, I <u>recognized</u> one of my teachers.
understand—to grasp the meaning of. I <u>understand</u> a few words in French.

L

like (v)—to be pleased with; to be satisfied with; to find agreeable. I <u>like</u> to be with pleasant companions.
admire—to regard with pleasure, wonder, and approval. I <u>admire</u> the crews of the Space Shuttle.
appreciate—to think highly of; to recognize the quality or worth of; to enjoy. Because he <u>appreciates</u> figure skating, he often attends ice shows and skating exhibitions.
cherish—to hold dear; to treat with tenderness. Many people <u>cherish</u> childhood memories.
enjoy—to have or use with happiness; to take pleasure in. We <u>enjoyed</u> ourselves when we went roller skating last Friday.
prefer—to like better; to choose above another. Do you <u>prefer</u> chicken soup or vegetable soup?
treasure—to value highly; to cherish. I <u>treasure</u> our friendship because you really care very much about me.

ANTONYMS: abhor, detest, dislike (v), hate (v), loathe

look (v)—to try to see; to see; to direct a glance at. Please <u>look</u> both ways before crossing that busy street.
examine—to look at carefully and closely. The doctor <u>examined</u> Dad's eyes and found that his vision was excellent.
gaze—to look steadily and long. She <u>gazed</u> at a puffy cloud as it moved across the sky.
observe—to see and note; to notice; to examine carefully; to watch; to study. Becky often <u>observes</u> the seagulls as they circle near the sandy beach.
peek—to look slyly and quickly; to peep. If you <u>peek</u> into that room, you will see the sleeping kittens.
stare—to look directly and long with the eyes wide open; to gaze fixedly. John <u>stares</u> into space while he is daydreaming.
watch—to look at; to observe with interest or care. While you were at the airport, did you <u>watch</u> the airplanes take off and land?
See also *see* (v).
ANTONYMS: disregard (v), ignore, miss (v), overlook (v)

loud (adj)—making a great sound; not soft or quiet; noisy. I could hear <u>loud</u> laughter from our neighbor's party yesterday.
blaring—making a loud, harsh sound. Will you please turn down that <u>blaring</u> music.
deafening—that stuns or deafens with noise. With a <u>deafening</u> roar the huge jet aircraft lifted off the runway.
earsplitting—overpoweringly loud; deafening. The racket made by the machines at the construction site is <u>earsplitting</u>.
noisy—making much noise; full of noise. The <u>noisy</u> children were having fun playing baseball.
thunderous—producing thunder; making or accompanied by a noise like thunder. After the concert, the symphony orchestra received a <u>thunderous</u> ovation.
vociferous—noisy and loud; clamoring; shouting. The <u>vociferous</u> crowd cheered enthusiastically for the team.
ANTONYMS: gentle (adj), low (adj), mellow (adj), quiet (adj), soft (adj), subdued

THESAURUS

THESAURUS

M

make (v)—**1** to bring into being; to build, form, put together, or shape. She made a delicious meal from only a few ingredients. **2** to cause to; to force to. The teacher made me write my report over again.

build—to make by putting materials together; to construct. In my spare time I build model airplanes.

compel—to urge or drive with force; to force. The fierce thunderstorm compelled the pilot to delay the takeoff.

construct—to put together; to fit together; to frame; to build. We carefully constructed the bookshelves according to the instructions that came in the box.

create—to make something that has not been made before; to bring into being. The artist created a beautiful landscape painting.

manufacture—to make by hand or by machine; to make into something useful. Many companies in this area manufacture electrical appliances.

pressure [informal]—to urge or force by exerting a compelling influence. She was pressured by the approaching deadline to work even faster.

See also *do* (v).
ANTONYMS: demolish, destroy, ruin (v), wreck (v)

N

need (n)—**1** the lack of a desired or useful thing; a want; a lack. We have a need for volunteers to help in the hospital. **2** something that has to be; a requirement; a necessity. There is a need for quiet in the library.

absence—the state of being without; a lack. Darkness is the absence of light.

deficiency—an absence or lack of something needed; an incompleteness. A balanced diet can help to prevent a vitamin deficiency.

lack—the condition of being without; not having enough; a shortage. Because of a lack of interest, a course in our town's adult school was cancelled.

necessity—that which cannot be done without; a needed thing. Flour is a necessity for many baked items.

requirement—something needed; a necessity.

Writing a book report is a requirement in this class.

shortage—too small an amount; a deficiency; a lack. We are fortunate not to have a shortage of food.
ANTONYMS: abundance, adequacy, affluence, excess (n), wealth

new (adj)—now first made, thought out, known, felt, or discovered; never having existed before; now first used; not used up or worn. Your new car is just beautiful.

current—of the present time. What are some of the current trends in fashion?

fledgling—just beginning; new or inexperienced. The fledgling store manager soon became quite good at her work.

fresh—newly made, gathered, or arrived; recent; not known, seen, or used before; new. If the cream is not fresh, I do not want it.

modern—of the present time; of times not long past; not old-fashioned; up-to-date. I do not think the telephone is a modern invention.

novel—of a new nature or kind; not known before; unfamiliar; new. Automobiles were novel to people living in the early twentieth century.

recent—made or done not long ago; not long past; modern. Did you see the recent movie that was on television last night?
ANTONYMS: ancient (adj), antique (adj), old (adj), outdated, outmoded, stale (adj)

noise (n)—loud, confused, or irritating sounds. The noise of traffic in the street made sleep impossible.

clamor—a loud noise, especially shouting, that goes on continuously. The clamor of the crowd filled the air.

clatter—a rapid succession of sharp, rattling sounds. An awful clatter was coming from the kitchen.

din—loud noise that goes on without letup. The din from the stadium could be heard blocks away.

hubbub—a general confused noise, as of many voices. The speaker waited for the hubbub to die down.

racket—loud, confused noise; loud talk. The sound of everyone talking made quite a racket.

noise (continued)

ruckus [informal]—a noisy uproar. After the game, the winning team raised a ruckus in the locker room.

See also *sound* (n).

ANTONYMS: calm (n), quiet (n), silence (n), tranquility

P

place (n)—the part of space occupied by or intended for a person or thing; a definite position in space; a particular portion of space. The corner of this room is a perfect place for my desk.

district—a part of a larger area; a region; a part of a state or city marked off for a special purpose, such as providing schools or law courts. Everyone living in this district attends Mountain Avenue School.

location—a place or position; a locality. Inspiration Point in Yellowstone National Park is an excellent location for taking breathtaking photographs.

region—a place, space, or area; any large part of the earth's surface. Does the northwestern region of the United States receive much snow?

residence—a home or house; a place where a person lives; an abode. My residence is on the other side of town.

site—the place or area upon which something has been, is being, or will be built, done, or made to happen. The site of the monument is right in front of the municipal building.

territory—a geographical area; land. The ancient Roman Empire included a vast amount of territory.

put (v)—to cause to be in some place or position; to place; to lay. I put my shoes under my bed.

deposit—to put or lay down; to put in a place for safekeeping. Carol deposited her paycheck at the local bank.

place—to set in a specified position; to put in a particular place. I placed the mixing bowl on the table for just a moment.

position—to put in a particular place. I will position the painting on this wall.

rest—to place on or against a support. Please rest those boards against the wall.

set—to put in some place. I will set the tray of sandwiches on this table.

situate—to locate or place. Their cabin is situated among the tall pines near the lake.

Q

quiet (adj)—with little or no noise; making no sound; hushed; silent. The class was quiet during the final exam.

inaudible—not loud enough to be heard; that cannot be heard. Can dogs hear sounds that are inaudible to human beings?

noiseless—making no noise; silent; making very little noise; nearly quiet. The noiseless spider was spinning a web.

reserved—showing or having self-restraint; disposed to say little or keep silent. Being a reserved individual, Brian does not dominate a discussion.

silent—quiet; noiseless; not speaking; saying little or nothing. Cynthia usually keeps silent on matters that do not pertain to her.

soft—not loud; subdued; quiet. When I arrived at the store, there was soft music playing in the background.

unvoiced—not expressed in words; not spoken. Although his opinion was unvoiced, I could tell how he felt by the expression on his face.

ANTONYMS: boisterous, clamorous, loquacious, noisy, verbose

R

rest (n)—a state of ease and quiet; repose; sleep; ease after effort or work; freedom from anything that tires, troubles, or pains. Do you mind if I take a brief rest before we continue walking up the path?

leisure—time free from required work, in which a person may rest and do enjoyable things. What kinds of hobbies do you pursue at your leisure?

recess—a time during which work stops. We plan to play basketball during recess.

relaxation—relief from effort or work; amusement; recreation. I get relaxation from sketching in the park.

repose—sleep or rest; ease; quietness. At this late hour most of the birds are at repose.

THESAURUS

respite—a time of rest and relief; a lull. During the afternoon we had a brief <u>respite</u> from the difficult work we were doing.

letup [informal]—a pause or stop; a lessening of effort. As closing time approached, there was a <u>letup</u> in the store clerk's busy job.

ANTONYMS: activity, disquiet (n), excitement, restlessness, toil (n), work (n)

right (adj)—**1** agreeing with what is just, lawful, or good. It is <u>right</u> to help others who are in need. **2** conforming to facts or truth; correct; true. My watch does not have the <u>right</u> time.

accurate—without mistakes or errors; exactly right; precisely correct. Electronic devices used to time running races are <u>accurate</u> to a fraction of a second.

correct—free from faults or mistakes; right; true. Most of the class had <u>correct</u> answers on the quiz.

decent—right and proper. A <u>decent</u> person treats others fairly.

precise—accurate; exact; definite. In order to repair the engine, the mechanic needed to know the <u>precise</u> size of the defective part.

proper—right for the occasion; correct; fitting. What are the <u>proper</u> clothes to wear to a job interview?

true—agreeing with fact; not false. Everything you heard on the radio about the accident was <u>true</u>.

See also *true* (adj).

ANTONYMS: erroneous, improper, unethical, unfair, unsatisfactory, wrong (adj)

run (v)—to go steadily by moving the legs quickly; to go faster than a walk; to go in a hurry; to hasten. Sheila <u>ran</u> in order to catch the early bus.

hurry—to move quickly or with more than easy or natural speed. People <u>hurry</u> everywhere during the rush hour.

jog—to run at a leisurely pace. Many people <u>jog</u> every day in order to keep in shape.

race—to run swiftly; to run to see who will win; to engage in a contest of speed. I <u>raced</u> my friend to the end of the block and back.

scamper—to run quickly; to go hastily. The chipmunk <u>scampered</u> across the front lawn.

sprint—to run at full speed, especially over a short distance. The runners <u>sprinted</u> across the finish line.

trot—(for four-legged animals) to go at a moderately fast gait by lifting the right forefoot and the left hind foot at about the same time and then the other two feet in the same way. As the horses <u>trotted</u> around the track, they pulled two-wheeled vehicles called sulkies.

ANTONYMS: crawl (v), creep (v), stroll (v), walk (v)

s

say (v)—to speak; to put into words. I <u>said</u> that I thought the meal was delicious.

affirm—to say firmly; to assert; to declare to be true. He <u>affirmed</u> that his decision about leaving the club was final.

declare—to announce formally or publicly; to make known. Did she <u>declare</u> her candidacy for public office?

express—to put into words; to utter; to state. I have <u>expressed</u> my feelings on this matter many times.

impart—to communicate; to tell; to reveal. He <u>imparted</u> to me a great deal of knowledge about gardening.

mention—to speak about; to refer to. Paul <u>mentioned</u> that he had traveled extensively.

respond—to reply in words; to answer. Who will <u>respond</u> to that challenging question?

See also *talk* (v).

see (v)—**1** to perceive by use of the eyes. Yesterday morning I <u>saw</u> a deer in my backyard. **2** to form a mental picture of. I still <u>see</u> last year's parade as if it were yesterday.

behold—to look at; to observe. We <u>beheld</u> the colorful sunset from the summit of that mountain.

distinguish—to see clearly. Even though the night sky was flooded with stars, Maryann <u>distinguished</u> many constellations.

notice—to give attention to; to observe; to perceive. I <u>noticed</u> that he has not been in school for a couple of days.

view—to look at; to see; to behold; to scan. The class <u>viewed</u> a film based upon a book that they had read.

see (*continued*)

visualize—to form a mental picture of. Can an artist <u>visualize</u> a painting even before it is begun?

witness—to perceive; to see. I know someone who <u>witnessed</u> the Olympic Games in person.

See also *look* (v).

sleek (adj)—smooth and shiny; soft and glossy. My cat's fur is <u>sleek</u>.

glassy—smooth; like glass. The ice-covered pond had a <u>glassy</u> appearance.

gleaming—sending forth flashes or beams of light. After it was waxed, the car once again had a <u>gleaming</u> finish.

glossy—having a shiny surface; smooth and shiny. It is difficult to read anything written on that <u>glossy</u> sheet of paper.

lustrous—having a bright and shining surface; shining; glossy. Regular brushing and proper diet keep my dog's coat <u>lustrous</u>.

shiny—reflecting light; bright; shining. The sunlight reflected off the <u>shiny</u> surface of the lake.

silky—soft and smooth; of or like silk; glossy. That black and white kitten has <u>silky</u> fur.

ANTONYMS: coarse (adj), dull (adj), rough (adj)

small (adj)—**1** not large or great; not large as compared with other things of the same kind; little in size. That <u>small</u> television set would fit almost anywhere in the house. **2** not great in amount, degree, strength, or value. Only a <u>small</u> number of people attended the outdoor ceremony in the rain.

insignificant—having little influence or importance; too small to be important. You added such an <u>insignificant</u> amount of spice that I can hardly detect its flavor in the stew.

microscopic—too small to be seen without a microscope; extremely small. Are there <u>microscopic</u> specks of dust in the air?

miniature—made or done on a very small scale; tiny. Many people collect <u>miniature</u> dollhouses and furniture.

minor—less important; smaller. That <u>minor</u> error will not affect the completion of the work.

—not important; not much; small. My

Chihuahua is so <u>slight</u> that I can carry him in my pocket.

teeny [informal]—tiny, very small. Please put a <u>teeny</u> amount of sugar in my tea.

ANTONYMS: big (adj), enormous, great (adj), immense, large (adj), significant

sound (n)—that which is heard; sensation perceived in the organs of hearing. That strange <u>sound</u> came from the other room.

intonation—the manner of producing musical notes, especially with regard to pitch; the manner of speaking, especially with regard to the rise and fall in the pitch of the voice. What <u>intonation</u> would you use in your voice to express surprise?

monotone—a manner of singing or speaking without change of pitch; unvaried sound. The guest lecturer spoke with such a <u>monotone</u> that many in the audience became drowsy.

noise—loud, confused, or irritating sounds. There was so much <u>noise</u> in the park that I could not concentrate on my book.

pitch—the degree of highness or lowness of a tone or sound. The notes of a musical scale vary in <u>pitch</u>.

reverberation—the fact or act of echoing back sound; echo. When the car horn sounded in the tunnel, there was a great <u>reverberation</u> of sound.

tone—any sound considered with reference to its quality, pitch, or strength; in music, a sound of definite pitch and character. That violin certainly has beautiful <u>tone</u>.

See also *noise* (n).

ANTONYMS: quiet (n), silence (n)

T

take (v)—**1** to grasp; to lay hold of; to seize; to capture. Please <u>take</u> your little brother's hand when crossing the street. **2** to carry; to convey. Is that the plane that will <u>take</u> us to Chicago?

acquire—to get by one's own actions or efforts; to attain; to gain. The museum <u>acquired</u> a valuable piece of sculpture.

confiscate—to seize for the public treasury; to seize by authority. Does the city government <u>confiscate</u> abandoned buildings?

grasp—to seize and hold fast by closing the fingers around; to grip, clutch, or grab. You must grasp the jar firmly to open it.

procure—to get by effort or care; to secure; to obtain. Some people procure large fortunes through wise investment of their money.

seize—to take hold of suddenly; to grasp; to clutch. A long time ago on the high seas, many ships were overrun by pirates who seized valuable cargo.

transport—to carry from one place to another; to convey. The movers will transport all of our furniture to our new home.

ANTONYMS: give (v), relinquish, return (v), surrender (v)

talk (v)—to speak; to use words; to exchange words or engage in conversation. I will talk with him after I finish my work.

chat—to talk in an informal and familiar way. My sister and I chat with one another over the phone.

communicate—to give information or news by speaking or writing. You should communicate your feelings to your parents.

converse—to talk in an informal way; to engage in conversation. While he stood in line at the supermarket, Bill conversed with another shopper.

discuss—to talk over; to consider a topic from various points of view. We discussed poetry in class today.

report—to give an account of something seen, heard, read, or done; to relate or tell. Tomorrow I will report on stamp collecting.

speak—to say words; to converse; to talk. Have you spoken to anyone about the class trip?

See also *say* (v).

think (v)—to have an idea or thought in the mind; to picture in the mind. I think it would be a better idea to paint the apartment blue.

conceive—to form in the mind; to think up; to imagine. The writer conceived an unusual plot for his next mystery novel.

contemplate—to think about for a long time; to study carefully. I often contemplate things while walking in the woods.

deliberate—to think over carefully; to consider. The judges of the talent contest deliberated for some time before choosing a winner.

imagine—to form a picture of in the mind; to have an idea of; to think; to fancy. I imagined that I was living in a far off country a long time ago.

reason—to think things out; to think logically; to solve new problems. The members of the touring group who were lost reasoned that if they remained in the museum, someone would come back and find them.

suppose—to consider as possible; to consider as possibly true. I suppose that someday everyone will be able to travel to distant places in outer space.

true (adj)—agreeing with fact; not false; genuine; real. That movie is based on a true story that occurred during the nineteenth century.

authentic—coming from the stated source; not copied; genuine; worthy of acceptance or belief; reliable. That is an authentic document from the eighteenth century.

certain—without any doubt; sure. It is certain that birch trees will grow in this part of the country if given the proper conditions.

correct—free from faults or mistakes; right; true. Justin had seventeen correct answers on the test.

factual—concerned with or consisting of facts; of the nature of fact. The factual accounts of the hardships endured by many of the pioneers are fascinating.

historical—of or having to do with history; according to history; known to be true or real. I enjoy reading about historical events because in doing so I learn about people in other times and places.

real—not imagined or made up; existing as a fact; actual; genuine. Is that a real diamond or an imitation?

See also *right* (adj).

ANTONYMS: artificial, false (adj), fictitious, inaccurate, incorrect, untrue

U

understand (v)—to grasp the meaning of; to know the meaning or idea of; to know well. Because I understood the material, I easily answered the question.

understand *(continued)*

apprehend—to grasp with the mind; to understand; to be aware of; to perceive. After carefully examining the broken motor, Margaret apprehended why it was not running.

comprehend—to understand the nature or meaning of something. I cannot comprehend what you are saying about the math problem.

fathom—to get to the bottom of; to fully understand. Can you fathom the incredible distances to the stars.

grasp—to lay hold of with the mind; to understand. Donna immediately grasped the impact that the decision would have.

know—to have understanding of the facts of; to have firmly in the mind or memory. The attorney knew the case quite well.

realize—to be fully aware of; to understand clearly. On my way to the beach I suddenly realized that I had left my sunglasses on a table at home.

ANTONYM: misunderstand

use (v)—**1** to put into action or service; to utilize; to practice or employ actively; to exercise, especially customarily or habitually. May I use your pen for just a moment? **2** to consume or take regularly; to expend or spend by using. Did you use all of the fertilizer on the lawn?

deplete—to exhaust or empty by using up strength, resources, vitality, or the like. The once abundant coal deposits in this part of the state have been depleted by many years of mining.

employ—to use; to use the services of. We employed a whole new set of tactics to help us win the game.

exercise—to actively use something to cause improvement or to give practice and training. I exercise every day in order to stay in good condition.

exhaust—to empty completely; to drain; to expend. By the end of our three-week vacation in Europe, we had exhausted our funds.

manipulate—to handle or treat with the hands or by mechanical means, especially in a skillful manner. The operator manipulated the power shovel, making it move as if it were a giant animal.

utilize—to make use of; to put to a practical use. When I see the clutter in this office, I wonder if we are utilizing all of our space properly.

ANTONYMS: conserve (v), preserve (v), save (v)

W

well (adv)—in a good, favorable, or satisfactory manner; thoroughly; fully; satisfactorily. I am doing well in most of my subjects.

competently—in an able manner. The new carpenter competently performed every task that had to be done.

proficiently—in an advanced or skillful manner; expertly. Janet speaks proficiently in both French and Spanish.

satisfactorily—in a satisfactory, pleasing, or adequate manner; so as to give satisfaction or contentment. Last year I satisfactorily completed a course in first aid.

skillfully—with skill; expertly. The bus driver skillfully eased the large bus around the hairpin turns.

successfully—in a manner that achieves a favorable result or accomplishes what is intended or desired. My older brother successfully completed high school last year.

fine [informal]—excellently; very well. Stacy was ill for a little while, but now she is doing fine.

ANTONYMS: badly, imperfectly, inadequately, poorly, unacceptably, unsatisfactorily

win (v)—to gain a victory in a contest; to succeed; to get possession of by work or fortune. If our basketball team wins the tournament tomorrow, we will become the new league champions.

achieve—to carry out successfully; to accomplish. Dana achieved her goal this marking period by getting an A in science.

acquire—to get by one's own actions or efforts; to gain; to attain. Since I saw you last year, have you acquired any more merit badges for your Scout work?

earn—to receive in return for work or service; to come to be worthy of or entitled to. I earned enough money from my paper route to buy the radio I want.

prevail—to win the victory; to gain supremacy

THESAURUS

through strength or superiority. At the international competition the superior gymnasts <u>prevailed</u> over their less skillful counterparts.

reap—to obtain as the result of action or effort. In victory we <u>reaped</u> the fruit of our long hours of practice.

triumph—to be victorious; to win success. Almost every day we read about courageous people who have <u>triumphed</u> over disease or misfortune.

ANTONYMS: fail (v), fall (v), flop (v), forfeit (v), lose

wonderful (adj)—causing wonder, or surprise or astonishment; remarkable; marvelous; surprisingly excellent. We had <u>wonderful</u> weather throughout our two-week vacation.

astonishing—very surprising; amazing. The daring feats of the trapeze artist in the circus were <u>astonishing</u>.

extraordinary—beyond what is ordinary; remarkable or very unusual. Pete did an <u>extraordinary</u> job in restoring that old furniture to its present excellent condition.

marvelous—causing wonder; extraordinary. The twinkling stars are a <u>marvelous</u> sight.

remarkable—worthy of notice; unusual. The person who ran into the burning building to save the little child showed truly <u>remarkable</u> courage.

superb—stately and grand; majestic; magnificent. This is a <u>superb</u> hotel.

terrific [informal]—very great or severe; extraordinary; remarkable; very good. My friends are <u>terrific</u> people to talk with as well as to have fun with.

ANTONYMS: average (adj), common (adj), mediocre, ordinary (adj), uninteresting, usual (adj)

work (v)—**1** to labor; to do or make something through effort; to do or make something for pay; to be employed. My cousin <u>works</u> for an electronics company. **2** to act; to operate, especially effectively. Does the new farm tractor <u>work</u> as well as the old one?

function—to work; to act; to be in action; to operate. That machine will <u>function</u> properly after it is lubricated.

labor—to do work, especially hard work; to toil. The farmer <u>labored</u> for many hours in order to harvest the wheat.

operate—to be at work; to run; to function. The commuter trains on this line generally <u>operate</u> on schedule.

perform—to do; to go through and finish; to accomplish. The symphony orchestra <u>performed</u> well yesterday evening in the first concert of the season.

toil—to work hard and long; to labor. The workers <u>toiled</u> for several years until the tunnel was completed.

tick [informal]—to function, go, or work. Somehow this complicated mass of gears and valves <u>ticks</u>.

ANTONYM: play (v)

wrong (adj)—**1** not right; bad; unlawful; unjust. It is <u>wrong</u> to tell a lie. **2** not true; not correct; not according to truth or facts; incorrect; inaccurate. The final score of the game as printed in this morning's newspaper is <u>wrong</u>. **3** not proper or right according to a code or standard; unsuitable. Yellow socks are <u>wrong</u> for a blue suit.

illegal—not lawful; forbidden by law; against the law. It is <u>illegal</u> to park a car in front of a fire hydrant.

innacurate—not without errors or mistakes; not exact. You should not make <u>inaccurate</u> statements in a report.

inappropriate—not right or proper; not suitable; improper. It is <u>inappropriate</u> to wear a tennis outfit to a formal dinner party.

incorrect—not correct; containing mistakes or errors; wrong. Your answers for the last two math problems are <u>incorrect</u>.

unethical—not morally right; not in accordance with professional or formal rules for right conduct or practice. It is <u>unethical</u> for a lawyer to discuss with anyone the confidential aspects of a client's case.

unsuitable—not right or fitting; inappropriate. That person is <u>unsuitable</u> for the position in management because he lacks the necessary education.

See also *bad* (adj).

ANTONYMS: correct (adj), ethical, proper (adj), right (adj), suitable, true (adj)

THESAURUS

1 — Diagraming Subjects and Verbs

> ● A **diagram** is a line drawing that explains something.

When you assemble a kite or bicycle, you use a diagram to see how the parts fit together. Similarly, a sentence diagram can help you see how all the words of a sentence fit together.

To begin a sentence diagram, draw a horizontal line. On this line write the subject and the verb of the sentence you wish to diagram. Then draw a vertical line to separate the subject and the verb.

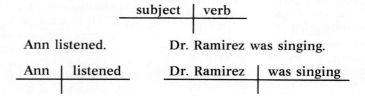

When you diagram an interrogative sentence, write the subject of the sentence before the complete verb.

May we enter?

| we | May enter |

Did Mrs. Peterson finish?

| Mrs. Peterson | Did finish |

The subject of an imperative sentence is usually understood to be *you*. In a diagram, write *you* in parentheses in the subject place.

Stop!

| (you) | Stop |

Do enter.

| (you) | Do enter |

Notice that a sentence diagram shows the capital letters of a sentence. Punctuation marks, however, are not shown.

Skills Tryout

Tell how you would diagram each of the following sentences.

1. Birds call.
2. Jason is laughing.
3. Did Denise arrive?
4. Leave!
5. Has anyone gone?
6. Gina can dance.
7. She may watch.
8. Do continue.
9. May I speak?
10. Listen.

Practice

A. Diagram each sentence.

11. Are you reading?
12. Mrs. Haggerty will sing.
13. Help!
14. Ian was following.
15. Run.
16. Lisa called.
17. Was she working?
18. He has tried.
19. Explain.
20. Will it hurt?

B. Locate the subject and the verb in each sentence. Write the subject and verb on a horizontal line. Then divide them with a vertical line.

EXAMPLE: In the class the boys were coloring.

ANSWER: boys | were coloring

21. People seldom walk near the dark castle.
22. A statue of an elf was standing on the lawn.
23. Listen to this tale about a white stag.
24. Always divide carefully.
25. Does this antique globe turn on its axis?
26. During October, the group of actors may travel to Canada and England.
27. The snow on the roads swirled playfully.
28. The children in the movie theater cheered loudly.
29. At the more difficult parts, the teacher paused.
30. Any friend of John's may join, too.

2 — Diagraming Sentence Parts

> ● Adjectives, adverbs, and prepositional phrases are diagramed below the words they modify.

Every sentence part can be shown in a sentence diagram. An adjective is written on a slanting line connected to the noun or pronoun it modifies. The articles *a, an,* and *the* are also diagramed in this way.

Many guests had arrived.   **A big hungry bear growled.**

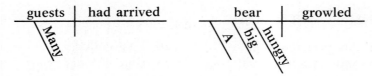

Adverbs are also diagramed on slanting lines. An adverb that modifies a verb appears directly under the verb.

The canary sang merrily.   **One pigeon flew here yesterday.**

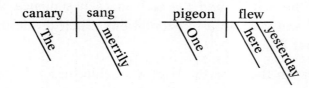

Diagram an adverb that modifies an adjective or another adverb on a slanting line connected to the word modified.

A very unusual comet was sighted quite recently.

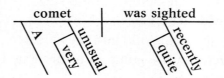

A prepositional phrase is diagramed below the word it modifies. Place the preposition on a slanting line connected to the modified word. Place the object of the preposition on a horizontal line connected to the slanting line.

The skier with the hat fell.   **An eagle soared near the tree.**

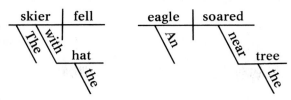

Skills Tryout

Tell how you would diagram each sentence.

1. The happy baby giggled gleefully.
2. Listen very carefully.
3. Several gold coins glistened in the well.

Practice

A. Diagram each sentence. First write the subject and the verb. Then write each adjective and adverb below the word it modifies.

1. The old kettle whistled shrilly.
2. A tall, thin boy was busily sweeping.
3. Did the heavy wrench work well?
4. Speak more clearly.
5. Several rather important books sold quickly.
6. The colorful flag flew proudly.
7. Will the other brother come, too?
8. Three young coyotes stood nearby.
9. The very hungry workers ate quite rapidly.
10. Write soon.

B. Diagram each sentence. Be sure each prepositional phrase is placed below the word it modifies.

11. The tall brown bear lumbered into the forest.
12. We ate on the patio.
13. The girl with the kite was singing.
14. Is the floor of the basement still settling?
15. The young explorers walked quite bravely toward the cave.

3 — Diagraming Other Sentence Parts

● Direct objects, predicate nominatives, and predicate adjectives appear after the verb in a sentence diagram.

A direct object receives the action of a verb. (See pages 94–95.) To diagram a direct object, write it on the horizontal line after the verb. Separate it from the verb with a vertical line that does not cut through the horizontal line.

| subject | verb | direct object |

Rita sculpted a wooden elephant.　　**Did you see it?**

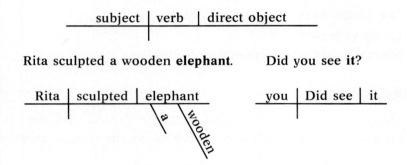

A predicate nominative is a noun or pronoun that renames the subject of the sentence. (See pages 140–141.) In a diagram, place the predicate nominative on the horizontal line after the verb. A line that slants backward separates it from the verb. This slanting line does not cross the horizontal one.

| subject | verb \ predicate nominative |

Rod became an excellent painter.　　**Is it he?**

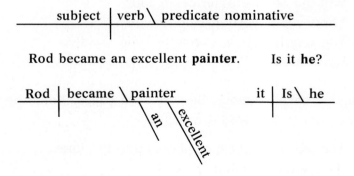

A predicate adjective follows a linking verb and describes the subject. (See pages 182–183.) It also appears after a slanting line in a sentence diagram.

The painting appears so **lifelike**!   Are they **new**?

painting | appears \ lifelike   they | Are \ new

Skills Tryout

Tell how you would diagram each sentence below.

1. Ed dug the garden.
2. We were flying the kite yesterday.
3. Did the child lose a sandal?
4. Rocky is a gentle horse.
5. The juicy red strawberries were delicious.

Practice

A. Diagram each sentence. Be sure your diagrams indicate which words are direct objects.

1. The teacher left the room.
2. The tiny kitten grabbed the red ribbon.
3. Did you understand the question?
4. Follow the leader.
5. You may give the correct answer now.
6. A lost dog followed me yesterday.
7. Martin cleaned the entire house.
8. Has anyone seen the new movie?
9. The young girl chased the pony into the barn.
10. May I borrow a book about sailboats?

B. Diagram each sentence. Be sure your diagrams indicate the predicate nominatives and the predicate adjectives.

11. Ms. Rivera is an excellent leader.
12. The oral report was quite interesting.
13. The sweater on the bed looks handmade.
14. The tall woman with the gray hair is a poet.
15. Is he a professional actor?

PLANNING AHEAD

- The **indirect object** comes before the direct object. It tells to whom or for whom the action of the verb is being done.

In Unit 3 on pages 94–95, you learned that a direct object receives the action of the verb. In the sentence below, the direct object *letter* receives the action of the verb *mailed.*

Pam mailed a letter.

Some sentences have an indirect object and a direct object. The indirect object comes before the direct object. It does not receive the action of the verb. Instead, it tells to whom or for whom something is being done. In the sentences below, the indirect objects are underlined.

Pam mailed <u>Bill</u> a letter.   **I left the <u>plumber</u> a note.**

A word used as an indirect object can also be used as an object of the preposition *to* or *for.*

Pam mailed a letter to Bill.   **I left a note for the plumber.**

A noun or a pronoun can be an indirect object.

Maggie gave <u>him</u> the wrench.

Often, an indirect object follows one of these verbs: *tell, throw, bring, buy, give, lend, offer, owe, sell, send, show.*

Skills Tryout

Identify the indirect object in each sentence.

1. Ellen threw Annie the football.
2. Buy Dad a birthday present tonight.
3. The old man gave us a warm smile.
4. I told Dr. Franklin the exact time.
5. I wrote the carpenter a long letter of complaint.

Practice

A. Write the indirect object in each sentence.

1. The circus owner had offered the clown a good job.
2. We told the hikers the best route to Bull Mountain.
3. I gave the dog a bath.
4. Aileen's great-grandmother had sent her the postcard from South America.
5. My sister will lend Mary her bicycle for the summer.
6. The guide showed them the ruins of a castle.
7. Can anyone give me change for a dollar?
8. Don't sell anyone the house until next spring.
9. We must buy the baby a crib and a high chair.
10. Father never brought me this.

B. Rewrite each sentence below. Use an indirect object instead of the prepositional phrase.

EXAMPLE: I gave the money to the clerk.
ANSWER: I gave the clerk the money.

11. I sent the package to Dr. Garufalo.
12. He has brought a large picnic lunch for the girls.
13. Have you shown your report card to your parents?
14. Did Aunt Gerri buy both records for you?
15. She offered the sandwich to you first.
16. He will show the movie to the class on Friday.
17. The manager flashed a signal to the base runner.
18. Mr. Braun bought the tickets for us.
19. I owe one hour's baby-sitting time to my neighbor.
20. Father got cool drinks for the players.

Application WRITING SENTENCES

Write four sentences. Use a prepositional phrase with *to* or *for* in each. Then rewrite the sentences. Use an indirect object instead of the prepositional phrase.

5 — Perfect Tenses of Verbs

> ● The tense of a verb shows time.

This lesson introduces three important verb tenses—the present perfect, the past perfect, and the future perfect. Before beginning, you may want to review the simple present, past, and future tenses in Unit 3, pages 96–97. The principal parts of verbs are on pages 98–103.

The **present perfect tense** expresses an action that occurred at an indefinite time in the past. This action may still be going on. The present perfect is formed with the helping verb *have* or *has* and the past participle of the main verb.

> **The car has worked perfectly.   We have studied hard.**

The **past perfect tense** expresses an action that was completed before some other past action. It is formed with the helping verb *had* and the past participle of the main verb.

> **They had called the fire department before you arrived.**

The **future perfect tense** expresses an action that will be completed in the future before some other future action or event. It is formed with *will have* or *shall have* and the past participle of the main verb.

> **By the time summer ends, I shall have run 500 miles.**
> **Everyone will have finished the book by next Thursday.**

Skills Tryout

Identify the tense of the underlined verb in each sentence.

1. When Sue returns from Iowa, Jay will have finished school.
2. The boys had eaten before they went to bed.
3. She has complained frequently about the barking dogs.
4. Have any tourists visited the museum recently?
5. By next week they will have talked to all the voters.

Practice

A. Write *present perfect, past perfect,* or *future perfect* to indicate the tense of each underlined verb.

   1. It happened after they <u>had gone</u> for help.
   2. Almost all the snow <u>has melted.</u>
   3. The dogs <u>have followed</u> us many, many times.
   4. Before we begin dessert, we <u>shall have finished</u> dinner.
   5. Next June you <u>will have lived</u> here four years.

B. Using the pronoun and verb given, write the tense form indicated in parentheses.

EXAMPLE: he studies (future perfect)
ANSWER: he will have studied

   6. he tries (present perfect)
   7. I answer (past perfect)
   8. you walk (future perfect)
   9. she laughs (past perfect)
  10. it cooks (present perfect)
  11. I play (future perfect)
  12. it works (past perfect)
  13. he spells (past perfect)
  14. we cook (present perfect)
  15. she rubs (future perfect)

C. Use each of the following perfect tense verbs in a sentence.

EXAMPLE: had gone
ANSWER: Before we returned home, we had gone to Dan's house.

  16. shall have taken
  17. has received
  18. will have begun
  19. had finished
  20. have tried
  21. will have given
  22. has thrown
  23. have thrown
  24. had accepted
  25. shall have won

Application LISTENING SKILLS

While listening to TV, radio, or personal conversation, record three sentences in which a speaker used a perfect tense. Then explain why each perfect tense was used.

6 — Clauses

> ● A **clause** is a group of words that has a subject and a verb.

You know that a prepositional phrase is a sentence part that is made up of a group of words. A clause is another sentence part made up of a group of words. Unlike a phrase, however, a clause has a subject and a verb.

Phrases	Clauses
after the party	after Jason arrived
before the dinner	before Rita had eaten dinner

There are two types of clauses. An **independent clause** has a subject and a verb and expresses a complete thought. An independent clause can stand by itself as a complete sentence.

We must leave. **Mother slept for an hour.**

A **subordinate clause** also has a subject and a verb. However, it does not express a complete thought and cannot stand by itself as a sentence.

because we are late **while I was working**

Often a sentence contains one independent clause and one or more subordinate clauses.

We must leave because we are late.
Mother slept for an hour while I was working.

Skills Tryout

Tell whether each word group is a phrase or a clause.

1. although he tried
2. after last night
3. snow is falling
4. through the storm's terrible fury
5. while we are waiting

Practice

A. Write *phrase* if the word group is a phrase. Write *clause* if the word group is a clause.

1. since the first steps were taken
2. before the parade was finally over
3. after the final attempt
4. everyone enjoyed the book very much
5. at the dark forest's center

B. Write *independent* if the clause is independent. Write *subordinate* if it is subordinate.

6. while their father went home
7. since the sun had already set in the west
8. Anita and Michael explained the unusual sounds
9. before any work can begin this summer
10. the birds had already flown away

C. Write each sentence. Underline the subordinate clause once. Underline the independent clause twice.

11. When we hear from Arthur, we will leave.
12. You may leave whenever you finish the job.
13. Since I don't like pizza, Mom left me at home.
14. If I had known French, I could have spoken with Michelle and Claude.
15. Everyone enjoyed the movie very much because the story was true.

Application WRITING SENTENCES

Write five subordinate clauses. Use the following words to begin the clauses: *after, wherever, while, since, although.* Then combine each subordinate clause with an independent clause to form a sentence. (Use a comma after a subordinate clause when that clause begins the sentence. A subordinate clause at the end of a sentence is not set off with a comma.)

Index

Abbreviations, 56–57, 64, 82, 85, 173, 404–406
    definition of, 56
    of state names, 397
Action verbs, 88–89, 110, 348, 350–351
    definition of, 88
Addresses
    in business letters, 120–121, 393
    on envelopes, 396
    in friendly letters, 118–119, 391
Adjective phrases, 262–263, 273, 290, 329, 378, 380
Adjectives
    and adverbs (usage), 222–223, 227, 252, 329, 374, 377
    articles, 178–179, 192, 210, 370–371
    comparison of, 186–187, 188–189, 193, 210, 255, 370, 373
    definition of, 178, 268, 370
    demonstrative, 184–185, 193, 210, 255, 328, 370, 372
    predicate, 182–183, 210, 255, 328, 370, 372
    proper, 180–181, 192, 210, 370–371
    spelling, 186–187
    suffixes added to, 190–191, 193, 211
    that tell how many, 178–179, 192, 370–371
    that tell what kind, 178–179, 192, 210, 370–371
    writing with, 194–195
Adverb phrases, 264–265, 273, 290, 329, 378, 380
Adverbs
    and adjectives (usage), 222–223, 227, 252, 329, 374, 377
    comparison of, 218–219, 226, 252, 255, 374, 376
    definition of, 214, 268, 374
    locations in sentences, 216–217, 226, 374
    negative words, 220–221, 227, 252, 374, 376–377
    that describe adjectives, 214–215, 216–217, 226, 252, 255, 329, 374–375
    that describe other adverbs, 214–215, 216–217, 226, 252, 255, 329, 374–375
    that describe verbs, 214–215, 226, 252, 255, 329, 374–375
    writing with, 228–229
Agreement, subject-verb, 298–299, 300–301, 308, 324, 326, 386–387
Alliteration, 314–315, 325
Almanac, 236–237, 253
Among, between, 266–267, 273, 290, 378, 381
Analogies, 280–281, 291
Antonyms, 20–21, 23, 47
    as context clues, 224–225, 227, 253
    See also Thesaurus.

Apostrophes
    in contractions, 144–145, 170, 404, 406, 408
    in possessive nouns, 60–61, 83, 85, 173, 327, 408
Articles *(a, an, the),* 178–179, 192, 210, 370–371
Atlas, 236–237, 253
Audience, for writing, 38, 122–123

Be
    and agreement with subject, 298–299, 308
    forms of, 88–89
    as helping verb, 92–93
    as linking verb, 90–91
    principal parts of, 356–359
    See also Helping verbs; Linking verbs.
Between, among, 266–267, 273, 290, 378, 381
Book reports
    form for, 395
    oral, 163
    written, 162–163, 171, 395
Books
    finding, in library, 232–233
    parts of, 238–239
    writing titles of, 162–163, 171, 395, 400, 402
Brainstorming, 40–41
Building Bridges
    to computers, 289
    to health, 81
    to mathematics, 169
    to music, 323
    to science, 127, 251
    to social studies, 45, 209
Business letters
    parts of, 120–121, 129, 393
    writing, 120–121, 393

Can, may, 104–105, 111, 128, 174, 362–363
Capitalization
    of abbreviations, 56–57, 82, 404–406
    of calendar words, 400, 402
    first word of sentence, 8–9, 46, 84, 172, 326, 333–335
    of initials, 56–57, 400–401
    in letters, 118–119, 120–121, 129, 391
    of names, 400–401
    in outlines, 242–243, 394
    of place names, 400–401
    of pronoun *I,* 134, 400, 402
    of proper adjectives, 180–181, 210
    of proper nouns, 54–55, 64, 82, 85, 173, 400–402
    in quotations, 154–155, 171
    of special groups, 400–401

of titles
    of books, 162–163, 171, 400, 402
    for people, 400–401
    of poems, 400, 402
    of reports, 400, 402
    of stories, 400, 402
Card catalog, 232–233, 253
Cause-and-effect paragraph, 284–287
Character sketch, writing a, 204–207
Choosing and narrowing a topic, 230–231
Classifying, 45
Colons
    between hours and minutes, 404, 406
    in business letters, 120–121, 129, 393, 404
Commands. *See* Imperative sentences.
Commas
    in addresses, 152–153, 382, 384
    in compound sentences, 296, 403
    in dates, 18–19, 23, 46, 84, 118–119, 172, 403, 405
    in letters, 118–119, 120–121, 129, 391
    in quotations, 154–155, 404, 406
    to separate last name and first name, 304–305, 403, 405
    to separate name of city from state or country, 18–19, 23, 46, 84, 118–119, 172, 403, 405
    in series, 18–19, 23, 46, 84, 172, 326, 403, 405
    to set off name of person spoken to, 304–305, 309, 324, 326, 403, 405
    after *yes, no, well,* 304–305, 309, 324, 326, 403, 405

Common nouns, 52–53, 64, 82, 85, 173, 254, 327, 340–343
Common-sense decisions, 282–283
Comparison
    of adjectives, 186–187, 188–189, 193, 210, 255, 370, 373
    of adverbs, 218–219, 226, 252, 255, 374, 376
    with metaphors, 316–317, 325
    with similes, 316–317, 325
Composition. *See* Writing.
Compound predicates, 294–295, 308, 324, 326, 382–383, 384–385
Compound sentences, 296–297, 308, 324, 384–385
    commas in, 296, 403
Compound subjects, 294–295, 308, 324, 326, 382–383, 384–385
    agreement with verbs, 300–301, 308, 326
Compounds, 62–63, 65, 83
Conjunctions, 258–259, 272, 290, 329, 378–381
    definition of, 258, 268, 378
Connotation, 306–307, 309, 325
Content areas, language in. *See* Building Bridges.
Context clues, 224–225, 227, 253
Contractions, 144–145, 148, 170, 175, 404, 406, 408
    apostrophes in, 144–145, 170, 404, 406, 408
Contrast, paragraph of, 40–43
Copyright page, of a book, 238–239

Dates, 18–19, 23, 46, 118–119, 172
Decisions, common-sense, 282–283
Declarative sentences, 6–7, 22, 46, 84, 172, 326, 332–335
    definition of, 6, 332
    end punctuation for, 8–9, 46, 84, 172, 326, 332–335
Demonstrative adjectives, 184–185, 193, 210, 255, 328, 370, 372
Descriptions, details in, 196–197, 198–199, 211
Descriptive paragraph, 196–197
Details
    arranging, in space order, 200–201, 211
    in descriptions, 196–197, 198–199, 211
    listening for, 198–199
    as subtopics in outlines, 242–243
    in supporting sentences, 34–35, 211, 390
Dewey decimal system, 232–233
Dictionary
    entry words, 26–27
    guide words, 26–27
    pronunciation key, 28–29
    using a, 26–27, 28–29, 47
    See also Thesaurus.
Direct object, 94–95, 110, 128, 142–143, 174, 328, 348–351
Directional words, 276–277
Directions, writing, 276–277, 291
Discussions, 70–71
Double negatives, 220–221, 227, 252, 374, 376–377

Editing, 39. *See also* Writing Projects.
Editing marks, 398
    See also Writing Projects.
Editorials, newspaper
    definition of, 74–75
    writing, 76–79
Encyclopedias, using, 234–235
Entry words, 26–27
Envelopes, addressing, 396
Exclamation marks
    in exclamatory sentences, 8–9, 46, 84, 172, 326, 332–335
    after interjections, 268–269, 273, 290, 378
Exclamatory sentences, 6–7, 22, 46, 84, 172, 326, 332–335
    definition of, 6, 332
    end punctuation for, 8–9, 46, 84, 172, 326, 332–335
Explanatory paragraph, 114–115, 129

Fact and opinion, 68–69, 83
Fiction and nonfiction, 232–233

Figures of speech
metaphors, 316–317, 325
similes, 316–317, 325
Friendly letters
parts of, 118–119, 129, 391
writing, 118–119, 391
Future tense, 96–97, 111, 128, 174, 328, 352–355

Good, better, best, 188–189, 255
Good, well, 222–223, 227, 329, 377
Grammar and Writing Workshops
Sentence Combining, 24–25, 274–275, 310–311
Writing with Adjectives, 194–195
Writing with Adverbs, 228–229
Writing with Nouns, 66–67
Writing with Pronouns, 150–151
Writing with Verbs, 112–113
Grammar Handbook, 332–389
Guide words, 26–27

Handwriting models, 411–412
Have, 356–359
Helping verbs, 92–93, 110, 128, 174, 255, 328, 348–351
definition of, 92, 348
Homographs, 146–147
Homophones, 146–147, 171
Hyphens, 62, 65, 83

Idioms, 270–271, 291
Imperative sentences, 6–7, 16–17, 22, 23, 46, 84, 172, 326, 332–335, 336, 338–339
definition of, 6, 332
end punctuation for, 8–9, 46, 84, 172, 326, 332–335
subject of, 16–17, 23, 46, 84, 172, 326, 336, 338–339
Indenting
in letters, 118–119, 391
paragraphs, 32–33, 390
Index, using an, 234–235, 238–239
Initials, 56–57, 400–401
Interjections, 268–269, 273, 290, 378, 381
Interrogative sentences, 6–7, 16–17, 22, 23, 46, 84, 172, 326, 332–335, 336, 338–339
definition of, 6, 332
end punctuation for, 8–9, 46, 84, 172, 332–335
locating subjects of, 16–17, 23, 46, 84, 172, 326, 336, 338–339

Interviewing, 202–203
Inverted word order, 266–267, 378, 381
Invitations, 392
Irregular verbs, 100–103, 356–361
See also Verbs, irregular.

Learn, teach, 106–107, 111, 128, 174, 362–363
Leave, let, 104–105, 111, 128, 174, 362–363
Letters
business, 120–121, 129, 393
friendly, 118–119, 129, 391
of information, 122–125
invitations, 392
thank-you notes, 392
See also Envelopes, addressing.
Library
card catalog, 232–233, 253
Dewey decimal system, 232–233
fiction and nonfiction, 232–233
reference materials, 236–237, 253
Life skills
directions, 277
filling out forms, 19, 55, 57, 305
preparing for trips, 237
using a telephone directory, 116–117
Linking verbs, 90–91, 110, 128, 174, 348–351
definition of, 90, 348
See also Predicate adjective; Predicate nominative.
Listening
for descriptive details, 198–199
for facts and opinions, 68–69
group discussions, 70–71
for main idea, 198–199
to oral reports, 245
to poetry, 314–315
for propaganda techniques, 278–279
on telephone, 116–117
Literature. *See* Poems; Stories.

Magazines, 236–237
Main idea
listening for, 198–199
as main topic in outline, 242–243
in paragraph, 32–33
See also Topic sentence.
Main verbs, 92–93, 110, 128, 174, 255, 328, 348–351
Maps, 276–277
May, can, 104–105, 111, 128, 174, 362–363
Messages, telephone, 116–117
Metaphors, 316–317, 325

Narrative, personal, 164–167
Narrative paragraph, 152–153, 171
Negative words, 220–221, 227, 252, 374, 376–377
Newspaper
    editorials, writing, 76–79
    parts of, 74–75, 83
Newspapers, as reference materials, 236–237
Nonfiction. *See* Fiction and nonfiction.
Notes, taking, 240–241, 253
Nouns
    common, 52–53, 64, 82, 85, 173, 254, 327, 340–343
    compounds, 62–63, 65
    definition of, 50, 268, 340
    identifying, 50–51
    plural, 58–59, 65, 82, 85, 173, 327, 344–347
    possessive, 60–61, 65, 83, 85, 173, 327, 340–343
    as predicate nominatives, 140–141, 148, 170
    proper, 52–53, 54–55, 56–57, 64, 82, 85, 173, 254, 327, 340–343
        capitalization of, 54–55, 64, 82, 85, 173, 400–402
    singular, 58–59, 65, 85, 173, 327, 344–347
    spelling of, 58–59, 82, 85, 344–347, 408
    writing with, 66–67

Object pronouns, 136–137, 142–143, 148, 149, 170, 175, 327, 364–367, 368–369
    in prepositional phrases, 266–267, 273, 290, 378, 381
Objects
    direct, 94–95, 110, 128, 142–143, 174, 328, 348–351
    of prepositions, 260–261, 272, 290, 378–381
        in prepositional phrases, 266–267, 273, 290, 378, 381
Onomatopoeia, 314–315, 325
Opinion. *See* Fact and opinion.
Oral language. *See* Speaking.
Oral reports, 244–245
Outlining, 242–243, 394

Paragraphs
    cause-and-effect, 284–287
    of contrast, 40–43
    definition of, 32, 390
    descriptive, 196–197
    explanatory, 114–115, 129
    indenting, 32–33, 390
    narrative, 152–153, 171
    persuasive, 72–73, 83
    space order in, 200–201, 211
    structure, 34–35, 390
    time order in, 152–153, 171
    writing, 32–33, 34–35, 390

Paraphrasing, 240–241, 253
Parts of speech, 268–269
    words as different, 184–185, 372
Past participle, 98–99, 111, 128, 174, 255, 352–355
    See also Verbs, irregular.
Past tense, 96–97, 111, 128, 174, 328, 352–355
Periodicals, 236–237, 253
Periods
    after abbreviations, 56–57, 404–406
    ending sentences, 8–9, 46, 84, 172, 326, 332–335
    after initials, 56–57
    in outlines, 242–243, 394
Personal narrative, 164–167
Persuasive paragraph, 72–73, 83
Photo essay, "The Writing Process," 36–39
Poems
    "Advice to a Bird, Species Unknown"
        by Georgie Starbuck Galbraith, 2
    "The Bells" by Edgar Allan Poe, 315
    "Cat" by Mary Britton Miller, 138
    "Fog" by Carl Sandburg, 312
    "I Wouldn't" by John Ciardi, 176
    "The Kayak" anonymous, 48
    "The Loon" by Lew Sare, 314
    "Onomatopoeia" by Eve Merriam, 314
    "The Pasture" by Robert Frost, 130
    "Shells" by Lilian Moore, 256
    "Southbound on the Freeway" by May Swenson, 313
    "Steam Shovel" by Charles Malam, 312
    "Summer Rain" by Lilian Moore, 292
    "Swallows" by Thomas Hornsby Ferril, 212
    "Water" by Hilda Conkling, 312
    "The Wind" by James Reeves, 86
Poetry
    alliteration, 314–315, 325
    listening to, 314–315
    onomatopoeia, 314–315, 325
    reading, 312–313
    repetition, 314–315
    rhyme, 314–315, 325
    rhythm, 314–315
    titles
        capitalization of, 400, 402
        quotation marks around, 404, 406
    writing, 318–321
Possessive nouns, 60–61, 65, 83, 85, 173, 327, 340–343
Possessive pronouns, 138–139, 148, 170, 175, 254, 327, 364–367
Predicate
    complete, 10–11, 22, 46, 84, 172, 254, 336–339
    compound, 294–295, 308, 324, 326, 382–383, 384–385
    simple, 14–15, 22, 46, 84, 172, 254, 336–339
Predicate adjectives, 182–183, 210, 255, 328, 370, 372
Predicate nominatives, 140–141, 142–143, 148, 170, 327, 364, 366–367

Prefixes
- *dis-*, 108–109, 129
- *im-*, 108–109, 129
- *in-*, 108–109, 129
- *mis-*, 108–109, 129
- *pre-*, 108–109, 129
- *re-*, 108–109, 129
- *un-*, 108–109, 129

Prepositional phrases, 260–261, 272, 290, 378–381
- as adjective phrases, 262–263, 273, 290, 329, 378, 380
- as adverb phrases, 264–265, 273, 290, 329, 378, 380
- definition of, 260
- inverted word order in, 266–267, 378, 381
- using *between* and *among*, 266–267, 273, 290, 378, 381
- using object pronouns, 266–267, 273, 290, 378, 381

Prepositions, 260–261, 272, 290, 378–381
- definition of, 260, 268, 378
- objects of, 260–261, 272, 290, 378–381
- *See also* Prepositional phrases.

Present tense, 96–97, 111, 352–355

Prewriting, 37
- *See also* Writing Projects.

Principal parts, of verbs, 98–99, 111, 128, 174, 255, 352–355
- *See also* Verbs, irregular.

Pronouns
- definition of, 132, 268, 364
- forming contractions with, 144–145, 148, 170, 175, 404, 406
- *I*, capitalization of, 134, 400, 402
- object, 136–137, 142–143, 148, 149, 170, 175, 327, 364–367, 368–369
  - in prepositional phrases, 266–267, 273, 290, 378, 381
- plural, 132–133
- possessive, 138–139, 148, 170, 175, 254, 327, 364–367
- as predicate nominatives, 140–141, 175, 364, 366–367
- singular, 132–133
- subject, 134–135, 142–143, 148, 149, 170, 175, 327, 364–367, 368–369
- *this, that, these, those,* 184–185, 372
- usage, 142–143, 149, 170, 175, 254, 368–369
- writing with, 150–151

Pronunciation key, using, 28–29

Proofreading. *See* Writing Projects.

Propaganda techniques, 278–279, 291

Proper adjectives, 180–181, 192, 210, 370–371

Proper nouns, 52–53, 54–55, 56–57, 64, 82, 85, 173, 254, 327, 340–343

Publishing, 39
- *See also* Writing Projects.

Punctuation
- apostrophes, 60–61, 83, 85, 144–145, 170, 173, 327, 404, 406, 408
- colons, 120–121, 129, 393, 404, 406
- commas, 18–19, 23, 46, 84, 118–119, 120–121, 129, 154–155, 172, 296, 304–305, 391, 403–406
- exclamation marks, 8–9, 46, 84, 172, 268–269, 273, 290, 326, 332–335, 378
- periods, 8–9, 46, 56–57, 84, 172, 242–243, 326, 332–335, 394, 404–406
- question marks, 8–9, 46, 84, 172, 332–335
- quotation marks, 154–155, 171, 326, 404, 406
- underlining, 162–163, 171, 395, 404, 406

Purpose for writing, 38

Question marks, 8–9, 46, 84, 172, 332–335

Questions. *See* Interrogative sentences.

Quotation marks, 154–155, 171, 326, 404, 406

Quotations, writing, 154–155, 171, 404, 406

Readers' Guide to Periodical Literature, 236–237, 253

Reading
- poetry, 312–313
- story, 156–161

Reasoning. *See* Thinking skills.

Reference materials, 236–237, 253
- *See also* Dictionary; Encyclopedia.

Reports
- choosing and narrowing a topic, 230–231
- oral, 244–245
- outlining, 242–243
- research skills, 232–233, 234–235, 236–237, 238–239
- taking notes, 240–241
- titles of
  - capitalization of, 400, 402
  - quotation marks around, 404, 406
- writing, 246–249
- *See also* Book reports.

Review and Practice Handbooks
- Grammar Handbook, 332–389
- Young Writer's Handbook, 390–413

Revising, 39
- *See also* Writing Projects.

Rhyme, 314–315, 325

Rhythm, 314–315

Sentence errors, 302–303, 309, 324, 388–389

Sentences
- agreement of subject and verb, 298–299, 300–301, 308, 324, 326, 386–387
- capitalization of, 8–9, 46, 84, 172, 326, 333–335

combining, 24–25, 274–275, 310–311
complete, 4–5, 332
compound, 296–297, 308, 324, 384–385
    commas in, 296, 403
declarative, 6–7, 22, 46, 84, 172, 326, 332–335
end punctuation of, 8–9, 46, 84, 172, 326, 332–335
exclamatory, 6–7, 22, 46, 84, 172, 326, 332–335
fragments, 302–303, 309, 324, 332, 388–389
imperative, 6–7, 16–17, 22, 23, 46, 84, 172, 326,
    332–335, 336, 338–339
interrogative, 6–7, 16–17, 22, 23, 46, 84, 172, 326,
    332–335, 336, 338–339
inverted word order in, 266–267, 378, 381
predicate in, complete, 10–11, 22, 46, 84, 172, 254,
    336–339
predicate in, compound, 294–295, 308, 324, 326,
    382–383, 384–385
predicate in, simple, 14–15, 22, 46, 84, 172, 254,
    336–339
run-on, 302–303, 309, 324, 388–389
simple, 296–297, 308, 324
subject in, complete, 10–11, 22, 46, 84, 172, 254,
    336–339
subject in, compound, 294–295, 308, 324, 326,
    382–383, 384–385
subject in, simple, 12–13, 22, 46, 84, 172, 254, 336–339
supporting, 34–35, 47, 390
topic, 34–35, 47, 72–73, 114–115, 196–197, 390
Set, sit, 106–107, 111, 128, 174, 362–363
Similes, 316–317, 325
Simple sentences, 296–297, 308, 324
Space order, 200–201, 211
Speaking
    group discussions, 70–71
    interviewing, 202–203
    oral reports, 163, 244–245
    on telephone, 116–117
Spelling
    adjectives, comparative and superlative forms, 186–187
    demons, 409–410
    homographs, 146–147
    plural nouns, 58–59, 82, 85, 344–347, 407–408
    rules, 407–408
    verbs, 98–99, 407–408
State-of-being verbs, 88–89, 348–351
    See also Linking verbs.
Stories
    "The Key Word" by Isaac Asimov, 156–161
Story titles
    capitalization of, 400, 402
    quotation marks around, 404, 406
Study skills
    choosing and narrowing a topic, 230–231
    dictionary, 26–27, 28–29, 47
    encyclopedia, 234–235

outlining, 242–243, 394
paraphrasing, 240–241, 253
parts of a book, 238–239
reference materials, 236–237, 253
taking notes, 240–241, 253
taking tests, 413
using a thesaurus, 30–31, 47
using the library, 232–233, 252
Subject
    agreement with verb, 298–299, 300–301, 308, 324, 326,
        386–387
    complete, 10–11, 22, 46, 84, 172, 254, 336–339
    compound, 294–295, 308, 324, 326, 382–383, 384–385
        agreement with verb, 300–301, 308, 326
    of imperative sentence, 16–17, 23, 46, 84, 172, 326, 336,
        338–339
    of interrogative sentence, 16–17, 23, 46, 84, 172, 326,
        336, 338–339
    simple, 12–13, 22, 46, 84, 172, 254, 336–339
Subject pronouns, 134–135, 142–143, 148, 149, 170, 175,
    327, 364–367, 368–369
Subject-verb agreement, 298–299, 300–301, 308, 324,
    326, 386–387
Suffixes
    -able, 190–191, 193
    -al, 190–191, 193
    -ful, 190–191, 193, 210
    -ive, 190–191, 193
    -less, 190–191, 193, 210
    -ous, 190–191, 193, 210
    -y, 190–191, 193, 210
Superlative forms
    of adjectives, 186–187, 188–189, 193, 210, 255, 370, 373
    of adverbs, 218–219, 226, 252, 255, 374, 376
Supporting sentences, 34–35, 47, 390
Synonyms, 20–21, 23, 47
    as context clues, 224–225, 227, 253
    definition of, 20
    See also Thesaurus.

Table of contents, using a, 238–239
Taking notes, 240–241, 253
Teach, learn, 106–107, 111, 128, 174, 362–363
Telephone
    directory, using a, 116–117
    messages, 116–117
    speaking/listening on a, 116–117
Tenses, of verbs, 96–97, 111, 128, 174, 352–355
Tests, taking, 413
Thank-you notes, 392
Thesaurus, 414–433
    using a, 30–31, 47, 67, 113, 151, 195, 229

Thinking skills
analogies, 280–281, 291
cause-and-effect relationships, 284–285
classifying, 45
fact and opinion, 68–69, 83
making common-sense decisions, 282–283
recognizing propaganda techniques, 278–279, 291
Time Order, 152–153, 171
Title page, of a book, 238–239
Titles
of articles, 404
of books
capitalization of, 162–163, 171, 400, 402
underlining, 162–163, 171, 395, 404, 406
of magazines, newspapers, movies, 404, 406
of stories, poems, reports
capitalization of, 400, 402
quotation marks around, 404, 406
Topic, choosing and narrowing, 230–231
Topic sentence, 34–35, 47, 72–73, 114–115, 196–197, 390

Underlining, 162–163, 171, 395, 404, 406
Usage
adverbs and adjectives, 222–223, 227, 252, 329, 374, 377
bad, worse, worst, 188–189, 210
badly, worse, worst, 218–219
be, 88–89
agreement with subject, 298–299, 308
as helping verb, 92–93
as linking verb, 90–91
principal parts of, 356–359
between, among, 266–267, 273, 290, 378, 381
can, may, 104–105, 111, 128, 174, 362–363
comparison of adjectives, 186–187, 188–189, 193, 210, 255, 370, 373
comparison of adverbs, 218–219, 226, 252, 255, 374, 376
double negatives, 220–221, 227, 252, 374, 376–377
good, better, best, 188–189, 255
good, well, 222–223, 227, 329, 377
irregular verbs, 100–101, 102–103, 356–361
See also Verbs, irregular.
learn, teach, 106–107, 111, 128, 174, 362–363
leave, let, 104–105, 111, 128, 174, 362–363
prepositional phrases, object pronouns in, 266–267, 273, 290, 378, 381
sit, set, 106–107, 111, 128, 174, 362–363
subject pronouns and object pronouns, 142–143, 149, 170, 175, 254, 368–369
subject-verb agreement, 298–299, 300–301, 308, 324, 326, 386–387
well, better, best, 218–219, 255

Verbs
action, 88–89, 110, 348, 350–351
agreement with subject, 298–299, 300–301, 308, 324, 326, 386–387
be, 88–89, 90–91, 92–93, 298–299, 308, 356–359
definition of, 88, 268, 348
forming contractions with, 144–145, 148, 170, 175, 404, 406
future tense, 96–97, 111, 128, 174, 328, 352–355
have, 356–359
helping, 92–93, 110, 128, 174, 255, 328, 348–351
irregular
become, became, become, 102–103, 111, 360–361
begin, began, begun, 100–101, 128, 356–359
blow, blew, blown, 100–101, 356–359
break, broke, broken, 102–103, 174, 360–361
bring, brought, brought, 102–103, 360–361
catch, caught, caught, 102–103, 174, 360–361
choose, chose, chosen, 102–103, 128, 255, 360–361
come, came, come, 102–103, 111, 360–361
do, did, done, 100–101, 128, 356–359
drink, drank, drunk, 100–101, 174, 356–359
eat, ate, eaten, 100–101, 356–359
fly, flew, flown, 100–101, 356–359
freeze, froze, frozen, 102–103, 360–361
give, gave, given, 100-101, 111, 356–359
go, went, gone, 100–101, 356–359
grow, grew, grown, 100–101, 128, 356–359
know, knew, known, 100–101, 111, 174, 356–359
ring, rang, rung, 100–101, 356–359
run, ran, run, 102–103, 111, 360–361
say, said, said, 102–103, 255, 360–361
sing, sang, sung, 100–101, 356–359
speak, spoke, spoken, 102–103, 111, 360–361
swim, swam, swum, 100–101, 255, 356–359
take, took, taken, 100–101, 111, 356–359
teach, taught, taught, 102–103, 111, 360–361
think, thought, thought, 102–103, 360–361
throw, threw, thrown, 100–101, 356–359
write, wrote, written, 100–101, 111, 174, 356–359

linking, 90–91, 110, 128, 174, 348–351
main, 92–93, 110, 128, 174, 255, 328, 348–351
past participle, 98–99, 111, 128, 174, 255, 352–355
past tense, 96–97, 111, 128, 174, 328, 352–355
present tense, 96–97, 111, 352–355
principal parts, 98–99, 111, 128, 174, 255, 352–355
as simple predicates, 14–15, 88–89
spelling of, 98–99, 407–408
state-of-being, 88–89, 348–351
tenses, 96–97, 111, 128, 174, 352–355
troublesome pairs of
can, may, 104–105, 111, 128, 174, 362–363
leave, let, 104–105, 111, 128, 174, 362–363
sit, set, 106–107, 111, 128, 174, 362–363

teach, learn, 106–107, 111, 128, 174, 362–363
    writing with, 112–113
Vocabulary
    antonyms, 20–21, 23, 47
    compounds, 62–63, 65, 83
    connotation, 306–307, 309, 325
    context clues, 224–225, 227, 253
    homographs, 146–147
    homophones, 146–147, 171
    idioms, 270–271, 291
    prefixes, 108–109, 129
    suffixes, 190–191, 193, 210
    synonyms, 20–21, 23, 47

Well, better, best, 218–219, 255
Well, good, 222–223, 227
Worktables
    A Call Number Guide, 250
    A Class Story Chart, 168
    A Coat of Arms, 208
    A Commemorative Stamp, 126
    A. Dictionary Calendar, 44
    A Greeting Card, 322
    Persuasive Advertisements, 80
    A Puzzle Potpourri, 288
Writing
    book reports, 162–163, 395
    business letters, 120–121, 393
    cause-and-effect paragraph, 284–287
    character sketch, 204–207
    descriptive paragraph, 196–197
    directions, 276–277, 291
    explanatory paragraph, 114–115
    friendly letters, 118–119, 391
    invitations, 392

letter of information, 122–125
    narrative paragraph, 152–153, 171
    newspaper editorial, 76–79
    outlines, 242–243, 394
    paragraph of contrast, 40–43
    paragraphs, 32–33, 34–35, 390
    personal narrative, 164–167
    persuasive paragraph, 72–73
    poem, 318–321
    sentences, 5, 7, 9, 11, 13, 15, 17, 24–25, 274–275, 295, 310–311
    similes and metaphors, 316–317
    thank-you notes, 392
    three-paragraph report, 246–249
    topic sentences, 34–35, 47, 72–73, 114–115, 196–197, 390
Writing process
    editing. *See* Writing Projects.
    four steps of, (prewriting, writing, revising, publishing). *See* Writing Projects.
    photo essay, 36–39
    proofreading. *See* Writing Projects.
Writing Projects (Prewriting, writing, editing, revising, proofreading, and publishing are taught in each Writing Project listed below.)
    Writing a Cause-and-Effect Paragraph, 284–287
    Writing a Character Sketch, 204–207
    Writing a Letter of Information, 122–125
    Writing a Newspaper Editorial, 76–79
    Wiring a Paragraph of Contrast, 40–43
    Writing a Personal Narrative, 164–167
    Writing a Poem, 318–321
    Writing a Three-Paragraph Report, 246–249

Young Writer's Handbook, 390–413